Programming Languages: A Modern Approach

Programming Languages: A Modern Approach

Edited by Katy Spalding

Clanrye International
www.clanryeinternational.com

Clanrye International,
750 Third Avenue, 9th Floor,
New York, NY 10017, USA

ISBN: 978-1-64726-585-4

Cataloging-in-publication Data

Programming languages : a modern approach / edited by Katy Spalding.
p. cm.
Includes bibliographical references and index.
ISBN 978-1-64726-585-4
1. Programming languages (Electronic computers). 2. Languages, Artificial.
3. Electronic data processing. 4. Computer science. I. Spalding, Katy.
QA76.7 .H36 2023
005.13--dc23

For information on all Clanrye International publications visit our website at www.clanryeinternational.com

CLANRYE INTERNATIONAL

Contents

Preface

In my initial years as a student, I used to run to the library at every possible instance to grab a book and learn something new. Books were my primary source of knowledge and I would not have come such a long way without all that I learnt from them. Thus, when I was approached to edit this book; I became understandably nostalgic. It was an absolute honor to be considered worthy of guiding the current generation as well as those to come. I put all my knowledge and hard work into making this book most beneficial for its readers.

A programming language is a computer language which is utilized for communicating with computers by programmers. It comprises of instructions written in a particular language to accomplish a specific task. A programming language is primarily used to create mobile applications, desktop applications, software and websites. There are various types of programming languages including low-level programming language, middle-level programming language, and high-level programming language. Some of the popular programming languages are C#, R, Go, C++, Python, Ruby, C, JavaScript, Java, Swift and PHP. Modern programming languages are designed to take advantage of large data sets, modern computer hardware, rapid networking, mobile devices and cloud networking. Majority of the advanced programming languages also provide better developer ergonomics. This book contains some path-breaking studies on programming languages. It will prove to be immensely beneficial to students and researchers in the field of computer science and software engineering.

I wish to thank my publisher for supporting me at every step. I would also like to thank all the authors who have contributed their researches in this book. I hope this book will be a valuable contribution to the progress of the field.

Editor

1

Handling Polymorphic Algebraic Effects

Taro Sekiyama[1(✉)] and Atsushi Igarashi[2(✉)]

[1] National Institute of Informatics, Tokyo, Japan
tsekiyama@acm.org
[2] Kyoto University, Kyoto, Japan
igarashi@kuis.kyoto-u.ac.jp

Abstract. Algebraic effects and handlers are a powerful abstraction mechanism to represent and implement control effects. In this work, we study their extension with parametric polymorphism that allows abstracting not only expressions but also effects and handlers. Although polymorphism makes it possible to reuse and reason about effect implementations more effectively, it has long been known that a naive combination of polymorphic effects and let-polymorphism breaks type safety. Although type safety can often be gained by restricting let-bound expressions—e.g., by adopting value restriction or weak polymorphism—we propose a complementary approach that restricts handlers instead of let-bound expressions. Our key observation is that, informally speaking, a handler is safe if resumptions from the handler do not interfere with each other. To formalize our idea, we define a call-by-value lambda calculus $\lambda_{\mathrm{eff}}^{\mathrm{let}}$ that supports let-polymorphism and polymorphic algebraic effects and handlers, design a type system that rejects interfering handlers, and prove type safety of our calculus.

1 Introduction

Algebraic effects [20] and handlers [21] are a powerful abstraction mechanism to represent and implement control effects, such as exceptions, interactive I/O, mutable states, and nondeterminism. They are growing in popularity, thanks to their success in achieving modularity of effects, especially the clear separation between their interfaces and their implementations. An interface of effects is given as a set of *operations*—e.g., an interface of mutable states consists of two operations, namely, put and get—with their signatures. An implementation is given by a *handler* H, which provides a set of interpretations of the operations (called *operation clauses*), and a handle–with expression $\mathsf{handle}\, M \,\mathsf{with}\, H$ associates effects invoked during the computation of M with handler H. Algebraic effects and handlers work as *resumable exceptions*: when an effect operation is invoked, the run-time system tries to find the nearest handler that handles the invoked operation; if it is found, the corresponding operation clause is evaluated by using the argument to the operation invocation and the continuation up to the handler. The continuation gives the ability to resume the computation from the point where the operation was invoked, using the result from the operation clause. Another modularity that algebraic effects provide is flexible composition: multiple algebraic effects can be combined freely [13].

In this work, we study an extension of algebraic effects and handlers with another type-based abstraction mechanism—parametric polymorphism [22]. In general, parametric polymorphism is a basis of generic programming and enhance code reusability by abstracting expressions over types. This work allows abstracting not only expressions but also effect operations and handlers, which makes it possible to reuse and reason about effect implementations that are independent of concrete type representations. Like in many functional languages, we introduce polymorphism in the form of *let-polymorphism* for its practically desirable properties such as decidable typechecking and type inference.

As is well known, however, a naive combination of polymorphic effects and let-polymorphism breaks type safety [11, 23]. Many researchers have attacked this classical problem [1, 2, 10, 12, 14, 17, 23, 24], and their common idea is to restrict the form of let-bound expressions. For example, value restriction [23, 24], which is the standard way to make ML-like languages with imperative features and let-polymorphism type safe, allows only syntactic values to be polymorphic.

In this work, we propose a new approach to achieving type safety in a language with let-polymorphic and polymorphic effects and handlers: the idea is to restrict handlers instead of let-bound expressions. Since a handler gives an implementation of an effect, our work can be viewed as giving a criterion that suggests what effects can cooperate safely with (unrestricted) let-polymorphism and what effects cannot. Our key observation for type safety is that, informally speaking, an invocation of a polymorphic effect in a let-bound expression is safe if resumptions in the corresponding operation clause do not interfere with each other. We formalize this discipline into a type system and show that typeable programs do not get stuck.

Our contributions are summarized as follows.

- We introduce a call-by-value, statically typed lambda calculus $\lambda_{\text{eff}}^{\text{let}}$ that supports let-polymorphism and polymorphic algebraic effects and handlers. The type system of $\lambda_{\text{eff}}^{\text{let}}$ allows any let-bound expressions involving effects to be polymorphic, but, instead, disallows handlers where resumptions interfere with each other.
- To give the semantics of $\lambda_{\text{eff}}^{\text{let}}$, we formalize an intermediate language $\lambda_{\text{eff}}^{\Lambda}$ wherein type information is made explicit and define a formal elaboration from $\lambda_{\text{eff}}^{\text{let}}$ to $\lambda_{\text{eff}}^{\Lambda}$.
- We prove type safety of $\lambda_{\text{eff}}^{\text{let}}$ by type preservation of the elaboration and type soundness of $\lambda_{\text{eff}}^{\Lambda}$.

We believe that our approach is complementary to the usual approach of restricting let-bound expressions: for handlers that are considered unsafe by our criterion, the value restriction can still be used.

The rest of this paper is organized as follows. Section 2 provides an overview of our work, giving motivating examples of polymorphic effects and handlers, a problem in naive combination of polymorphic effects and let-polymorphism, and our solution to gain type safety with those features. Section 3 defines the surface language $\lambda_{\text{eff}}^{\text{let}}$, and Sect. 4 defines the intermediate language $\lambda_{\text{eff}}^{\Lambda}$ and the elaboration from $\lambda_{\text{eff}}^{\text{let}}$ to $\lambda_{\text{eff}}^{\Lambda}$. We also state that the elaboration is type-preserving and that $\lambda_{\text{eff}}^{\Lambda}$ is type sound in Sect. 4. Finally, we discuss related work in Sect. 5 and conclude in Sect. 6. The proofs of the stated properties and the full definition of the elaboration are given in the full version at https://arxiv.org/abs/1811.07332.

2 Overview

We start with reviewing how monomorphic algebraic effects and handlers work through examples and then extend them to a polymorphic version. We also explain why polymorphic effects are inconsistent with let-polymorphism, if naively combined, and how we resolve it.

2.1 Monomorphic Algebraic Effects and Handlers

Exception. Our first example is exception handling, shown in an ML-like language below.

```
1  effect fail : unit ↪ unit
2
3  let div100 (x:int) : int =
4    if x = 0 then (#fail(); -1)
5    else 100 / x
6
7  let f (y:int) : int option =
8    handle (div_100 y) with
9      return z → Some z
10     fail   z → None
```

`Some` and `None` are constructors of datatype α `option`. Line 1 declares an effect operation `fail`, which signals that an anomaly happens, with its signature `unit` ↪ `unit`, which means that the operation is invoked with the unit value `()`, causes some effect, and may return the unit value. The function `div100`, defined in Lines 3–5, is an example that uses `fail`; it returns the number obtained by dividing 100 by argument `x` if `x` is not zero; otherwise, if `x` is zero, it raises an exception by calling effect operation `fail`.[1] In general, we write `#op(`M`)` for invoking effect operation `op` with argument M. The function `f` (Lines 7–10) calls `div_100` inside a `handle`–`with` expression, which returns `Some` n if `div_100` returns integer n normally and returns `None` if it invokes `fail`.

An expression of the form `handle` M `with` H handles effect operations invoked in M (which we call *handled expression*) according to the effect interpretations given by handler H. A handler H consists of two parts: a single *return*

[1] Here, "`; -1`" is necessary to make the types of both branches the same; it becomes unnecessary when we introduce polymorphic effects.

clause and zero or more *operation clauses*. A return clause `return x` $\rightarrow M'$ will be executed if the evaluation of M results in a value v. Then, the value of M' (where `x` is bound to v) will be the value of the entire `handle–with` expression. For example, in the program above, if a nonzero number n is passed to `f`, the `handle–with` expression would return `Some` $(100/n)$ because `div100` n returns $100/n$. An operation clause `op x` $\rightarrow M'$ defines an implementation of effect `op`: if the evaluation of handled expression M invokes effect `op` with argument v, expression M' will be evaluated after substituting v for `x` and the value of M' will be the value of the entire `handle–with` expression. In the program example above, if zero is given to `f`, then `None` will be returned because `div100 0` invokes `fail`.

As shown above, algebraic effect handling is similar to exception handling. However, a distinctive feature of algebraic effect handling is that it allows *resumption* of the computation from the point where an effect operation was invoked. The next example demonstrates such an ability of algebraic effect handlers.

Choice. The next example is effect `choose`, which returns one of the given two arguments.

```
1 effect choose : int × int ↪ int
2
3 handle (#choose(1,2) + #choose(10,20)) with
4     return x → x
5     choose x → resume (fst x)
```

As usual, $A_1 \times A_2$ is a product type, (M_1, M_2) is a pair expression, and `fst` is the first projection function. The first line declares that effect `choose` is for choosing integers. The handled expression `#choose(1,2) + #choose(10,20)` intuitively suggests that there would be four possible results—11, 21, 12, and 22—depending on which value each invocation of `choose` returns. The handler in this example always chooses the first element of a given pair[2] and returns it by using a `resume` expression, and, as a result, the expression in Lines 3–5 evaluates to 11.

A resumption expression `resume` M in an operation clause makes it possible to return a value of M to the point where an effect operation was invoked. This behavior is realized by constructing a *delimited continuation* from the point of the effect invocation up to the `handle–with` expression that deals with the effect and passing the value of M to the continuation. We illustrate it by using the program above. When the handled expression `#choose(1,2) + #choose(10,20)` is evaluated, continuation $c \stackrel{\text{def}}{=} [\,]$ `+ #choose(10,20)` is constructed. Then, the body `resume (fst x)` of the operation clause is evaluated after binding `x` to the invocation argument `(1,2)`. Receiving the value `1` of `fst (1,2)`, the resumption

[2] We can think of more practical implementations, which choose one of the two arguments by other means, say, random values.

expression passes it to the continuation c and $c[1] =$ `1 + #choose(10,20)` is evaluated under the same handler. Next, `choose` is invoked with argument `(10,20)`. Similarly, continuation $c' \stackrel{\text{def}}{=}$ `1 + []` is constructed and the operation clause for `choose` is executed again. Since `fst (10,20)` evaluates to `10`, $c'[10] =$ `1 + 10` is evaluated under the same handler. Since the **`return`** clause returns what it receives, the entire expression evaluates to `11`.

Finally, we briefly review how an operation clause involving resumption expressions is typechecked [3,13,16]. Let us consider operation clause `op(x)` $\rightarrow M$ for `op` of type signature $A \hookrightarrow B$. The typechecking is performed as follows. First, argument `x` is assigned the domain type A of the signature as it will be bound to an argument of an effect invocation. Second, for resumption expression **`resume`** M' in M, (1) M' is required to have the codomain type B of the signature because its value will be passed to the continuation as the result of the invocation and (2) the resumption expression is assigned the same type as the return clause. Third, the type of the body M has to be the same as that of the return clause because the value of M is the result of the entire **`handle`**–**`with`** expression. For example, the above operation clause for `choose` is typechecked as follows: first, argument `x` is assigned type `int` $\times$ `int`; second, it is checked whether the argument `fst x` of the resumption expression has `int`, the codomain type of `choose`; third, it is checked whether the body **`resume`** `(fst x)` of the clause has the same type as the return clause, i.e., `int`. If all the requirements are satisfied, the clause is well typed.

2.2 Polymorphic Algebraic Effects and Handlers

This section discusses motivation for polymorphism in algebraic effects and handlers. There are two ways to introduce polymorphism: by *parameterized effects* and by *polymorphic effects*.

The former is used to parameterize the declaration of an effect by types. For example, one might declare:

`effect` α `choose` : $\alpha \times \alpha \hookrightarrow \alpha$

An invocation `#choose` involves a parameterized effect of the form A `choose` (where A denotes a type), according to the type of arguments: For example, `#choose(true,false)` has the effect `bool choose` and `#choose(1,-1)` has `int choose`. Handlers are required for each effect A `choose`.

The latter is used to give a polymorphic type to an effect. For example, one may declare

`effect` `choose` : $\forall\alpha.\ \alpha \times \alpha \hookrightarrow \alpha$

In this case, the effect can be invoked with different types, but all invocations have the same effect `choose`. One can implement a single operation clause that can handle all invocations of `choose`, regardless of argument types. Koka supports both styles [16] (with the value restriction); we focus, however, on the latter in this paper. A type system for parameterized effects lifting the value restriction is studied by Kammar and Pretnar [14] (see Sect. 5 for comparison).

In what follows, we show a polymorphic version of the examples we have seen, along with brief discussions on how polymorphic effects help with reasoning about effect implementations. Other practical examples of polymorphic effects can be found in Leijen's work [16].

Polymorphic Exception. First, we extend the exception effect `fail` with polymorphism.

```
1  effect fail∀ : ∀α. unit ↪ α
2
3  let div100∀ (x:int) : int =
4    if x = 0 then #fail∀()
5    else 100 / x
```

The polymorphic type signature of effect `fail`$^\forall$, given in Line 1, means that the codomain type α can be any. Thus, we do not need to append the dummy value `-1` to the invocation of `fail`$^\forall$ by instantiating the bound type variable α with `int` (the shaded part).

Choice. Next, let us make `choose` polymorphic.

```
 1  effect choose∀ : ∀α. α × α ↪ α
 2
 3  let rec random_walk (x:int) : int =
 4    let b = #choose∀(true,false) in
 5    if b then random_walk (x + #choose∀(1,-1))
 6    else x
 7
 8  let f (s:int) =
 9    handle random_walk s with
10      return x   → x
11      choose∀ y → if rand() < 0.0 then resume (fst y)
12                                   else resume (snd y)
```

The function `random_walk` implements random walk; it takes the current coordinate `x`, chooses whether it stops, and, if it decides to continue, recursively calls itself with a new coordinate. In the definition, `choose`$^\forall$ is used twice with different types: `bool` and `int`. Lines 11–12 give `choose`$^\forall$ an interpretation, which calls `rand` to obtain a random `float`,[3] and returns either the first or the second element of `y`.

Typechecking of operation clauses could be extended in a straightforward manner. That is, an operation clause `op(x)` $\rightarrow M$ for an effect operation of signature $\forall\alpha.A \hookrightarrow B$ would be typechecked as follows: first, α is locally bound in the clause and x is assigned type A; second, an argument of a resumption

[3] One might implement `rand` as another effect operation.

expression must have type B (which may contain type variable α); third, M must have the same type as that of the return clause (its type cannot contain α as α is local) under the assumption that resumption expressions have the same type as the return clause. For example, let us consider typechecking of the above operation clause for `choose`$^\forall$. First, the typechecking algorithm allocates a local type variable α and assigns type $\alpha \times \alpha$ to `y`. The body has two resumption expressions, and it is checked whether the arguments `fst y` and `snd y` have the codomain type α of the signature. Finally, it is checked whether the body is typed at `int` assuming that the resumption expressions have type `int`. The operation clause meets all the requirements, and, therefore, it would be well typed.

An obvious advantage of polymorphic effects is reusability. Without polymorphism, one has to declare many versions of `choose` for different types.

Another pleasant effect of polymorphic effects is that, thanks to parametricity, inappropriate implementations for an effect operation can be excluded. For example, it is not possible for an implementation of `choose`$^\forall$ to resume with values other than the first or second element of `y`. In the monomorphic version, however, it is possible to resume with any integer, as opposed to what the name of the operation suggests. A similar argument applies to `fail`$^\forall$; since the codomain type is α, which does not appear in the domain type, it is not possible to resume! In other words, the signature $\forall\alpha.$ `unit` $\hookrightarrow \alpha$ enforces that no invocation of `fail`$^\forall$ will return.

2.3 Problem in Naive Combination with Let-Polymorphism

Although polymorphic effects and handlers provide an ability to abstract and restrict effect implementations, one may easily expect that their unrestricted use with naive *let-polymorphism*, which allows any let-bound expressions to be polymorphic, breaks type safety. Indeed, it does.

We develop a counterexample, inspired by Harper and Lillibridge [11], below.

```
effect get_id : ∀α. unit ↪ (α → α)

let f () : int =
  let g = #get_id() in (* g : ∀α.α → α *)
  if (g true) then ((g 0) + 1) else 2
```

The function `f` first binds `g` to the invocation result of `op`. The expression `#get_id()` is given type $\alpha \rightarrow \alpha$ and the naive let-polymorphism would assign type scheme $\forall\alpha.\alpha \rightarrow \alpha$ to `g`, which makes both `g true` and `g 0` (and thus the definition of `f`) well typed.

An intended use of `f` is as follows:

```
handle f () with
  return x → x
  get_id y → resume (λz. z)
```

The operation clause for `get_id` resumes with the identity function `λz.z`. It would be well typed under the typechecking procedure described in Sect. 2.2 and it safely returns `1`.

However, the following strange expression

```
handle f () with
  return x → x
  get_id y → resume (λz1. (resume (λz2. z1)); z1)
```

will get stuck, although this expression would be well typed: both `λz1. ··· ;z1` and `λz2. z1` could be given type $\alpha \to \alpha$ by assigning both `z1` and `z2` type α, which is the type variable local to this clause. Let us see how the evaluation gets stuck in detail. When the handled expression `f ()` invokes effect `get_id`, the following continuation will be constructed:

$$c \stackrel{\text{def}}{=} \texttt{let g = [] in if (g true) then ((g 0) + 1) else 2}\,.$$

Next, the body of the operation clause `get_id` is evaluated. It immediately resumes and reduces to

$$c'[(\lambda\texttt{z1.}\ c'[(\lambda\texttt{z2.z1})];\ \texttt{z1})]$$

where

```
        handle c with
c' def=   return x → x
          get_id y → resume (λz1. (resume (λz2.z1)); z1) ,
```

which is the continuation c under the same handler. The evaluation proceeds as follows (here, $k \stackrel{\text{def}}{=} \lambda\texttt{z1.}\ c'[(\lambda\texttt{z2.z1})];\ \texttt{z1}$):

```
   c'[(λz1. c'[(λz2.z1)]; z1)]
 = handle let g = k in if (g true) then ((g 0) + 1) else 2 with ...
 → handle if (k true) then ((k 0) + 1) else 2 with ...
 → handle if c'[(λz2.true)]; true then ((k 0) + 1) else 2 with ...
```

Here, the hole in c' is filled by function `(λz2.true)`, which returns a Boolean value, *though the hole is supposed to be filled by a function of* $\forall\alpha.\,\alpha \to \alpha$. This weird gap triggers a run-time error:

```
    c'[(λz2.true)]
    handle
 =    let g = λz2.true in if (g true) then ((g 0) + 1) else 2
    with ...
 →* handle if true then (((λz2.true) 0) + 1) else 2 with ...
 →  handle ((λz2.true) 0) + 1 with ...
 →  handle true + 1 with ...
```

We stop here because `true + 1` cannot reduce.

2.4 Our Solution

A standard approach to this problem is to restrict the form of let-bound expressions by some means such as the (relaxed) value restriction [10,23,24] or weak polymorphism [1,12]. This approach amounts to restricting how effect operations can be *used*.

In this paper, we seek for a complementary approach, which is to restrict how effect operations can be *implemented*.[4] More concretely, we develop a type system such that let-bound expressions are polymorphic as long as they invoke only "safe" polymorphic effects and the notion of safe polymorphic effects is formalized in terms of typing rules (for handlers).

To see what are "safe" effects, let us examine the above counterexample to type safety. The crux of the counterexample is that

1. continuation c uses `g` polymorphically, namely, as `bool` $\rightarrow$ `bool` in `g true` and as `int` $\rightarrow$ `int` in `g 1`;
2. c is invoked twice; and
3. the use of `g` as `bool` $\rightarrow$ `bool` in the first invocation of c—where `g` is bound to λ`z1.`$\cdots$`; z1`—"alters" the type of λ`z2. z1` (passed to `resume`) from $\alpha \rightarrow \alpha$ to $\alpha \rightarrow$ `bool`, contradicting the second use of `g` as `int` $\rightarrow$ `int` in the second invocation of c.

The last point is crucial—if λz2.z1 were, say, λz2.z2, there would be no influence from the first invocation of c and the evaluation would succeed. The problem we see here is that the naive type system mistakenly allows *interference* between the arguments to the two resumptions by assuming that `z1` and `z2` share the same type.

Based on this observation, the typing rule for resumption is revised to disallow interference between different resumptions by separating their types: for each `resume` M in the operation clause for `op` : $\forall \alpha_1 \cdots \alpha_n . A \hookrightarrow B$, M has to have type B' obtained by renaming all type variables α_i in B with *fresh* type variables α'_i. In the case of `get_id`, the two resumptions should be called with $\beta \rightarrow \beta$ and $\gamma \rightarrow \gamma$ for fresh β and γ; for the first `resume` to be well typed, `z1` has to be of type β, although it means that the return type of λ`z2.z1` (given to the second resumption) is β, making the entire clause ill typed, as we expect. If a clause does not have interfering resumptions like

```
get_id y  → resume (λz1.z1)
```

or

```
get_id y  → resume (λz1. (resume (λz2.z2)); z1),
```

it will be well typed.

[4] We compare our approach with the standard approaches in Sect. 5 in detail.

3 Surface Language: $\lambda_{\text{eff}}^{\text{let}}$

We define a lambda calculus $\lambda_{\text{eff}}^{\text{let}}$ that supports let-polymorphism, polymorphic algebraic effects, and handlers without interfering resumptions. This section introduces the syntax and the type system of $\lambda_{\text{eff}}^{\text{let}}$. The semantics is given by a formal elaboration to intermediate calculus $\lambda_{\text{eff}}^{\Lambda}$, which will be introduced in Sect. 4.

Effect operations	op		**Type variables** α, β, γ
Effects	ϵ	::=	sets of effect operations
Base types	ι	::=	$\mathsf{bool} \mid \mathsf{int} \mid ...$
Types	A, B, C, D	::=	$\alpha \mid \iota \mid A \rightarrow_\epsilon B$
Type schemes	σ	::=	$A \mid \forall \alpha.\sigma$
Constants	c	::=	$\mathsf{true} \mid \mathsf{false} \mid 0 \mid + \mid ...$
Terms	M	::=	$x \mid c \mid \lambda x.M \mid M_1\, M_2 \mid \mathsf{let}\, x = M_1 \,\mathsf{in}\, M_2 \mid$ $\#\mathsf{op}(M) \mid \mathsf{handle}\, M \,\mathsf{with}\, H \mid \mathsf{resume}\, M$
Handlers	H	::=	$\mathsf{return}\, x \rightarrow M \mid H; \mathsf{op}(x) \rightarrow M$
Typing contexts	Γ	::=	$\emptyset \mid \Gamma, x : \sigma \mid \Gamma, \alpha$

Fig. 1. Syntax of $\lambda_{\text{eff}}^{\text{let}}$.

3.1 Syntax

The syntax of $\lambda_{\text{eff}}^{\text{let}}$ is given in Fig. 1. Effect operations are denoted by op and type variables by α, β, and γ. An effect, denoted by ϵ, is a finite set of effect operations. We write $\langle\rangle$ for the empty effect set. A type, denoted by A, B, C, and D, is a type variable; a base type ι, which includes, e.g., bool and int; or a function type $A \rightarrow_\epsilon B$, which is given to functions that take an argument of type A and compute a value of type B possibly with effect ϵ. A type scheme σ is obtained by abstracting type variables. Terms, denoted by M, consist of variables; constants (including primitive operations); lambda abstractions $\lambda x.M$, which bind x in M; function applications; let-expressions $\mathsf{let}\, x = M_1 \,\mathsf{in}\, M_2$, which bind x in M_2; effect invocations $\#\mathsf{op}(M)$; handle–with expressions $\mathsf{handle}\, M \,\mathsf{with}\, H$; and resumption expressions $\mathsf{resume}\, M$. All type information in $\lambda_{\text{eff}}^{\text{let}}$ is implicit; thus the terms have no type annotations. A handler H has a single return clause $\mathsf{return}\, x \rightarrow M$, where x is bound in M, and zero or more operation clauses of the form $\mathsf{op}(x) \rightarrow M$, where x is bound in M. A typing context Γ binds a sequence of variable declarations $x : \sigma$ and type variable declarations α.

We introduce the following notations used throughout this paper. We write $\forall \boldsymbol{\alpha}^{i \in I}.A$ for $\forall \alpha_1 .... \forall \alpha_n.A$ where $I = \{1, ..., n\}$. We often omit indices (i and j) and index sets (I and J) if they are not important: e.g., we often abbreviate $\forall \boldsymbol{\alpha}^{i \in I}.A$ to $\forall \boldsymbol{\alpha}^{I}.A$ or even to $\forall \boldsymbol{\alpha}.A$. Similarly, we use a bold font for other sequences ($\boldsymbol{A}^{i \in I}$ for a sequence of types, $\boldsymbol{v}^{i \in I}$ for a sequence of values, etc.).

We sometimes write $\{\boldsymbol{\alpha}\}$ to view the sequence $\boldsymbol{\alpha}$ as a set by ignoring the order. Free type variables $ftv(\sigma)$ in a type scheme σ and type substitution $B[\boldsymbol{A}/\boldsymbol{\alpha}]$ of $\boldsymbol{A}$ for type variables $\boldsymbol{\alpha}$ in B are defined as usual (with the understanding that the omitted index sets for $\boldsymbol{A}$ and $\boldsymbol{\alpha}$ are the same).

We suppose that each constant c is assigned a first-order closed type $ty(c)$ of the form $\iota_1 \to \langle\rangle \cdots \to \langle\rangle \iota_n$ and that each effect operation op is assigned a signature of the form $\forall\boldsymbol{\alpha}.A \hookrightarrow B$, which means that an invocation of op with type instantiation $\boldsymbol{C}$ takes an argument of $A[\boldsymbol{C}/\boldsymbol{\alpha}]$ and returns a value of $B[\boldsymbol{C}/\boldsymbol{\alpha}]$. We also assume that, for $ty(\mathsf{op}) = \forall\boldsymbol{\alpha}.A \hookrightarrow B$, $ftv(A) \subseteq \{\boldsymbol{\alpha}\}$ and $ftv(B) \subseteq \{\boldsymbol{\alpha}\}$.

3.2 Type System

The type system of $\lambda_{\mathrm{eff}}^{\mathrm{let}}$ consists of four judgments: well-formedness of typing contexts $\vdash \Gamma$; well formedness of type schemes $\Gamma \vdash \sigma$; term typing judgment $\Gamma; R \vdash M : A \,|\, \epsilon$, which means that M computes a value of A possibly with effect ϵ under typing context Γ and resumption type R (discussed below); and handler typing judgment $\Gamma; R \vdash H : A \,|\, \epsilon \Rightarrow B \,|\, \epsilon'$, which means that H handles a computation that produces a value of A with effect ϵ and that the clauses in H compute a value of B possibly with effect ϵ' under Γ and R.

A resumption type R contains type information for resumption.

Definition 1 (Resumption type). *Resumption types in* $\lambda_{\mathrm{eff}}^{\mathrm{let}}$, *denoted by* R, *are defined as follows:*

$$R ::= \mathsf{none} \mid (\boldsymbol{\alpha}, A, B \to \epsilon\; C)$$
$$(\text{if } ftv(A) \cup ftv(B) \subseteq \{\boldsymbol{\alpha}\} \text{ and } ftv(C) \cap \{\boldsymbol{\alpha}\} = \emptyset)$$

If M is not a subterm of an operation clause, it is typechecked under $R = \mathsf{none}$, which means that M cannot contain resumption expressions. Otherwise, suppose that M is a subterm of an operation clause $\mathsf{op}(x) \to M'$ that handles effect op of signature $\forall\boldsymbol{\alpha}.A \hookrightarrow B$ and computes a value of C possibly with effect ϵ. Then, M is typechecked under $R = (\boldsymbol{\alpha}, x : A, B \to \epsilon\; C)$, which means that argument x to the operation clause has type A and that resumptions in M are effectful functions from B to C with effect ϵ. Note that type variables $\boldsymbol{\alpha}$ occur free only in A and B but not in C.

Figure 2 shows the inference rules of the judgments (except for $\Gamma \vdash \sigma$, which is defined by: $\Gamma \vdash \sigma$ if and only if all free type variables in σ are bound by Γ). For a sequence of type schemes $\boldsymbol{\sigma}$, we write $\Gamma \vdash \boldsymbol{\sigma}$ if and only if every type scheme in $\boldsymbol{\sigma}$ is well formed under Γ.

Well-formedness rules for typing contexts, shown at the top of Fig. 2, are standard. A typing context is well formed if it is empty (WF_EMPTY) or a variable in the typing context is associated with a type scheme that is well formed in the remaining typing context (WF_VAR) and a type variable in the typing context is not declared (WF_TVAR). For typing context Γ, $dom(\Gamma)$ denotes the set of type and term variables declared in Γ.

Well-formed rules for typing contexts

$\boxed{\vdash \Gamma}$

$$\frac{}{\vdash \emptyset}\ \textsc{WF\_Empty} \qquad \frac{\vdash \Gamma \quad x \notin \mathit{dom}(\Gamma) \quad \Gamma \vdash \sigma}{\vdash \Gamma, x : \sigma}\ \textsc{WF\_Var}$$

$$\frac{\vdash \Gamma \quad \alpha \notin \mathit{dom}(\Gamma)}{\vdash \Gamma, \alpha}\ \textsc{WF\_TyVar}$$

Typing rules

$\boxed{\Gamma; R \vdash M : A \,|\, \epsilon}$

$$\frac{\vdash \Gamma \quad x : \forall \boldsymbol{\alpha}.A \in \Gamma \quad \Gamma \vdash \boldsymbol{B}}{\Gamma; R \vdash x : A[\boldsymbol{B}/\boldsymbol{\alpha}] \,|\, \epsilon}\ \textsc{TS\_Var} \qquad \frac{\vdash \Gamma}{\Gamma; R \vdash c : \mathit{ty}(c) \,|\, \epsilon}\ \textsc{TS\_Const}$$

$$\frac{\Gamma, x : A; R \vdash M : B \,|\, \epsilon'}{\Gamma; R \vdash \lambda x.M : A \to^{\epsilon'} B \,|\, \epsilon}\ \textsc{TS\_Abs}$$

$$\frac{\Gamma; R \vdash M_1 : A \to^{\epsilon'} B \,|\, \epsilon \quad \Gamma; R \vdash M_2 : A \,|\, \epsilon \quad \epsilon' \subseteq \epsilon}{\Gamma; R \vdash M_1\, M_2 : B \,|\, \epsilon}\ \textsc{TS\_App}$$

$$\frac{\Gamma, \boldsymbol{\alpha}; R \vdash M_1 : A \,|\, \epsilon \quad \Gamma, x : \forall \boldsymbol{\alpha}.A; R \vdash M_2 : B \,|\, \epsilon}{\Gamma; R \vdash \mathsf{let}\ x = M_1\ \mathsf{in}\ M_2 : B \,|\, \epsilon}\ \textsc{TS\_Let}$$

$$\frac{\Gamma; R \vdash M : A \,|\, \epsilon' \quad \epsilon' \subseteq \epsilon}{\Gamma; R \vdash M : A \,|\, \epsilon}\ \textsc{TS\_Weak}$$

$$\frac{\mathit{ty}(\mathsf{op}) = \forall \boldsymbol{\alpha}.A \hookrightarrow B \quad \mathsf{op} \in \epsilon \quad \Gamma; R \vdash M : A[\boldsymbol{C}/\boldsymbol{\alpha}] \,|\, \epsilon \quad \Gamma \vdash \boldsymbol{C}}{\Gamma; R \vdash \#\mathsf{op}(M) : B[\boldsymbol{C}/\boldsymbol{\alpha}] \,|\, \epsilon}\ \textsc{TS\_Op}$$

$$\frac{\Gamma; R \vdash M : A \,|\, \epsilon \quad \Gamma; R \vdash H : A \,|\, \epsilon \Rightarrow B \,|\, \epsilon'}{\Gamma; R \vdash \mathsf{handle}\ M\ \mathsf{with}\ H : B \,|\, \epsilon'}\ \textsc{TS\_Handle}$$

$$\frac{\begin{array}{c}\vdash \Gamma_1, x : D, \Gamma_2 \quad \boldsymbol{\alpha} \in \Gamma_1 \quad \epsilon \subseteq \epsilon' \\ \Gamma_1, \Gamma_2, \boldsymbol{\beta}, x : A[\boldsymbol{\beta}/\boldsymbol{\alpha}]; (\boldsymbol{\alpha}, x : A, B \to^{\epsilon} C) \vdash M : B[\boldsymbol{\beta}/\boldsymbol{\alpha}] \,|\, \epsilon'\end{array}}{\Gamma_1, x : D, \Gamma_2; (\boldsymbol{\alpha}, x : A, B \to^{\epsilon} C) \vdash \mathsf{resume}\ M : C \,|\, \epsilon'}\ \textsc{TS\_Resume}$$

$\boxed{\Gamma; R \vdash H : A \,|\, \epsilon \Rightarrow B \,|\, \epsilon'}$

$$\frac{\Gamma, x : A; R \vdash M : B \,|\, \epsilon' \quad \epsilon \subseteq \epsilon'}{\Gamma; R \vdash \mathsf{return}\ x \to M : A \,|\, \epsilon \Rightarrow B \,|\, \epsilon'}\ \textsc{THS\_Return}$$

$$\frac{\begin{array}{c}\Gamma; R \vdash H : A \,|\, \epsilon \Rightarrow B \,|\, \epsilon' \\ \mathit{ty}(\mathsf{op}) = \forall \boldsymbol{\alpha}.C \hookrightarrow D \quad \Gamma, \boldsymbol{\alpha}, x : C; (\boldsymbol{\alpha}, x : C, D \to^{\epsilon'} B) \vdash M : B \,|\, \epsilon'\end{array}}{\Gamma; R \vdash H; \mathsf{op}(x) \to M : A \,|\, \epsilon \uplus \{\mathsf{op}\} \Rightarrow B \,|\, \epsilon'}\ \textsc{THS\_Op}$$

Fig. 2. Typing rules.

Typing rules for terms are given in the middle of Fig. 2. The first six rules are standard for the lambda calculus with let-polymorphism and a type-and-effect system. If a variable x is introduced by a let-expression and has type scheme $\forall \boldsymbol{\alpha}.A$ in Γ, it is given type $A[\boldsymbol{B}/\boldsymbol{\alpha}]$, obtained by instantiating type variables $\boldsymbol{\alpha}$ with well-formed types $\boldsymbol{B}$. If x is bound by other constructors (e.g., a lambda abstraction), x is always bound to a monomorphic type and both $\boldsymbol{\alpha}$ and $\boldsymbol{B}$ are the empty sequence. Note that (TS_VAR) gives any effect ϵ to the typing judgment for x. In general, ϵ in judgment $\Gamma; R \vdash M : A \mid \epsilon$ means that the evaluation of M *may* invoke effect operations in ϵ. Since a reference to a variable involves no effect, it is given any effect; for the same reason, value constructors are also given any effect. The rule (TS_CONST) means that the type of a constant is given by (meta-level) function ty. The typing rules for lambda abstractions and function applications are standard in the lambda calculus equipped with a type-and-effect system. The rule (TS_ABS) gives lambda abstraction $\lambda x.M$ function type $A \rightarrow \epsilon' B$ if M computes a value of B possibly with effect ϵ' by using x of type A. The rule (TS_APP) requires that (1) the argument type of function part M_1 be equivalent to the type of actual argument M_2 and (2) effect ϵ' invoked by function M_1 be contained in the whole effect ϵ. The rule (TS_WEAK) allows weakening of effects.

The next two rules are mostly standard for algebraic effects and handlers. The rule (TS_OP) is applied to effect invocations. Since $\lambda_{\mathrm{eff}}^{\mathrm{let}}$ supports implicit polymorphism, an invocation #op(M) of polymorphic effect op of signature $\forall \boldsymbol{\alpha}.A \hookrightarrow B$ also accompanies implicit type substitution of well-formed types $\boldsymbol{C}$ for $\boldsymbol{\alpha}$. Thus, the type of argument M has to be $A[\boldsymbol{C}/\boldsymbol{\alpha}]$ and the result of the invocation is given type $B[\boldsymbol{C}/\boldsymbol{\alpha}]$. In addition, effect ϵ contains op. The typeability of handle–with expressions depends on the typing of handlers (TS_HANDLE), which will be explained below shortly.

The last typing rule (TS_RESUME) is the key to gaining type safety in this work. Suppose that we are given resumption type $(\boldsymbol{\alpha}, x : A, B \rightarrow \epsilon\ C)$. Intuitively, $B \rightarrow \epsilon\ C$ is the type of the continuation for resumption and, therefore, argument M to resume is required to have type B. As we have discussed in Sect. 2, we avoid interference between different resumptions by renaming $\boldsymbol{\alpha}$, the type parameters to the effect operation, to fresh type variables $\boldsymbol{\beta}$, in typechecking M. Freshness of $\boldsymbol{\beta}$ will be ensured when well-formedness of typing contexts $\Gamma_1, \Gamma_2, \boldsymbol{\beta}, \ldots$ is checked at the leaves of the type derivation. The type variables $\boldsymbol{\alpha}$ in the type of x, the parameter to the operation, are also renamed for x to be useful in M. To see why this renaming is useful, let us consider an extension of the calculus with pairs and typechecking of an operation clause for choose$^\forall$ of signature $\forall \alpha.\alpha \times \alpha \hookrightarrow \alpha$:

$$\mathsf{choose}^\forall(x) \rightarrow \mathsf{resume}\,(\mathsf{fst}\,x)$$

Variable x is assigned product type $\alpha \times \alpha$ for fresh type variable α and the body resume (fst x) is typechecked under the resumption type $(\alpha, x : \alpha \times \alpha, \alpha \rightarrow \epsilon\ A)$ for some ϵ and A (see the typing rules for handlers for details). To typecheck resume (fst x), the argument fst x is required to have type β, freshly generated for this resume. Without applying renaming also to x, the clause would not typecheck. Finally, (TS_RESUME) also requires that (1) the typing context contains $\boldsymbol{\alpha}$, which should have been declared at an application of the typing rule for the operation clause that surrounds this resume and (2) effect ϵ, which may be invoked by resumption of a continuation, be contained in the whole effect ϵ'. The binding $x : D$ in the conclusion means that parameter x to the operation clause is declared outside the resumption expression.

The typing rules for handlers are standard [3, 13, 16]. The rule (THS_RETURN) for a return clause $\mathsf{return}\, x \rightarrow M$ checks that the body M is given a type under the assumption that argument x has type A, which is the type of the handled expression. The effect ϵ stands for effects that are not handled by the operation clauses that follow the return clause and it must be a subset of the effect ϵ' that M may cause.[5] A handler having operation clauses is typechecked by (THS_OP), which checks that the body of the operation clause $\mathsf{op}(x) \rightarrow M$ for op of signature $\forall \boldsymbol{\alpha}.C \hookrightarrow D$ is typed at the result type B, which is the same as the type of the return clause, under the typing context extended with fresh assigned type variables $\boldsymbol{\alpha}$ and argument x of type C, together with the resumption type $(\boldsymbol{\alpha}, x : C, D \rightarrow_{\epsilon'} B)$. The effect $\epsilon \uplus \{\mathsf{op}\}$ in the conclusion means that the effect operation op is handled by this clause and no other clauses (in the present handler) handle it. Our semantics adopts deep handlers [13], i.e., when a handled expression invokes an effect operation, the continuation, which passed to the operation clause, is wrapped by the same handler. Thus, resumption may invoke the same effect ϵ' as the one possibly invoked by the clauses of the handler, hence $D \rightarrow_{\epsilon'} B$ in the resumption type.

Finally, we show how the type system rejects the counterexample given in Sect. 2. The problem is in the following operation clause.

$$\mathsf{op}(y) \rightarrow \mathsf{resume}\, \lambda z_1.(\mathsf{resume}\, \lambda z_2.z_1); z_1$$

where op has effect signature $\forall \alpha.\mathsf{unit} \hookrightarrow (\alpha \rightarrow_{\langle\rangle} \alpha)$. This clause is typechecked under resumption type $(\alpha, y : \mathsf{unit}, \alpha \rightarrow_{\epsilon} \alpha)$ for some ϵ. By (TS_RESUME), the two resumption expressions are assigned two different type variables γ_1 and γ_2, and the arguments $\lambda z_1.(\mathsf{resume}\, \lambda z_2.z_1); z_1$ and $\lambda z_2.z_1$ are required to have $\gamma_1 \rightarrow_{\epsilon} \gamma_1$ and $\gamma_2 \rightarrow_{\epsilon} \gamma_2$, respectively. However, $\lambda z_2.z_1$ cannot because z_1 is associated with γ_1 but not with γ_2.

Remark. The rule (TS_RESUME) allows only the type of the argument to an operation clause to be renamed. Thus, other variables bound by, e.g., lambda abstractions and let-expressions outside the resumption expression cannot be used as such a type. As a result, more care may be required as to where to introduce a new variable. For example, let us consider the following operation clause (which is a variant of the example of $\mathsf{choose}^{\forall}$ above).

$$\mathsf{choose}^{\forall}(x) \rightarrow \mathsf{let}\, y = \mathsf{fst}\, x\, \mathsf{in}\, \mathsf{resume}\, y$$

The variable x is assigned $\alpha \times \alpha$ first and the resumption requires y to be typed at fresh type variable β. This clause would be rejected in the current type system

[5] Thus, handlers in $\lambda_{\mathsf{eff}}^{\mathsf{let}}$ are open [13] in the sense that a handle–with expression does not have to handle *all* effects caused by the handled expression.

because fst x appears outside resume and, therefore, y is given type α, not β. This inconvenience may be addressed by moving down the let-binding in some cases: e.g., resume (let y = fst x in y) is well typed.

4 Intermediate Language: $\lambda_{\text{eff}}^{\Lambda}$

The semantics of $\lambda_{\text{eff}}^{\text{let}}$ is given by a formal elaboration to an intermediate language $\lambda_{\text{eff}}^{\Lambda}$, wherein type abstraction and type application appear explicitly. We define the syntax, operational semantics, and type system of $\lambda_{\text{eff}}^{\text{let}}$ and the formal elaboration from $\lambda_{\text{eff}}^{\text{let}}$ to $\lambda_{\text{eff}}^{\Lambda}$. Finally, we show type safety of $\lambda_{\text{eff}}^{\text{let}}$ via type preservation of the elaboration and type soundness of $\lambda_{\text{eff}}^{\Lambda}$.

Values	v	::=	$c \mid \lambda x.e$
Polymorphic values	w	::=	$v \mid \Lambda\alpha.w$
Terms	e	::=	$x\,\boldsymbol{A} \mid c \mid \lambda x.e \mid e_1\,e_2 \mid \mathsf{let}\,x = \Lambda\boldsymbol{\alpha}.e_1\,\mathsf{in}\,e_2 \mid$ $\#\mathsf{op}(\boldsymbol{A}, e) \mid \#\mathsf{op}(\boldsymbol{\sigma}, w, E) \mid \mathsf{handle}\,e\,\mathsf{with}\,h \mid$ $\mathsf{resume}\,\boldsymbol{\alpha}\,x.e$
Handlers	h	::=	$\mathsf{return}\,x \rightarrow e \mid h; \Lambda\boldsymbol{\alpha}.\mathsf{op}(x) \rightarrow e$
Evaluation contexts	$E^{\boldsymbol{\alpha}^I}$	::=	$[\,]\ (\text{if } \boldsymbol{\alpha}^I = \emptyset) \mid E^{\boldsymbol{\alpha}^I}\,e_2 \mid v_1\,E^{\boldsymbol{\alpha}^I} \mid$ $\mathsf{let}\,x = \Lambda\boldsymbol{\beta}^{J_1}.E^{\boldsymbol{\gamma}^{J_2}}\,\mathsf{in}\,e_2\ (\text{if } \boldsymbol{\alpha}^I = \boldsymbol{\beta}^{J_1}, \boldsymbol{\gamma}^{J_2}) \mid$ $\#\mathsf{op}(\boldsymbol{A}^J, E^{\boldsymbol{\alpha}^I}) \mid \mathsf{handle}\,E^{\boldsymbol{\alpha}^I}\,\mathsf{with}\,h$

Fig. 3. Syntax of $\lambda_{\text{eff}}^{\Lambda}$.

4.1 Syntax

The syntax of $\lambda_{\text{eff}}^{\Lambda}$ is shown in Fig. 3. Values, denoted by v, consist of constants and lambda abstractions. Polymorphic values, denoted by w, are values abstracted over types. Terms, denoted by e, and handlers, denoted by h, are the same as those of $\lambda_{\text{eff}}^{\text{let}}$ except for the following three points. First, type abstraction and type arguments are explicit in $\lambda_{\text{eff}}^{\Lambda}$: variables and effect invocations are accompanied by a sequence of types and let-bound expressions, resumption expressions, and operation clauses bind type variables. Second, a new term constructor of the form $\#\mathsf{op}(\boldsymbol{\sigma}, w, E)$ is added. It represents an intermediate state in which an effect invocation is capturing the continuation up to the closest handler for op. Here, E is an evaluation context [6] and denotes a continuation to be resumed by an operation clause handling op. In the operational semantics, an operation invocation $\#\mathsf{op}(\boldsymbol{A}, v)$ is first transformed to $\#\mathsf{op}(\boldsymbol{A}, v, [\,])$ (where $[\,]$ denotes the empty context or the identity continuation) and then it bubbles up by capturing its context and pushing it onto the third argument. Note that $\boldsymbol{\sigma}$ and w of $\#\mathsf{op}(\boldsymbol{\sigma}, w, E)$ become polymorphic when it bubbles up from the body of a type abstraction. Third, each resumption expression $\mathsf{resume}\,\boldsymbol{\alpha}\,x.e$ declares distinct (type) variables $\boldsymbol{\alpha}$ and x to denote the (type) argument to an operation

Reduction rules $\boxed{e_1 \rightsquigarrow e_2}$

$$c_1\, c_2 \rightsquigarrow \zeta(c_1, c_2) \quad (\text{R\_Const}) \qquad (\lambda x.e)\, v \rightsquigarrow e[v/x] \; (\text{R\_Beta})$$

$$\mathsf{let}\, x = \Lambda \boldsymbol{\alpha}.v\, \mathsf{in}\, e \rightsquigarrow e[\Lambda \boldsymbol{\alpha}.v/x] \quad (\text{R\_Let}) \qquad \begin{array}{r} \mathsf{handle}\, v\, \mathsf{with}\, h \rightsquigarrow e[v/x] \; (\text{R\_Return}) \\ (\text{where } h^{\mathsf{return}} = \mathsf{return}\, x \rightarrow e) \end{array}$$

$$\#\mathsf{op}(\boldsymbol{A}, v) \rightsquigarrow \#\mathsf{op}(\boldsymbol{A}, v, [\,]) \; (\text{R\_Op})$$

$$\#\mathsf{op}(\boldsymbol{\sigma}, w, E)\, e_2 \rightsquigarrow \#\mathsf{op}(\boldsymbol{\sigma}, w, E\, e_2) \qquad (\text{R\_OpApp1})$$

$$v_1\, \#\mathsf{op}(\boldsymbol{\sigma}, w, E) \rightsquigarrow \#\mathsf{op}(\boldsymbol{\sigma}, w, v_1\, E) \qquad (\text{R\_OpApp2})$$

$$\#\mathsf{op}'(\boldsymbol{A}^I, \#\mathsf{op}(\boldsymbol{\sigma}^J, w, E)) \rightsquigarrow \#\mathsf{op}(\boldsymbol{\sigma}^J, w, \#\mathsf{op}'(\boldsymbol{A}^I, E)) \qquad (\text{R\_OpOp})$$

$$\begin{array}{r} \mathsf{handle}\, \#\mathsf{op}(\boldsymbol{\sigma}, w, E)\, \mathsf{with}\, h \rightsquigarrow \#\mathsf{op}(\boldsymbol{\sigma}, w, \mathsf{handle}\, E\, \mathsf{with}\, h) \\ (\text{where } \mathsf{op} \notin ops(h)) \end{array} \qquad (\text{R\_OpHandle})$$

$$\begin{array}{l} \mathsf{let}\, x = \Lambda \boldsymbol{\alpha}^I.\#\mathsf{op}(\boldsymbol{\sigma}^J, w, E)\, \mathsf{in}\, e_2 \rightsquigarrow \\ \qquad \#\mathsf{op}(\forall\, \boldsymbol{\alpha}^I.\boldsymbol{\sigma}^J, \Lambda \boldsymbol{\alpha}^I.w, \mathsf{let}\, x = \Lambda \boldsymbol{\alpha}^I.E\, \mathsf{in}\, e_2) \end{array} \qquad (\text{R\_OpLet})$$

$$\begin{array}{l} \mathsf{handle}\, \#\mathsf{op}(\forall\, \boldsymbol{\beta}^J.\boldsymbol{A}^I, \Lambda \boldsymbol{\beta}^J.v, E^{\boldsymbol{\beta}^J})\, \mathsf{with}\, h \rightsquigarrow \\ \quad e[\mathsf{handle}\, E^{\boldsymbol{\beta}^J}\, \mathsf{with}\, h/\mathsf{resume}]^{\forall \boldsymbol{\beta}^J.\boldsymbol{A}^I}_{\Lambda \boldsymbol{\beta}^J.v} [\boldsymbol{A}^I[\bot/\boldsymbol{\beta}^J]/\boldsymbol{\alpha}^I][v[\bot/\boldsymbol{\beta}^J]/x] \\ \qquad (\text{where } h^{\mathsf{op}} = \Lambda \boldsymbol{\alpha}^I.\mathsf{op}(x) \rightarrow e) \end{array} \qquad (\text{R\_Handle})$$

Evaluation rules $\boxed{e_1 \longrightarrow e_2}$

$$\frac{e_1 \rightsquigarrow e_2}{E[e_1] \longrightarrow E[e_2]}\ \text{E\_Eval}$$

Fig. 4. Semantics of $\lambda^{\Lambda}_{\mathsf{eff}}$.

clause, whereas a single variable declared at $\mathsf{op}(x) \rightarrow M$ and implicit type variables are used for the same purpose in $\lambda^{\mathsf{let}}_{\mathsf{eff}}$. For example, the $\lambda^{\mathsf{let}}_{\mathsf{eff}}$ operation clause $\mathsf{choose}^{\forall}(x) \rightarrow \mathsf{resume}\,(\mathsf{fst}\, x)$ is translated to $\Lambda\alpha.\mathsf{choose}^{\forall}(x) \rightarrow \mathsf{resume}\, \beta\, y.(\mathsf{fst}\, y)$. This change simplifies the semantics.

Evaluation contexts, denoted by $E^{\boldsymbol{\alpha}}$, are standard for the lambda calculus with call-by-value, left-to-right evaluation except for two points. First, they contain the form $\mathsf{let}\, x = \Lambda \boldsymbol{\alpha}.E^{\boldsymbol{\beta}}\, \mathsf{in}\, e_2$, which allows the body of a type abstraction to be evaluated. Second, the metavariable E for evaluation contexts is indexed by type variables $\boldsymbol{\alpha}$, meaning that the hole in the context appears under type abstractions binding $\boldsymbol{\alpha}$. For example, $\mathsf{let}\, x = \Lambda\alpha.\mathsf{let}\, y = \Lambda\beta.[\,]\, \mathsf{in}\, e_2\, \mathsf{in}\, e_1$ is denoted by $E^{\alpha,\beta}$ and, more generally, $\mathsf{let}\, x = \Lambda \boldsymbol{\beta}^{J_1}.E^{\boldsymbol{\gamma}^{J_2}}\, \mathsf{in}\, e$ is denoted by $E^{\boldsymbol{\beta}^{J_1}, \boldsymbol{\gamma}^{J_2}}$. (Here, $\boldsymbol{\beta}^{J_1}, \boldsymbol{\gamma}^{J_2}$ stands for the concatenation of the two sequences $\boldsymbol{\beta}^{J_1}$ and $\boldsymbol{\gamma}^{J_2}$.) If $\boldsymbol{\alpha}$ is not important, we simply write E for $E^{\boldsymbol{\alpha}}$. We often use the term "continuation" to mean "evaluation context," especially when it is expected to be resumed.

As usual, substitution $e[w/x]$ of w for x in e is defined in a capture-avoiding manner. Since variables come along with type arguments, the case for variables is defined as follows:

$$(x\ \boldsymbol{A})[\Lambda\boldsymbol{\alpha}.v/x] \stackrel{\text{def}}{=} v[\boldsymbol{A}/\boldsymbol{\alpha}]$$

Application of substitution $[\Lambda\boldsymbol{\alpha}^I.v/x]$ to $x\ \boldsymbol{A}^J$, where $I \neq J$, is undefined. We define free type variables $\mathit{ftv}(e)$ and $\mathit{ftv}(E)$ in e and E, respectively, as usual.

4.2 Semantics

The semantics of $\lambda_{\mathrm{eff}}^{\Lambda}$ is given in the small-step style and consists of two relations: the reduction relation $\rightsquigarrow$, which is for basic computation, and the evaluation relation $\longrightarrow$, which is for top-level execution. Figure 4 shows the rules for these relations. In what follows, we write h^{return} for the return clause of handler h, $\mathit{ops}(h)$ for the set of effect operations handled by h, and h^{op} for the operation clause for op in h.

Most of the reduction rules are standard [13,16]. A constant application $c_1\ c_2$ reduces to $\zeta(c_1, c_2)$ (R_Const), where function ζ maps a pair of constants to another constant. A function application $(\lambda x.e)\ v$ and a let-expression $\mathsf{let}\ x = \Lambda\boldsymbol{\alpha}.v\ \mathsf{in}\ e$ reduce to $e[v/x]$ (R_Beta) and $e[\Lambda\boldsymbol{\alpha}.v/x]$ (R_Let), respectively. If a handled expression is a value v, the handle–with expression reduces to the body of the return clause where v is substituted for the parameter x (R_Return). An effect invocation $\#\mathsf{op}(\boldsymbol{A}, v)$ reduces to $\#\mathsf{op}(\boldsymbol{A}, v, [\,])$ with the identity continuation, as explained above (R_Op); the process of capturing its evaluation context is expressed by the rules (R_OpApp1), (R_OpApp2), (R_OpOp), (R_OpHandle), and (R_OpLet). The rule (R_OpHandle) can be applied only if the handler h does *not* handle op. The rule (R_OpLet) is applied to a let-expression where $\#\mathsf{op}(\boldsymbol{\sigma}^J, w, E)$ appears under a type abstraction with bound type variables $\boldsymbol{\alpha}^I$. Since $\boldsymbol{\sigma}^J$ and w may refer to $\boldsymbol{\alpha}^I$, the reduction result binds $\boldsymbol{\alpha}^I$ in both $\boldsymbol{\sigma}^J$ and w. We write $\forall\boldsymbol{\alpha}^I.\boldsymbol{\sigma}^J$ for a sequence $\forall\boldsymbol{\alpha}^I.\sigma_{j_1}, \ldots, \forall\boldsymbol{\alpha}^I.\sigma_{j_n}$ of type schemes (where $J = \{j_1, \ldots, j_n\}$).

The crux of the semantics is (R_Handle): it is applied when $\#\mathsf{op}(\boldsymbol{\sigma}^I, w, E)$ reaches the handler h that handles op. Since the handled term $\#\mathsf{op}(\boldsymbol{\sigma}^I, w, E)$ is constructed from an effect invocation $\#\mathsf{op}(\boldsymbol{A}^I, v)$, if the captured continuation E binds type variables $\boldsymbol{\beta}^J$, the same type variables $\boldsymbol{\beta}^J$ should have been added to $\boldsymbol{A}^I$ and v along the capture. Thus, the handled expression on the left-hand side of the rule takes the form $\#\mathsf{op}(\forall\boldsymbol{\beta}^J.\boldsymbol{A}^I, \Lambda\boldsymbol{\beta}^J.v, E^{\boldsymbol{\beta}^J})$ (with the same type variables $\boldsymbol{\beta}^J$).

The right-hand side of (R_Handle) involves three types of substitution: continuation substitution $[\mathsf{handle}\ E^{\boldsymbol{\beta}^J}\ \mathsf{with}\ h/\mathsf{resume}]^{\forall\boldsymbol{\beta}^J.\boldsymbol{A}^I}_{\Lambda\boldsymbol{\beta}^J.v}$ for resumptions, type substitution for $\boldsymbol{\alpha}^I$, and value substitution for x. We explain them one by one below. In the following, let $h^{\mathsf{op}} = \Lambda\boldsymbol{\alpha}^I.\mathsf{op}(x) \rightarrow e$ and $E'^{\boldsymbol{\beta}^J} = \mathsf{handle}\ E^{\boldsymbol{\beta}^J}\ \mathsf{with}\ h$.

Continuation Substitution. Let us start with a simple case where the sequence $\boldsymbol{\beta}^J$ is empty. Intuitively, continuation substitution $[E'/\mathsf{resume}]_v^{\boldsymbol{A}^I}$ replaces a resumption expression $\mathsf{resume}\,\boldsymbol{\gamma}^I\, z.e'$ in the body e with $E'[v']$, where v' is the value of e', and substitutes $\boldsymbol{A}^I$ and v (arguments to the invocation of op) for $\boldsymbol{\gamma}^I$ and z, respectively. Therefore, assuming resume does not appear in e', we define $(\mathsf{resume}\,\boldsymbol{\gamma}^I\, z.e')[E'/\mathsf{resume}]_v^{\boldsymbol{A}^I}$ to be $\mathsf{let}\, y = e'[\boldsymbol{A}^I/\boldsymbol{\gamma}^I][v/z]\,\mathsf{in}\, E'[y]$ (for fresh y). Note that the evaluation of e' takes place outside of E so that an invocation of an effect in e' is *not* handled by handlers in E. When $\boldsymbol{\beta}^J$ is not empty,

$$(\mathsf{resume}\,\boldsymbol{\gamma}^I\, z.e')[E^{\boldsymbol{\beta}^J}/\mathsf{resume}]_{\Lambda\boldsymbol{\beta}^J.v}^{\forall\boldsymbol{\beta}^J.\boldsymbol{A}^I} \stackrel{\text{def}}{=}$$
$$\mathsf{let}\, y = \Lambda\boldsymbol{\beta}^J.\, e'[\boldsymbol{A}^I/\boldsymbol{\gamma}^I][v/z]\,\mathsf{in}\, E^{\boldsymbol{\beta}^J}[y\,\boldsymbol{\beta}^J]\,.$$

(The differences from the simple case are shaded.) The idea is to bind $\boldsymbol{\beta}^J$ that appear free in $\boldsymbol{A}^I$ and v by type abstraction at let and to instantiate with the same variables at $y\,\boldsymbol{\beta}^J$, where $\boldsymbol{\beta}^J$ are bound by type abstractions in $E^{\boldsymbol{\beta}^J}$.

Continuation substitution is formally defined as follows:

Definition 2 (Continuation substitution). *Substitution of continuation $E^{\boldsymbol{\beta}^J}$ for resumptions in e, written $e[E^{\boldsymbol{\beta}^J}/\mathsf{resume}]_{\Lambda\boldsymbol{\beta}^J.v}^{\forall\boldsymbol{\beta}^J.\boldsymbol{A}^I}$, is defined in a capture-avoiding manner, as follows (we describe only the important cases):*

$$(\mathsf{resume}\,\boldsymbol{\gamma}^I\, z.e)[E^{\boldsymbol{\beta}^J}/\mathsf{resume}]_{\Lambda\boldsymbol{\beta}^J.v}^{\forall\boldsymbol{\beta}^J.\boldsymbol{A}^I} \stackrel{\text{def}}{=}$$
$$\mathsf{let}\, y = \Lambda\boldsymbol{\beta}^J.e[E^{\boldsymbol{\beta}^J}/\mathsf{resume}]_{\Lambda\boldsymbol{\beta}^J.v}^{\forall\boldsymbol{\beta}^J.\boldsymbol{A}^I}[\boldsymbol{A}^I/\boldsymbol{\gamma}^I][v/z]\,\mathsf{in}\, E^{\boldsymbol{\beta}^J}[y\,\boldsymbol{\beta}^J]$$
$$\textit{(if } (\mathit{ftv}(e) \cup \mathit{ftv}(E^{\boldsymbol{\beta}^J})) \cap \{\boldsymbol{\beta}^J\} = \emptyset \textit{ and } y \textit{ is fresh)}$$
$$(\mathsf{return}\, x \rightarrow e)[E/\mathsf{resume}]_w^{\sigma} \stackrel{\text{def}}{=} \mathsf{return}\, x \rightarrow e[E/\mathsf{resume}]_w^{\sigma}$$
$$(h'; \Lambda\boldsymbol{\gamma}^J.\mathsf{op}(x) \rightarrow e)[E/\mathsf{resume}]_w^{\boldsymbol{\sigma}^I} \stackrel{\text{def}}{=} h'[E/\mathsf{resume}]_w^{\boldsymbol{\sigma}^I}; \Lambda\boldsymbol{\gamma}^J.\mathsf{op}(x) \rightarrow e$$

The second and third clauses (for a handler) mean that continuation substitution is applied only to return clauses.

Type and Value Substitution. The type and value substitutions $\boldsymbol{A}^I[\bot^J/\boldsymbol{\beta}^J]$ and $v[\bot^J/\boldsymbol{\beta}^J]$, respectively, in (R_HANDLE) are for (type) parameters in $h^{\mathsf{op}} = \Lambda\boldsymbol{\alpha}^I.\mathsf{op}(x) \rightarrow e$. The basic idea is to substitute $\boldsymbol{A}^I$ for $\boldsymbol{\beta}^I$ and v for x—similarly to continuation substitution. We erase free type variables $\boldsymbol{\beta}^J$ in $\boldsymbol{A}^I$ and v by substituting the designated base type $\bot$ for all of them. (We write $\boldsymbol{A}^I[\bot^J/\boldsymbol{\beta}^J]$ and $v[\bot^J/\boldsymbol{\beta}^J]$ for the types and value, respectively, after the erasure.)

The evaluation rule is ordinary: Evaluation of a term proceeds by reducing a subterm under an evaluation context.

4.3 Type System

The type system of $\lambda_{\text{eff}}^{\Lambda}$ is similar to that of $\lambda_{\text{eff}}^{\text{let}}$ and has five judgments: well-formedness of typing contexts $\vdash \Gamma$; well formedness of type schemes $\Gamma \vdash \sigma$; term typing judgment $\Gamma; r \vdash e : A \mid \epsilon$; handler typing judgment $\Gamma; r \vdash h : A \mid \epsilon \Rightarrow B \mid \epsilon'$; and continuation typing judgment $\Gamma \vdash E : \forall \boldsymbol{\alpha}.A \multimap B \mid \epsilon$. The first two are defined in the same way as those of $\lambda^{\text{let}}_{\text{eff}}$. The last judgment means that a term obtained by filling the hole of E with a term having A under $\Gamma, \boldsymbol{\alpha}$ is typed at B under Γ and possibly involves effect ϵ. A resumption type r is similar to R but does not contain an argument variable.

Definition 3 (Resumption type). *Resumption types in $\lambda^{\Lambda}_{\text{eff}}$, denoted by r, are defined as follows:*

$$r ::= \mathsf{none} \mid (\boldsymbol{\alpha}, A, B \rightarrow_\epsilon C) \quad (\text{if } \mathit{ftv}(A) \cup \mathit{ftv}(B) \subseteq \{\boldsymbol{\alpha}\} \text{ and } \mathit{ftv}(C) \cap \{\boldsymbol{\alpha}\} = \emptyset)$$

Typing rules

$\boxed{\Gamma; r \vdash e : A \mid \epsilon}$

$$\frac{\vdash \Gamma \quad x : \forall \boldsymbol{\alpha}.A \in \Gamma \quad \Gamma \vdash \boldsymbol{B}}{\Gamma; r \vdash x\, \boldsymbol{B} : A[\boldsymbol{B}/\boldsymbol{\alpha}] \mid \epsilon}\ \text{T\_Var} \qquad \frac{\vdash \Gamma}{\Gamma; r \vdash c : \mathit{ty}(c) \mid \epsilon}\ \text{T\_Const}$$

$$\frac{\Gamma, x : A; r \vdash e : B \mid \epsilon'}{\Gamma; r \vdash \lambda x.e : A \rightarrow_{\epsilon'} B \mid \epsilon}\ \text{T\_Abs}$$

$$\frac{\Gamma; r \vdash e_1 : A \rightarrow_{\epsilon'} B \mid \epsilon \quad \Gamma; r \vdash e_2 : A \mid \epsilon \quad \epsilon' \subseteq \epsilon}{\Gamma; r \vdash e_1\, e_2 : B \mid \epsilon}\ \text{T\_App}$$

$$\frac{\mathit{ty}(\mathsf{op}) = \forall \boldsymbol{\alpha}.A \hookrightarrow B \quad \mathsf{op} \in \epsilon \quad \Gamma; r \vdash e : A[\boldsymbol{C}/\boldsymbol{\alpha}] \mid \epsilon \quad \Gamma \vdash \boldsymbol{C}}{\Gamma; r \vdash \#\mathsf{op}(\boldsymbol{C}, e) : B[\boldsymbol{C}/\boldsymbol{\alpha}] \mid \epsilon}\ \text{T\_Op}$$

$$\frac{\begin{array}{c}\mathit{ty}(\mathsf{op}) = \forall \boldsymbol{\alpha}^I.A \hookrightarrow B \quad \mathsf{op} \in \epsilon \quad \Gamma \vdash \forall \boldsymbol{\beta}^J.\boldsymbol{C}^I \\ \Gamma, \boldsymbol{\beta}^J; r \vdash v : A[\boldsymbol{C}^I/\boldsymbol{\alpha}^I] \mid \epsilon \quad \Gamma \vdash E^{\boldsymbol{\beta}^J} : \forall \boldsymbol{\beta}^J.(B[\boldsymbol{C}^I/\boldsymbol{\alpha}^I]) \multimap D \mid \epsilon\end{array}}{\Gamma; r \vdash \#\mathsf{op}(\forall \boldsymbol{\beta}^J.\boldsymbol{C}^I, \Lambda \boldsymbol{\beta}^J.v, E^{\boldsymbol{\beta}^J}) : D \mid \epsilon}\ \text{T\_OpCont}$$

$$\frac{\Gamma; r \vdash e : A \mid \epsilon' \quad \epsilon' \subseteq \epsilon}{\Gamma; r \vdash e : A \mid \epsilon}\ \text{T\_Weak}$$

$$\frac{\Gamma; r \vdash e : A \mid \epsilon \quad \Gamma; r \vdash h : A \mid \epsilon \Rightarrow B \mid \epsilon'}{\Gamma; r \vdash \mathsf{handle}\, e\, \mathsf{with}\, h : B \mid \epsilon'}\ \text{T\_Handle}$$

$$\frac{\Gamma, \boldsymbol{\alpha}; r \vdash e_1 : A \mid \epsilon \quad \Gamma, x : \forall \boldsymbol{\alpha}.A; r \vdash e_2 : B \mid \epsilon}{\Gamma; r \vdash \mathsf{let}\, x = \Lambda \boldsymbol{\alpha}.e_1\, \mathsf{in}\, e_2 : B \mid \epsilon}\ \text{T\_Let}$$

$$\frac{\boldsymbol{\alpha} \in \Gamma \quad \Gamma, \boldsymbol{\beta}, x : A[\boldsymbol{\beta}/\boldsymbol{\alpha}]; (\boldsymbol{\alpha}, A, B \rightarrow_\epsilon C) \vdash e : B[\boldsymbol{\beta}/\boldsymbol{\alpha}] \mid \epsilon' \quad \epsilon \subseteq \epsilon'}{\Gamma; (\boldsymbol{\alpha}, A, B \rightarrow_\epsilon C) \vdash \mathsf{resume}\, \boldsymbol{\beta}\, x.e : C \mid \epsilon'}\ \text{T\_Resume}$$

Fig. 5. Typing rules for terms in $\lambda^{\Lambda}_{\text{eff}}$.

The typing rules for terms, shown in Fig. 5, and handlers, shown in the upper half of Fig. 6, are similar to those of $\lambda_{\text{eff}}^{\text{let}}$ except for a new rule (T_OpCont), which is applied to an effect invocation $\#\mathsf{op}(\forall \boldsymbol{\beta}^J.\boldsymbol{C}^I, \Lambda\boldsymbol{\beta}^J.v, E^{\boldsymbol{\beta}^J})$ with a continuation. Let $ty(\mathsf{op}) = \forall \boldsymbol{\alpha}^I.A \hookrightarrow B$. Since op should have been invoked with $\boldsymbol{C}^I$ and v under type abstractions with bound type variables $\boldsymbol{\beta}^J$, the argument v has type $A[\boldsymbol{C}^I/\boldsymbol{\alpha}^I]$ under the typing context extended with $\boldsymbol{\beta}^J$. Similarly, the hole of $E^{\boldsymbol{\beta}^J}$ expects to be filled with the result of the invocation, i.e., a value of $B[\boldsymbol{C}^I/\boldsymbol{\alpha}^I]$. Since the continuation denotes the context before the evaluation, its result type matches with the type of the whole term.

The typing rules for continuations are shown in the lower half of Fig. 6. They are similar to the corresponding typing rules for terms except that a subterm is replaced with a continuation. In (TE_Let), the continuation $\mathsf{let}\, x = \Lambda\boldsymbol{\alpha}.E \,\mathsf{in}\, e$ has type $\forall \boldsymbol{\alpha}.\sigma \multimap B$ because the hole of E appears inside the scope of $\boldsymbol{\alpha}$.

$$\boxed{\Gamma; r \vdash h : A \mid \epsilon \Rightarrow B \mid \epsilon'}$$

$$\frac{\Gamma, x : A; r \vdash e : B \mid \epsilon' \quad \epsilon \subseteq \epsilon'}{\Gamma; r \vdash \mathsf{return}\, x \rightarrow e : A \mid \epsilon \Rightarrow B \mid \epsilon'} \ \text{TH\_Return}$$

$$\frac{\begin{array}{c}\Gamma; r \vdash h : A \mid \epsilon \Rightarrow B \mid \epsilon' \\ ty(\mathsf{op}) = \forall \boldsymbol{\alpha}.C \hookrightarrow D \quad \Gamma, \boldsymbol{\alpha}, x : C; (\boldsymbol{\alpha}, C, D \rightarrow^{\epsilon'} B) \vdash e : B \mid \epsilon'\end{array}}{\Gamma; r \vdash h; \Lambda\boldsymbol{\alpha}.\mathsf{op}(x) \rightarrow e : A \mid \epsilon \uplus \{\mathsf{op}\} \Rightarrow B \mid \epsilon'} \ \text{TH\_Op}$$

$$\boxed{\Gamma \vdash E : \sigma \multimap A \mid \epsilon}$$

$$\frac{}{\Gamma \vdash [\,] : A \multimap A \mid \epsilon} \ \text{TE\_Hole}$$

$$\frac{\Gamma \vdash E : \sigma \multimap (A \rightarrow^{\epsilon'} B) \mid \epsilon \quad \Gamma; \mathsf{none} \vdash e_2 : A \mid \epsilon \quad \epsilon' \subseteq \epsilon}{\Gamma \vdash E\, e_2 : \sigma \multimap B \mid \epsilon} \ \text{TE\_App1}$$

$$\frac{\Gamma; \mathsf{none} \vdash v_1 : (A \rightarrow^{\epsilon'} B) \mid \epsilon \quad \Gamma \vdash E : \sigma \multimap A \mid \epsilon \quad \epsilon' \subseteq \epsilon}{\Gamma \vdash v_1\, E : \sigma \multimap B \mid \epsilon} \ \text{TE\_App2}$$

$$\frac{ty(\mathsf{op}) = \forall \boldsymbol{\alpha}.A \hookrightarrow B \quad \mathsf{op} \in \epsilon \quad \Gamma \vdash E : \sigma \multimap A[\boldsymbol{C}/\boldsymbol{\alpha}] \mid \epsilon \quad \Gamma \vdash \boldsymbol{C}}{\Gamma \vdash \#\mathsf{op}(\boldsymbol{C}, E) : \sigma \multimap B[\boldsymbol{C}/\boldsymbol{\alpha}] \mid \epsilon} \ \text{TE\_Op}$$

$$\frac{\Gamma \vdash E : \sigma \multimap A \mid \epsilon \quad \Gamma; \mathsf{none} \vdash h : A \mid \epsilon \Rightarrow B \mid \epsilon'}{\Gamma \vdash \mathsf{handle}\, E \,\mathsf{with}\, h : \sigma \multimap B \mid \epsilon'} \ \text{TE\_Handle}$$

$$\frac{\Gamma \vdash E : \sigma \multimap A \mid \epsilon' \quad \epsilon' \subseteq \epsilon}{\Gamma \vdash E : \sigma \multimap A \mid \epsilon} \ \text{TE\_Weak}$$

$$\frac{\Gamma, \boldsymbol{\alpha} \vdash E : \sigma \multimap A \mid \epsilon \quad \Gamma, x : \forall \boldsymbol{\alpha}.A; \mathsf{none} \vdash e : B \mid \epsilon}{\Gamma \vdash \mathsf{let}\, x = \Lambda\boldsymbol{\alpha}.E \,\mathsf{in}\, e : \forall \boldsymbol{\alpha}.\sigma \multimap B \mid \epsilon} \ \text{TE\_Let}$$

Fig. 6. Typing rules for handlers and continuations in $\lambda_{\text{eff}}^{\Lambda}$.

4.4 Elaboration

This section defines the elaboration from $\lambda_{\mathsf{eff}}^{\mathsf{let}}$ to $\lambda_{\mathsf{eff}}^{\Lambda}$. The important difference between the two languages from the viewpoint of elaboration is that, whereas the parameter of an operation clause is referred to by a single variable in $\lambda_{\mathsf{eff}}^{\mathsf{let}}$, it is done by one or more variables in $\lambda_{\mathsf{eff}}^{\Lambda}$. Therefore, one variable in $\lambda_{\mathsf{eff}}^{\mathsf{let}}$ is represented by multiple variables (required for each resume) in $\lambda_{\mathsf{eff}}^{\Lambda}$. We use S, a mapping from variables to variables, to make the correspondence between variable names. We write $S \circ \{x \mapsto y\}$ for the same mapping as S except that x is mapped to y.

Elaboration is defined by two judgments: term elaboration judgment $\Gamma; R \vdash M : A \mid \epsilon \rhd^S e$, which denotes elaboration from a typing derivation of judgment $\Gamma; R \vdash M : A \mid \epsilon$ to e with S, and handler elaboration judgment $\Gamma; R \vdash H : A \mid \epsilon \Rightarrow B \mid \epsilon' \rhd^S h$, which denotes elaboration from a typing derivation of judgment $\Gamma; R \vdash H : A \mid \epsilon \Rightarrow B \mid \epsilon'$ to h with S.

Term elaboration rules $\boxed{\Gamma; R \vdash M : A \mid \epsilon \rhd^S e}$

$$\frac{\vdash \Gamma \quad x : \forall \boldsymbol{\alpha}.A \in \Gamma \quad \Gamma \vdash \boldsymbol{B}}{\Gamma; R \vdash x : A[\boldsymbol{B}/\boldsymbol{\alpha}] \mid \epsilon \rhd^S S(x)\,\boldsymbol{B}}\ \textsc{Elab\_Var}$$

$$\frac{\Gamma, x : A; R \vdash M : B \mid \epsilon' \rhd^{S \circ \{x \mapsto x\}} e}{\Gamma; R \vdash \lambda x.M : A \to^{\epsilon'} B \mid \epsilon \rhd^S \lambda x.e}\ \textsc{Elab\_Abs}$$

$$\frac{\Gamma; R \vdash M : A \mid \epsilon \rhd^S e \quad \Gamma; R \vdash H : A \mid \epsilon \Rightarrow B \mid \epsilon' \rhd^S h}{\Gamma; R \vdash \mathsf{handle}\ M\ \mathsf{with}\ H : B \mid \epsilon' \rhd^S \mathsf{handle}\ e\ \mathsf{with}\ h}\ \textsc{Elab\_Handle}$$

$$\frac{\begin{array}{c}\Gamma, \boldsymbol{\alpha}; R \vdash M_1 : A \mid \epsilon \rhd^S e_1 \quad S' = S \circ \{x \mapsto x\} \\ \Gamma, x : \forall \boldsymbol{\alpha}.A; R \vdash M_2 : B \mid \epsilon \rhd^{S'} e_2\end{array}}{\Gamma; R \vdash \mathsf{let}\ x = M_1\ \mathsf{in}\ M_2 : B \mid \epsilon \rhd^S \mathsf{let}\ x = \Lambda \boldsymbol{\alpha}.e_1\ \mathsf{in}\ e_2}\ \textsc{Elab\_Let}$$

$$\frac{\begin{array}{c}R = (\boldsymbol{\alpha}, x : A, B \to^{\epsilon} C) \quad \vdash \Gamma_1, x : D, \Gamma_2 \quad \boldsymbol{\alpha} \in \Gamma_1 \quad \epsilon \subseteq \epsilon' \\ y \text{ is fresh} \quad S' = S \circ \{x \mapsto y\} \\ \Gamma_1, \Gamma_2, \boldsymbol{\beta}, x : A[\boldsymbol{\beta}/\boldsymbol{\alpha}]; R \vdash M : B[\boldsymbol{\beta}/\boldsymbol{\alpha}] \mid \epsilon' \rhd^{S'} e\end{array}}{\Gamma_1, x : D, \Gamma_2; R \vdash \mathsf{resume}\ M : C \mid \epsilon' \rhd^S \mathsf{resume}\ \boldsymbol{\beta}\ y.e}\ \textsc{Elab\_Resume}$$

Handler elaboration rules $\boxed{\Gamma; R \vdash H : A \mid \epsilon \Rightarrow B \mid \epsilon' \rhd^S h}$

$$\frac{\Gamma, x : A; R \vdash M : B \mid \epsilon' \rhd^{S \circ \{x \mapsto x\}} e \quad \epsilon \subseteq \epsilon'}{\Gamma; R \vdash \mathsf{return}\ x \to M : A \mid \epsilon \Rightarrow B \mid \epsilon' \rhd^S \mathsf{return}\ x \to e}\ \textsc{ElabH\_Return}$$

$$\frac{\begin{array}{c}ty(\mathsf{op}) = \forall \boldsymbol{\alpha}.C \hookrightarrow D \quad \Gamma; R \vdash H : A \mid \epsilon \Rightarrow B \mid \epsilon' \rhd^S h \\ \Gamma, \boldsymbol{\alpha}, x : C; (\boldsymbol{\alpha}, x : C, D \to^{\epsilon'} B) \vdash M : B \mid \epsilon' \rhd^{S \circ \{x \mapsto x\}} e\end{array}}{\Gamma; R \vdash H; \mathsf{op}(x) \to M : A \mid \epsilon \uplus \{\mathsf{op}\} \Rightarrow B \mid \epsilon' \rhd^S h; \Lambda \boldsymbol{\alpha}.\mathsf{op}(x) \to e}\ \textsc{ElabH\_Op}$$

Fig. 7. Elaboration rules (excerpt).

Selected elaboration rules are shown in Fig. 7; the complete set of the rules is found in the full version of the paper. The elaboration rules are straightforward except for the use of S. A variable x is translated to $S(x)$ (ELAB_VAR) and, every time a new variable is introduced, S is extended: see the rules other than (ELAB_VAR) and (ELAB_HANDLE).

4.5 Properties

We show type safety of $\lambda_{\text{eff}}^{\text{let}}$, i.e., a well-typed program in $\lambda_{\text{eff}}^{\text{let}}$ does not get stuck, by proving (1) type preservation of the elaboration from $\lambda_{\text{eff}}^{\text{let}}$ to $\lambda_{\text{eff}}^{\Lambda}$ and (2) type soundness of $\lambda_{\text{eff}}^{\Lambda}$. Term M is a well-typed program of A if and only if $\emptyset; \mathsf{none} \vdash M : A \mid \langle\rangle$.

The first can be shown easily. We write $\emptyset$ also for the identity mapping for variables.

Theorem 1 (Elaboration is type-preserving). *If M is a well-typed program of A, then $\emptyset; \mathsf{none} \vdash M : A \mid \langle\rangle \rhd^{\emptyset} e$ and $\emptyset; \mathsf{none} \vdash e : A \mid \langle\rangle$ for some e.*

We show the second—type soundness of $\lambda_{\text{eff}}^{\Lambda}$—via progress and subject reduction [25]. We write Δ for a typing context that consists only of type variables. Progress can be shown as usual.

Lemma 1 (Progress). *If $\Delta; \mathsf{none} \vdash e : A \mid \epsilon$, then (1) $e \longrightarrow e'$ for some e', (2) e is a value, or (3) $e = \#\mathsf{op}(\boldsymbol{\sigma}, w, E)$ for some $\mathsf{op} \in \epsilon$, $\boldsymbol{\sigma}$, w, and E.*

A key lemma to show subject reduction is type preservation of continuation substitution.

Lemma 2 (Continuation substitution). *Suppose that $\Gamma \vdash \forall \boldsymbol{\beta}^J.\boldsymbol{C}^I$ and $\Gamma \vdash E^{\boldsymbol{\beta}^J} : \forall \boldsymbol{\beta}^J.(B[\boldsymbol{C}^I/\boldsymbol{\alpha}^I]) \multimap D \mid \epsilon$ and $\Gamma, \boldsymbol{\beta}^J \vdash v : A[\boldsymbol{C}^I/\boldsymbol{\alpha}^I]$.*

1. *If $\Gamma; (\boldsymbol{\alpha}^I, A, B \to_\epsilon D) \vdash e : D' \mid \epsilon'$, then $\Gamma; \mathsf{none} \vdash e[E^{\boldsymbol{\beta}^J}/\mathsf{resume}]^{\forall \boldsymbol{\beta}^J.\boldsymbol{C}^I}_{\Lambda \boldsymbol{\beta}^J.v} : D' \mid \epsilon'$.*
2. *If $\Gamma; (\boldsymbol{\alpha}^I, A, B \to_\epsilon D) \vdash h : D_1 \mid \epsilon_1 \Rightarrow D_2 \mid \epsilon_2$, then $\Gamma; \mathsf{none} \vdash h[E^{\boldsymbol{\beta}^J}/\mathsf{resume}]^{\forall \boldsymbol{\beta}^J.\boldsymbol{C}^I}_{\Lambda \boldsymbol{\beta}^J.v} : D_1 \mid \epsilon_1 \Rightarrow D_2 \mid \epsilon_2$.*

Using the continuation substitution lemma as well as other lemmas, we show subject reduction.

Lemma 3 (Subject reduction)

1. *If $\Delta; \mathsf{none} \vdash e_1 : A \mid \epsilon$ and $e_1 \rightsquigarrow e_2$, then $\Delta; \mathsf{none} \vdash e_2 : A \mid \epsilon$.*
2. *If $\Delta; \mathsf{none} \vdash e_1 : A \mid \epsilon$ and $e_1 \longrightarrow e_2$, then $\Delta; \mathsf{none} \vdash e_2 : A \mid \epsilon$.*

We write $e \not\longrightarrow$ if and only if e cannot evaluate further. Moreover, $\longrightarrow^*$ denotes the reflexive and transitive closure of the evaluation relation $\longrightarrow$.

Theorem 2 (Type soundness of $\lambda_{\mathbf{eff}}^{\Lambda}$). *If Δ; none $\vdash e : A \mid \epsilon$ and $e \longrightarrow^* e'$ and $e' \not\longrightarrow$, then (1) e' is a value or (2) $e' = \#\mathsf{op}(\boldsymbol{\sigma}, w, E)$ for some $\mathsf{op} \in \epsilon$, $\boldsymbol{\sigma}$, w, and E.*

Now, type safety of $\lambda_{\mathrm{eff}}^{\mathrm{let}}$ is obtained as a corollary of Theorems 1 and 2.

Corollary 1 (Type safety of $\lambda_{\mathbf{eff}}^{\mathbf{let}}$). *If M is a well-typed program of A, there exists some e such that $\emptyset$; none $\vdash M : A \mid \langle\rangle \rhd^{\emptyset} e$ and e does not get stuck.*

5 Related Work

5.1 Polymorphic Effects and Let-Polymorphism

Many researchers have attacked the problem of combining effects—not necessarily algebraic—and let-polymorphism so far [1,2,10,12,14,17,23,24]. In particular, most of them have focused on ML-style polymorphic references. The algebraic effect handlers dealt with in this paper seem to be unable to implement general ML-style references—i.e., give an appropriate implementation to a set of effect operations `new` with the signature $\forall\alpha.\alpha \hookrightarrow \alpha\,\mathsf{ref}$, `get` with $\forall\alpha.\alpha\,\mathsf{ref} \hookrightarrow \alpha$, and `put` with $\forall\alpha.\alpha \times \alpha\,\mathsf{ref} \hookrightarrow \mathsf{unit}$ for abstract datatype $\alpha\,\mathsf{ref}$—even without the restriction on handlers because each operation clause in a handler assigns type variables locally and it is impossible to share such type variables between operation clauses.[6] Nevertheless, their approaches would be applicable to algebraic effects and handlers.

A common idea in the literature is to restrict the form of expressions bound by polymorphic let. Thus, they are complementary to our approach in that they restrict how effect operations are used whereas we restrict how effect operations are implemented.

Value restriction [23,24], a standard way adopted in ML-like languages, restricts polymorphic let-bound expressions to syntactic values. Garrigue [10] relaxes the value restriction so that, if a let-bound expression is not a syntactic value, type variables that appear only at positive positions in the type of the expression can be generalized. Although the (relaxed) value restriction is a quite clear criterion that indicates what let-bound expressions can be polymorphic safely and it even accepts interfering handlers, it is too restrictive in some cases. We give an example for such a case below.

```
effect choose∀ : ∀α. α × α ↪ α

let f1 () =
  let g = #choose∀(fst, snd) in
  if g (true,false) then g (-1,1) else g (1,-1)
```

6 One possible approach to dealing with ML-style references is to extend algebraic effects and handlers so that a handler for *parameterized* effects can be connected with dynamic resources [3].

In the definition of function `f1`, variable `g` is used polymorphically. Execution of this function under an appropriate handler would succeed, and in fact our calculus accepts it. By contrast, the (relaxed) value restriction rejects it because the let-bound expression `#choose`$^\forall$`(fst,snd)` is not a syntactic value and the type variable appear in both positive and negative positions, and so `g` is assigned a monomorphic type. A workaround for this problem is to make a function wrapper that calls either of `fst` or `snd` depending on the Boolean value chosen by `choose`$^\forall$:

```
let f2 () =
  let b = #choose∀(true,false) in
  let g = λx. if b then (fst x) else (snd x) in
  if g (true,false) then g (-1,1) else g (1,-1)
```

However, this workaround makes the program complicated and incurs additional run-time cost for the branching and an extra call to the wrapper function.

Asai and Kameyama [2] study a combination of let-polymorphism with delimited control operators shift/reset [4]. They allow a let-bound expression to be polymorphic if it invokes no control operation. Thus, the function `f1` above would be rejected in their approach.

Another research line to restrict the use of effects is to allow only type variables unrelated to effect invocations to be generalized. Tofte [23] distinguishes between applicative type variables, which cannot be used for effect invocations, and imperative ones, which can be used, and proposes a type system that enforces restrictions that (1) type variables of imperative operations can be instantiated only with types wherein all type variables are imperative and (2) if a let-bound expression is not a syntactic value, only applicative type variables can be generalized. Leroy and Weis [17] allow generalization only of type variables that do not appear in a parameter type to the reference type in the type of a let-expression. To detect the hidden use of references, their type system gives a term not only a type but also the types of free variables used in the term. Standard ML of New Jersey (before ML97) adopted weak polymorphism [1], which was later formalized and investigated deeply by Hoang et al. [12]. Weak polymorphism equips a type variable with the number of function calls after which a value of a type containing the type variable will be passed to an imperative operation. The type system ensures that type variables with positive numbers are not related to imperative constructs, and so such type variables can be generalized safely. In this line of research, the function `f1` above would not typecheck because generalized type variables are used to instantiate those of the effect signature, although it could be rewritten to an acceptable one by taking care not to involve type variables in effect invocation.

```
let f3 () =
  let g = if #choose∀(true,false) then fst then snd in
  if g (true,false) then g (-1,1) else g (1,-1)
```

More recently, Kammar and Pretnar [14] show that *parameterized* algebraic effects and handlers do not need the value restriction *if* the type variables used in an effect invocation are not generalized. Thus, as the other work that restricts generalized type variables, their approach would reject function `f1` but would accept `f3`.

5.2 Algebraic Effects and Handlers

Algebraic effects [20] are a way to represent the denotation of an effect by giving a set of operations and an equational theory that capture their properties. Algebraic effect handlers, introduced by Plotkin and Pretnar [21], make it possible to provide user-defined effects. Algebraic effect handlers have been gaining popularity owing to their flexibility and have been made available as libraries [13,15,26] or as primitive features of languages, such as Eff [3], Koka [16], Frank [18], and Multicore OCaml [5]. In these languages, let-bound expressions that can be polymorphic are restricted to values or pure expressions.

Recently, Forster et al. [9] investigate the relationships between algebraic effect handlers and other mechanisms for user-defined effects—delimited control shift0 [19] and monadic reflection [7,8]—conjecturing that there would be no type-preserving translation from a language with delimited control or monadic reflection to one with algebraic effect handlers. It would be an interesting direction to export our idea to delimited control and monadic reflection.

6 Conclusion

There has been a long history of collaboration between effects and let-polymorphism. This work focuses on polymorphic algebraic effects and handlers, wherein the type signature of an effect operation can be polymorphic and an operation clause has a type binder, and shows that a naive combination of polymorphic effects and let-polymorphism breaks type safety. Our novel observation to address this problem is that any let-bound expression can be polymorphic safely if resumptions from a handler do not interfere with each other. We formalized this idea by developing a type system that requires the argument of each resumption expression to have a type obtained by renaming the type variables assigned in the operation clause to those assigned in the resumption. We have proven that a well-typed program in our type system does not get stuck via elaboration to an intermediate language wherein type information appears explicitly.

There are many directions for future work. The first is to address the problem, described at the end of Sect. 3, that renaming the type variables assigned in an operation clause to those assigned in a resumption expression is allowed for the argument of the clause but not for variables bound by lambda abstractions and let-expressions outside the resumption expression. Second, we are interested in incorporating other features from the literature on algebraic effect handlers, such as dynamic resources [3] and parameterized algebraic effects, and restriction techniques that have been developed for type-safe imperative programming with let-polymorphism such as (relaxed) value restriction [10,23,24]. For example, we would like to develop a type system that enforces the non-interfering restriction only to handlers implementing effect operations invoked in polymorphic computation. We also expect that it is possible to determine whether implementations of an effect operation have no interfering resumption from the type signature of the operation, as relaxed value restriction makes it possible to find safely generalizable type variables from the type of a let-bound expression [10]. Finally, we are also interested in implementing our idea for a language with effect handlers such as Koka [16] and in applying the idea of analyzing handlers to other settings such as dependent typing.

Acknowledgments. We would like to thank the anonymous reviewers for their valuable comments. This work was supported in part by ERATO HASUO Metamathematics for Systems Design Project (No. JPMJER1603), JST (Sekiyama), and JSPS KAKENHI Grant Number JP15H05706 (Igarashi).

References

1. Appel, A.W., MacQueen, D.B.: Standard ML of New Jersey. In: Maluszyński, J., Wirsing, M. (eds.) PLILP 1991. LNCS, vol. 528, pp. 1–13. Springer, Heidelberg (1991). https://doi.org/10.1007/3-540-54444-5_83
2. Asai, K., Kameyama, Y.: Polymorphic delimited continuations. In: Shao, Z. (ed.) APLAS 2007. LNCS, vol. 4807, pp. 239–254. Springer, Heidelberg (2007). https://doi.org/10.1007/978-3-540-76637-7_16
3. Bauer, A., Pretnar, M.: Programming with algebraic effects and handlers. J. Log. Algebr. Methods Program. **84**(1), 108–123 (2015). https://doi.org/10.1016/j.jlamp.2014.02.001
4. Danvy, O., Filinski, A.: Abstracting control. In: LISP and Functional Programming, pp. 151–160 (1990). https://doi.org/10.1145/91556.91622
5. Dolan, S., Eliopoulos, S., Hillerström, D., Madhavapeddy, A., Sivaramakrishnan, K.C., White, L.: Concurrent system programming with effect handlers. In: Wang, M., Owens, S. (eds.) TFP 2017. LNCS, vol. 10788, pp. 98–117. Springer, Cham (2018). https://doi.org/10.1007/978-3-319-89719-6_6
6. Felleisen, M., Hieb, R.: The revised report on the syntactic theories of sequential control and state. Theor. Comput. Sci. **103**(2), 235–271 (1992). https://doi.org/10.1016/0304-3975(92)90014-7
7. Filinski, A.: Representing monads. In: Proceedings of the 21st ACM SIGPLAN-SIGACT Symposium on Principles of Programming Languages, pp. 446–457 (1994). https://doi.org/10.1145/174675.178047
8. Filinski, A.: Monads in action. In: Proceedings of the 37th ACM SIGPLAN-SIGACT Symposium on Principles of Programming Languages, POPL 2010, pp. 483–494 (2010). https://doi.org/10.1145/1706299.1706354
9. Forster, Y., Kammar, O., Lindley, S., Pretnar, M.: On the expressive power of user-defined effects: effect handlers, monadic reflection, delimited control. PACMPL **1**(ICFP), 13:1–13:29 (2017). https://doi.org/10.1145/3110257
10. Garrigue, J.: Relaxing the value restriction. In: Kameyama, Y., Stuckey, P.J. (eds.) FLOPS 2004. LNCS, vol. 2998, pp. 196–213. Springer, Heidelberg (2004). https://doi.org/10.1007/978-3-540-24754-8_15
11. Harper, R., Lillibridge, M.: Polymorphic type assignment and CPS conversion. Lisp Symb. Comput. **6**(3–4), 361–380 (1993)

12. Hoang, M., Mitchell, J.C., Viswanathan, R.: Standard ML-NJ weak polymorphism and imperative constructs. In: Proceedings of the Eighth Annual Symposium on Logic in Computer Science, LICS 1993 (1993)
13. Kammar, O., Lindley, S., Oury, N.: Handlers in action. In: ACM SIGPLAN International Conference on Functional Programming, ICFP 2013, pp. 145–158 (2013). https://doi.org/10.1145/2500365.2500590
14. Kammar, O., Pretnar, M.: No value restriction is needed for algebraic effects and handlers. J. Funct. Program. **27**, e7 (2017). https://doi.org/10.1017/S0956796816000320
15. Kiselyov, O., Ishii, H.: Freer monads, more extensible effects. In: Proceedings of the 8th ACM SIGPLAN Symposium on Haskell, Haskell 2015, pp. 94–105 (2015). https://doi.org/10.1145/2804302.2804319
16. Leijen, D.: Type directed compilation of row-typed algebraic effects. In: Proceedings of the 44th ACM SIGPLAN Symposium on Principles of Programming Languages, POPL 2017, pp. 486–499 (2017). http://dl.acm.org/citation.cfm?id=3009872
17. Leroy, X., Weis, P.: Polymorphic type inference and assignment. In: Proceedings of the 18th Annual ACM Symposium on Principles of Programming Languages, pp. 291–302 (1991). https://doi.org/10.1145/99583.99622
18. Lindley, S., McBride, C., McLaughlin, C.: Do be do be do. In: Proceedings of the 44th ACM SIGPLAN Symposium on Principles of Programming Languages, POPL 2017, pp. 500–514 (2017). http://dl.acm.org/citation.cfm?id=3009897
19. Materzok, M., Biernacki, D.: A dynamic interpretation of the CPS hierarchy. In: Jhala, R., Igarashi, A. (eds.) APLAS 2012. LNCS, vol. 7705, pp. 296–311. Springer, Heidelberg (2012). https://doi.org/10.1007/978-3-642-35182-2_21
20. Plotkin, G.D., Power, J.: Algebraic operations and generic effects. Appl. Categ. Struct. **11**(1), 69–94 (2003). https://doi.org/10.1023/A:1023064908962
21. Plotkin, G.D., Pretnar, M.: Handlers of algebraic effects. In: Castagna, G. (ed.) ESOP 2009. LNCS, vol. 5502, pp. 80–94. Springer, Heidelberg (2009). https://doi.org/10.1007/978-3-642-00590-9_7
22. Reynolds, J.C.: Types, abstraction and parametric polymorphism. In: IFIP Congress, pp. 513–523 (1983)
23. Tofte, M.: Type inference for polymorphic references. Inf. Comput. **89**(1), 1–34 (1990). https://doi.org/10.1016/0890-5401(90)90018-D
24. Wright, A.K.: Simple imperative polymorphism. Lisp Symb. Comput. **8**(4), 343–355 (1995)
25. Wright, A.K., Felleisen, M.: A syntactic approach to type soundness. Inf. Comput. **115**(1), 38–94 (1994). https://doi.org/10.1006/inco.1994.1093
26. Wu, N., Schrijvers, T., Hinze, R.: Effect handlers in scope. In: Proceedings of the 2014 ACM SIGPLAN Symposium on Haskell, Haskell 2014, pp. 1–12 (2014). https://doi.org/10.1145/2633357.2633358

2

Fixing Incremental Computation Derivatives of Fixpoints and the Recursive Semantics of Datalog

Mario Alvarez-Picallo[1(✉)], Alex Eyers-Taylor[2], Michael Peyton Jones[2(✉)], and C.-H. Luke Ong[1]

[1] University of Oxford, Oxford, UK
{mario.alvarez-picallo,luke.ong}@cs.ox.ac.uk
[2] Semmle Ltd., Oxford, UK
alexet@semmle.com, me@michaelpj.com

Abstract. Incremental computation has recently been studied using the concepts of *change structures* and *derivatives* of programs, where the derivative of a function allows updating the output of the function based on a change to its input. We generalise change structures to *change actions*, and study their algebraic properties. We develop change actions for common structures in computer science, including directed-complete partial orders and Boolean algebras. We then show how to compute derivatives of fixpoints. This allows us to perform incremental evaluation and maintenance of recursively defined functions with particular application generalised Datalog programs. Moreover, unlike previous results, our techniques are *modular* in that they are easy to apply both to variants of Datalog and to other programming languages.

Keywords: Incremental computation · Datalog · Semantics · Fixpoints

1 Introduction

Consider the following classic Datalog program[1], which computes the transitive closure of an edge relation e:

$$tc(x, y) \leftarrow e(x, y)$$
$$tc(x, y) \leftarrow e(x, z) \wedge tc(z, y)$$

The semantics of Datalog tells us that the denotation of this program is the least fixpoint of the rule tc. Kleene's fixpoint Theorem tells us that we can compute this fixpoint by repeatedly applying the rule until the output stops changing, starting from the empty relation. For example, supposing that $e = \{(1, 2), (2, 3), (3, 4)\}$, we get the following evaluation trace:

[1] See [1, part D] for an introduction to Datalog.

Iteration	Newly deduced facts	Accumulated data in tc
0	$\{\}$	$\{\}$
1	$\{(1,2),(2,3),(3,4)\}$	$\{(1,2),(2,3),(3,4)\}$
2	$\{(1,2),(2,3),(3,4),$ $(1,3),(2,4)\}$	$\{(1,2),(2,3),(3,4),$ $(1,3),(2,4)\}$
3	$\{(1,2),(2,3),(3,4),$ $(1,3),(2,4),(1,4),(1,4)\}$	$\{(1,2),(2,3),(3,4),$ $(1,3),(2,4),(1,4)\}$
4	(as above)	(as above)

At this point we have reached a fixpoint, and so we are done.

However, this process is quite wasteful. We deduced the fact $(1,2)$ at every iteration, even though we had already deduced it in the first iteration. Indeed, for a chain of n such edges we will deduce $O(n^2)$ facts along the way.

The standard improvement to this evaluation strategy is known as "semi-naive" evaluation (see [1, section 13.1]), where we transform the program into a *delta* program with two parts:

- A *delta* rule that computes the *new* facts at each iteration.
- An *accumulator* rule that accumulates the delta at each iteration to compute the final result.

In this case our delta rule is simple: we only get new transitive edges at iteration $n+1$ if we can deduce them from transitive edges we deduced at iteration n.

$$\begin{aligned} \Delta tc_0(x,y) &\leftarrow e(x,y) \\ \Delta tc_{i+1}(x,y) &\leftarrow e(x,z) \wedge \Delta tc_i(z,y) \\ tc_0(x,y) &\leftarrow \Delta tc_0(x,y) \\ tc_{i+1}(x,y) &\leftarrow tc_i(x,y) \vee \Delta tc_{i+1}(x,y) \end{aligned}$$

Iteration	Δtc_i	tc_i
0	$\{(1,2),(2,3),(3,4)\}$	$\{(1,2),(2,3),(3,4)\}$
1	$\{(1,3),(2,4)\}$	$\{(1,2),(2,3),(3,4),$ $(1,3),(2,4)\}$
2	$\{(1,4)\}$	$\{(1,2),(2,3),(3,4),$ $(1,3),(2,4),(1,4)\}$
3	$\{\}$	(as above)

This is much better—we have turned a quadratic computation into a linear one. The delta transformation is a kind of *incremental computation*: at each stage we compute the changes in the rule given the previous changes to its inputs.

But the delta rule translation works only for traditional Datalog. It is common to liberalise the formula syntax with additional features, such as disjunction, existential quantification, negation, and aggregation.[2] This allows us to

[2] See, for example, LogiQL [26,32], Datomic [18], Souffle [38,42], and DES [36], which between them have all of these features and more. We do not here explore supporting extensions to the syntax of rule *heads*, although as long as this can be given a denotational semantics in a similar style our techniques should be applicable.

write programs like the following, where we compute whether all the nodes in a subtree given by *child* have some property p:

$$treeP(x) \leftarrow p(x) \wedge \neg\exists y.(child(x,y) \wedge \neg treeP(y))$$

The body of this predicate amounts to recursion through an *universal* quantifier (encoded as $\neg\exists\neg$). We would like to be able to use semi-naive evaluation for this rule too, but the standard definition of semi-naive transformation is not well defined for the extended program syntax, and it is unclear how to extend it (and the correctness proof) to handle such cases.

It is possible, however, to write a delta program for *treeP* by hand; indeed, here is a definition for the delta predicate (the accumulator is as before):[3]

$$\begin{aligned} \Delta_{i+1} treeP(x) \leftarrow & p(x) \\ & \wedge \exists y.(child(x,y) \wedge \Delta_i treeP(y)) \\ & \wedge \neg\exists y.(child(x,y) \wedge \neg treeP_i(y)) \end{aligned}$$

This is a *correct* delta program (in that using it to iteratively compute *treeP* gives the right answer), but it is not *precise* because it derives some facts repeatedly. We will show how to construct correct delta programs generally using a program transformation, and show how we have some freedom to optimize within a range of possible alternatives to improve precision or ease evaluation.

Handling extended Datalog is of more than theoretical interest—the research in this paper was carried out at Semmle, which makes heavy use of a commercial Datalog implementation to implement large-scale static program analysis [7,37, 39,40]. Semmle's implementation includes parity-stratified negation[4], recursive aggregates [34], and other non-standard features, so we are faced with a dilemma: either abandon the new language features, or abandon incremental computation.

We can tell a similar story about *maintenance* of Datalog programs. Maintenance means updating the results of the program when its inputs change, for example, updating the value of *tc* given a change to *e*. Again, this is a kind of incremental computation, and there are known solutions for traditional Datalog [25], but these break down when the language is extended.

There is a piece of folkloric knowledge in the Datalog community that hints at a solution: the semi-naive translation of a rule corresponds to the *derivative* of that rule [8,9, section 3.2.2]. The idea of performing incremental computation using derivatives has been studied recently by Cai et al. [14], who give an account using *change structures*. They use this to provide a framework for incrementally evaluating lambda calculus programs.

---

[3] This rule should be read as: we can newly deduce that x is in *treeP* if x satisfies the predicate, and we have newly deduced that one of its children is in *treeP*, and we currently believe that all of its children are in *treeP*.

[4] Parity-stratified negation means that recursive calls must appear under an even number of negations. This ensures that the rule remains monotone, so the least fixpoint still exists.

However, Cai et al.'s work isn't directly applicable to Datalog: the tricky part of Datalog's semantics are recursive definitions and the need for the *fixpoints*, so we need some additional theory to tell us how to handle incremental evaluation and maintenance of fixpoint computations.

This paper aims to bridge that gap by providing a solid semantic foundation for the incremental computation of Datalog, and other recursive programs, in terms of changes and differentiable functions.

Contributions. We start by generalizing change structures to *change actions* (Sect. 2). Change actions are simpler and weaker than change structures, while still providing enough structure to handle incremental computation, and have fruitful interactions with a variety of structures (Sects. 3 and 6.1).

We then show how change actions can be used to perform incremental evaluation and maintenance of non-recursive program semantics, using the formula semantics of generalized Datalog as our primary example (Sect. 4). Moreover, the structure of the approach is modular, and can accommodate arbitrary additional formula constructs (Sect. 4.3).

We also provide a method of incrementally computing and maintaining fixpoints (Sect. 6.2). We use this to perform incremental evaluation and maintenance of *recursive* program semantics, including generalized recursive Datalog (Sect. 7). This provides, to the best of our knowledge, the world's first incremental evaluation and maintenance mechanism for Datalog that can handle negation, disjunction, and existential quantification.

We have omitted the proofs from this paper. Most of the results have routine proofs, but the proofs of the more substantial results (especially those in Sect. 6.2) are included in an extended report [3], along with some extended worked examples, and additional material on the precision of derivatives.

2 Change Actions and Derivatives

Incremental computation requires understanding how values *change*. For example, we can change an integer by adding a natural to it. Abstractly, we have a set of values (the integers), and a set of changes (the naturals) which we can "apply" to a value (by addition) to get a new value.

This kind of structure is well-known—it is a set action. It is also very natural to want to combine changes sequentially, and if we do this then we find ourselves with a monoid action.

Using monoid actions for changes gives us a reason to think that change actions are an adequate representation of changes: any subset of $A \to A$ which is closed under composition can be represented as a monoid action on A, so we are able to capture all of these as change actions.

2.1 Change Actions

Definition 1. *A* change action *is a tuple:*

$$\hat{A} := (A, \Delta A, \oplus_A)$$

where A is a set, ΔA is a monoid, and $\oplus_A : A \times \Delta A \to A$ is a monoid action on A.[5]

We will call A the base set, and ΔA the change set *of the change action. We will use $\cdot$ for the monoid operation of ΔA, and $\mathbf{0}$ for its identity element. When there is no risk of confusion, we will simply write $\oplus$ for $\oplus_A$.*

Examples. A typical example of a change action is $(A^*, A^*, +\!\!+)$ where A^* is the set of finite words (or lists) of A. Here we represent changes to a word made by concatenating another word onto it. The changes themselves can be combined using $+\!\!+$ as the monoid operation with the empty word as the identity, and this is a monoid action: $(a +\!\!+ b) +\!\!+ c = a +\!\!+ (b +\!\!+ c)$.

This is a very common case: any monoid $(A, \cdot, \mathbf{0})$ can be seen as a change action $(A, (A, \cdot, \mathbf{0}), \cdot)$. Many practical change actions can be constructed in this way. In particular, for any change action $(A, \Delta A, \oplus)$, $(\Delta A, \Delta A, \cdot)$ is also a change action. This means that we do not have to do any extra work to talk about changes to changes—we can always take $\Delta\Delta A = \Delta A$ (although there may be other change actions available).

Three examples of change actions are of particular interest to us. First, whenever L is a Boolean algebra, we can give it the change actions $(L, L, \vee)$ and $(L, L, \wedge)$, as well as a combination of these (see Sect. 3.2). Second, the natural numbers with addition have a change action $\hat{\mathbb{N}} := (\mathbb{N}, \mathbb{N}, +)$, which will prove useful during inductive proofs.

Another interesting example of change actions is *semiautomata*. A semiautomaton is a triple (Q, Σ, T), where Q is a set of states, Σ is a (non-empty) finite input alphabet and $T : Q \times \Sigma \to Q$ is a transition function. Every semiautomaton corresponds to a change action (Q, Σ^*, T^*) on the free monoid over Σ^*, with T^* being the free extension of T. Conversely, every change action $\hat{A}$ whose change set ΔA is freely generated by a finite set corresponds to a semiautomaton.

Other recurring examples of change actions are:

- $\hat{A}_\perp := (A, M, \lambda(a, \delta a).a)$, where M is any monoid, which we call the *empty* change action on any base set, since it induces no changes at all.
- $\hat{A}_\top := (A, A \to A, \mathrm{ev})$, where A is an arbitrary set, $A \to A$ denotes the set of all functions from A into itself, considered as a monoid under composition and ev is the usual evaluation map. We will call this the "full" change action on A since it contains every possible non-redundant change.

These are particularly relevant because they are, in a sense, the "smallest" and "largest" change actions that can be imposed on an arbitrary set A.

Many other notions in computer science can be understood naturally in terms of change actions, *e.g.* databases and database updates, files and diffs, Git repositories and commits, even video compression algorithms that encode a frame as a series of changes to the previous frame.

[5] Why not just work with monoid actions? The reason is that while the category of monoid actions and the category of change actions have the same objects, they have different morphisms. See Sect. 8.1 for further discussion.

2.2 Derivatives

When we do incremental computation we are usually trying to save ourselves some work. We have an expensive function $f : A \to B$, which we've evaluated at some point a. Now we are interested in evaluating f after some change δa to a, but ideally we want to avoid actually computing $f(a \oplus \delta a)$ directly.

A solution to this problem is a function $f' : A \times \Delta A \to \Delta B$, which given a and δa tells us how to change $f(a)$ to $f(a \oplus \delta a)$. We call this a *derivative* of a function.

Definition 2. *Let $\hat{A}$ and $\hat{B}$ be change actions. A* derivative *of a function $f : A \to B$ is a function $f' : A \times \Delta A \to \Delta B$ such that*

$$f(a \oplus_A \delta a) = f(a) \oplus_B f'(a, \delta a)$$

A function which has a derivative is differentiable, *and we will write $\hat{A} \to \hat{B}$ for the set of differentiable functions between A and B.*[6]

Derivatives need not be unique in general, so we will speak of "a" derivative. Functions into "thin" change actions—where $a \oplus \delta a = a \oplus \delta b$ implies $\delta a = \delta b$—have unique derivatives, but many change actions are not thin. For example, $(\mathcal{P}(\mathbb{N}), \mathcal{P}(\mathbb{N}), \cap)$ is not thin because $\{0\} \cap \{1\} = \{0\} \cap \{2\}$.

Derivatives capture the structure of incremental computation, but there are important operational considerations that affect whether using them for computation actually saves us any work. As we will see in a moment (Proposition 1), for many change actions we will have the option of picking the "worst" derivative, which merely computes $f(a \oplus \delta a)$ directly and then works out the change that maps $f(a)$ to this new value. While this is formally a derivative, using it certainly does not save us any work! We will be concerned with both the possibility of constructing correct derivatives (Sects. 3.2 and 6.2 in particular), and also in giving ourselves a range of derivatives to choose from so that we can soundly optimize for operational value.

For our Datalog case study, we aim to cash out the folkloric idea that incremental computation functions via a derivative. We will construct a derivative of the semantics of Datalog in stages: first the non-recursive formula semantics (Sect. 4); and later the full, recursive, semantics (Sect. 7).

2.3 Useful Facts About Change Actions and Derivatives

The Chain Rule. The derivative of a function can be computed compositionally, because derivatives satisfy the standard chain rule.

6 Note that we do not require that $f'(a, \delta a \cdot \delta b) = f'(a, \delta a) \cdot f'(a \oplus \delta a, \delta b)$ nor that $f'(a, \mathbf{0}) = \mathbf{0}$. These are natural conditions, and all the derivatives we have studied also satisfy them, but none of the results on this paper require them to hold.

Theorem 1 (The Chain Rule). *Let* $f : \hat{A} \to \hat{B}$, $g : \hat{B} \to \hat{C}$ *be differentiable functions. Then* $g \circ f$ *is also differentiable, with a derivative given by*

$$(g \circ f)'(x, \delta x) = g'(f(x), f'(x, \delta x))$$

or, in curried form

$$(g \circ f)'(x) = g'(f(x)) \circ f'(x)$$

Complete change actions and minus operators. Complete change actions are an important class of change actions, because they have changes between *any* two values in the base set.

Definition 3. *A change action is* complete *if for any* $a, b \in A$, *there is a change* $\delta a \in \Delta A$ *such that* $a \oplus \delta a = b$.

Complete change actions have convenient "minus operators" that allow us to compute the difference between two values.

Definition 4. *A* minus operator *is a function* $\ominus : A \times A \to \Delta A$ *such that* $a \oplus (b \ominus a) = b$ *for all* $a, b \in A$.

Proposition 1. *Given a minus operator* $\ominus$, *and a function* f, *let*

$$f'_{\ominus}(a, \delta a) := f(a \oplus \delta a) \ominus f(a)$$

Then $f'_{\ominus}$ *is a derivative for* f.

Proposition 2. *Let* $\hat{A}$ *be a change action. Then the following are equivalent:*

- $\hat{A}$ *is complete.*
- *There is a minus operator on* $\hat{A}$.
- *For any change action* $\hat{B}$ *all functions* $f : B \to A$ *are differentiable.*

This last property is of the utmost importance, since we are often concerned with the differentiability of functions.

Products and sums. Given change actions on sets A and B, the question immediately arises of whether there are change actions on their Cartesian product $A \times B$ or disjoint union $A + B$. While there are many candidates, there is a clear "natural" choice for both.

Proposition 3 (Products). *Let* $\hat{A} = (A, \Delta A, \oplus_A)$ *and* $\hat{B} = (B, \Delta B, \oplus_B)$ *be change actions.*

Then $\hat{A} \times \hat{B} := (A \times B, \Delta A \times \Delta B, \oplus_\times)$ *is a change action, where* $\oplus_\times$ *is defined by:*

$$(a, b) \oplus_{A \times B} (\delta a, \delta b) := (a \oplus_A \delta a, b \oplus_B \delta b)$$

The projection maps π_1,π_2 are differentiable with respect to it. Furthermore, a function $f : A \times B \to C$ is differentiable from $\hat{A} \times \hat{B}$ into $\hat{C}$ if and only if, for every fixed $a \in A$ and $b \in B$, the partially applied functions

$$f(a, \cdot) : B \to C$$
$$f(\cdot, b) : A \to C$$

are differentiable.

Whenever $f : A \times B \to C$ is differentiable, we will sometimes use $\partial_1 f$ and $\partial_2 f$ to refer to derivatives of the partially applied versions, i.e. if $f'_a : B \times \Delta B \to \Delta C$ and $f'_b : A \times \Delta A \to \Delta C$ refer to derivatives for $f(a, \cdot), f(\cdot, b)$ respectively, then

$$\begin{aligned} \partial_1 f &: A \times \Delta A \times B \to \Delta C \\ \partial_1 f(a, \delta a, b) &:= f'_b(a, \delta a) \\ \partial_2 f &: A \times B \times \Delta B \to \Delta C \\ \partial_2 f(a, b, \delta b) &:= f'_a(b, \delta b) \end{aligned}$$

Proposition 4 (Disjoint unions). *Let $\hat{A} = (A, \Delta A, \oplus_A)$ and $\hat{B} = (B, \Delta B, \oplus_B)$ be change actions.*

Then $\hat{A} + \hat{B} := (A + B, \Delta A \times \Delta B, \oplus_+)$ is a change action, where $\oplus_+$ is defined as:

$$\begin{aligned} \iota_1 a \oplus_+ (\delta a, \delta b) &:= \iota_1(a \oplus_A \delta a) \\ \iota_2 b \oplus_+ (\delta a, \delta b) &:= \iota_2(b \oplus_B \delta b) \end{aligned}$$

The injection maps ι_1, ι_2 are differentiable with respect to $\hat{A}+\hat{B}$. Furthermore, whenever $\hat{C}$ is a change action and $f : A \to C, g : B \to C$ are differentiable, then so is $[f, g]$.

2.4 Comparing Change Actions

Much like topological spaces, we can compare change actions on the same base set according to coarseness. This is useful since differentiability of functions between change actions is characterized entirely by the coarseness of the actions.

Definition 5. *Let $\hat{A}_1$ and $\hat{A}_2$ be change actions on A. We say that $\hat{A}_1$ is* coarser *than $\hat{A}_2$ (or that $\hat{A}_2$ is* finer *than $\hat{A}_1$) whenever for every $x \in A$ and change $\delta a_1 \in \Delta A_1$, there is a change $\delta a_2 \in \Delta A_2$ such that $x \oplus_{A_1} \delta a_1 = x \oplus_{A_2} \delta a_2$.*

We will write $\hat{A}_1 \leq \hat{A}_2$ whenever $\hat{A}_1$ is coarser than $\hat{A}_2$. If $\hat{A}_1$ is both finer and coarser than $\hat{A}_2$, we will say that $\hat{A}_1$ and $\hat{A}_2$ are equivalent.

The relation $\leq$ defines a preorder (but not a partial order) on the set of all change actions over a fixed set A. Least and greatest elements do exist up to equivalence, and correspond respectively to the empty change action $\hat{A}_\bot$ and any complete change action, such as the full change action $\hat{A}_\top$, defined in Sect. 2.1.

Proposition 5. *Let $\hat{A}_2 \leq \hat{A}_1$, $\hat{B}_1 \leq \hat{B}_2$ be change actions, and suppose the function $f : A \to B$ is differentiable as a function from $\hat{A}_1$ into $\hat{B}_1$. Then f is differentiable as a function from $\hat{A}_2$ into $\hat{B}_2$.*

A consequence of this fact is that whenever two change actions are equivalent they can be used interchangeably without affecting which functions are differentiable. One last parallel with topology is the following result, which establishes a simple criterion for when a change action is coarser than another:

Proposition 6. *Let $\hat{A}_1, \hat{A}_2$ be change actions on A. Then $\hat{A}_1$ is coarser than $\hat{A}_2$ if and only if the identity function* $\mathrm{id} : A \to A$ *is differentiable from $\hat{A}_1$ to $\hat{A}_2$.*

3 Posets and Boolean Algebras

The semantic domain of Datalog is a complete Boolean algebra, and so our next step is to construct a good change action for Boolean algebras. Along the way, we will consider change actions over posets, which give us the ability to *approximate* derivatives, which will turn out to be very important in practice.

3.1 Posets

Ordered sets give us a constrained class of functions: monotone functions. We can define *ordered* change actions, which are those that are well-behaved with respect to the order on the underlying set.[7]

Definition 6. *A change action $\hat{A}$ is* ordered *if*

- *A and ΔA are posets.*
- *$\oplus$ is monotone as a map from $A \times \Delta A \to A$*
- *$\cdot$ is monotone as a map from $\Delta A \times \Delta A \to \Delta A$*

In fact, any change action whose base set is a poset induces a partial order on the corresponding change set:

Definition 7. *$\delta a \leq_\Delta \delta b$ iff for all $a \in A$ it is the case that $a \oplus \delta a \leq a \oplus \delta b$.*

Proposition 7. *Let $\hat{A}$ be a change action on a set A equipped with a partial order $\leq$ such that $\oplus$ is monotone in its first argument. Then $\hat{A}$ is an ordered change action when ΔA is equipped with the partial order $\leq_\Delta$.*

In what follows, we will extend the partial order $\leq_\Delta$ on some change set ΔB pointwise to functions from some A into ΔB. This pointwise order interacts nicely with derivatives, in that it gives us the following lemma:

[7] If we were giving a presentation that was generic in the base category, then this would simply be the definition of being a change action in the category of posets and monotone maps.

Theorem 2 (Sandwich lemma). *Let $\hat{A}$ be a change action, and $\hat{B}$ be an ordered change action, and let $f : A \to B$ and $g : A \times \Delta A \to \Delta B$ be function. If $f_\uparrow$ and $f_\downarrow$ are derivatives for f such that*

$$f_\downarrow \leq_\Delta g \leq_\Delta f_\uparrow$$

then g is a derivative for f.

If unique minimal and maximal derivatives exist, then this gives us a characterisation of all the derivatives for a function.

Theorem 3. *Let $\hat{A}$ and $\hat{B}$ be change actions, with $\hat{B}$ ordered, and let $f : A \to B$ be a function. If there exist $f_{\downarrow\downarrow}$ and $f_{\uparrow\uparrow}$ which are unique minimal and maximal derivatives of f, respectively, then the derivatives of f are precisely the functions f' such that*

$$f_{\downarrow\downarrow} \leq_\Delta f' \leq_\Delta f_{\uparrow\uparrow}$$

This theorem gives us the leeway that we need when trying to pick a derivative: we can pick out the bounds, and that tells us how much "wiggle room" we have above and below.

3.2 Boolean Algebras

Complete Boolean algebras are a particularly nice domain for change actions because they have a negation operator. This is very helpful for computing differences, and indeed Boolean algebras have a complete change action.

Proposition 8 (Boolean algebra change actions). *Let L be a complete Boolean algebra. Define*

$$\hat{L}_{\bowtie} := (L, L \bowtie L, \oplus_{\bowtie})$$

where

$$L \bowtie L := \{(a, b) \in L \times L \mid a \wedge b = \bot\}$$
$$a \oplus_{\bowtie} (p, q) := (a \vee p) \wedge \neg q$$

$$(p, q) \cdot (r, s) := ((p \wedge \neg s) \vee r, (q \wedge \neg r) \vee s)$$

with identity element $(\bot, \bot)$.

Then $\hat{L}_{\bowtie}$ is a complete change action on L.

We can think of $\hat{L}_{\bowtie}$ as tracking changes as pairs of "upwards" and "downwards" changes, where the monoid action simply applies one after the other, with an adjustment to make sure that the components remain disjoint.[8] For example,

[8] The intuition that $\hat{L}_{\bowtie}$ is made up of an "upwards" and a "downwards" change action glued together can in fact be made precise, but the specifics are outside the scope of this paper.

in the powerset Boolean algebra $\mathcal{P}(\mathbb{N})$, a change to $\{1,2\}$ might consist of *adding* $\{3\}$ and *removing* $\{1\}$, producing $\{2,3\}$. In $\mathcal{P}(\mathbb{N})_{\bowtie}$ this would be represented as $(\{1,2\}) \oplus (\{3\},\{1\}) = \{2,3\}$.

Boolean algebras also have unique maximal and minimal derivatives, under the usual partial order based on implication. The change set is, as usual, given the change partial order, which in this case corresponds to the natural order on $L \times L^{\text{op}}$.

Proposition 9. *Let L be a complete Boolean algebra with the $\hat{L}_{\bowtie}$ change action, and $f : A \to L$ be a function. Then, the following are minus operators:*

$$a \ominus_{\bot} b = (a \wedge \neg b, \neg a)$$
$$a \ominus_{\top} b = (a, b \wedge \neg a)$$

Additionally, $f'_{\ominus_\bot}$ and $f'_{\ominus_\top}$ define unique least and greatest derivatives for f.

Theorem 3 then gives us bounds for all the derivatives on Boolean algebras:

Corollary 1. *Let L be a complete Boolean algebra with the corresponding change action $\hat{L}_{\bowtie}$, $\hat{A}$ be an arbitrary change action, and $f : A \to L$ be a function. Then the derivatives of f are precisely those functions $f' : A \times \Delta A \to \Delta A$ such that*

$$f'_{\ominus_\bot} \leq_{\Delta} f' \leq_{\Delta} f'_{\ominus_\top}$$

This makes Theorem 3 actually usable in practice, since we have concrete definitions for our bounds (which we will make use of in Sect. 4.2).

4 Derivatives for Non-recursive Datalog

We now want to apply the theory we have developed to the specific case of the semantics of Datalog. Giving a differentiable semantics for Datalog will lead us to a strategy for performing incremental evaluation and maintenance of Datalog programs. To begin with, we will restrict ourselves to the non-recursive fragment of the language—the formulae that make up the right hand sides of Datalog rules. We will tackle the full program semantics in a later section, once we know how to handle fixpoints.

Although the techniques we are using should work for any language, Datalog provides a non-trivial case study where the need for incremental computation is real and pressing, as we saw in Sect. 1.

4.1 Semantics of Datalog Formulae

Datalog is usually given a logical semantics where formulae are interpreted as first-order logic predicates and the semantics of a program is the set of models of its constituent predicates. We will instead give a simple denotational semantics (as is typical when working with fixpoints, see e.g. [17]) that treats a Datalog formula as directly denoting a relation, i.e. a set of named tuples, with variables ranging over a finite schema.

Definition 8. *A* schema Γ *is a finite set of names. A* named tuple *over* Γ *is an assignment of a value* v_i *for each name* x_i *in* Γ*. Given disjoint schemata* $\Gamma = \{x_1, \ldots, x_n\}$ *and* $\Sigma = \{y_1, \ldots, y_m\}$*, the* selection function σ_Γ *is defined as*

$$\sigma_\Gamma(\{x_1 \mapsto v_1, \ldots, x_n \mapsto v_n, y_1 \mapsto w_1, \ldots, y_m \mapsto w_m\}) := \{x_1 \mapsto v_1, \ldots, x_n \mapsto v_n\}$$

i.e. σ_Γ *restricts a named tuple over* $\Gamma \cup \Sigma$ *into a tuple over* Γ *with the same values for the names in* Γ*. We denote the elementwise extension of* σ_Γ *to sets of tuples also as* σ_Γ*.*

We will adopt the usual closed-world assumption to give a denotation to negation.

Definition 9. *For any schema* Γ*, there exists a universal relation* $\mathcal{U}_\Gamma$*. Negation on relations can then be defined as*

$$\neg R := \mathcal{U}_\Gamma \setminus R$$

This makes $\mathbf{Rel}_\Gamma$, the set of all subsets of $\mathcal{U}_\Gamma$, a complete Boolean algebra.

Definition 10. *A Datalog formula* T *whose free term variables are contained in* Γ *denotes a function from* $\mathbf{Rel}_\Gamma^n$ *to* $\mathbf{Rel}_\Gamma$*.*

$$[\![\text{-}]\!]_\Gamma : \text{Formula} \to \mathbf{Rel}_\Gamma^n \to \mathbf{Rel}_\Gamma$$

If $\mathcal{R} = (\mathcal{R}_1, \ldots, \mathcal{R}_n)$ *is a choice of a relation* $\mathcal{R}_i$ *for each of the variables* R_i*,* $[\![T]\!](\mathcal{R})$ *is inductively defined according to the rules in Fig. 1.*

$$[\![\top]\!]_\Gamma(\mathcal{R}) := \mathcal{U}_\Gamma \qquad [\![T \wedge U]\!]_\Gamma(\mathcal{R}) := [\![T]\!]_\Gamma(\mathcal{R}) \cap [\![U]\!]_\Gamma(\mathcal{R})$$
$$[\![\bot]\!]_\Gamma(\mathcal{R}) := \emptyset \qquad [\![T \vee U]\!]_\Gamma(\mathcal{R}) := [\![T]\!]_\Gamma(\mathcal{R}) \cup [\![U]\!]_\Gamma(\mathcal{R})$$
$$[\![R_j]\!]_\Gamma(\mathcal{R}) := \mathcal{R}_j \qquad [\![\neg T]\!]_\Gamma(\mathcal{R}) := \neg [\![T]\!]_\Gamma(\mathcal{R})$$
$$[\![\exists x.T]\!]_\Gamma(\mathcal{R}) := \sigma_\Gamma([\![T]\!]_{\Gamma \cup \{x\}}(\mathcal{R}))$$

Fig. 1. Formula semantics for Datalog

Since $\mathbf{Rel}_\Gamma$ is a complete Boolean algebra, and so is $\mathbf{Rel}_\Gamma^n$, $[\![T]\!]_\Gamma$ is a function between complete Boolean algebras. For brevity, we will often leave the schema implicit, as it is clear from the context.

4.2 Differentiability of Datalog Formula Semantics

In order to actually perform our incremental computation, we first need to provide a concrete derivative for the semantics of Datalog formulae. Of course, since $[\![T]\!]_\Gamma$ is a function between the complete Boolean algebras $\mathbf{Rel}_\Gamma^n$ and $\mathbf{Rel}_\Gamma$, and

$$
\begin{aligned}
\Delta(\bot) &:= \bot & \nabla(\bot) &:= \bot \\
\Delta(\top) &:= \bot & \nabla(\top) &:= \bot \\
\Delta(R_j) &:= \Delta R_j & \nabla(R_j) &:= \nabla R_j \\
\Delta(T \vee U) &:= \Delta(T) \vee \Delta(U) & \nabla(T \vee U) &:= (\nabla(T) \wedge \neg \mathsf{X}(U)) \\
\Delta(T \wedge U) &:= (\Delta(T) \wedge \mathsf{X}(U)) & &\quad \vee (\nabla(U) \wedge \neg \mathsf{X}(T)) \\
&\quad \vee (\Delta(U) \wedge \mathsf{X}(T)) & \nabla(T \wedge U) &:= (\nabla(T) \wedge U) \vee (T \wedge \nabla(U)) \\
\Delta(\neg T) &:= \nabla(T) & \nabla(\neg T) &:= \Delta(T) \\
\Delta(\exists x.T) &:= \exists x.\Delta(T) & \nabla(\exists x.T) &:= \exists x.\nabla(T) \wedge \neg \exists x.\mathsf{X}(T)
\end{aligned}
$$

$$\mathsf{X}(R) := (R \vee \Delta(R)) \wedge \neg \nabla(R)$$

Fig. 2. Upwards and downwards formula derivatives for Datalog

we know that the corresponding change actions $\widehat{\mathbf{Rel}^n_{\Gamma\bowtie}}$ and $\widehat{\mathbf{Rel}_{\Gamma\bowtie}}$ are complete, this guarantees the existence of a derivative for $[\![T]\!]$.

Unfortunately, this does not necessarily provide us with an *efficient* derivative for $[\![T]\!]$. The derivatives that we know how to compute (Corollary 1) rely on computing $f(a \oplus \delta a)$ itself, which is the very thing we were trying to avoid computing!

Of course, given a concrete definition of a derivative we can simplify this expression and hopefully make it easier to compute. But we also know from Corollary 1 that *any* function bounded by $f'_{\ominus_\bot}$ and $f'_{\ominus_\top}$ is a valid derivative, and we can therefore optimize anywhere within that range to make a trade-off between ease of computation and precision.[9]

There is also the question of how to compute the derivative. Since the change set for $\widehat{\mathbf{Rel}_{\bowtie}}$ is a subset of $\mathbf{Rel} \times \mathbf{Rel}$, it is possible and indeed very natural to compute the two components via a pair of Datalog formulae, which allows us to reuse an existing Datalog formula evaluator. Indeed, if this process is occurring in an optimizing compiler, the derivative formulae can themselves be optimized. This is very beneficial in practice, since the initial formulae may be quite complex.

This does give us additional constraints that the derivative formulae must satisfy: for example, we need to be able to evaluate them; and we may wish to pick formulae that will be easy or cheap for our evaluation engine to compute, even if they compute a less precise derivative.

The upshot of these considerations is that the optimal choice of derivatives is likely to be quite dependent on the precise variant of Datalog being evaluated, and the specifics of the evaluation engine. Here is one possibility, which is the one used at Semmle.

---

9 The idea of using an approximation to the precise derivative, and a soundness condition, appears in Bancilhon [9].

A concrete Datalog formula derivative. In Fig. 2, we define a "symbolic" derivative operator as a pair of mutually recursive functions, Δ and ∇, which turn a Datalog formula T into new formulae that compute the upwards and downwards parts of the derivative, respectively. Our definition uses an auxiliary function, X, which computes the "neXt" value of a term by applying the upwards and downwards derivatives. As is typical for a derivative, the new formulae will have additional free relation variables for the upwards and downwards derivatives of the free relation variables of T, denoted as ΔR and ∇R respectively. Evaluating the formula as a derivative means evaluating it as a normal Datalog formula with the new relation variables set to the input relation changes.

While the definitions mostly exhibit the dualities we would expect between corresponding operators, there are a few asymmetries to explain.

The asymmetry between the cases for $\Delta(T \vee U)$ and $\nabla(T \wedge U)$ is for operational reasons. The symmetrical version of $\Delta(T \vee U)$ is $(\Delta(T) \wedge \neg U) \vee (\Delta(U) \wedge \neg T)$ (which is also precise). The reason we omit the negated conjuncts is simply that they are costly to compute and not especially helpful to our evaluation engine.

The asymmetry between the cases for $\exists$ is because our dialect of Datalog does not have a primitive universal quantifier. If we did have one, the cases for $\exists$ would be dual to the corresponding cases for $\forall$.

Theorem 4 (Concrete Datalog formula derivatives). *Let* Δ, ∇, X : $\mathsf{Formula} \rightarrow \mathsf{Formula}$ *be mutually recursive functions defined by structural induction as in Fig. 2.*

Then $\Delta(T)$ *and* $\nabla(T)$ *are disjoint, and for any schema* Γ *and any Datalog formula* T *whose free term variables are contained in* Γ, $[\![T]\!]'_\Gamma := ([\![\Delta(T)]\!]_\Gamma, [\![\nabla(T)]\!]_\Gamma)$ *is a derivative for* $[\![T]\!]_\Gamma$.

We can give a derivative for our *treeP* predicate by mechanically applying the recursive functions defined in Fig. 2.

$$\begin{aligned}&\Delta(treeP(x))\\&= p(x) \wedge \exists y.(child(x,y) \wedge \Delta(treeP(y))) \wedge \neg\exists y.(child(x,y) \wedge \neg\mathsf{X}(treeP(y)))\end{aligned}$$

$$\begin{aligned}&\nabla(treeP(x))\\&= p(x) \wedge \exists y.(child(x,y) \wedge \nabla(treeP(y)))\end{aligned}$$

The upwards difference in particular is not especially easy to compute. If we naively compute it, the third conjunct requires us to recompute the whole of the recursive part. However, the second conjunct gives us a guard: if it is empty we then the whole formula will be, so we only need to evaluate the third conjunct if the second conjunct is non-empty, i.e if there is *some* change in the body of the existential.

This shows that our derivatives aren't a panacea: it is simply *hard* to compute downwards differences for $\exists$ (and, equivalently, upwards differences for $\forall$) because we must check that there is no other way of deriving the same facts.[10] However,

[10] The "support" data structures introduced by [25] are an attempt to avoid this issue by tracking the number of derivations of each tuple.

we can still avoid the re-evaluation in many cases, and the inefficiency is local to this subformula.

4.3 Extensions to Datalog

Our formulation of Datalog formula semantics and derivatives is generic and modular, so it is easy to extend the language with new formula constructs: all we need to do is add cases for Δ and ∇.

In fact, because we are using a complete change action, we can *always* do this by using the maximal or minimal derivative. This justifies our claim that we can support *arbitrary* additional formula constructs: although the maximal and minimal derivatives are likely to be impractical, having them available as options means that we will never be completely stymied.

This is important in practice: here is a real example from Semmle's variant of Datalog. This includes a kind of aggregates which have well-defined recursive semantics. Aggregates have the form

$$r = \mathrm{agg}(p)(vs \mid T \mid U)$$

where agg refers to an aggregation function (such as "sum" or "min"), vs is a sequence of variables, p and r are variables, T is a formula possibly mentioning vs, and U is a formula possibly mentioning vs and p. The full details can been found in Moor and Baars [34], but for example this allows us to write

$$\begin{aligned} \mathit{height}(n, h) \longleftarrow & \neg\exists c.(\mathit{child}(n, c)) \land h = 0 \\ & \lor \exists h'.(h' = \max(p)(c \mid \mathit{child}(n, c) \mid \mathit{height}(c, p)) \land h = h' + 1) \end{aligned}$$

which recursively computes the height of a node in a tree.

Here is an upwards derivative for an aggregate formula:

$$\Delta(r = \mathrm{agg}(p)(vs \mid T \mid U)) := \exists vs.(T \land \Delta U) \land r = \mathrm{agg}(p)(vs \mid T \mid U)$$

While this isn't a precise derivative, it is still substantially cheaper than re-evaluating the whole subformula, as the first conjunct acts as a guard, allowing us to skip the second conjunct when U has not changed.

5 Changes on Functions

So far we have defined change actions for the kinds of things that typically make up *data*, but we would also like to have change actions on *functions*. This would allow us to define derivatives for higher-order languages (where functions are first-class); and for semantic operators like fixpoint operators $\mathbf{fix} : (A \to A) \to A$, which also operate on functions.

Function spaces, however, differ from products and disjoint unions in that there is no obvious "best" change action on $A \to B$. Therefore instead of trying to define a single choice of change action, we will instead pick out subsets of function spaces which have "well-behaved" change actions.

Definition 11 (Functional Change Action). *Given change actions $\hat{A}$ and $\hat{B}$ and a set $U \subseteq A \to B$, a change action $\hat{U} = (U, \Delta U, \oplus_U)$ is* functional *whenever the evaluation map* ev $: U \times A \to B$ *is differentiable, that is to say, whenever there exists a function* $\mathrm{ev}' : (U \times A) \times (\Delta U \times \Delta A) \to \Delta B$ *such that:*

$$(f \oplus_U \delta f)(a \oplus_A \delta a) = f(a) \oplus_B \mathrm{ev}'((f, a), (\delta f, \delta a))$$

We will write $\hat{U} \subseteq \hat{A} \Rightarrow \hat{B}$ whenever $U \subseteq A \to B$ and $\hat{U}$ is functional.

There are two reasons why functional change actions are usually associated with a *subset* of $U \subseteq A \to B$. Firstly, it allows us to restrict ourselves to spaces of monotone or continuous functions. But more importantly, functional change actions are necessarily made up of differentiable functions, and thus a functional change action may not exist for the entire function space $A \to B$.

Proposition 10. *Let $\hat{U} \subseteq \hat{A} \Rightarrow \hat{B}$ be a functional change action. Then every $f \in U$ is differentiable, with a derivative f' given by:*

$$f'(x, \delta x) = \mathrm{ev}'((f, x), (\mathbf{0}, \delta x))$$

5.1 Pointwise Functional Change Actions

Even if we restrict ourselves to the differentiable functions between $\hat{A}$ and $\hat{B}$ it is hard to find a concrete functional change action for this set. Fortunately, in many important cases there is a simple change action on the set of differentiable functions.

Definition 12 (Pointwise functional change action). *Let $\hat{A}$ and $\hat{B}$ be change actions. The* pointwise functional change action *$\hat{A} \Rightarrow_{pt} \hat{B}$, when it is defined, is given by $(\hat{A} \to \hat{B}, A \to \Delta B, \oplus_\to)$, with the monoid structure $(A \to \Delta B, \cdot_\to, \mathbf{0}_\to)$ and the action $\oplus_\to$ defined by:*

$$\begin{aligned}(f \oplus_\to \delta f)(x) &:= f(x) \oplus_B \delta f(x) \\ (\delta f \cdot_\to \delta g)(x) &:= \delta f(x) \cdot_B \delta g(x) \\ \mathbf{0}_\to(x) &:= \mathbf{0}_B\end{aligned}$$

That is, a change is given pointwise, mapping each point in the domain to a change in the codomain.

The above definition is not always well-typed, since given $f : \hat{A} \to \hat{B}$ and $\delta f : A \to \Delta B$ there is no guarantee that $f \oplus_\to \delta f$ is differentiable. We present two sufficient criteria that guarantee this.

Theorem 5. *Let $\hat{A}$ and $\hat{B}$ be change actions, and suppose that $\hat{B}$ satisfies one of the following conditions:*

- *$\hat{B}$ is a complete change action.*
- *The change action $\widehat{\Delta B} := (\Delta B, \Delta B, \cdot_B)$ is complete and $\oplus_B : B \times \Delta B \to B$ is differentiable.*

Then the pointwise functional change action $(\hat{A} \to \hat{B}, A \to \Delta B, \oplus_{\to})$ *is well defined.*[11]

As a direct consequence of this, it follows that whenever L is a Boolean algebra (and hence has a complete change action), the pointwise functional change action $\hat{A} \Rightarrow_{pt} \hat{L}_{\bowtie}$ is well-defined.

Pointwise functional change actions are functional in the sense of Definition 11. Moreover, the derivative of the evaluation map is quite easy to compute.

Proposition 11 (Derivatives of the evaluation map). *Let* $\hat{A}$ *and* $\hat{B}$ *be change actions such that the pointwise functional change action* $\hat{A} \Rightarrow_{pt} \hat{B}$ *is well defined, and let* $f : \hat{A} \to \hat{B}$, $a \in A$, $\delta a \in \Delta A$, $\delta f \in A \to \Delta B$.

Then the following are both derivatives of the evaluation map:

$$\mathrm{ev}'_1((f, a), (\delta f, \delta a)) := f'(a, \delta a) \cdot \delta f(a \oplus \delta a)$$
$$\mathrm{ev}'_2((f, a), (\delta f, \delta a)) := \delta f(a) \cdot (f \oplus \delta f)'(a, \delta a)$$

A functional change action merely tells us that a derivative of the evaluation map exists—a pointwise change action actually gives us a definition of it. In practice, this means that we will only be able to use the results in Sect. 6.2 (incremental computation and derivatives of fixpoints) when we have pointwise change actions, or where we have some other way of computing a derivative of the evaluation map.

6 Directed-Complete Partial Orders and Fixpoints

Directed-complete partial orders (dcpos) equipped with a least element, are an important class of posets. They allow us to take *fixpoints* of (Scott-)continuous maps, which is important for interpreting recursion in program semantics.

6.1 Dcpos

As before, we can define change actions on dcpos, rather than sets, as change actions whose base and change sets are endowed with a dcpo structure, and where the monoid operation and action are (Scott-)continuous.

Definition 13. *A change action* $\hat{A}$ *is* continuous *if*

- A *and* ΔA *are dcpos.*
- $\oplus$ *is Scott-continuous as a map from* $A \times \Delta A \to A$.
- $\cdot$ *is Scott-continuous as a map from* $\Delta A \times \Delta A \to \Delta A$.

[11] Either of these conditions is enough to guarantee that the pointwise functional change action is well defined, but it can be the case that $\hat{B}$ satisfies neither and yet pointwise change actions into $\hat{B}$ do exist. A precise account of when pointwise functional change actions exist is outside the scope of this paper.

Unlike posets, the change order $\leq_\Delta$ does *not*, in general, induce a dcpo on ΔA. As a counterexample, consider the change action $(\overline{\mathbb{N}}, \mathbb{N}, +)$, where $\overline{\mathbb{N}}$ denotes the dcpo of natural numbers extended with positive infinity.

A key example of a continuous change action is the $\hat{L}_{\bowtie}$ change action on Boolean algebras.

Proposition 12 (Boolean algebra continuity). *Let L be a Boolean algebra. Then $\hat{L}_{\bowtie}$ is a continuous change action.*

For a general overview of results in domain theory and dcpos, we refer the reader to an introductory work such as [2], but we state here some specific results that we shall be using, such as the following, whose proof can be found in [2, Lemma 3.2.6]:

Proposition 13. *A function $f : A \times B \to C$ is continuous iff it is continuous in each variable separately.*

It is a well-known result in standard calculus that the limit of an absolutely convergent sequence of differentiable functions $\{f_i\}$ is itself differentiable, and its derivative is equal to the limit of the derivatives of the f_i. A consequence of Proposition 13 is the following analogous result:

Corollary 2. *Let $\hat{A}$ and $\hat{B}$ be change actions, with $\hat{B}$ continuous and let $\{f_i\}$ and $\{f_i'\}$ be I-indexed directed sets of functions in $A \to B$ and $A \times \Delta A \to \Delta B$ respectively.*

Then, if for every $i \in I$ it is the case that f_i' is a derivative of f_i, then $\bigsqcup_{i \in I} f_i'$ is a derivative of $\bigsqcup_{i \in I} f_i$.

6.2 Fixpoints

Fixpoints appear frequently in the semantics of languages with recursion. If we can give a generic account of how to compute fixpoints using change actions, then this gives us a compositional way of extending a derivative for the non-recursive semantics of a language to a derivative that can also handle recursion. We will later apply this technique to create a derivative for the semantics of full recursive Datalog (Sect. 7.2).

Iteration functions. Over directed-complete partial orders we can define a least fixpoint operator **lfp** in terms of the iteration function **iter**:

$$
\begin{aligned}
&\mathbf{iter} : (A \to A) \times \mathbb{N} \to A \\
&\mathbf{iter}(f, 0) := \bot \\
&\mathbf{iter}(f, n) := f^n(\bot) \\
&\mathbf{lfp} : (A \to A) \to A \\
&\mathbf{lfp}(f) := \bigsqcup_{n \in \mathbb{N}} \mathbf{iter}(f, n) && \text{(where } f \text{ is continuous)}
\end{aligned}
$$

The iteration function is the basis for all the results in this section: we can take a partial derivative with respect to n, and this will give us a way to get to the next iteration incrementally; and we can take the partial derivative with respect to f, and this will give us a way to get from iterating f to iterating $f \oplus \delta f$.

Incremental computation of fixpoints. The following theorems provide a generalization of semi-naive evaluation to any differentiable function over a continuous change action. Throughout this section we will assume that we have a continuous change action $\hat{A}$, and any reference to the change action $\hat{\mathbb{N}}$ will refer to the monoidal change action on the naturals defined in Sect. 2.1.

Since we are trying to incrementalize the iterative step, we start by taking the partial derivative of **iter** with respect to n.

Proposition 14 (Derivative of the iteration map with respect to n). *Let $\hat{A}$ be a complete change action and let $f : A \to A$ be a differentiable function. Then* **iter** *is differentiable with respect to its second argument, and a partial derivative is given by:*

$$\begin{aligned}
&\partial_2\mathbf{iter} : (A \to A) \times \mathbb{N} \times \Delta\mathbb{N} \to \Delta A\\
&\partial_2\mathbf{iter}(f, \mathbf{0}, m) := \mathbf{iter}(f, m) \ominus \mathbf{iter}(f, 0)\\
&\partial_2\mathbf{iter}(f, n+1, m) := f'(\mathbf{iter}(f, n), \partial_2\mathbf{iter}(f, n, m))
\end{aligned}$$

By using the following recurrence relation, we can then compute ∂_2**iter** along with **iter** simultaneously:

$$\begin{aligned}
&\mathbf{recur}_f : A \times \Delta A \to A \times \Delta A\\
&\mathbf{recur}_f(\bot, \bot) := (\bot, f(\bot) \ominus \bot)\\
&\mathbf{recur}_f(a, \delta a) := (a \oplus \delta a, f'(a, \delta a))
\end{aligned}$$

Which has the property that

$$\mathbf{recur}_f^n(\bot, \bot) = (\mathbf{iter}(f, n), \partial_2\mathbf{iter}(f, n, 1))$$

This gives us a way to compute a fixpoint incrementally, by adding successive changes to an accumulator until we reach it. This is exactly how semi-naive evaluation works: you compute the delta relation and the accumulator simultaneously, adding the delta into the accumulator at each stage until it becomes the final output.

Theorem 6 (Incremental computation of least fixpoints). *Let $\hat{A}$ be a complete, continuous change action, $f : \hat{A} \to \hat{A}$ be continuous and differentiable.*

Then $\mathbf{lfp}(f) = \bigsqcup_{n \in \mathbb{N}}(\pi_1(\mathbf{recur}_f^n(\bot, \bot)))$.[12]

[12] Note that we have *not* taken the fixpoint of $\mathbf{recur}_f$, since it is not continuous.

Derivatives of fixpoints. In the previous section we have shown how to use derivatives to compute fixpoints more efficiently, but we also want to take the derivative of the fixpoint operator itself. A typical use case for this is where we have calculated some fixpoint

$$F_E := \mathbf{fix}(\lambda X.F(E, X))$$

then update the parameter E with some change δE and wish to compute the new value of the fixpoint, i.e.

$$F_{E \oplus \delta E} := \mathbf{fix}(\lambda X.F(E \oplus \delta E, X))$$

This can be seen as applying a change to the *function* whose fixpoint we are taking. We go from computing the fixpoint of $F(E, \_)$ to computing the fixpoint of $F(E \oplus \delta E, \_)$. If we have a pointwise functional change action then we can express this change as a function giving the change at each point, that is:

$$\lambda X.F(E \oplus \delta E, X) \ominus F(E, X)$$

In Datalog this would allow us to update a recursively defined relation given an update to one of its non-recursive dependencies, or the extensional database. For example, we might want to take the transitive closure relation and update it by changing the edge relation e.

However, to compute these examples would requires us to provide a derivative for the fixpoint operator **fix**: we want to know how the resulting fixpoint changes given a change to its input function.

Definition 14 (Derivatives of fixpoints). *Let $\hat{A}$ be a change action, let $\hat{U} \subseteq \hat{A} \Rightarrow \hat{A}$ be a functional change action (not necessarily pointwise) and suppose $\mathbf{fix}_U$ and $\mathbf{fix}_{\Delta A}$ are fixpoint operators for endofunctions on U and ΔA respectively.*

Then we define

$$\begin{aligned}
&\mathbf{adjust} : U \times \Delta U \to (\Delta A \to \Delta A)\\
&\mathbf{adjust}(f, \delta f) := \lambda\ \delta a.\, \mathrm{ev}'((f, \mathbf{fix}_U(f)), (\delta f, \delta a))\\
&\mathbf{fix}'_U : U \times \Delta U \to \Delta A\\
&\mathbf{fix}'_U(f, \delta f) := \mathbf{fix}_{\Delta A}(\mathbf{adjust}(f, \delta f))
\end{aligned}$$

The suggestively named $\mathbf{fix}'_U$ will in fact turn out to be a derivative—for *least* fixpoints. The appearance of ev$'$, a derivative of the evaluation map, in the definition of **adjust** is also no coincidence: as evaluating a fixpoint consists of many steps of applying the evaluation map, so computing the derivative of a fixpoint consists of many steps of applying the derivative of the evaluation map.[13]

[13] Perhaps surprisingly, the authors first discovered an expanded version of this formula, and it was only later that we realised the remarkable connection to ev$'$.

Since **lfp** is characterized as the limit of a chain of functions, Corollary 2 suggests a way to compute its derivative. It suffices to find a derivative $\mathbf{iter}'_n$ of each iteration map such that the resulting set $\{\mathbf{iter}'_n \mid n \in \mathbb{N}\}$ is directed, which will entail that $\bigsqcup_{n\in\mathbb{N}} \mathbf{iter}'_n$ is a derivative of **lfp**.

These correspond to the first partial derivative of **iter**—this time with respect to f. While we are differentiating with respect to f, we are still going to need to define our derivatives inductively in terms of n.

Proposition 15 (Derivative of the iteration map with respect to f). **iter** *is differentiable with respect to its first argument and a derivative is given by:*

$$\begin{aligned}
&\partial_1\mathbf{iter} : (A \to A) \times \Delta(A \to A) \times \mathbb{N} \to \Delta A \\
&\partial_1\mathbf{iter}(f, \delta f, \mathbf{0}) := \bot_{\Delta A} \\
&\partial_1\mathbf{iter}(f, \delta f, n+1) := \mathrm{ev}'((f, \mathbf{iter}(f, n)), (\delta f, \partial_1\mathbf{iter}(f, \delta f, n)))
\end{aligned}$$

As before, we can now compute $\partial_1\mathbf{iter}$ together with **iter** by mutual recursion.[14]

$$\begin{aligned}
&\mathbf{recur}_{f,\delta f} : A \times \Delta A \to A \times \Delta A \\
&\mathbf{recur}_{f,\delta f}(a, \delta a) := (f(a), \mathrm{ev}'((f, a), (\delta f, \delta a)))
\end{aligned}$$

Which has the property that

$$\mathbf{recur}^n_{f,\delta f}(\bot, \bot) = (\mathbf{iter}(f, n), \partial_1\mathbf{iter}(f, \delta f, n)).$$

This indeed provides us with a function whose limit we can take. If we do so we will discover that it is exactly $\mathbf{lfp}'$ (defined as in Definition 14), showing that $\mathbf{lfp}'$ is a true derivative.

Theorem 7 (Derivatives of least fixpoint operators). *Let*

- $\hat{A}$ *be a continuous change action*
- U *be the set of continuous functions* $f : A \to A$*, with a functional change action* $\hat{U} \subseteq \hat{A} \Rightarrow \hat{A}$
- $f \in U$ *be a continuous, differentiable function*
- $\delta f \in \Delta U$ *be a function change*
- ev' *be a derivative of the evaluation map which is continuous with respect to* a *and* δa.

Then $\mathbf{lfp}'$ *is a derivative of* **lfp**.

Computing this derivative still requires computing a fixpoint—over the change lattice—but this may still be significantly less expensive than recomputing the full new fixpoint.

---

[14] In fact, the recursion here is not *mutual*: the first component does not depend on the second. However, writing it in this way makes it amenable to computation by fixpoint, and we will in fact be able to avoid the recomputation of $\mathbf{iter}_n$ when we show that it is equivalent to $\mathbf{lfp}'$.

7 Derivatives for Recursive Datalog

Given the non-recursive semantics for a language, we can extend it to handle recursive definitions using fixpoints. Section 6.2 lets us extend our derivative for the non-recursive semantics to a derivative for the recursive semantics, as well as letting us compute the fixpoints themselves incrementally.

Again, we will demonstrate the technique with Datalog, although the approach is generic.

7.1 Semantics of Datalog Programs

First of all, we define the usual "immediate consequence operator" which computes "one step" of our program semantics.

Definition 15. *Given a program $\mathbb{P} = (P_1, \ldots, P_n)$, where P_i is a predicate, with schema Γ_i, the* immediate consequence operator $\mathcal{I} : \mathbf{Rel}^n \to \mathbf{Rel}^n$ *is defined as follows:*

$$\mathcal{I}(\mathcal{R}_1, \ldots, \mathcal{R}_n) = (\llbracket P_1 \rrbracket_{\Gamma_1}(\mathcal{R}_1, \ldots, \mathcal{R}_n), \ldots, \llbracket P_n \rrbracket_{\Gamma_n}(\mathcal{R}_1, \ldots, \mathcal{R}_n))$$

That is, given a value for the program, we pass in all the relations to the denotation of each predicate, to get a new tuple of relations.

Definition 16. *The semantics of a program $\mathbb{P}$ is defined to be*

$$\llbracket \mathbb{P} \rrbracket := \mathbf{lfp}_{\mathbf{Rel}^n}(\mathcal{I})$$

and may be calculated by iterative application of $\mathcal{I}$ to $\bot$ until fixpoint is reached.

Whether or not this program semantics exists will depend on whether the fixpoint exists. Typically this is ensured by constraining the program such that $\mathcal{I}$ is monotone (or, in the context of a dcpo, continuous). We do not require monotonicity to apply Theorem 6 (and hence we can incrementally compute fixpoints that happen to exist even though the generating function is not monotonic), but it is required to apply Theorem 7.

7.2 Incremental Evaluation of Datalog

We can easily extend a derivative for the formula semantics to a derivative for the immediate consequence operator $\mathcal{I}$. Putting this together with the results from Sect. 6.2, we have now created *modular* proofs for the two main results, which allows us to preserve them in the face of changes to the underlying language.

Corollary 3. *Datalog program semantics can be evaluated incrementally.*

Corollary 4. *Datalog program semantics can be incrementally maintained with changes to relations.*

Note that our approach makes no particular distinction between changes to the *extensional* relations (adding or removing facts), and changes to the *intensional* relations (changing the definition). The latter simply amounts to a change to the denotation of that relation, which can be incrementally propagated in exactly the same way as we would propagate a change to the extensional relations.

8 Related Work

8.1 Change Actions and Incremental Computation

Change structures. The seminal paper in this area is Cai et al. [14]. We deviate from that excellent paper in three regards: the inclusion of minus operators, the nature of function changes, and the use of dependent types.

We have omitted minus operators from our definition because there are many interesting change actions that are not complete and so cannot have a minus operator. Where we can find a change structure with a minus operator, often we are forced to use unwieldy representations for change sets, and Cai et al. cite this as their reason for using a dependent type of changes. For example, the monoidal change actions on sets and lists are clearly useful for incremental computation on streams, yet they do not admit minus operators—instead, one would be forced to work with e.g. multisets admitting negative arities, as Cai et al. do.

Our function changes (when well behaved) correspond to what Cai et al. call *pointwise differences* (see [14, section 2.2]). As they point out, you can reconstruct their function changes from pointwise changes and derivatives, so the two formulations are equivalent.

The equivalence of our presentations means that our work should be compatible with their Incremental Lambda Calculus (see [14, section 3]). The derivatives we give in Sect. 4.2 are more or less a "change semantics" for Datalog (see [14, section 3.5]).

S-acts. S-acts (i.e the category of monoid actions on sets) and their categorical structure have received a fair amount of attention over the years (Kilp, Knauer, and Mikhalev [30] is a good overview). However, there is a key difference between change actions considered as a category (**CAct**) and the category of S-acts (**SAct**): the objects of **SAct** all maintain the same monoid structure, whereas we are interested in changing both the base set *and* the structure of the action.

Derivatives of fixpoints. Arntzenius [5] gives a derivative operator for fixpoints based on the framework in Cai et al. [14]. However, since we have different notions of function changes, the result is inapplicable as stated. In addition, we require a somewhat different set of conditions; in particular, we do not require our changes to always be increasing.

8.2 Datalog

Incremental evaluation. The earliest interpretation of semi-naive evaluation as a derivative appears in Bancilhon [8]. The idea of using an approximate derivative and the requisite soundness condition appears as a throwaway comment in Bancilhon and Ramakrishnan [9, section 3.2.2], and it would appear that nobody has since developed that approach.

As far as we know, traditional semi-naive is the state of the art in incremental, bottom-up, Datalog evaluation, and there are no strategies that accommodate additional language features such as parity-stratified negation and aggregates.

Incremental maintenance. There is existing literature on incremental maintenance of relational algebra expressions.

Griffin, Libkin, and Trickey [24] following Qian and Wiederhold [35] compute differences with both an "upwards" and a "downwards" component, and produce a set of rules that look quite similar to those we derive in Theorem 4. However, our presentation is significantly more generic, handles recursive expressions, and works on set semantics rather than bag semantics.[15]

Several approaches [25, 27]—most notably DReD—remove facts until one can start applying the rules again to reach the new fixpoint. Given a good way of deciding what facts to remove this can be quite efficient. However, such techniques tend to be tightly coupled to the domain. Although we know of no theoretical reason why either approach should give superior performance when both are applicable, an empirical investigation of this could prove interesting.

Other approaches [19, 43] consider only restricted subsets of Datalog, or incur other substantial constraints.

Embedding Datalog. Datafun (Arntzenius and Krishnaswami [6]) is a functional programming language that embeds Datalog, allowing significant improvements in genericity, such as the use of higher-order functions. Since we have directly defined a change action and derivative operator for Datalog, our work could be used as a "plugin" in the sense of Cai et al., allowing Datafun to compute its internal fixpoints incrementally, but also allowing Datafun expressions to be fully incrementally maintained.

In a different direction, Cathcart Burn, Ong, and Ramsay [15] have proposed *higher-order constrained Horn clauses* (HoCHC), a new class of constraints for the automatic verification of higher-order programs. HoCHC may be viewed as a higher-order extension of Datalog. Change actions can be readily applied to organise an efficient semi-naive method for solving HoCHC systems.

8.3 Differential λ-calculus

Another setting where derivatives of arbitrary higher-order programs have been studied is the *differential λ-calculus* [20, 21]. This is a higher-order, simply-typed

[15] The same approach of finding derivatives would work with bag semantics, although unfortunately the Boolean algebra structure is missing.

λ-calculus which allows for computing the derivative of a function, in a similar way to the notion of derivative in Cai's work and the present paper.

While there are clear similarities between the two systems, the most important difference is the properties of the derivatives themselves: in the differential λ-calculus, derivatives are guaranteed to be linear in their second argument, whereas in our approach derivatives do not have this restriction but are instead required to satisfy a strong relation to the function that is being differentiated (see Definition 2).

Families of denotational models for the differential λ-calculus have been studied in depth [12,13,16,29], and the relationship between these and change actions is the subject of ongoing work.

8.4 Higher-Order Automatic Differentiation

Automatic differentiation [23] is a technique that allows for efficiently computing the derivative of arbitrary programs, with applications in probabilistic modeling [31] and machine learning [10] among other areas. In recent times, this technique has been successfully applied to higher-order languages [11,41]. While some approaches have been suggested [28,33], a general theoretical framework for this technique is still a matter of open research.

To this purpose, some authors have proposed the incremental λ-calculus as a foundational framework on which models of automatic differentiation can be based [28]. We believe our change actions are better suited to this purpose than the incremental λ-calculus, since one can easily give them a synthetic differential geometric reading (by interpreting $\hat{A}$ as an Euclidean module and ΔA as its corresponding spectrum, for example).

9 Conclusions and Future Work

We have presented change actions and their properties, and used them to provide novel, compositional, strategies for incrementally evaluating and maintaining recursive functions, in particular the semantics of Datalog.

The main avenue for future theoretical work is the categorical structure of change actions. This has begun to be explored by the authors in [4], where change actions are generalized to arbitrary Cartesian base categories and a construction is provided to obtain "canonical" Cartesian closed categories of change actions and differentiable maps.

We hope that these generalizations would allow us to extend the theory of change actions towards other classes of models, such as synthetic differential geometry and domain theory. Some early results in [4] also indicate a connection between 2-categories and change actions which has yet to be fully mapped.

The compositional nature of these techniques suggest that an approach like that used in [22] could be used for an even more generic approach to automatic differentiation.

In addition, there is plenty of scope for practical application of the techniques given here to languages other than Datalog.

References

1. Abiteboul, S., Hull, R., Vianu, V.: Foundations of Databases: The Logical Level. Addison-Wesley Longman Publishing Co., Inc., Boston (1995)
2. Abramsky, S., Jung, A.: Domain theory. In: Handbook of Logic in Computer Science. Oxford University Press, New York (1994)
3. Alvarez-Picallo, M., Eyers-Taylor, A., Jones, M.P., Ong, C.L.: Fixing incremental computation: derivatives of fixpoints, and the recursive semantics of datalog. CoRR abs/1811.06069 (2018). http://arxiv.org/abs/1811.06069
4. Alvarez-Picallo, M., Ong, C.H.L.: Change actions: models of generalised differentiation. In: International Conference on Foundations of Software Science and Computation Structures. Springer (2019, in press)
5. Arntzenius, M.: Static differentiation of monotone fixpoints (2017). http://www.rntz.net/files/fixderiv.pdf
6. Arntzenius, M., Krishnaswami, N.R.: Datafun: a functional datalog. In: Proceedings of the 21st ACM SIGPLAN International Conference on Functional Programming, pp. 214–227. ACM (2016)
7. Avgustinov, P., de Moor, O., Jones, M.P., Schäfer, M.: QL: object-oriented queries on relational data. In: LIPIcs-Leibniz International Proceedings in Informatics, vol. 56. Schloss Dagstuhl-Leibniz-Zentrum fuer Informatik (2016)
8. Bancilhon, F.: Naive evaluation of recursively defined relations. In: Brodie, M.L., Mylopoulos, J. (eds.) On Knowledge Base Management Systems. TINF, pp. 165–178. Springer, New York (1986). https://doi.org/10.1007/978-1-4612-4980-1_17
9. Bancilhon, F., Ramakrishnan, R.: An amateur's introduction to recursive query processing strategies, vol. 15. ACM (1986)
10. Baydin, A.G., Pearlmutter, B.A.: Automatic differentiation of algorithms for machine learning. arXiv preprint arXiv:1404.7456 (2014)
11. Baydin, A.G., Pearlmutter, B.A., Siskind, J.M.: DiffSharp: an AD library for .NET languages. arXiv preprint arXiv:1611.03423 (2016)
12. Blute, R., Ehrhard, T., Tasson, C.: A convenient differential category. arXiv preprint arXiv:1006.3140 (2010)
13. Bucciarelli, A., Ehrhard, T., Manzonetto, G.: Categorical models for simply typed resource calculi. Electron. Notes Theor. Comput. Sci. **265**, 213–230 (2010)
14. Cai, Y., Giarrusso, P.G., Rendel, T., Ostermann, K.: A theory of changes for higher-order languages: incrementalizing λ-calculi by static differentiation. In: ACM SIGPLAN Notices, vol. 49, pp. 145–155. ACM (2014)
15. Cathcart Burn, T., Ong, C.L., Ramsay, S.J.: Higher-order constrained horn clauses for verification. PACMPL **2**(POPL), 11:1–11:28 (2018). https://doi.org/10.1145/3158099
16. Cockett, J.R.B., Gallagher, J.: Categorical models of the differential λ-calculus revisited. Electron. Notes Theor. Comput. Sci. **325**, 63–83 (2016)
17. Compton, K.J.: Stratified least fixpoint logic. Theor. Comput. Sci. **131**(1), 95–120 (1994)
18. Datomic website (2018). https://www.datomic.com. Accessed 01 Jan 2018
19. Dong, G., Su, J.: Incremental maintenance of recursive views using relational calculus/SQL. ACM SIGMOD Rec. **29**(1), 44–51 (2000)
20. Ehrhard, T.: An introduction to differential linear logic: proof-nets, models and antiderivatives. Math. Struct. Comput. Sci. 1–66 (2017)
21. Ehrhard, T., Regnier, L.: The differential lambda-calculus. Theor. Comput. Sci. **309**(1–3), 1–41 (2003)

22. Elliott, C.: The simple essence of automatic differentiation. Proc. ACM Program. Lang. **2**(ICFP), 70 (2018)
23. Griewank, A., Walther, A.: Evaluating Derivatives: Principles and Techniques of Algorithmic Differentiation, vol. 105. SIAM, Philadelphia (2008)
24. Griffin, T., Libkin, L., Trickey, H.: An improved algorithm for the incremental recomputation of active relational expressions. IEEE Trans. Knowl. Data Eng. **3**, 508–511 (1997)
25. Gupta, A., Mumick, I.S., Subrahmanian, V.S.: Maintaining views incrementally. ACM SIGMOD Rec. **22**(2), 157–166 (1993)
26. Halpin, T., Rugaber, S.: LogiQL: A Query Language for Smart Databases. CRC Press, Boca Raton (2014)
27. Harrison, J.V., Dietrich, S.W.: Maintenance of materialized views in a deductive database: an update propagation approach. In: Workshop on Deductive Databases, JICSLP, pp. 56–65 (1992)
28. Kelly, R., Pearlmutter, B.A., Siskind, J.M.: Evolving the incremental λ calculus into a model of forward automatic differentiation (AD). arXiv preprint arXiv:1611.03429 (2016)
29. Kerjean, M., Tasson, C.: Mackey-complete spaces and power series-a topological model of differential linear logic. Math. Struct. Comput. Sci. 1–36 (2016)
30. Kilp, M., Knauer, U., Mikhalev, A.V.: Monoids, Acts and Categories: With Applications to Wreath Products and Graphs. A Handbook for Students and Researchers, vol. 29. Walter de Gruyter, Berlin (2000)
31. Kucukelbir, A., Tran, D., Ranganath, R., Gelman, A., Blei, D.M.: Automatic differentiation variational inference. J. Mach. Learn. Res. **18**(1), 430–474 (2017)
32. LogicBlox Inc. website (2018). http://www.logicblox.com. Accessed 01 Jan 2018
33. Manzyuk, O.: A simply typed λ-calculus of forward automatic differentiation. Electron. Notes Theor. Comput. Sci. **286**, 257–272 (2012)
34. de Moor, O., Baars, A.: Doing a doaitse: simple recursive aggregates in datalog. In: Liber Amicorum for Doaitse Swierstra, pp. 207–216 (2013). http://www.staff.science.uu.nl/~hage0101/liberdoaitseswierstra.pdf. Accessed 01 Jan 2018
35. Qian, X., Wiederhold, G.: Incremental recomputation of active relational expressions. IEEE Trans. Knowl. Data Eng. **3**(3), 337–341 (1991)
36. Sáenz-Pérez, F.: DES: a deductive database system. Electron. Notes Theor. Comput. Sci. **271**, 63–78 (2011)
37. Schäfer, M., de Moor, O.: Type inference for datalog with complex type hierarchies. In: ACM SIGPLAN Notices, vol. 45, pp. 145–156. ACM (2010)
38. Scholz, B., Jordan, H., Subotić, P., Westmann, T.: On fast large-scale program analysis in datalog. In: Proceedings of the 25th International Conference on Compiler Construction, pp. 196–206. ACM (2016)
39. Semmle Ltd. website (2018). https://semmle.com. Accessed 01 Jan 2018
40. Sereni, D., Avgustinov, P., de Moor, O.: Adding magic to an optimising datalog compiler. In: Proceedings of the 2008 ACM SIGMOD International Conference on Management of Data, pp. 553–566. ACM (2008)
41. Siskind, J.M., Pearlmutter, B.A.: Nesting forward-mode AD in a functional framework. High.-Order Symb. Comput. **21**(4), 361–376 (2008)
42. Souffle language website (2018). http://souffle-lang.org. Accessed 01 Jan 2018
43. Urpi, T., Olive, A.: A method for change computation in deductive databases. In: VLDB, vol. 92, pp. 225–237 (1992)

3

Data Races and Static Analysis for Interrupt-Driven Kernels

Nikita Chopra, Rekha Pai(✉), and Deepak D'Souza

Indian Institute of Science, Bangalore, India
{nikita,rekhapai,deepakd}@iisc.ac.in

Abstract. We consider a class of interrupt-driven programs that model the kernel API libraries of some popular real-time embedded operating systems and the synchronization mechanisms they use. We define a natural notion of data races and a happens-before ordering for such programs. The key insight is the notion of *disjoint blocks* to define the synchronizes-with relation. This notion also suggests an efficient and effective lockset based analysis for race detection. It also enables us to define efficient "sync-CFG" based static analyses for such programs, which exploit data race freedom. We use this theory to carry out static analysis on the FreeRTOS kernel library to detect races and to infer simple relational invariants on key kernel variables and data-structures.

Keywords: Static analysis · Interrupt-driven programs · Data races

1 Introduction

Embedded software is widespread and increasingly employed in safety-critical applications in medical, automobile, and aerospace domains. These programs are typically multi-threaded applications, running on uni-processor systems, that are compiled along with a kernel library that provides priority-based scheduling, and other task management and communication functionality. The applications themselves are similar to classical multi-threaded programs (using lock, semaphore, or queue based synchronization) although they are distinguished by their priority-based execution semantics. The kernel on the other hand typically makes use of non-standard low-level synchronization mechanisms (like disabling-enabling interrupts, suspending the scheduler, and flag-based synchronization) to ensure thread-safe access to its data-structures. In the literature such software (both applications and kernels) are referred to as *interrupt-driven* programs. Our interest in this paper is in the subclass of interrupt-driven programs corresponding to kernel libraries.

Efficient static analysis of concurrent programs is a challenging problem. One could carry out a precise analysis by considering the *product* of the control flow graphs (CFGs) of the threads, however this is prohibitively expensive due to the exponential number of program points in the product graph. A promising direction is to focus on the subclass of *race-free* programs. This is an important class of programs, as most developers aim to write race-free code, and one could try to exploit this property to give an efficient way of analyzing programs that fall in this class. In recent years there have been many techniques [7, 11, 12, 18, 21] that exploit the race-freedom property to perform sound and efficient static analysis. In particular [11, 21] create an appealing structure called a "sync-CFG" which is the *union* of the control flow graphs of the threads augmented with possible "synchronization" edges, and essentially perform sequential analysis on this graph to obtain sound facts about the concurrent program. However these techniques are all for classical lock-based concurrent programs. A natural question asks if we can analyze interrupt-driven programs in a similar way.

There are several challenges in doing this. Firstly one needs to define *what* constitutes a data race in a generalized setting that includes these programs. Secondly, how does one define the happens-before order, and in particular the *synchronizes-with* relation that many of the race-free analysis techniques rely on, given the ad-hoc synchronization mechanisms used in these programs.

A natural route that suggests itself is to translate a given interrupt-driven program into one that uses classical locks, and faithfully captures the interleaved executions of the original program. One could then use existing techniques for lock-based concurrency to analyze these programs. However, this route is fraught with many challenges. To begin with, it is not clear how one would handle flag-based synchronization which is one of the main synchronization mechanisms used in these programs. Even if one could handle this, such a translation *may not* preserve data races, in that the original program might have had a race but the translated program does not. Finally, some of the synchronizes-with edges in the translated program are clearly unnecessary, leading to imprecise data-flow facts in the analyses.

In this paper, we show that it is possible to take a more organic route and address these challenges in a principled way that could apply to other non-standard classes of concurrent systems as well. Firstly, we propose a general definition of a data race that is not based on a happens-before order, but on the operational semantics of the class of programs under consideration. The definition essentially says that two statements s and t can race, if two notional "blocks" around them can *overlap* in time during an execution. We believe that this definition accurately captures what it is that a programmer tries to avoid while dealing with shared variables whose values matter. Secondly we propose a way of defining the *synchronizes-with* relation, based on the notion of *disjoint blocks*. These are statically identifiable pairs of path segments in the CFGs of different threads that are guaranteed to never overlap (in time) during an execution of the program, much like blocks of code that lie between an acquire and release of the same lock. This relation now suggests a natural sync-CFG structure on which we can perform analyses like value-set (including interval, null-deference, and points-to analysis), and region-based relational invariant analysis, in a sound and efficient manner. We also use the notion of disjoint blocks to define an efficient and precise lock-set-based analysis for detecting races in interrupt-driven programs.

We implement some of these analyses on the FreeRTOS kernel library [3] which is one of the most widely used open-source real-time kernels for embedded systems, comprising about 3,500 lines of C code. Our race-detection analysis reports a total of 64 races in kernel methods, of which 18 turn out to be true positives. We also carry out a region-based relational analysis using an implementation based on CIL [22]/Apron [15], to prove several relational invariants on the kernel variables and abstracted data-structures.

2 Overview

We give an overview of our contributions via an illustrative example modelled on a portion of the FreeRTOS kernel library. Figure 1 shows an interrupt-driven program that contains a main thread that first initializes the kernel variables. The variables represent components of a message queue, like `msgw` (the number of messages waiting in the queue), `len` (max length of the queue), `wtosend` (the number of tasks waiting to send to the queue), `wtorec` (the number of tasks waiting to receive from the queue), and `RxLock` (a counter which also acts as a synchronization flag that mediates access to the waiting queues). The main thread then creates (or spawns) two threads: *qsend* which models the kernel API method for sending a message to the queue, and *qrec_ISR* which models a method for receiving a message, and which is meant to be called from an interrupt-service routine. The basic semantics of this program is that the ISR thread can interrupt *qsend* at any time (provided interrupts are not disabled), but always runs to completion itself. The threads use `disableint`/`enableint` to disable and enable interrupts, `suspendsch`/`resumesch` to suspend/resume the scheduler (thereby preventing preemption by another non-ISR thread), and finally flag-based synchronization (using the `RxLock` variable), as different means to ensure mutual exclusion.

Our first contribution is a general notion of data races which is applicable to such programs. We say that two conflicting statements s and t in two different threads are involved in a data race if assuming s and t were enclosed in a notional "block" of skip statements, there is an execution in which the two blocks "overlap" in time. The given program can be seen to be free of races. However if we were to remove the `disableint` statement of line 10, then the statements accessing `msgw` in lines 12 and 42 would be racy, since soon after the access of `msgw` in *qsend* at line 12, there could be preemption by *qrec_ISR* which goes on to execute line 42.

Next we illustrate the notion of "disjoint blocks" which is the key to defining synchronizes-with edges, which we need in our sync-CFG analysis as well as to define an appropriate happens-before relation. Disjoint blocks are also used in our race-detection algorithm. A pair of blocks of code (for example any of the like-shaded blocks of code in the figure) are *disjoint* if they can never overlap during an execution. For example, the block comprising lines 11–14 in *qsend* and the whole of *qrec_ISR*, form a pair of disjoint blocks.

Next we give an analysis for checking race-freedom, by adapting the standard lockset analysis [24] for classical concurrent programs. We associate a unique

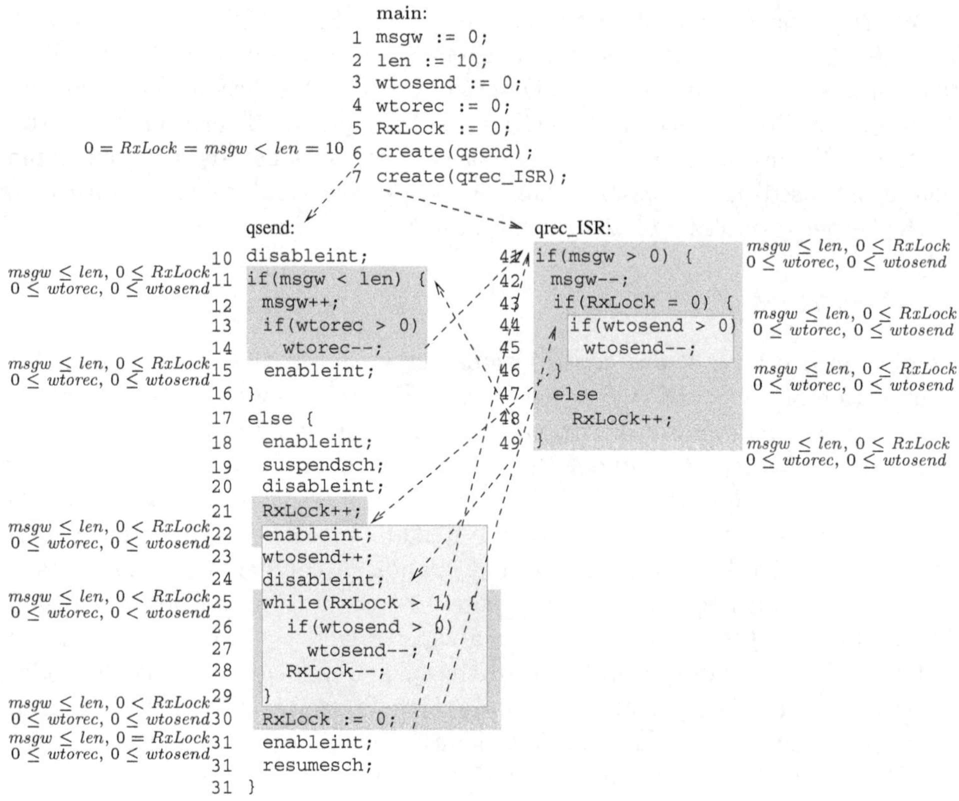

Fig. 1. An interrupt-driven program modelled on the FreeRTOS kernel library. Similarly shaded blocks denote disjoint blocks. Some of the sync-with edges are shown in dashed lines. Some edges like 22 → 41 and 49 → 20 have been omitted for clarity.

lock with each pair of disjoint blocks, and add notional acquires and releases of this lock at the beginning and end (respectively) of these blocks. We now do the standard lockset analysis on this version of the program, and declare two accesses to be non-racy if they hold sets of locks with a non-empty intersection.

Finally, we show how to do data-flow analysis for such programs in a sound and efficient way. The basic idea is to construct a "sync-CFG" for the program by unioning the control-flow graphs of the threads, and adding *sync* edges that capture the synchronizes-with edges (going from the end of a block to the beginning of its paired block), for example line 14 to line 41 and line 49 to line 11. The sync-edges are shown by dashed arrows in the figure. We now do a standard "value-set" analysis (for example interval analysis) on this graph, keeping track of a set of values each variable can take. The resulting facts about a variable are guaranteed to be sound at points where the variable is accessed (or even "owned" in the sense that a notional read of the variable at that point is non-racy). For example an interval analysis on this program would give us that $0 <$ `msgw` at line 14. Finally, we could do a region-based value-set analysis, by identifying regions of variables that are accessed as a unit – for example `msgw` and `len` could be in one region, while `wtosend` and `wtorec` could be in another. The figure shows some facts inferred by a polyhedral analysis based on these regions, for the given program.

3 Interrupt-Driven Programs

The programs we consider have a finite number of (static) threads, with a designated "main" thread in which execution begins. The threads access a set of shared global variables, some of which are used as "synchronization flags", using a standard set of commands like assignment statements of the form `x := e`, conditional statements (`if-then-else`), loop statements (`while`), etc. In addition, the threads can use commands like `disableint`, `enableint` (to disable and enable interrupts, respectively), `suspendsch`, `resumesch` (to suspend and resume the scheduler, respectively), while the main thread can also `create` a thread (enable it for execution). Table 1 shows the set of basic statements $cmd_{V,T}$ over a set of variables V and a set of threads T.

We allow standard integer and Boolean expressions over a set of variables V. For an integer expression e over V, and an environment ϕ for V, we denote by $[\![e]\!]_\phi$ the integer value that e evaluates to in ϕ. Similarly for a Boolean expression b, we denote the Boolean value (*true* or *false*) that b evaluates to in ϕ by $[\![b]\!]_\phi$. For a set of environments Φ for a set of variables V, we define the set of integer values that e can evaluate to in an environment in Φ, by $[\![e]\!]_\Phi = \{[\![e]\!]_\phi \mid \phi \in \Phi\}$. Similarly, for a boolean expression b, we define the set of environments in Φ that satisfy b to be $[\![b]\!]_\Phi = \{\phi \in \Phi \mid [\![b]\!]_\phi = true\}$.

Each thread is of one of two *types*: "task" threads that are like standard threads, and "ISR" threads that represent threads that run as interrupt service routines. The *main* thread is a task thread, which is the only task thread enabled initially. The *main* thread can enable other threads (both task and ISR) for execution using the `create` command. Task threads can be preempted by other task threads (whenever interrupts are not disabled, and the scheduler is not suspended) or by ISR threads (whenever interrupts are not disabled). On the other hand ISR threads cannot be preempted and are assumed to run to completion.

Only task threads are allowed to use `disableint`, `enableint`, `suspendsch` and `resumesch` commands. Similarly, if flag-based synchronization is used, only task threads can modify the flag variable, while an ISR can only check whether the flag is set or not, and perform some actions accordingly.

Formally we represent an interrupt-driven program P as a tuple (V, T) where V is a finite set of integer variables, and T is a finite set of named threads. Each thread $t \in T$ has a *type* which is one of *task* or *ISR*, and an associated control-flow graph of the form $G_t = (L_t, s_t, inst_t)$ where L_t is a finite set of *locations* of thread t, $s_t \in L_t$ is the *start* location of thread t, $inst_t \subseteq L_t \times cmd_{V,T} \times L_t$ is a finite set of *instructions* of thread t.

Some definitions related to threads will be useful going forward. We denote by $L_P = \biguplus_{t \in T} L_t$ the disjoint union of the thread locations. Whenever P is clear

Table 1. Basic statements $cmd_{V,T}$ over variables V and threads T

Command	Description
`skip`	Do nothing
`x := e`	Assign the value of expression e to variable $x \in V$
`assume`(b)	Enabled only if expression b evaluates to *true*, acts like `skip`
`create(t)`	Enable thread $t \in T$ for execution
`disableint`	Disable interrupts and context switches
`enableint`	Enable interrupts and context switches
`suspendsch`	Suspend the scheduler (other task threads cannot preempt the current thread); Also sets `ssflag` variable
`resumesch`	Resume the scheduler (other task threads can now preempt the current thread); Also unsets `ssflag` variable

from the context we will drop the subscript of P from L_P and its decorations. For a location $l \in L$ we denote by $tid(l)$ the thread t which contains location l. We denote the set of instructions of P by $inst_P = \bigcup_{t \in T} inst_t$. For an instruction $\iota \in inst_t$, we will also write $tid(\iota)$ to mean the thread t. For an instruction $\iota = \langle l, c, l' \rangle$, we call l the *source* location, and l' the *target* location of ι.

We denote the set of commands appearing in program P by $cmd(P)$. We will consider an assignment `x := e` as a *write-access* to x, and as a *read-access* to every variable that appears in the expression e. Similarly, `assume`(b) is considered to be a read-access of every variable that occurs in expression b. We say two accesses are *conflicting* accesses if they are read/write accesses to the same variable, and at least one of them is a write. We assume that the control-flow graph of each thread comes from a well-structured program. Finally, we assume that the *main* thread begins by initializing the variables to constant values. Figure 2 shows an example program and the control-flow-graphs of its threads.

We define the operational semantics of an interrupt-driven program using a labeled transition system (LTS). Let $P = (V, T)$ be a program. We define an LTS $\mathcal{T}_P = (Q, \Sigma, s, \Rightarrow)$ corresponding to P, where:

- Q is a set of states of the form $(pc, \phi, enab, rt, it, id, ss)$, where $pc \in T \rightarrow L$ is the program counter giving the current location of each thread, $\phi \in V \rightarrow \mathbb{Z}$ is a valuation for the variables, $enab \subseteq T$ is the set of enabled threads, $rt \in T$ is the currently running thread; $it \in T$ is the task thread which is interrupted when the scheduler is suspended; and id and ss are Boolean values telling us whether interrupts are disabled ($id = true$) or not ($id = false$) and whether the scheduler is suspended ($ss = true$) or not ($ss = false$).
- The set of labels Σ is the set of instructions $inst_P$ of P.
- The initial state s is $(\lambda t.s_t, \lambda x.0, \{main\}, main, main, false, false)$. Thus all threads are at their entry locations, the initial environment sets all variables to 0, only the main thread is enabled and running, the interrupted task is

```
main:
1. x := 0;
2. y := 0;
3. t := 0;
4. create(t1);
5. create(t2);
6.

t1:                 t2:
7. x := x + 1;       9. disableint;
8.                  10. y := t;
                    11. t := x;
                    12. if(t > 0) {
                    13.    y := y + 1;
                    14. }
                    15. else {
                    16.    t := t + 1;
                    17. }
                    18. enableint;
                    19.
```

(a) Example program

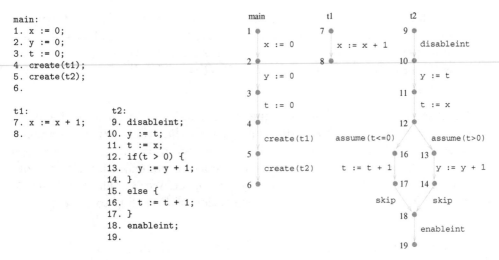

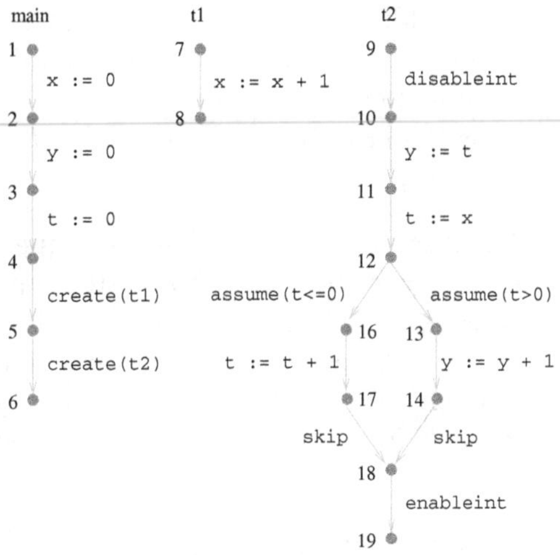

(b) Control-flow-graph representation

Fig. 2. An example program and its CFG representation.

set to *main* (this is a dummy value as it is used only when the scheduler is suspended), interrupts are enabled, and the scheduler is not suspended.

– For an instruction $\iota = \langle l, c, l' \rangle$ in $inst_P$, with $tid(\iota) = t$, we define

$$(pc, \phi, enab, rt, it, id, ss) \Rightarrow_\iota (pc', \phi', enab', rt', it', id', ss')$$

iff the following conditions are satisfied:
  - $t \in enab$; $pc(t) = l$; $pc' = pc[t \mapsto l']$;
  - if id is true or rt is an ISR then $t = rt$;
  - if ss is true, then either $t = rt$ or t is an ISR thread;
  - Based on the command c, the following conditions must be satisfied:
    * If c is the **skip** command then $\phi' = \phi$, $enab' = enab$, $id' = id$, and $ss' = ss$.
    * If c is an assignment statement of the form $x := e$ then $\phi' = \phi[x \mapsto [\![e]\!]_\phi]$, $enab' = enab$, $id' = id$, and $ss' = ss$.
    * If c is a command of the form **assume**(b) then $[\![b]\!]_\phi = true$, $\phi' = \phi$, $enab' = enab$, $id' = id$, and $ss' = ss$.
    * If c is a **create**(u) command then $t = main$, $\phi' = \phi$, $enab' = enab \cup \{u\}$, $id' = id$, and $ss' = ss$.
    * If c is the **disableint** command then $\phi' = \phi$, $enab' = enab$, $id' = true$, and $ss' = ss$.
    * If c is the **enableint** command then $\phi' = \phi$, $enab' = enab$, $id' = false$, and $ss' = ss$.
    * If c is the **suspendsch** command then $\phi' = \phi[ssflag \mapsto 1]$, $enab' = enab$, $id' = id$, and $ss' = true$.
    * If c is the **resumesch** command then $\phi' = \phi[ssflag \mapsto 0]$, $enab' = enab$, $id' = id$, and $ss' = false$.

- In addition, the transitions set the new running thread rt' and interrupted task it' as follows. If t is an ISR thread, ss is true, and ι is the first statement of t then $it' = rt$, $rt' = t$. If t is an ISR thread, ss is true, and ι is the last statement of t then $it' = it$, $rt' = it$. In all other cases, $rt' = t$ and $it' = it$.

An execution σ of P is a finite sequence of transitions in $\mathcal{T}_P$ from the initial state s: $\sigma = \tau_0, \tau_1, \ldots, \tau_n$ $(n \geq 0)$ from $\Rightarrow$, such that there exists a sequence of states $q_0, q_1, \ldots, q_{n+1}$ from Q, with $q_0 = s$ and $\tau_i = (q_i, \iota_i, q_{i+1})$ for each $0 \leq i \leq n$. Wherever convenient we will also represent an execution like σ above as a sequence of the form $q_0 \Rightarrow_{\iota_0} q_1 \Rightarrow_{\iota_1} \cdots \Rightarrow_{\iota_n} q_{n+1}$. We say that a state $q \in Q$ is *reachable* in program P if there is an execution of P leading to state q.

4 Data Races and Happens-Before Ordering

In this section we propose a definition of a data race which has general applicability, and also define a natural happens-before order for interrupt-driven programs.

4.1 Data Races

Data races have typically been defined in the literature in terms of a *happens-before* order on program executions. In the classical setting of lock-based synchronization, the happens-before relation is a partial order on the instructions in an execution, that is reflexive-transitive closure of the union of the *program-order* relation between two instructions in the same thread, and the *synchronizes-with* relation which relates a release of a lock in a thread to the next acquire of the same lock in another thread. Two instructions in an execution are then defined to be involved in a data race if they are conflicting accesses to a shared variable and are *not* ordered by the happens-before relation.

We feel it is important to have a definition of a data race that is based on the operational semantics of the class of programs we are interested in, and not on a happens-before relation. Such a definition would more tangibly capture what it is that a programmer typically tries to avoid when dealing with shared variables whose consistency she is worried about. Moreover, when coming up with a definition of the happens-before order (the synchronizes-with relation in particular) for non-standard concurrent programs like interrupt-driven programs, it is useful to have a reference notion to relate to. For instance, one could show that a proposed happens-before order is strong enough to ensure the absence of races.

We propose to define a race between two conflicting statements in a program in terms of whether two imaginary blocks enclosing each of these statements can *overlap* in an execution. Let us consider a multi-threaded program P in a class of concurrent programs with a certain operational execution semantics. Consider a block of contiguous instructions in a thread t of a program P and another block in thread t' of P. We say that these two blocks are involved in a *high-level race* in an execution of P if they *overlap* with each other during the execution, in that one block begins *in between* the beginning and ending of the other. We say two conflicting statements s and t in P are involved in a *data race* (or are *racy*), if the following condition is true: Consider the program P' which is obtained from P by replacing the statement s by the block "**skip**; s; **skip**", and similarly for statement t. Then there is an execution of P' in which the two blocks containing s and t are involved in a high-level race. The definition is illustrated in Fig. 3. We say a program P is *race-free* if no pair of instructions in it are racy.

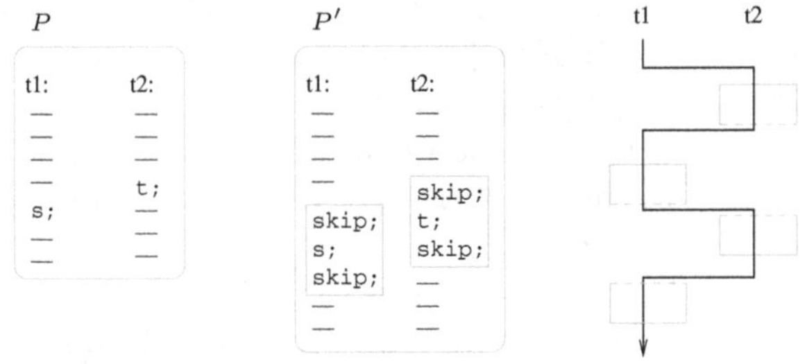

Fig. 3. Illustrating the definition of a data race on statements s and t. A program P, its transformation P', and an execution of P' in which the blocks overlap.

The rationale for this definition is that the concerned statements s and t may be compiled down to a sequence of instructions (represented by the blocks with `skip`'s around s and t) depending on the underlying processor and compiler, and if these instructions interleave in an execution, it may lead to undesirable results.

To illustrate the definition, consider the program in Fig. 2a. The accesses to x in line 7 and line 11 can be seen to be racy, since there is an execution of the augmented program P' in which *t1* performs the `skip` followed by the increment to x at line 7, followed by a context switch to thread *t2* which goes on to execute lines 9 and 10 and then the read of x in line 11. On the other hand, the version of the program in which line 7 is enclosed in a `disableint-enableint` block, does *not* contain a race.

We note that for classical concurrent programs, it might suffice to define a race as *consecutive* occurrences of conflicting accesses in an execution, as done in [4,17]. However, this definition is not general enough to apply to interrupt-driven programs. By this definition, the statements in lines 7 and 11 of the program in Fig. 2a are *not* racy, as there is *no* execution in which they happen consecutively. This is because the `disableint-enableint` block containing the access in line 11 is "atomic" in that the statements in the block must happen contiguously in any execution, and hence the instructions corresponding to line 7 and line 11 can never happen immediately one after another.

4.2 Disjoint Blocks and the Happens-Before Relation

Now that we have a proposed definition of races, we can proceed to give a principled way to define the happens-before relation for our class of interrupt-driven programs. The main question is how does one define the synchronizes-with relation. Our insight here is that the key to defining the synchronizes-with relation lies in identifying what we call *disjoint blocks* for the class of programs. Disjoint blocks are statically identifiable pairs of path segments in the CFGs of different threads, which are guaranteed by the execution semantics of the class of programs never to *overlap* in an execution of the program. Disjoint block structures – for example in the form of blocks enclosed between locks/unlocks of the same lock – are the primary mechanism used by developers to ensure race-freedom. The synchronizes-with relation in an execution can then be defined as relating, for every pair (A, B) of disjoint blocks in the program, the end of block A to the beginning of the succeeding occurrence of block B in the execution. The happens-before order for an execution can now be defined, as before, in terms of the program order and the synchronizes-with order, and is easily seen to be sufficient to ensure non-raciness.

Let us illustrate this hypothesis on classical lock-based programs. The disjoint block pairs for this class of programs are segments of code enclosed between acquires and releases of the *same* lock; or the portion of a thread's code before it spawns a thread t, and the whole of thread t's code; and similarly for joins. The synchronizes-with relation between instructions in an execution essentially goes from a release to the succeeding acquire of the same lock. If two accesses are related by the resulting happens-before order, they clearly cannot be involved in a race.

We now focus on defining a happens-before relation based on disjoint blocks for our class of interrupt-driven programs. We have identified eight pairs of disjoint block patterns for this class of programs, which are depicted in Fig. 4. We use the following types of blocks to define the pairs. A block of type D is a path segment in a task thread that begins with a `disableint` and ends with an `enableint` with no intervening `enableint` in between. A block of type S is a path segment in a task thread that begins with a `suspendsch` and ends with a `resumesch` with no intervening `resumesch`. An I block is an initial and terminating path segment in an ISR thread (i.e. begins with the first instruction and ends with a terminating instruction). Similarly, for a task thread t, T_t is an initial and terminating path in t, while M_t is an initial segment of the main thread that ends with a `create`(t) command. A block of type C_{ssflag} is a path segment in an ISR thread corresponding to the `then` block of a conditional that checks if $ssflag = 0$. For a synchronization flag f, C_f is the path segment in an ISR thread corresponding to the `then` block of a conditional that checks if $f = 0$. Finally F_f is a segment between statements that set f to 1 and back to 0, in a task thread. We also require that an F_f segment be within the scope of a `suspendsch` command.

We can now describe the pairs of disjoint blocks depicted in Fig. 4. Case (a) says that two D blocks in different task threads are disjoint. Clearly two such blocks can never overlap in an execution, since once one of the blocks begins execution no context-switch can occur until interrupts are enabled again. Case (b) says that D and I blocks are disjoint. Once again this is because once the D block

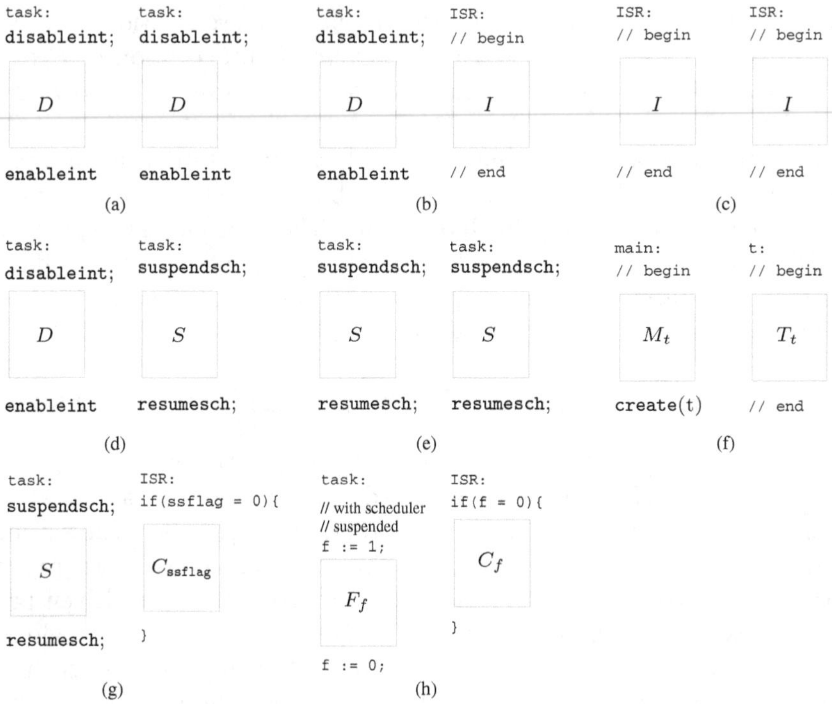

Fig. 4. Disjoint blocks in an interrupt-driven program.

begins execution no ISR can run until interrupts are enabled again, and once an ISR begins execution it runs to completion without any context-switches. Case (e) says that S blocks in different task threads are disjoint, because once the scheduler is suspended no context-switch to another task thread can occur. Case (f) says that M_t and T_t blocks are disjoint, since a thread cannot begin execution before it is created in main. Case (g) says that an S block is disjoint from a $C_{\texttt{ssflag}}$ block. This is because once the scheduler is suspended by the `suspendsch` command, and even if a context-switch to an ISR occurs, the `then` block of the `if` statement will not execute. Conversely, if the ISR is running there can be no context-switch to another thread. Finally, case (h) is similar to case (g). We note that the disjoint block pairs are not ordered (the relation is symmetric).

We can now define the synchronizes-with relation as follows. Let $\sigma = q_0 \Rightarrow_{\iota_0} q_1 \Rightarrow_{\iota_1} \cdots \Rightarrow_{\iota_n} q_{n+1}$ be an execution of P. We say instruction ι_i *synchronizes-with* an instruction ι_j of P in σ, if $i < j$, $tid(\iota_i) \neq tid(\iota_j)$, and there exists a pair of disjoint blocks A and B, with ι_i ending block A and ι_j beginning block B. As usual we say ι_i is *program-order* related to ι_j iff $i < j$ and $tid(\iota_i) = tid(\iota_j)$. We define the *happens-before* relation on σ as the reflexive-transitive closure of the union of the program-order and synchronizes-with relations for σ.

We can now define a *HB-race* in an execution σ of P as follows: we say that two instructions ι_i and ι_j in σ are involved in a *HB-race* if they are conflicting instructions that are *not* ordered by the happens-before relation in σ. We say that two instructions in P are *HB-racy* if there is an execution of P in which they are involved in a HB-race. Finally, we say a program P is *HB-race-free* if no two of its instructions are HB-racy.

Once again, it is fairly immediate to see that if two statements of a program are not involved in a HB-race, they cannot be involved in a race. Further, if two statements belong to disjoint blocks, then they are clearly happens-before ordered in every execution. Hence belonging to disjoint blocks is sufficient to ensure that the statements are happens-before ordered, which in turn ensures that the statements cannot be involved in a race.

5 Sync-CFG Analysis for Interrupt-Driven Programs

In this section we describe a way of lifting a sequential value-set analysis in a sound way for a HB-race free interrupt-driven program, in a similar way to how it is done for lock-based concurrent programs in [11]. A value-set analysis keeps track of the set of values each variable can take at each program point. The basic idea is to create a "sync-CFG" for a given interrupt-driven program P, which is essentially the union of the CFGs of each thread of P, along with "may-synchronize-with" edges between statements that may be synchronizes-with related in an execution of P, and then perform the value-set analysis on the resulting graph. Whenever the given program is *HB-race free*, the result of the analysis is guaranteed to be sound, in a sense made clear in Theorem 1.

5.1 Sync-CFG

We begin by defining the "sync-CFG" for an interrupt-driven program. It is on this structure that we will do the value-set analysis. Let $P = (V, T)$ be an interrupt-driven program, and let G be the disjoint union (over threads $t \in T$) of the CFGs G_t. We define a set of *may-synchronize-with* edges in G, denoted $MSW(G)$, as follows. The edges correspond to the pairs of disjoint blocks depicted in Fig. 4, in that they connect the ending of one block to the beginning of the other block in the pair. Consider two instructions $\iota = \langle l, c, m\rangle \in inst_t$ and $\kappa = \langle l', c', m'\rangle \in inst_{t'}$, with $t \neq t'$. We add the edge (m, l') in $MSW(G)$, iff for some pair of disjoint blocks (A, B), ι ends a block of type A in thread t and κ begins a block of type B in thread t'. For example, corresponding to a (D, D) pair of disjoint blocks, we add the edge (m, l') when c is an `enableint` command, and c' is a `disableint` command.

The sync-CFG induced by P is the control flow graph given by G along with the additional edges in MSW(G). Figure 6 shows a program P_2 and its induced sync-CFG.

5.2 Value Set Analysis

We first spell out the particular form of abstract interpretation we will be using. It is similar to the standard formulation of [9], except that it is a little more general to accommodate non-standard control-flow graphs like the sync-CFG.

An *abstract interpretation* of a program $P = (V, T)$ is a structure of the form $\mathcal{A} = (D, \leq, d_o, F)$ where

- D is the set of *abstract states*.
- $(D, \leq)$ forms a complete lattice. We denote the join (least upper bound) in this lattice by $\sqcup_{\leq}$, or simply $\sqcup$ when the ordering is clear from the context.
- $d_0 \in D$ is the initial abstract state.
- $F : inst_P \rightarrow (D \rightarrow D)$ associates a *transfer function* $F(\iota)$ (or simply F_ι) with each instruction ι of P. We require each transfer function F_ι to be *monotonic*, in that whenever $d \leq d'$ we have $F_\iota(d) \leq F_\iota(d')$.

An abstract interpretation $\mathcal{A} = (D, \leq, d_0, F)$ of P induces a "global" transfer function $\mathcal{F}_\mathcal{A} : D \rightarrow D$, given by $\mathcal{F}_\mathcal{A}(d) = d_0 \sqcup \bigsqcup_{\iota \in inst_P} F_\iota(d)$. This transfer function can also be seen to be monotonic. By the Knaster-Tarski theorem [28], $\mathcal{F}_\mathcal{A}$ has a least fixed point (LFP) in D, which we denote by $LFP(\mathcal{F}_\mathcal{A})$, and refer to as the resulting value of the analysis.

A *value set* for a set of variables V is a map $vs : V \rightarrow 2^\mathbb{Z}$, associating a set of integer values with each variable in V. A value set vs induces a set of environments Φ_{vs} in a natural way: $\Phi_{vs} = \{\phi \mid \text{for all } x \in V,\ \phi(x) \in vs(x)\}$ (i.e. essentially the Cartesian product of the values sets). Conversely, a set of environments Φ for V, induces a value set $valset(\Phi)$ given by $valset(\Phi)(x) = \{v \in \mathbb{Z} \mid \exists\phi \in \Phi,\ \phi(x) = v\}$, which is the "projection" of the environments to each variable $x \in V$. Finally, we define a point-wise ordering on value sets as follows: $vs \preceq vs'$ iff $vs(x) \subseteq vs'(x)$ for each variable x in V. We denote the least element in this ordering by $vs_\bot = \lambda x.\emptyset$.

We can now define the value-set analysis $\mathcal{A}_{vset}$ for an interrupt-driven program $P = (V, T)$ as follows. Let $\mathcal{A}_{vset} = (D, \leq, d_0, F)$ where

- D is the set $L_P \rightarrow (V \rightarrow 2^\mathbb{Z})$ (thus an element of D associates a value-set with each program location)
- The ordering $d \leq d'$ holds iff $d(l) \preceq d'(l)$ for each $l \in L_P$
- The initial abstract value d_0 is given by:

$$d_0 = \lambda l. \begin{cases} \lambda x.\{0\} & \text{if } l = s_{main} \\ vs_\bot & \text{otherwise.} \end{cases}$$

- The transfer functions are given as follows. Given an abstract value d, and a location $l \in L_P$, we define vs_l^d to be the join of the value-set at l, and the value-set at all may-synchronizes-with edges coming into l. Thus $vs_l^d = d(l) \sqcup_{\preceq} \bigsqcup_{(n,l) \in MSW(G)} d(n)$. Below we will use Φ as an abbreviation of the set $\Phi_{vs_l^d}$ of environments induced by vs_l^d. Let $\iota = \langle l, c, l' \rangle$ be an instruction in P.
  - If c is the command `x := e` then $F_\iota(d) = d'$ where

$$d'(m) = \begin{cases} vs_l^d[x \mapsto [\![e]\!]_\Phi] & \text{if } m = l' \\ vs_\bot & \text{otherwise.} \end{cases}$$

- If c is the command `assume`(b), then $F_\iota(d) = d'$ where

$$d'(m) = \begin{cases} valset([\![b]\!]_\Phi) & \text{if } m = l' \\ vs_\bot & \text{otherwise.} \end{cases}$$

- If c is any other command (`skip`, `disableint`, `enableint`, `suspendsch`, `resumesch`, or `create`) then $F_\iota(d) = d'$ where

$$d'(m) = \begin{cases} vs_l^d & \text{if } m = l' \\ vs_\bot & \text{otherwise.} \end{cases}$$

Figure 6 shows the results of a value-set analysis on the sync-CFG of program P_2. The data-flow facts are shown just before a statement, at selected points in the program.

Soundness. The value-set analysis is sound in the following sense: if P is a *HB-race free* program, and we have a reachable state of P at a location l in a thread where a variable x is *read*; then the value of x in this state is contained in the value-set for x, obtained by the analysis at point l. More formally:

Theorem 1. *Let $P = (V, T)$ be an HB-race free interrupt-driven program, and let d^* be the result of the analysis $\mathcal{A}_{vset}$ on P. Let l be a location in a thread $t \in T$ where a variable x is read (i.e. P contains an instruction of the form $\langle l, c, l' \rangle$ where c is a read access of x). Let ϕ be an environment at l reachable via some execution of P. Then $\phi(x) \in d^*(l)(x)$.*

The proof of this theorem is similar to the one for classical concurrent programs in [11] (see [10] for a more accurate proof). The soundness claim can be extended to locations where a variable is "owned" (which includes locations where it is read). We say a variable x is *owned* by a thread t at location l, if an inserted read of x at this point is non-HB-racy in the resulting program.

Region-Based Analysis. One problem with the value-set analysis is that it may not be able to prove *relational* invariants (like $x \leq y$) for a program. One way to remedy this is to exploit the fact that concurrent programs often ensure race-free access to a *region* of variables, and to essentially do a region-based value-set analysis, as originally done in [21]. More precisely, let us say we have a partition of the set of variables V of a program P into a set of regions $R_1, \ldots, R_n$. We classify each read (write) access to a variable x in a region R, as an read (write) access to region R. We say that two instructions in an execution of P are involved in a *HB-region-race*, if the two instructions are conflicting accesses to the same region R, and are *not* happens-before ordered in the execution. A program is *HB-region-race free* if none of its executions contain a HB-region-race.

We can now define a region-based version of the value-set analysis for a program P, which we call $\mathcal{A}_{rvset}$. The value-set for a region R is a set of valuations (or sub-environments) for the variables in R. The transfer functions are defined in an analogous way to the value-set analysis. The analogue of Theorem 1 for regions gives us that for a HB-region-race free program, at any location where a region R is accessed, the region-value-set computed by the analysis at that point will contain every sub-environment of R reachable at that point.

6 Translation to Classical Lock-Based Programs

In this section we address the question of why an execution-preserving translation to a classical lock-based program is not a fruitful route to take. In a nutshell, such a translation would not preserve races and would induce a sync-CFG with many unnecessary MSW edges, leading to much more imprecise facts than the analysis on the native sync-CFG described in the previous section. We also describe how our approach can be viewed as a *lightweight* translation of an interrupt-driven program to a classical lock-based one. The translation is "lightweight" in the sense that it does *not* attempt to preserve the execution semantics of the given interrupt-driven program, but instead preserves races and the sync-CFG structure of the original program.

6.1 Execution-Preserving Lock Translation

One could try to translate a given interrupt-driven program P into a classical lock-based program P^L in a way that preserves the interleaved execution semantics of P. By this we mean that every execution of P has a corresponding execution in P^L that follows essentially the same sequence of interleaved instructions from the different threads (modulo of course the synchronization statements which may differ); and vice-versa. For example, to capture the semantics of `disableint-enableint`, one could introduce an "execution" lock E which is acquired in place of disabling interrupts, and released in place of enabling interrupts. Every instruction in a task thread outside a `disableint-enableint` block must also acquire and release E immediately before and after the instruction. Note that the latter step is necessary if we want to capture the fact that once a thread disables interrupts it cannot be preempted by any thread. Figure 5a shows an interrupt-driven program P_1 and its lock translation P_1^L in Fig. 5b. There are still issues with the translation related to re-entrancy of locks and it is not immediately clear how one would handle flag-based synchronization – but let us keep this aside for now.

The first problem with this translation is that it does not preserve race information. Consider the program P_1 in Fig. 5a and its translation P_1^L. The original program clearly has a race on x in statements 4 and 9. However the translation P_1^L does *not* have a race as the accesses are protected by the lock E. Hence checking for races in P^L does not substitute for checking in P. An alternative around this would be to first construct P' (recall that this is the version of P in which we introduce the `skip`-blocks around statements we want to check for races), then construct its lock translation $(P')^L$, and check this program for *high-level* races on the introduced `skip`-blocks. However this is expensive as it involves a 3x blow-up in going from P to P' and another 3x blow-up in going from P' to $(P')^L$. Further, checking for high-level races (for example using a lock-set analysis) is more expensive than just checking for races. In contrast, as we show next, our lock-set analysis on the native program P does not incur any of these expenses.

```
main:
1. x := y := t := 0;
2. create(t1);
3. create(t2);

t1:                  t2:
4. x := x + 1;       8. disableint;
5. disableint;       9. t := x;
6. x := y;           10. enableint;
7. enableint;
```

(a) Example program P_1

```
main:
1. x := y := t := 0;
2. spawn(t1);
3. spawn(t2);

t1:                  t2:
4. lock(E)           10. lock(E);
5. x := x + 1;       11. t := x;
6. unlock(E)         12. unlock(E);
7. lock(E)
8. x := y;
9. unlock(E)
```

(b) Exec-preserving trans. P_1^L

```
main:
1. x := y := t := 0;
2. spawn(t1);
3. spawn(t2);

t1:                  t2:
4. x := x + 1;       8. lock(A);
5. lock(A);          9. t := x;
6. x := y;           10. unlock(A);
7. unlock(A);
```

(c) Lightweight trans. P_1^W

Fig. 5. Example program P_1, and its lock and lightweight translations P_1^L, P_1^W.

The second problem with a precise lock translation is that the sync-CFG of the translated program has many unnecessary MSW-edges, leading to imprecision in the ensuing analysis. Consider the program P_2 in Fig. 6, and its lock translation P_2^L in Fig. 7. P_2 is similar to P_1 except that line 4 is now an increment of y instead of x, and the resulting program is race-free (in fact HB-race-free). Notice that the may-sync-with edges from line 13 to 4, and line 6 to 10 in the sync-CFG of P_2^L in Fig. 7 are *unnecessary* (they are not present in the native sync-CFG) and lead to imprecise facts in an interval analysis on this graph. Some of the final facts in an interval analysis on these graphs are shown alongside the programs in Figs. 6 and 7. In particular the analysis on P_2^L is unable to prove the assertion in line 10 of the original program.

6.2 A Lightweight Lock-Translation

Our disjoint block-based approach of Sect. 5 can be viewed as a *lightweight* lock translation which does not attempt to preserve execution semantics, but preserves disjoint blocks and hence also races and the sync-CFG structure of the original interrupt-driven program.

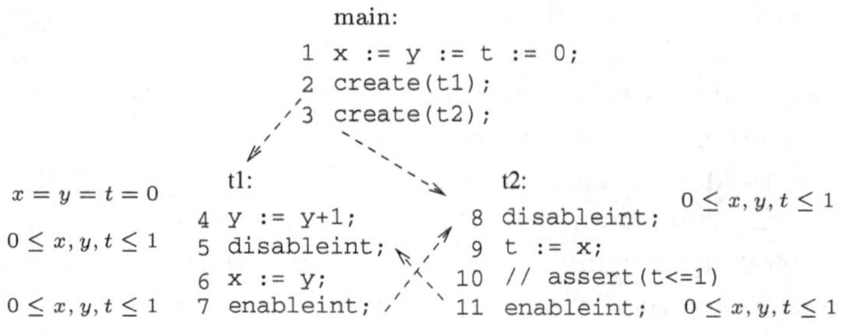

Fig. 6. Program P_2 with its Sync-CFG and facts from an interval analysis

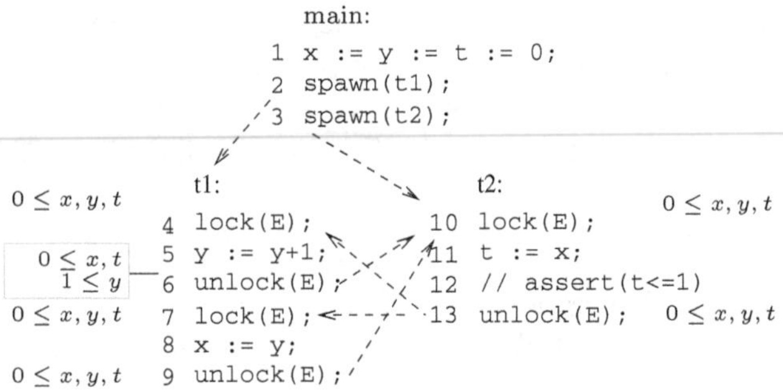

Fig. 7. Lock translation P_2^L of P_2, with its Sync-CFG and interval analysis facts

Let us first spell out the translation. Let us fix an interrupt-driven program $P = (V, T)$. The idea is simply to introduce a lock corresponding to each pattern of disjoint block pairs listed in Fig. 4, and to insert at the entry and exit to these blocks an acquire and release (respectively) of the corresponding lock. For each of the cases (a) through (h) we introduce locks named A through H, with some exceptions. Firstly, for case (f) regarding the `create` of a thread t, we simply translate these as a `spawn`(t) command in a classical lock-based programming language, which has a standard acquire-release semantics. Secondly, for case (h), we need a copy of H for *each* thread t, which we call H_t. This is because the concerned blocks (say between a set and unset of the flag f) are *not* disjoint across *task* threads, but only with the "then" block of an ISR thread statement that checks if $f = 0$. The ISR thread now acquires the set of locks $\{H_t \mid t \in T\}$ at the beginning of the "then" block of the `if` statement, and releases them at the end of that block. We call the resulting classical lock-based program P^W. Figure 5c shows this translation for the program P_1.

Figure 8 shows this translation along with the sync-CFG edges and some of the final facts in an interval analysis for the program P_2.

It is not difficult to see that P^W allows all executions that are possible in P. However it also allows more: for example the execution of P_1^W (Fig. 5c) in which thread $t1$ preempts $t2$ at line 9 to execute the statement at line 4, is *not* allowed in P_1. Thus it only *weakly* captures the execution semantics of P. However, every race in P is also a race in P^W. To see this, suppose we have a race on statements s and t in P. This means there is a high-level race on the two skip blocks around s and t in the augmented program P'. Since an execution exhibiting the high-level race on these blocks would also be present in $(P')^W$ which is identical to $(P^W)'$, it follows that the corresponding statements are racy in P^W as well.

Further, since our translation preserves disjoint blocks by construction, if s and t are in disjoint blocks in P, the corresponding statements will be in disjoint blocks in P^W; and vice-versa. It follows that the sync-CFGs induced by P and P^W are essentially isomorphic (modulo the synchronization statements). As a result, any value-set-based analysis will produce identical results on the two graphs.

Finally, if statements s and t are HB-racy in P, they must also be HB-racy in P^W. This is because disjoint blocks are preserved and the synchronizes-with relation is inherited from the disjoint blocks. Hence the execution witnessing the HB-race in P would also be present in P^W, and would also witness a HB-race on the corresponding statements.

We summarize these observations below:

Proposition 1. *Let P be an interrupt-driven program and P^W the classical lock program obtained using our lightweight lock translation. Then:*

1. *If statements s and t are racy in P, the corresponding statements are racy in P^W as well.*
2. *If statements s and t are HB-racy in P, the corresponding statements are HB-racy in P^W as well.*
3. *The sync-CFGs induced by P and P^W are essentially isomorphic. As a result the final facts in a value-set-based analysis on these graphs will be identical.*

□

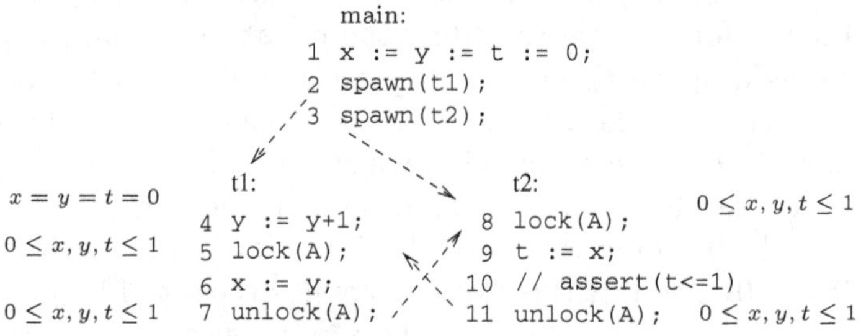

Fig. 8. Our lightweight translation P_2^W of P_2, with its Sync-CFG and interval analysis facts

6.3 Lockset Analysis for Race Detection

For classical lock-based programs, the lockset analysis [24] essentially tracks whether two statements are in disjoint blocks. Here two blocks are disjoint if they hold the same lock for the duration of the block. When two statements are in disjoint blocks, they are necessarily happens-before ordered, and hence this gives us a way to declare pairs of statements to be non-HB-racy.

A lockset analysis computes the set of locks held at each program point as follows: at program entry it is assumed that no locks are held. When a call to acquire(l) is encountered, the analysis adds the lock l at the *out* point of the call. When a call to release(l) is encountered the lockset at the *out* point of the call is the lockset computed at the *in* point with the lock l removed. For any other statement, the lockset from the *in* point of the statement is copied to its *out* point. The *join* operation is the simple intersection of the input locksets. Once locksets are computed at each point, a pair of conflicting statements s and

t in different threads are declared to *may* HB-race if the locksets held at these points have no lock in common.

Using our lock translation above, we can detect races as follows. Given an interrupt-driven program P, we first translate it to the lock-based program P^W, and do a lockset analysis on P^W. If any pair of conflicting statements s and t are found to be may-HB-racy in P^W, we declare them to be may-HB-racy in P. By Proposition 1(2), it follows that this is a sound analysis for interrupt-driven programs.

7 Analyzing the FreeRTOS Kernel Library

We now perform an experimental evaluation of the proposed race detection algorithm and sync-CFG-based relational analysis for interrupt-driven programs. We use the FreeRTOS kernel library [3], on which our interrupt-driven program semantics are based, to perform our evaluation. FreeRTOS is a collection of functions mostly written in C, that an application developer compiles with and invokes in the application code. We view the FreeRTOS kernel library as an interrupt-driven program as follows: we build an interrupt-driven program out of the FreeRTOS kernel as shown in the figure alongside. The main thread is responsible for initializing the kernel data structures and then creating two threads: a *task* thread which branches out calling each task kernel API function, and loops on this; and an *ISR* thread which similarly branches and loops on the ISR kernel API functions. FreeRTOS provides versions of API functions that can be called from interrupt service routines. These functions have "FromISR" appended to their name. While it is sufficient to have one ISR thread, we assume (in the analysis) that there could be any number of task threads running. To achieve this we simply add sync-edges *within* each task kernel function, in addition to the usual sync-edges between task functions. We used FreeRTOS version 10.0.0 for our experiments. We conducted these experiments on an Intel Core i7 machine with 32 GB RAM running Ubuntu 16.04.

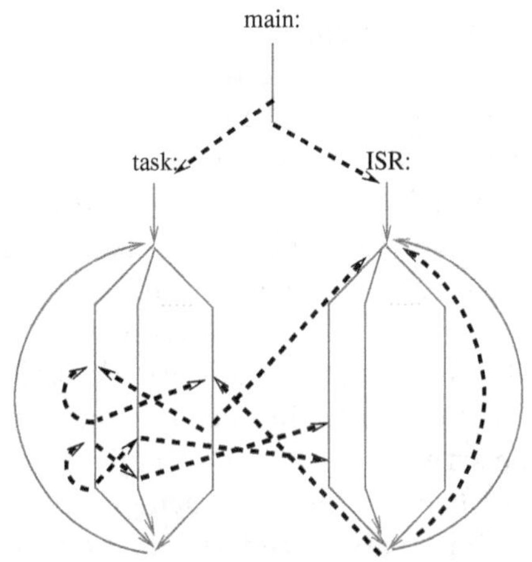

7.1 Race Detection

We consider 49 task and queue API functions that can be called from an application (termed top-level functions) for race detection. The functions operating on semaphores and mutexes were not considered.

We prepared the API functions for analysis, in two steps: (1) inlining and (2) lock insertion, as follows: The function `vTaskStartScheduler` and the queue initialization code in the function `xQueueGenericCreate` were treated as part of the main thread, which initializes kernel data structures. All the helper function calls made inside the top-level functions were inlined. After inlining, the functions are modified to acquire and release locks using the strategy explained in Sect. 6.2. We consider each pair of disjoint blocks as taking the same distinct lock. For example, the pair of disjoint blocks protected by `disableint-enableint` take lock A. That is `disableint` is replaced with `acquire`(A) and `enableint` is replaced with `release`(A). A total of 9 locks corresponding to disjoint blocks were employed in the modification of the FreeRTOS code. The two steps outlined above are automated. Inlining is achieved using the `inline` pass in the CIL framework [22]. Lock insertion is accomplished using a script.

The modified code, which has over 3.5K lines of code, is used for race detection. We tracked 24 variables and check whether the statements accessing them are racy. These variables include fields in the queue data-structure, task control block, and queue registry, as well as variables related to tasks. FreeRTOS maintains lists for the states of the tasks like "ready", "suspended", "waiting to send", etc. The pointers to these lists are also analysed. Access to any portion of a list (like the delayed list) is treated as an access of a corresponding variable of the same name.

Races are detected in this modified FreeRTOS code in three steps - (1) compute locks held, (2) identify whether access of a variable is a read or write, and (3) report potential races. First a lockset analysis, as explained in Sect. 6.3, to compute locks held at each access to variables, is implemented as a pass in CIL. The modified FreeRTOS code is analyzed using this new pass and the lockset at each access to the 24 variables of interest is computed. Then, a `writes` pass to identify whether accesses to variables are "read" or "write", also implemented in CIL, is run on the modified FreeRTOS code. Finally, a shell script to interpret both the results in the previous steps and report potential races is employed. The script identifies the conflicting access pairs (using the `writes` pass) and the locks held by the conflicting accesses (using lockset pass).

Our analysis reports 64 pairs of conflicting accesses as being potentially racy. On manual inspection we classified 18 of them are real races and the rest as false positives. Table 2 summarizes our findings. The second column in the table lists the variables of interest involved in the race, like various task list pointers, queue registry fields `pcQueueName` and `xHandle`, task variable `uxCurrentNumberOfTasks`, tick count `xTickCount`, etc. The third column lists the functions in which the conflicting accesses are made and the fourth gives the number of racing pairs. The fifth column assesses the potential races based on our manual inspection of the code. The analysis took 3.91 s.

The false positives were typically due to the fact that we had abstracted data-structures (like the delayed list which is a linked-list) by a synonymous variable. Thus even if the accesses were to different parts of the structure (like the container field of a list item and the next pointer of a different list item) our analysis flagged them as races.

We were in touch with the developers of FreeRTOS regarding the 18 pairs we classified as true positives. The 14 races on the queue registry were deemed to be non-issues as the queue delete function is usually invoked only once the application is about to terminate. The 2 races on `uxCurrentNumberOfTasks` are known (going by comments in the code) but are considered benign as the variable is of "base type". The remaining couple of races on the delayed task lists appear to be real issues as they have been fixed (independent of our work) in v10.1.1.

7.2 Region-Based Relational Analysis

Our aim here is to do a region-based interval and polyhedral analysis of a region-race-free subset of the FreeRTOS kernel APIs, and to prove some simple assertions about the kernel variables in each region.

We first identified six regions for this purpose. One region corresponds to variables protected by disabling interrupts (like `xTickCount`, `xNextTaskUnblockTime`, etc.), while variables protected by suspend and resume scheduler commands (like `uxPendedTicks`, `xPendingReadyList`, etc.) are in another region. Fields of the queue structure like `pcHead`, `pcTail`, etc. are in a third region, while the waiting lists for a queue form another region. The queue registry fields like `pcQueueName` and `xHandle` are in region 5. The pointer variable `pxCurrentTCB`, pointing to the current Task Control Block (TCB), is put in the sixth region.

The FreeRTOS code was modified further to reflect access to regions. For this new variables $R_1, \ldots, R_6$, are declared. Wherever there is a write (or read) access to a variable in region i an assignment statement that defines (or reads from) variable R_i is inserted just before the access. This is done using a script which takes the result of the `writes` pass to find where in the source code an appropriate assignment statement has to be inserted. We selected 15 APIs that did not contain any region races.

Next, we prepared the API functions for the analysis in two steps. They are described below:

Abstraction of FreeRTOS API Functions. We abstracted the FreeRTOS source code to prepare it for the relational analysis. In this abstraction, we basically model the various lists (ready list, delayed list) by their lengths and the value at the head of the list (if required). Using this abstraction, we are able to convert list operations to operations on integers.

Similarly, to model insertion into a list, we abstract it by incrementing the variable which represents the length of the list. We abstracted all the API functions in a similar fashion.

Creation of the Sync-CFG. The next step is to create a sync-CFG out of the abstracted program. For doing this, we used the abstracted version of the FreeRTOS code (along with acquire-release added as explained in Sect. 7.1).

Table 2. Potential races

Variables	Functions	#Race pairs	Remark
pxDelayedTaskList	eTaskGetState xTaskIncrementTick	1	Real race. Read of **pxDelayedTaskList** in **eTaskGetState** while it is written to in **xTaskIncrementTick**
pxOverflowDelayedTaskList	eTaskGetState xTaskIncrementTick	1	Real race. (similar as above)
uxCurrentNumberOfTasks	xTaskCreate uxTaskGetNumberOfTasks	2	Real race. Unprotected read in **uxTaskGetNumberOfTasks** while it is written to in **xTaskCreate**
pcQueueName xHandle	vQueueDelete pcQueueGetName vQueueAddToRegistry	14	Real race. Unprotected accesses in queue registry functions
xTasksWaitingToSend xTasksWaitingToReceive	eTaskGetState xQueueGenericReset	2	False positive. Initialization of vars when queue is created
pxDelayedTaskList pxOverflowDelayedTaskList xSuspendedTaskList pxCurrentTCB	9 functions like xTaskCreate, eTaskGetState, etc.	11	False positive. Initialization of vars when the first task is created
pxDelayedTaskList pxOverflowDelayedTaskList xSuspendedTaskList xTasksWaitingToSend xTasksWaitingToReceive	13 functions like vTaskDelay, eTaskGetState, etc.	33	False positive. The accesses are to disjoint portions of the lists

Next, we used a script to insert non-deterministic gotos from the point of release of a lock to the acquire of the same lock. Since we are using gotos for creation of sync-CFG, we keep all the API functions in main itself and evaluate a non-deterministic "if" condition before entering the code for an API function.

Results. For the purpose of analysis we listed out some numerical relations between kernel variables in the same region, which we believed should hold. We identified a total of 15 invariants including 4 invariants which involve relations between kernel variables. We then inserted assertions for these invariants at the key points in our source code like the exit of a block protecting a region.

We have implemented an interval-based value-set analysis and a region-based octagon and polyhedral analysis for C programs using CIL [22] as the front-end and the Apron library (version 0.9.11) [16]. We represent the sync-with edges of the sync-CFG of a program using goto statements from the source (release) to the target (acquire) of the may-synchronizes-with (MSW) edges.

We ran our implementation on the abstracted version of the FreeRTOS kernel library, with the aim of checking how many of the invariants it was able to prove. The abstracted code along with addition of gotos is about 1500 lines of code. We did a preliminary interval analysis on this abstracted sync-CFG and were able to prove 11 out of these 15 invariants. With a widening threshold of 30, the interval analysis takes under 5 min to run. As expected, the interval analysis could not prove the relational invariants.

We then did a region-based polyhedral analysis using the six regions identified above. For the region-based analysis, we used convex polyhedra domain with a widening threshold of 30. It is able to prove all the assertions we believed to be true. The analysis takes about 30 min to complete with the convex polyhedra domain and about 20 min with the octagon domain.

The results obtained by our analysis are shown in Table 3.

Table 3. Relational analysis results

Assertion	Interval Anal	Region Anal (Oct/Polyhedral)
xTickCount $\leq$ xNextTaskUnblockTime	No	Yes
head(pxDelayedTaskList) = xNextTaskUnblockTime	No	Yes
head(pxDelayedTaskList) $\geq$ TickCount	No	Yes
uxMessagesWaiting $\leq$ uxLength	No	Yes
uxMessagesWaiting ≥ 0	Yes	Yes
uxCurrentNumberOfTasks ≥ 0	Yes	Yes
lenpxReadyTasksLists ≥ 0	Yes	Yes
uxTopReadyPriority ≥ 0	Yes	Yes
lenpxDelayedTaskList ≥ 0	Yes	Yes
lenxPendingReadyList ≥ 0	Yes	Yes
lenxSuspendedTaskList ≥ 0	Yes	Yes
cRxLock ≥ -1	Yes	Yes
cTxLock ≥ -1	Yes	Yes
lenxTasksWaitingToSend ≥ 0	Yes	Yes
lenxTasksWaitingToReceive ≥ 0	Yes	Yes

8 Related Work

We classify related work based on the main topics touched upon in this paper.

Data Races. Adve and Hill [1] introduce the notion of a data race using a happens-before relation, and identify instructions that form release-acquire pairs, for low-level concurrent programs. Boehm and Adve [4] define races in terms of consecutive occurrences in a sequentially consistent execution, as well as using a happens-before order, in the context of the C++ semantics. They show their notions are equivalent as far as race-free programs go. As pointed out earlier, the definition of races as consecutive occurrences is inadequate in our setting. Schwarz *et al.* [26] define a notion of data race for priority-based interrupt-driven programs, where there is a single main task and multiple ISRs. A race occurs when the main thread is accessing a variable at a certain dynamic priority, and an ISR thread with higher priority also accesses the variable. Our definition can be seen to be stronger and more accurately captures racy situations. In particular, if the ISR thread with higher priority does not actually execute the conflicting access, due to say a condition not being enabled, then we would *not* call it a race. The term "high-level" race was coined by Artho *et al.* [2]. Our definition of a high-level race follows that of [20].

Analysis of Interrupt-Driven Programs. Regehr and Cooprider [23] describe a source-to-source translation of an interrupt-driven program to a standard multi-threaded program, and analyze the translated program for races. Their translation is inadequate for our setting in many ways: in particular, disable-enable of interrupts is translated by acquiring and releasing all ISR-specific locks; however this does not prevent interaction with another task while one task has disabled interrupts. In [8] they also describe an analysis framework for constant-propagation analysis on TinyOS applications. They use a similar idea of adding "control-flow" edges between disable-enable blocks and ISRs. However no soundness argument is given, and other kinds of blocks (suspend/resume, flag-based synchronization) are not handled. The works in [5,6,13] analyze timing properties, interrupt-latency, and stack sizes for interrupt-driven programs, using model-checking, algebraic, and algorithmic approaches. Schwarz *et al.* [25,26] give analyses for race-detection and invariants based on linear-equalities for their aforementioned class of priority-based interrupt-driven programs. Our work differs in several ways: Their analysis is directed towards *applications* (we target *libraries* where task priorities do not matter), their analyses are specific (we provide a basis for carrying out a variety of value-set and relational analyses, targeting race-free programs), they consider priority and flag-based synchronization (but not disable-enable and suspend-resume based synchronization). Sung and others [27] consider interrupt-driven applications in the form of ISRs with different priorities, and perform interval-based static analysis for checking assertions. They do not handle libraries and do not leverage race-freedom. Finally, [20] uses a model-checking approach to find all high-level races in FreeRTOS with a completeness guarantee.

Analysis of Race-Free Programs. Chugh *et al.* [7] use race information to do thread-modular null-dereference analysis, by killing facts at a point whenever a notional read of a variable is found to be racy. De *et al.* [11] propose the sync-CFG and value-set analysis for race-free programs, while Mukherjee *et al.* [21] extend the framework to region and relational analyses. Gotsman *et al.* [12] and Miné *et al.* [18,19] define relational shape/value analyses for concurrent programs that exploit race-freedom and lock invariants respectively. All these works are for classical lock-based synchronization while we target interrupt-driven programs.

9 Conclusion

In this paper our aim has been to give efficient static analyses for classes of non-standard concurrent programs like interrupt-driven kernels, that exploit the property of race-freedom. Towards this goal, we have proposed a definition of data races which we feel is applicable to general concurrent programs. We have also proposed a general principle for defining synchronizes-with edges, which is the key ingredient of a happens-before relation, based on the notion of disjoint blocks. We have implemented our theory to perform sound and effective static analysis for race-detection and invariant inference, on the popular real-time kernel FreeRTOS.

We feel this framework should be applicable to other kinds of concurrent systems, like other embedded kernels (for example TI-RTOS [14]) and application programs, and event-driven programs. There are additional challenges in these systems like priority-based preemption and priority inheritance conventions which need to be addressed. Apart from investigating these systems we would like to apply this theory to perform other static analyses like null-dereference, points-to, and shape analysis, for these non-standard classes of concurrent programs.

References

1. Adve, S.V., Hill, M.D.: A unified formalization of four shared-memory models. IEEE Trans. Parallel Distrib. Syst. **4**(6), 613–624 (1993)
2. Artho, C., Havelund, K., Biere, A.: High-level data races. J. Softw. Test. Verif. Reliab. **13**, 207–227 (2003)
3. Barry, R.: The FreeRTOS kernel, v10.0.0 (2017). https://freertos.org
4. Boehm, H., Adve, S.V.: Foundations of the C++ concurrency memory model. In: Proceedings of the ACM SIGPLAN 2008 Conference on Programming Language Design and Implementation, Tucson, USA, pp. 68–78. ACM (2008)
5. Brylow, D., Damgaard, N., Palsberg, J.: Static checking of interrupt-driven software. In: Proceedings of the 23rd International Conference on Software Engineering, ICSE 2001, Toronto, Ontario, Canada, 12–19 May 2001, pp. 47–56 (2001)
6. Chatterjee, K., Ma, D., Majumdar, R., Zhao, T., Henzinger, T.A., Palsberg, J.: Stack size analysis for interrupt-driven programs. In: Cousot, R. (ed.) SAS 2003. LNCS, vol. 2694, pp. 109–126. Springer, Heidelberg (2003). https://doi.org/10.1007/3-540-44898-5_7
7. Chugh, R., Voung, J.W., Jhala, R., Lerner, S.: Dataflow analysis for concurrent programs using data race detection. In: Proceedings of the ACM SIGPLAN 2008 Conference on Programming Language Design and Implementation, Tucson, AZ, USA, 7–13 June 2008, pp. 316–326 (2008)
8. Cooprider, N., Regehr, J.: Pluggable abstract domains for analyzing embedded software. In: Proceedings of the ACM SIGPLAN/SIGBED Conference on Languages, Compilers, and Tools for Embedded Systems (LCTES 2006), Ottawa, Canada, 14–16 June 2006, pp. 44–53 (2006)
9. Cousot, P., Cousot, R.: Abstract interpretation: a unified lattice model for static analysis of programs by construction or approximation of fixpoints. In: Proceedings of the ACM SIGACT-SIGPLAN Symposium on Principles of Programming Languages, pp. 238–252. ACM (1977)
10. De, A.: Access path based dataflow analysis for sequential and concurrent programs. Ph.D. thesis, Indian Institute of Science, Bangalore, December 2012

11. De, A., D'Souza, D., Nasre, R.: Dataflow analysis for data race-free programs. In: Proceedings of the 20th European Symposium on Programming ESOP 2011, Saarbrücken, Germany, 26 March – 3 April 2011, pp. 196–215 (2011)
12. Gotsman, A., Berdine, J., Cook, B., Sagiv, M.: Thread-modular shape analysis. In: Proceedings of the ACM SIGPLAN 2007 Conference on Programming Language Design and Implementation, San Diego, California, USA, 10–13 June 2007, pp. 266–277 (2007)
13. Huang, Y., Zhao, Y., Shi, J., Zhu, H., Qin, S.: Investigating time properties of interrupt-driven programs. In: Gheyi, R., Naumann, D. (eds.) SBMF 2012. LNCS, vol. 7498, pp. 131–146. Springer, Heidelberg (2012). https://doi.org/10.1007/978-3-642-33296-8_11
14. Texas Instruments: TI-RTOS: A Real-Time Operating System for Microcontrollers (2017). http://www.ti.com/tool/ti-rtos
15. Jeannet, B., Miné, A.: APRON: a library of numerical abstract domains for static analysis. In: Bouajjani, A., Maler, O. (eds.) CAV 2009. LNCS, vol. 5643, pp. 661–667. Springer, Heidelberg (2009). https://doi.org/10.1007/978-3-642-02658-4_52
16. Jeannet Bertrand, M.A.: Apron numerical abstract domain library (2009). http://apron.cri.ensmp.fr/library/
17. Kini, D., Mathur, U., Viswanathan, M.: Dynamic race prediction in linear time. In: Proceedings of the 38th ACM SIGPLAN Conference on Programming Language Design and Implementation, PLDI 2017, pp. 157–170. ACM, New York (2017)
18. Miné, A.: Relational thread-modular static value analysis by abstract interpretation. In: McMillan, K.L., Rival, X. (eds.) VMCAI 2014. LNCS, vol. 8318, pp. 39–58. Springer, Heidelberg (2014). https://doi.org/10.1007/978-3-642-54013-4_3
19. Monat, R., Miné, A.: Precise thread-modular abstract interpretation of concurrent programs using relational interference abstractions. In: Bouajjani, A., Monniaux, D. (eds.) VMCAI 2017. LNCS, vol. 10145, pp. 386–404. Springer, Cham (2017). https://doi.org/10.1007/978-3-319-52234-0_21
20. Mukherjee, S., Kumar, A., D'Souza, D.: Detecting all high-level dataraces in an RTOS kernel. In: Bouajjani, A., Monniaux, D. (eds.) VMCAI 2017. LNCS, vol. 10145, pp. 405–423. Springer, Cham (2017). https://doi.org/10.1007/978-3-319-52234-0_22
21. Mukherjee, S., Padon, O., Shoham, S., D'Souza, D., Rinetzky, N.: Thread-local semantics and its efficient sequential abstractions for race-free programs. In: Ranzato, F. (ed.) SAS 2017. LNCS, vol. 10422, pp. 253–276. Springer, Cham (2017). https://doi.org/10.1007/978-3-319-66706-5_13
22. Necula, G.: CIL – infrastructure for c program analysis and transformation (v. 1.3.7) (2002). http://people.eecs.berkeley.edu/~necula/cil/
23. Regehr, J., Cooprider, N.: Interrupt verification via thread verification. Electr. Notes Theor. Comput. Sci. **174**(9), 139–150 (2007)
24. Savage, S., Burrows, M., Nelson, G., Sobalvarro, P., Anderson, T.E.: Eraser: a dynamic data race detector for multithreaded programs. ACM Trans. Comput. Syst. **15**(4), 391–411 (1997)
25. Schwarz, M.D., Seidl, H., Vojdani, V., Apinis, K.: Precise analysis of value-dependent synchronization in priority scheduled programs. In: McMillan, K.L., Rival, X. (eds.) VMCAI 2014. LNCS, vol. 8318, pp. 21–38. Springer, Heidelberg (2014). https://doi.org/10.1007/978-3-642-54013-4_2
26. Schwarz, M.D., Seidl, H., Vojdani, V., Lammich, P., Müller-Olm, M.: Static analysis of interrupt-driven programs synchronized via the priority ceiling protocol. In: Proceedings of the ACM SIGPLAN-SIGACT Principles of Programming Languages (POPL), pp. 93–104 (2011)

27. Sung, C., Kusano, M., Wang, C.: Modular verification of interrupt-driven software. In: Proceedings of the 32nd IEEE/ACM International Conference on Automated Software Engineering, ASE 2017, Urbana, IL, USA, 30 October – 3 November 2017, pp. 206–216 (2017)
28. Tarski, A., et al.: A lattice-theoretical fixpoint theorem and its applications. Pac. J. Math. **5**, 285–309 (1955)

4

Distributive Disjoint Polymorphism for Compositional Programming

Xuan Bi[1(✉)], Ningning Xie[1], Bruno C. d. S. Oliveira[1], and Tom Schrijvers[2]

[1] The University of Hong Kong, Hong Kong, China
{xbi,nnxie,bruno}@cs.hku.hk
[2] KU Leuven, Leuven, Belgium
tom.schrijvers@cs.kuleuven.be

Abstract. Popular programming techniques such as *shallow embeddings* of Domain Specific Languages (DSLs), *finally tagless* or *object algebras* are built on the principle of *compositionality*. However, existing programming languages only support simple compositional designs well, and have limited support for more sophisticated ones.

This paper presents the F_i^+ calculus, which supports highly modular and compositional designs that improve on existing techniques. These improvements are due to the combination of three features: *disjoint intersection types* with a *merge operator*; *parametric (disjoint) polymorphism*; and *BCD-style distributive subtyping*. The main technical challenge is F_i^+'s proof of coherence. A naive adaptation of ideas used in System F's *parametricity* to *canonicity* (the logical relation used by F_i^+ to prove coherence) results in an ill-founded logical relation. To solve the problem our canonicity relation employs a different technique based on immediate substitutions and a restriction to predicative instantiations. Besides coherence, we show several other important meta-theoretical results, such as type-safety, sound and complete algorithmic subtyping, and decidability of the type system. Remarkably, unlike $\mathsf{F}_{<:}$'s *bounded polymorphism*, disjoint polymorphism in F_i^+ supports decidable type-checking.

1 Introduction

Compositionality is a desirable property in programming designs. Broadly defined, it is the principle that a system should be built by composing smaller subsystems. For instance, in the area of programming languages, compositionality is a key aspect of *denotational semantics* [48, 49], where the denotation of a program is constructed from the denotations of its parts. Compositional definitions have many benefits. One is ease of reasoning: since compositional definitions are recursively defined over smaller elements they can typically be reasoned about using induction. Another benefit is that compositional definitions are easy to extend, without modifying previous definitions.

Programming techniques that support compositional definitions include: *shallow embeddings* of Domain Specific Languages (DSLs) [20], *finally tagless* [11], *polymorphic embeddings* [26] or *object algebras* [35]. These techniques allow us to create compositional definitions, which are easy to extend without modifications. Moreover, when modeling semantics, both finally tagless and object algebras support *multiple interpretations* (or denotations) of syntax, thus offering a solution to the well-known *Expression Problem* [53]. Because of these benefits these techniques have become popular both in the functional and object-oriented programming communities.

However, programming languages often only support simple compositional designs well, while support for more sophisticated compositional designs is lacking. For instance, once we have multiple interpretations of syntax, we may wish to compose them. Particularly useful is a *merge* combinator, which composes two interpretations [35,37,42] to form a new interpretation that, when executed, returns the results of both interpretations.

The merge combinator can be manually defined in existing programming languages, and be used in combination with techniques such as finally tagless or object algebras. Moreover variants of the merge combinator are useful to model more complex combinations of interpretations. A good example are so-called *dependent* interpretations, where an interpretation does not depend *only* on itself, but also on a different interpretation. These definitions with dependencies are quite common in practice, and, although they are not orthogonal to the interpretation they depend on, we would like to model them (and also mutually dependent interpretations) in a modular and compositional style.

Defining the merge combinator in existing programming languages is verbose and cumbersome, requiring code for every new kind of syntax. Yet, that code is essentially mechanical and ought to be automated. While using advanced meta-programming techniques enables automating the merge combinator to a large extent in existing programming languages [37,42], those techniques have several problems: error messages can be problematic, type-unsafe reflection is needed in some approaches [37] and advanced type-level features are required in others [42]. An alternative to the merge combinator that supports modular multiple interpretations and works in OO languages with support for some form of multiple inheritance and covariant type-refinement of fields has also been recently proposed [55]. While this approach is relatively simple, it still requires a lot of manual boilerplate code for composition of interpretations.

This paper presents a calculus and polymorphic type system with *(disjoint) intersection types* [36], called F_i^+. F_i^+ supports our broader notion of compositional designs, and enables the development of highly modular and reusable programs. F_i^+ has a built-in merge operator and a powerful subtyping relation that are used to automate the composition of multiple (possibly dependent) interpretations. In F_i^+ subtyping is coercive and enables the automatic generation of coercions in a *type-directed* fashion. This process is similar to that of other type-directed code generation mechanisms such as *type classes* [52], which eliminate boilerplate code associated to the *dictionary translation* [52].

F_i^+ continues a line of research on disjoint intersection types. Previous work on *disjoint polymorphism* (the F_i calculus) [2] studied the combination of parametric polymorphism and disjoint intersection types, but its subtyping relation does not support BCD-style distributivity rules [3] and the type system also prevents unrestricted intersections [16]. More recently the NeColus calculus (or λ_i^+) [5] introduced a system with *disjoint intersection types* and BCD-style distributivity rules, but did not account for parametric polymorphism. F_i^+ is unique in that it combines all three features in a single calculus: *disjoint intersection types* and a *merge operator*; *parametric (disjoint) polymorphism*; and a BCD-style subtyping relation with *distributivity rules.* The three features together allow us to improve upon the finally tagless and object algebra approaches and support advanced compositional designs. Moreover previous work on disjoint intersection types has shown various other applications that are also possible in F_i^+, including: *first-class traits* and *dynamic inheritance* [4], *extensible records* and *dynamic mixins* [2], and *nested composition* and *family polymorphism* [5].

Unfortunately the combination of the three features has non-trivial complications. The main technical challenge (like for most other calculi with disjoint intersection types) is the proof of coherence for F_i^+. Because of the presence of BCD-style distributivity rules, our coherence proof is based on the recent approach employed in λ_i^+ [5], which uses a *heterogeneous* logical relation called *canonicity.* To account for polymorphism, which λ_i^+'s canonicity does not support, we originally wanted to incorporate the relevant parts of System F's logical relation [43]. However, due to a mismatch between the two relations, this did not work. The parametricity relation has been carefully set up with a delayed type substitution to avoid ill-foundedness due to its impredicative polymorphism. Unfortunately, canonicity is a heterogeneous relation and needs to account for cases that cannot be expressed with the delayed substitution setup of the homogeneous parametricity relation. Therefore, to handle those heterogeneous cases, we resorted to immediate substitutions and *predicative instantiations.* We do not believe that predicativity is a severe restriction in practice, since many source languages (e.g., those based on the Hindley-Milner type system like Haskell and OCaml) are themselves predicative and do not require the full generality of an impredicative core language. Should impredicative instantiation be required, we expect that step-indexing [1] can be used to recover well-foundedness, though at the cost of a much more complicated coherence proof.

The formalization and metatheory of F_i^+ are a significant advance over that of F_i. Besides the support for distributive subtyping, F_i^+ removes several restrictions imposed by the syntactic coherence proof in F_i. In particular F_i^+ supports unrestricted intersections, which are forbidden in F_i. Unrestricted intersections enable, for example, encoding certain forms of bounded quantification [39]. Moreover the new proof method is more robust with respect to language extensions. For instance, F_i^+ supports the bottom type without significant complications in the proofs, while it was a challenging open problem in F_i. A final interesting aspect is that F_i^+'s type-checking is decidable. In the design space of languages with polymorphism and subtyping, similar mechanisms have been known to lead to undecidability. Pierce's seminal paper "*Bounded quantification is undecidable*" [40] shows that the contravariant subtyping rule for bounded quantification in $\mathsf{F}_{<:}$ leads to undecidability of subtyping. In F_i^+ the contravariant rule for disjoint quantification retains decidability. Since with unrestricted intersections F_i^+ can express several use cases of bounded quantification, F_i^+ could be an interesting and decidable alternative to $\mathsf{F}_{<:}$.

In summary the contributions of this paper are:

- **The F_i^+ calculus,** which is the first calculus to combine disjoint intersection types, BCD-style distributive subtyping and disjoint polymorphism. We show several meta-theoretical results, such as *type-safety*, *sound and complete algorithmic subtyping*, *coherence* and *decidability* of the type system. F_i^+ includes the *bottom type*, which was considered to be a significant challenge in previous work on disjoint polymorphism [2].
- **An extension of the canonicity relation with polymorphism,** which enables the proof of coherence of F_i^+. We show that the ideas of System F's *parametricity* cannot be ported to F_i^+. To overcome the problem we use a technique based on immediate substitutions and a predicativity restriction.
- **Improved compositional designs:** We show that F_i^+'s combination of features enables improved compositional programming designs and supports automated composition of interpretations in programming techniques like object algebras and finally tagless.
- **Implementation and proofs:** All of the metatheory of this paper, except some manual proofs of decidability, has been mechanically formalized in Coq. Furthermore, F_i^+ is implemented and all code presented in the paper is available. The implementation, Coq proofs and extended version with appendices can be found in https://github.com/bixuanzju/ESOP2019-artifact.

2 Compositional Programming

To demonstrate the compositional properties of F_i^+ we use Gibbons and Wu's shallow embeddings of parallel prefix circuits [20]. By means of several different shallow embeddings, we first illustrate the short-comings of a state-of-the-art compositional approach, popularly known as a *finally tagless* encoding [11], in Haskell. Next we show how parametric polymorphism and distributive intersection types provide a more elegant and compact solution in SEDEL [4], a source language built on top of our F_i^+ calculus.

2.1 A Finally Tagless Encoding in Haskell

The circuit DSL represents networks that map a number of inputs (known as the width) of some type A onto the same number of outputs of the same type. The outputs combine (with repetitions) one or more inputs using a binary associative operator $\oplus : A \times A \rightarrow A$. A particularly interesting class of circuits that can be expressed in the DSL are *parallel prefix circuits*. These represent computations that take $n > 0$ inputs $x_1, \ldots, x_n$ and produce n outputs $y_1, \ldots, y_n$, where $y_i = x_1 \oplus x_2 \oplus \ldots \oplus x_i$.

The DSL features 5 language primitives: two basic circuit constructors and three circuit combinators. These are captured in the Haskell type class `Circuit`:

```
data Width = W { width :: Int }
instance Circuit Width where
  identity n   = W n
  fan n        = W n
  beside c1 c2 =
    W (width c1 + width c2)
  above c1 c2  = c1
  stretch ws c = W (sum ws)
```

(a) Width embedding

```
data Depth = D { depth :: Int }
instance Circuit Depth where
  identity n   = D 0
  fan n        = D 1
  beside c1 c2 =
    D (max (depth c1) (depth c2))
  above c1 c2  = D (depth c1 + depth c2)
  stretch ws c = c
```

(b) Depth embedding

Fig. 1. Two finally tagless embeddings of circuits.

```
class Circuit c where
  identity :: Int → c
  fan      :: Int → c
  beside   :: c → c → c
  above    :: c → c → c
  stretch  :: [Int] → c → c
```

An `identity` circuit with n inputs x_i, has n outputs $y_i = x_i$. A `fan` circuit has n inputs x_i and n outputs y_i, where $y_1 = x_1$ and $y_j = x_1 \oplus x_j \, (j > 1)$. The binary `beside` combinator puts two circuits in parallel; the combined circuit takes the inputs of both circuits to the outputs of both circuits. The binary `above` combinator connects the outputs of the first circuit to the inputs of the second; the width of both circuits has to be same. Finally, `stretch ws c` interleaves the wires of circuit `c` with bundles of additional wires that map their input straight on their output. The `ws` parameter specifies the width of the consecutive bundles; the ith wire of `c` is preceded by a bundle of width $ws_i - 1$.

Basic width and depth embeddings. Figure 1 shows two simple shallow embeddings, which represent a circuit respectively in terms of its width and its depth. The former denotes the number of inputs/outputs of a circuit, while the latter is the maximal number of $\oplus$ operators between any input and output. Both definitions follow the same setup: a new Haskell datatype (`Width`/`Depth`) wraps the primitive result value and provides an instance of the `Circuit` type class that interprets the 5 DSL primitives accordingly. The following code creates a so-called Brent-Kung parallel prefix circuit [9]:

```
e1 :: Width
e1 = above (beside (fan 2) (fan 2))
       (above (stretch [2, 2] (fan 2))
         (beside (beside (identity 1) (fan 2)) (identity 1)))
```

Here `e1` evaluates to `W {width = 4}`. If we want to know the depth of the circuit, we have to change type signature to `Depth`.

Interpreting multiple ways. Fortunately, with the help of polymorphism we can define a type of circuits that support multiple interpretations at once.

```
type DCircuit = forall c. Circuit c ⇒ c
```

This way we can provide a single Brent-Kung parallel prefix circuit definition that can be reused for different interpretations.

```
brentKung :: DCircuit
brentKung = above (beside (fan 2) (fan 2))
              (above (stretch [2, 2] (fan 2))
                (beside (beside (identity 1) (fan 2)) (identity 1)))
```

A type annotation then selects the desired interpretation. For instance, `brentKung :: Width` yields the width and `brentKung :: Depth` the depth.

Composition of embeddings. What is not ideal in the above code is that the same `brentKung` circuit is processed twice, if we want to execute both interpretations. We can do better by processing the circuit only once, computing both interpretations simultaneously. The finally tagless encoding achieves this with a boilerplate instance for tuples of interpretations.

```
instance (Circuit c1, Circuit c2) ⇒ Circuit (c1, c2) where
  identity n    = (identity n, identity n)
  fan n         = (fan n, fan n)
  beside c1 c2  = (beside (fst c1) (fst c2), beside (snd c1) (snd c2))
  above c1 c2   = (above (fst c1) (fst c2), above (snd c1) (snd c2))
  stretch ws c  = (stretch ws (fst c), stretch ws (snd c))
```

Now we can get both embeddings simultaneously as follows:

```
e12 :: (Width, Depth)
e12 = brentKung
```

This evaluates to `(W {width = 4}, D {depth = 2})`.

Composition of dependent interpretations. The composition above is easy because the two embeddings are orthogonal. In contrast, the composition of dependent interpretations is rather cumbersome in the standard finally tagless setup. An example of the latter is the interpretation of circuits as their well-sizedness, which captures whether circuits are well-formed. This interpretation depends on the interpretation of circuits as their width.[1]

```
data WellSized = WS { wS :: Bool, ox :: Width }
instance Circuit WellSized where
 identity n   = WS True (identity n)
 fan n        = WS True (fan n)
 beside c1 c2 = WS (wS c1 && wS c2) (beside (ox c1) (ox c2))
```

[1] Dependent recursion schemes are also known as *zygomorphism* [18] after the ancient Greek word ζυγον for yoke. We have labeled the `Width` field with `ox` because it is pulling the yoke.

```
above c1 c2   = WS (wS c1 && wS c2 && width (ox c1) == width (ox c2))
                   (above (ox c1) (ox c2))
stretch ws c = WS (wS c && length ws==width (ox c)) (stretch ws (ox c))
```

The WellSized datatype represents the well-sizedness of a circuit with a Boolean, and also keeps track of the circuit's width. The 5 primitives compute the well-sizedness in terms of both the width and well-sizedness of the subcomponents. What makes the code cumbersome is that it has to explicitly delegate to the Width interpretation to collect this additional information.

With the help of a substantially more complicated setup that features a dozen Haskell language extensions, and advanced programming techniques, we can make the explicit delegation implicit (see the appendix). Nevertheless, that approach still requires *a lot of boilerplate* that needs to be repeated for each DSL, as well as explicit projections that need to be written in each interpretation. Another alternative Haskell encoding that also enables multiple dependent interpretations is proposed by Zhang and Oliveira [55], but it does not eliminate the explicit delegation and still requires substantial amounts of boilerplate. A final remark is that adding new primitives (e.g., a "right stretch" rstretch combinator [25]) can also be easily achieved [46].

2.2 The SEDEL Encoding

SEDEL is a source language that elaborates to F_i^+, adding a few convenient source level constructs. The SEDEL setup of the circuit DSL is similar to the finally tagless approach. Instead of a Circuit c type class, there is a Circuit[C] type that gathers the 5 circuit primitives in a record. Like in Haskell, the type parameter C expresses that the interpretation of circuits is a parameter.

```
type Circuit[C] = {
  identity : Int → C, fan : Int → C, beside : C → C → C,
  above : C → C → C, stretch : List[Int] → C → C };
```

As a side note if a new constructor (e.g., rstretch) is needed, then this is done by means of intersection types (& creates an intersection type) in SEDEL:

```
type NCircuit[C] = Circuit[C] & { rstretch : List[Int] → C → C };
```

Figure 2 shows the two basic shallow embeddings for width and depth. In both cases, a named SEDEL definition replaces the corresponding unnamed Haskell type class instance in providing the implementations of the 5 language primitives for a particular interpretation.

The use of the SEDEL embeddings is different from that of their Haskell counterparts. Where Haskell implicitly selects the appropriate type class instance based on the available type information, in SEDEL the programmer explicitly selects the implementation following the style used by object algebras. The following code does this by building a circuit with l1 (short for language1).

```
l1 = language1;
e1 = l1.above (l1.beside (l1.fan 2) (l1.fan 2))
```

```
type Width = { width : Int };
language1 : Circuit[Width] = {
  identity (n : Int) = { width = n },
  fan      (n : Int) = { width = n },
  beside   (c1 : Width) (c2 : Width) = { width = c1.width + c2.width },
  above    (c1 : Width) (c2 : Width) = { width = c1.width },
  stretch  (ws : List[Int]) (c : Width) = { width = sum ws } };
```

```
type Depth = { depth : Int };
language2 : Circuit[Depth] = {
  identity (n : Int) = { depth = 0 },
  fan      (n : Int) = { depth = 1 },
  beside   (c1 : Depth) (c2 : Depth) = { depth = max c1.depth c2.depth},
  above    (c1 : Depth) (c2 : Depth) = { depth = c1.depth + c2.depth},
  stretch  (ws : List[Int]) (c : Depth) = { depth = c.depth } };
```

Fig. 2. Two SEDEL embeddings of circuits.

```
  (l1.above (l1.stretch (cons 2 (cons 2 nil)) (l1.fan 2))
    (l1.beside (l1.beside (l1.identity 1) (l1.fan 2)) (l1.identity 1)));
```

Here `e1` evaluates to `{width = 4}`. If we want to know the depth of the circuit, we have to replicate the code with `language2`.

Dynamically reusable circuits. Just like in Haskell, we can use polymorphism to define a type of circuits that can be interpreted with different languages.

```
type DCircuit = { accept : forall C. Circuit[C] → C };
```

In contrast to the Haskell solution, this implementation explicitly accepts the implementation.

```
brentKung : DCircuit = {
  accept C l = l.above (l.beside (l.fan 2) (l.fan 2))
    (l.above (l.stretch (cons 2 (cons 2 nil)) (l.fan 2))
      (l.beside (l.beside (l.identity 1) (l.fan 2)) (l.identity 1))) };
e1 = brentKung.accept Width language1;
e2 = brentKung.accept Depth language2;
```

Automatic composition of languages. Of course, like in Haskell we can also compute both results simultaneously. However, unlike in Haskell, the composition of the two interpretation requires no boilerplate whatsoever—in particular, there is no SEDEL counterpart of the `Circuit (c1, c2)` instance. Instead, we can just compose the two interpretations with the term-level merge operator (`,,`) and specify the desired type `Circuit[Width & Depth]`.

```
language3 : Circuit[Width & Depth] = language1 ,, language2;
e3 = brentKung.accept (Width & Depth) language3;
```

Here the use of the merge operator creates a term with the intersection type `Circuit[Width] & Circuit[Depth]`. Implicitly, the SEDEL type system takes care of the details, turning this intersection type into `Circuit[Width & Depth]`. This is possible because intersection (`&`) distributes over function and record types (a distinctive feature of BCD-style subtyping).

Composition of dependent interpretations. In SEDEL the composition scales nicely to dependent interpretations. For instance, the well-sizedness interpretation can be expressed without explicit projections.

```
type WellSized = { wS : Bool };
language4 = {
  identity (n : Int) = { wS = true },
  fan      (n : Int) = { wS = true },
  above (c1 : WellSized & Width) (c2 : WellSized & Width) =
    { wS = c1.wS && c2.wS && c1.width == c2.width },
  beside (c1 : WellSized) (c2 : WellSized) = { wS  = c1.wS && c2.wS  },
  stretch (ws : List[Int]) (c : WellSized & Width) =
    { wS = c.wS && length ws == c.width  } };
```

Here the `WellSized & Width` type in the `above` and `stretch` cases expresses that both the well-sizedness and width of subcircuits must be given, and that the width implementation is left as a dependency—when `language4` is used, then the width implementation must be provided. Again, the distributive properties of `&` in the type system take care of merging the two interpretations.

```
e4   = brentKung.accept (WellSized & Width) (language1 ,, language4);
main = e4.wS -- Output: true
```

Disjoint polymorphism and dynamic merges. While it may seem from the above examples that definitions have to be merged statically, SEDEL in fact supports dynamic merges. For instance, we can encapsulate the merge operator in the `combine` function while abstracting over the two components `x` and `y` that are merged as well as over their types `A` and `B`.

```
combine A [B * A] (x : A) (y : B) = x ,, y;
```

This way the components `x` and `y` are only known at runtime and thus the merge can only happen at that time. The types `A` and `B` cannot be chosen entirely freely. For instance, if both components would contribute an implementation for the same method, which implementation is provided by the combination would be ambiguous. To avoid this problem the two types `A` and `B` have to be *disjoint*. This is expressed in the disjointness constraint `* A` on the quantifier of the type variable `B`. If a quantifier mentions no disjointness constraint, like that of `A`, it defaults to the trivial $*\ \top$ constraint which implies no restriction.

3 Semantics of the F_i^+ Calculus

This section gives a formal account of F_i^+, the first typed calculus combining disjoint polymorphism [2] (and disjoint intersection types) with BCD subtyping [3].

Types	A, B, C	$::= \mathsf{Int} \mid \top \mid \bot \mid A \to B \mid A \,\&\, B \mid \{l : A\} \mid \alpha \mid \forall(\alpha * A).\, B$
Expressions	E	$::= x \mid i \mid \top \mid \lambda x.\, E \mid E_1\, E_2 \mid E_1 \,,,\, E_2 \mid E : A \mid \{l = E\} \mid E.l$
		$\mid \Lambda(\alpha * A).\, E \mid E\, A$
Term contexts Γ		$::= \bullet \mid \Gamma, x : A$
Type contexts Δ		$::= \bullet \mid \Delta, \alpha * A$

Fig. 3. Syntax of F_i^+

The main differences to F_i are in the subtyping, well-formedness and disjointness relations. F_i^+ adds BCD subtyping and unrestricted intersections, and also closes an open problem of F_i by including the bottom type. The dynamic semantics of F_i^+ is given by elaboration to the target calculus F_{co}—a variant of System F extended with products and explicit coercions.

3.1 Syntax and Semantics

Figure 3 shows the syntax of F_i^+. Metavariables A, B, C range over types. Types include standard constructs from prior work [2,36]: integers Int, the top type $\top$, arrows $A \to B$, intersections $A \,\&\, B$, single-field record types $\{l : A\}$ and disjoint quantification $\forall(\alpha * A).\, B$. One novelty in F_i^+ is the addition of the uninhabited bottom type $\bot$. Metavariable E ranges over expressions. Expressions are integer literals i, the top value $\top$, lambda abstractions $\lambda x.\, E$, applications $E_1\, E_2$, merges $E_1 \,,,\, E_2$, annotated terms $E : A$, single-field records $\{l = E\}$, record projections $E.l$, type abstractions $\Lambda(\alpha * A).\, E$ and type applications $E\, A$.

Well-formedness and unrestricted intersections. F_i^+'s well-formedness judgment of types $\Delta \vdash A$ is standard, and only enforces well-scoping. This is one of the key differences from F_i, which uses well-formedness to also ensure that all intersection types are disjoint. In other words, while in F_i all valid intersection types must be disjoint, in F_i^+ unrestricted intersection types such as $\mathsf{Int} \,\&\, \mathsf{Int}$ are allowed. More specifically, the well-formedness of intersection types in F_i^+ and F_i is:

$$\frac{\Delta \vdash A \qquad \Delta \vdash B}{\Delta \vdash A \,\&\, B}\ \textsc{wf-}\mathsf{F}_i^+ \qquad\qquad \frac{\Delta \vdash A \qquad \Delta \vdash B \qquad \Delta \vdash A * B}{\Delta \vdash A \,\&\, B}\ \textsc{wf-}\mathsf{F}_i$$

Notice that F_i has an extra disjointness condition $\Delta \vdash A * B$ in the premise. This is crucial for F_i's syntactic method for proving coherence, but also burdens the calculus with various syntactic restrictions and complicates its metatheory. For example, it requires extra effort to show that F_i only produces disjoint intersection types. As a consequence, F_i features a *weaker* substitution lemma (note the gray part in Proposition 1) than F_i^+ (Lemma 1).

Proposition 1 (Type substitution in F_i). *If $\Delta \vdash A$, $\Delta \vdash B$, $(\alpha * C) \in \Delta$, $\Delta \vdash B * C$ and well-formed context $[B/\alpha]\Delta$, then $[B/\alpha]\Delta \vdash [B/\alpha]A$.*

Lemma 1 (Type substitution in F_i^+). *If $\Delta \vdash A$, $\Delta \vdash B$, $(\alpha * C) \in \Delta$ and well-formed context $[B/\alpha]\Delta$, then $[B/\alpha]\Delta \vdash [B/\alpha]A$.*

$\boxed{A <: B \rightsquigarrow co}$ *(Declarative subtyping)*

$$\textsc{S-Refl}\quad \frac{}{A <: A \rightsquigarrow \mathsf{id}} \qquad \textsc{S-Trans}\quad \frac{A_2 <: A_3 \rightsquigarrow co_1 \qquad A_1 <: A_2 \rightsquigarrow co_2}{A_1 <: A_3 \rightsquigarrow co_1 \circ co_2} \qquad \textsc{S-Top}\quad \frac{}{A <: \top \rightsquigarrow \mathsf{top}}$$

$$\textsc{S-Rcd}\quad \frac{A <: B \rightsquigarrow co}{\{l : A\} <: \{l : B\} \rightsquigarrow co} \qquad \textsc{S-AndL}\quad \frac{}{A_1 \,\&\, A_2 <: A_1 \rightsquigarrow \pi_1} \qquad \textsc{S-AndR}\quad \frac{}{A_1 \,\&\, A_2 <: A_2 \rightsquigarrow \pi_2}$$

$$\textsc{S-Arr}\quad \frac{B_1 <: A_1 \rightsquigarrow co_1 \qquad A_2 <: B_2 \rightsquigarrow co_2}{A_1 \to A_2 <: B_1 \to B_2 \rightsquigarrow co_1 \to co_2} \qquad \textsc{S-And}\quad \frac{A_1 <: A_2 \rightsquigarrow co_1 \qquad A_1 <: A_3 \rightsquigarrow co_2}{A_1 <: A_2 \,\&\, A_3 \rightsquigarrow \langle co_1, co_2 \rangle}$$

$$\textsc{S-DistArr}\quad \frac{}{(A_1 \to A_2) \,\&\, (A_1 \to A_3) <: A_1 \to A_2 \,\&\, A_3 \rightsquigarrow \mathsf{dist}_{\to}} \qquad \textsc{S-TopArr}\quad \frac{}{\top <: \top \to \top \rightsquigarrow \mathsf{top}_{\to}}$$

$$\textsc{S-DistRcd}\quad \frac{}{\{l : A\} \,\&\, \{l : B\} <: \{l : A \,\&\, B\} \rightsquigarrow \mathsf{id}} \qquad \textsc{S-TopRcd}\quad \frac{}{\top <: \{l : \top\} \rightsquigarrow \mathsf{id}} \qquad \textsc{S-Bot}\quad \frac{}{\bot <: A \rightsquigarrow \mathsf{bot}}$$

$$\textsc{S-Forall}\quad \frac{B_1 <: B_2 \rightsquigarrow co \qquad A_2 <: A_1}{\forall(\alpha * A_1).\, B_1 <: \forall(\alpha * A_2).\, B_2 \rightsquigarrow co_{\forall}} \qquad \textsc{S-TopAll}\quad \frac{}{\top <: \forall(\alpha * \top).\, \top \rightsquigarrow \mathsf{top}_{\forall}}$$

$$\textsc{S-DistAll}\quad \frac{}{(\forall(\alpha * A).\, B_1) \,\&\, (\forall(\alpha * A).\, B_2) <: \forall(\alpha * A).\, B_1 \,\&\, B_2 \rightsquigarrow \mathsf{dist}_{\forall}}$$

Fig. 4. Declarative subtyping

Declarative subtyping. F_i^+'s subtyping judgment is another major difference to F_i, because it features BCD-style subtyping and a rule for the bottom type. The full set of subtyping rules are shown in Fig. 4. The reader is advised to ignore the gray parts for now. Our subtyping rules extend the BCD-style subtyping rules from λ_i^+ [5] with a rule for parametric (disjoint) polymorphism (rule S-FORALL). Moreover, we have three new rules: rule S-BOT for the bottom type, and rules S-DISTALL and S-TOPALL for distributivity of disjoint quantification. The subtyping relation is a partial order (rules S-REFL and S-TRANS). Most of the rules are quite standard. $\bot$ is a subtype of all types (rule S-BOT). Subtyping of disjoint quantification is covariant in its body, and contravariant in its disjointness constraints (rule S-FORALL). Of particular interest are those so-called "distributivity" rules: rule S-DISTARR says intersections distribute over arrows; rule S-DISTRCD says intersections distribute over records. Similarly, rule S-DISTALL dictates that intersections may distribute over disjoint quantifiers.

$$\boxed{\Delta; \Gamma \vdash E \Rightarrow A \rightsquigarrow e} \qquad \textit{(Inference)}$$

$$\textsc{T-top}\ \frac{\vdash \Delta \qquad \Delta \vdash \Gamma}{\Delta; \Gamma \vdash \top \Rightarrow \top \rightsquigarrow \langle\rangle} \qquad \textsc{T-nat}\ \frac{\vdash \Delta \qquad \Delta \vdash \Gamma}{\Delta; \Gamma \vdash i \Rightarrow \mathsf{Int} \rightsquigarrow i} \qquad \textsc{T-var}\ \frac{\vdash \Delta \qquad \Delta \vdash \Gamma \qquad (x : A) \in \Gamma}{\Delta; \Gamma \vdash x \Rightarrow A \rightsquigarrow x}$$

$$\textsc{T-app}\ \frac{\Delta; \Gamma \vdash E_1 \Rightarrow A_1 \to A_2 \rightsquigarrow e_1 \qquad \Delta; \Gamma \vdash E_2 \Leftarrow A_1 \rightsquigarrow e_2}{\Delta; \Gamma \vdash E_1\, E_2 \Rightarrow A_2 \rightsquigarrow e_1\, e_2} \qquad \textsc{T-merge}\ \frac{\Delta; \Gamma \vdash E_1 \Rightarrow A_1 \rightsquigarrow e_1 \qquad \Delta; \Gamma \vdash E_2 \Rightarrow A_2 \rightsquigarrow e_2 \qquad \Delta \vdash A_1 * A_2}{\Delta; \Gamma \vdash E_1 \,,,\, E_2 \Rightarrow A_1 \,\&\, A_2 \rightsquigarrow \langle e_1, e_2 \rangle}$$

$$\textsc{T-anno}\ \frac{\Delta; \Gamma \vdash E \Leftarrow A \rightsquigarrow e}{\Delta; \Gamma \vdash E : A \Rightarrow A \rightsquigarrow e} \qquad \textsc{T-rcd}\ \frac{\Delta; \Gamma \vdash E \Rightarrow A \rightsquigarrow e}{\Delta; \Gamma \vdash \{l = E\} \Rightarrow \{l : A\} \rightsquigarrow e}$$

$$\textsc{T-proj}\ \frac{\Delta; \Gamma \vdash E \Rightarrow \{l : A\} \rightsquigarrow e}{\Delta; \Gamma \vdash E.l \Rightarrow A \rightsquigarrow e} \qquad \textsc{T-tabs}\ \frac{\Delta, \alpha * A; \Gamma \vdash E \Rightarrow B \rightsquigarrow e \qquad \Delta \vdash A \qquad \Delta \vdash \Gamma}{\Delta; \Gamma \vdash \Lambda(\alpha * A).\, E \Rightarrow \forall(\alpha * A).\, B \rightsquigarrow \Lambda\alpha.\, e}$$

$$\textsc{T-tapp}\ \frac{\Delta; \Gamma \vdash E \Rightarrow \forall(\alpha * B).\, C \rightsquigarrow e \qquad \Delta \vdash A * B}{\Delta; \Gamma \vdash E\, A \Rightarrow [A/\alpha]C \rightsquigarrow e\, |A|}$$

$$\boxed{\Delta; \Gamma \vdash E \Leftarrow A \rightsquigarrow e} \qquad \textit{(Checking)}$$

$$\textsc{T-abs}\ \frac{\Delta \vdash A \qquad \Delta; \Gamma, x : A \vdash E \Leftarrow B \rightsquigarrow e}{\Delta; \Gamma \vdash \lambda x.\, E \Leftarrow A \to B \rightsquigarrow \lambda x.\, e} \qquad \textsc{T-sub}\ \frac{\Delta; \Gamma \vdash E \Rightarrow B \rightsquigarrow e \qquad B <: A \rightsquigarrow co}{\Delta; \Gamma \vdash E \Leftarrow A \rightsquigarrow co\, e}$$

Fig. 5. Bidirectional type system

Typing rules. F_i^+ features a bidirectional type system inherited from F_i. The full set of typing rules are shown in Fig. 5. Again we ignore the gray parts and explain them in Sect. 3.3. The inference judgment $\Delta; \Gamma \vdash E \Rightarrow A$ says that we can synthesize the type A under the contexts Δ and Γ. The checking judgment $\Delta; \Gamma \vdash E \Leftarrow A$ asserts that E checks against the type A under the contexts Δ and Γ. Most of the rules are quite standard in the literature. The merge expression $E_1 \,,,\, E_2$ is well-typed if both sub-expressions are well-typed, and their types are *disjoint* (rule T-MERGE). The disjointness relation will be explained in Sect. 3.2. To infer a type abstraction (rule T-TABS), we add disjointness constraints to the type context. For a type application (rule T-TAPP), we check that the type argument satisfies the disjointness constraints. Rules T-MERGE and T-TAPP are the only rules checking disjointness.

$\boxed{\rceil A \lceil}$ *(Top-like types)*

$$\text{TL-TOP}\ \frac{}{\rceil \top \lceil} \qquad \text{TL-AND}\ \frac{\rceil A \lceil \quad \rceil B \lceil}{\rceil A \,\&\, B \lceil} \qquad \text{TL-ARR}\ \frac{\rceil B \lceil}{\rceil A \to B \lceil} \qquad \text{TL-RCD}\ \frac{\rceil A \lceil}{\rceil \{l : A\} \lceil} \qquad \text{TL-ALL}\ \frac{\rceil B \lceil}{\rceil \forall (\alpha * A).\, B \lceil}$$

$\boxed{\Delta \vdash A * B}$ *(Disjointness)*

$$\text{D-TOPL}\ \frac{\rceil A \lceil}{\Delta \vdash A * B} \qquad \text{D-TOPR}\ \frac{\rceil B \lceil}{\Delta \vdash A * B} \qquad \text{D-ARR}\ \frac{\Delta \vdash A_2 * B_2}{\Delta \vdash A_1 \to A_2 * B_1 \to B_2}$$

$$\text{D-ANDL}\ \frac{\Delta \vdash A_1 * B \qquad \Delta \vdash A_2 * B}{\Delta \vdash A_1 \,\&\, A_2 * B} \qquad \text{D-ANDR}\ \frac{\Delta \vdash A * B_1 \qquad \Delta \vdash A * B_2}{\Delta \vdash A * B_1 \,\&\, B_2}$$

$$\text{D-RCDEQ}\ \frac{\Delta \vdash A * B}{\Delta \vdash \{l : A\} * \{l : B\}} \qquad \text{D-RCDNEQ}\ \frac{l_1 \neq l_2}{\Delta \vdash \{l_1 : A\} * \{l_2 : B\}} \qquad \text{D-TVARL}\ \frac{(\alpha * A) \in \Delta \qquad A <: B}{\Delta \vdash \alpha * B}$$

$$\text{D-TVARR}\ \frac{(\alpha * A) \in \Delta \qquad A <: B}{\Delta \vdash B * \alpha} \qquad \text{D-FORALL}\ \frac{\Delta, \alpha * A_1 \,\&\, A_2 \vdash B_1 * B_2}{\Delta \vdash \forall (\alpha * A_1).\, B_1 * \forall (\alpha * A_2).\, B_2} \qquad \text{D-AX}\ \frac{A *_{ax} B}{\Delta \vdash A * B}$$

Fig. 6. Selected rules for disjointness

3.2 Disjointness

We now turn to another core judgment of F_i^+—the disjointness relation, shown in Fig. 6. The disjointness rules are mostly inherited from F_i [2], but the new bottom type requires a notable change regarding disjointness with *top-like types.*

Top-like types. Top-like types are all types that are isomorphic to $\top$ (i.e., simultaneously sub- and supertypes of $\top$). Hence, they are inhabited by a single value, isomorphic to the $\top$ value. Figure 6 captures this notion in a syntax-directed fashion in the $\rceil A \lceil$ predicate. As a historical note, the concept of top-like types was already known by Barendregt et al. [3]. The λ_i calculus [36] re-discovered it and coined the term "top-like types"; the F_i calculus [2] extended it with universal quantifiers. Note that in both calculi, top-like types are solely employed for enabling a syntactic method of proving coherence, and due to the lack of BCD subtyping, they do not have a type-theoretic interpretation of top-like types.

Disjointness rules. The disjointness judgment $\Delta \vdash A * B$ is helpful to check whether the merge of two expressions of type A and B preserves coherence. Incoherence arises when both expressions produce distinct values for the same type, either directly when they are both of that same type, or through implicit

Types	τ	$::= \mathsf{Int} \mid \langle\rangle \mid \tau_1 \to \tau_2 \mid \tau_1 \times \tau_2 \mid \alpha \mid \forall \alpha.\, \tau$
Terms	e	$::= x \mid i \mid \langle\rangle \mid \lambda x.\, e \mid e_1\, e_2 \mid \langle e_1, e_2 \rangle \mid \Lambda \alpha.\, e \mid e\, \tau \mid co\, e$
Coercions	co	$::= \mathsf{id} \mid co_1 \circ co_2 \mid \mathsf{top} \mid \mathsf{bot} \mid co_1 \to co_2 \mid \langle co_1, co_2 \rangle \mid \pi_1 \mid \pi_2$
		$\mid co_\forall \mid \mathsf{dist}_\to \mid \mathsf{top}_\to \mid \mathsf{top}_\forall \mid \mathsf{dist}_\forall$
Values	v	$::= i \mid \langle\rangle \mid \lambda x.\, e \mid \langle v_1, v_2 \rangle \mid \Lambda \alpha.\, e \mid (co_1 \to co_2)\, v \mid co_\forall\, v$
		$\mid \mathsf{dist}_\to\, v \mid \mathsf{top}_\to\, v \mid \mathsf{top}_\forall\, v \mid \mathsf{dist}_\forall\, v$
Term contexts	Ψ	$::= \bullet \mid \Psi, x : \tau$
Type contexts	Φ	$::= \bullet \mid \Phi, \alpha$
Evaluation contexts	$\mathcal{E}$	$::= [\cdot] \mid \mathcal{E}\, e \mid v\, \mathcal{E} \mid \langle \mathcal{E}, e \rangle \mid \langle v, \mathcal{E} \rangle \mid co\, \mathcal{E} \mid \mathcal{E}\, \tau$

Fig. 7. Syntax of F_{co}

upcasting to a common supertype. Of course we can safely disregard top-like types in this matter because they do not have two distinct values. In short, it suffices to check that the two types have only top-like supertypes in common.

Because $\bot$ and any another type A always have A as a common supertype, it follows that $\bot$ is only disjoint to A when A is top-like. More generally, if A is a top-like type, then A is disjoint to any type. This is the rationale behind the two rules D-TOPL and D-TOPR, which generalize and subsume $\Delta \vdash \top * A$ and $\Delta \vdash A * \top$ from F_i, and also cater to the bottom type. Two other interesting rules are D-TVARL and D-TVARR, which dictate that a type variable α is disjoint with some type B if its disjointness constraints A is a subtype of B. Disjointness axioms $A *_{ax} B$ (appearing in rule D-AX) take care of two types with different type constructors (e.g., Int and records). Axiom rules can be found in the appendix. Finally we note that the disjointness relation is symmetric.

3.3 Elaboration and Type Safety

The dynamic semantics of F_i^+ is given by elaboration into a target calculus. The target calculus F_{co} is the standard call-by-value System F extended with products and coercions. The syntax of F_{co} is shown in Fig. 7.

Type translation. Definition 1 defines the type translation function $|\cdot|$ from F_i^+ types A to F_{co} types τ. Most cases are straightforward. For example, $\bot$ is mapped to an uninhabited type $\forall \alpha.\, \alpha$; disjoint quantification is mapped to universal quantification, dropping the disjointness constraints. $|\cdot|$ is naturally extended to work on contexts as well.

Definition 1. *Type translation* $|\cdot|$ *is defined as follows:*

$\lvert\mathsf{Int}\rvert = \mathsf{Int}$	$\lvert\top\rvert = \langle\rangle$	$\lvert A \to B\rvert = \lvert A\rvert \to \lvert B\rvert$
$\lvert A \,\&\, B\rvert = \lvert A\rvert \times \lvert B\rvert$	$\lvert\{l : A\}\rvert = \lvert A\rvert$	$\lvert\alpha\rvert = \alpha$
$\lvert\bot\rvert = \forall \alpha.\, \alpha$	$\lvert\forall(\alpha * A).\, B\rvert = \forall \alpha.\, \lvert B\rvert$	

$\boxed{e \longrightarrow e'}$ *(Single-step reduction)*

$$\text{R-FORALL}\quad \frac{}{(co_{\forall}\, v)\, \tau \longrightarrow co\,(v\, \tau)} \qquad \text{R-TOPALL}\quad \frac{}{(\mathsf{top}_{\forall}\, \langle\rangle)\, \tau \longrightarrow \langle\rangle} \qquad \text{R-DISTALL}\quad \frac{}{(\mathsf{dist}_{\forall}\, \langle v_1, v_2\rangle)\, \tau \longrightarrow \langle v_1\, \tau, v_2\, \tau\rangle}$$

$$\text{R-TAPP}\quad \frac{}{(\Lambda\alpha.\, e)\, \tau \longrightarrow [\tau/\alpha]e} \qquad \text{R-APP}\quad \frac{}{(\lambda x.\, e)\, v \longrightarrow [v/x]e} \qquad \text{R-CTXT}\quad \frac{e \longrightarrow e'}{\mathcal{E}[e] \longrightarrow \mathcal{E}[e']}$$

Fig. 8. Selected reduction rules

Coercions and coercive subtyping. We follow prior work [5,6] by having a syntactic category for coercions [22]. In Fig. 7, we have several new coercions: bot, $co_{\forall}$, $\mathsf{dist}_{\forall}$ and $\mathsf{top}_{\forall}$ due to the addition of polymorphism and bottom type. As seen in Fig. 4 the coercive subtyping judgment has the form $A <: B \rightsquigarrow co$, which says that the subtyping derivation for $A <: B$ produces a coercion co that converts terms of type $|A|$ to $|B|$.

F_{co} *static semantics.* The typing rules of F_{co} are quite standard. We have one rule T-CAPP regarding coercion application, which uses the judgment $co{::}\tau \rhd \tau'$ to type coercions. We show two representative rules CT-FORALL and CT-BOT.

$$\text{T-CAPP}\quad \frac{\Phi; \Psi \vdash e : \tau \qquad co :: \tau \rhd \tau'}{\Phi; \Psi \vdash co\, e : \tau'} \qquad \text{CT-FORALL}\quad \frac{co :: \tau_1 \rhd \tau_2}{co_{\forall} :: \forall\alpha.\, \tau_1 \rhd \forall\alpha.\, \tau_2} \qquad \text{CT-BOT}\quad \frac{}{\mathsf{bot} :: \forall\alpha.\, \alpha \rhd \tau}$$

F_{co} *dynamic semantics.* The dynamic semantics of F_{co} is mostly unremarkable. We write $e \longrightarrow e'$ to mean one-step reduction. Figure 8 shows selected reduction rules. The first line shows three representative rules regarding coercion reductions. They do not contribute to computation but merely rearrange coercions. Our coercion reduction rules are quite standard but not efficient in terms of space. Nevertheless, there is existing work on space-efficient coercions [23,50], which should be applicable to our work as well. Rule R-APP is the usual β-rule that performs actual computation, and rule R-CTXT handles reduction under an evaluation context. As usual, $\longrightarrow^*$ is the reflexive, transitive closure of $\longrightarrow$. Now we can show that F_{co} is type safe:

Theorem 1 (Preservation). *If* $\bullet; \bullet \vdash e : \tau$ *and* $e \longrightarrow e'$, *then* $\bullet; \bullet \vdash e' : \tau$.

Theorem 2 (Progress). *If* $\bullet; \bullet \vdash e : \tau$, *either* e *is a value, or* $\exists e'.\ e \longrightarrow e'$.

Elaboration. Now consider the translation parts in Fig. 5. The key idea of the translation follows the prior work [2,5,16,36]: merges are elaborated to pairs (rule T-MERGE); disjoint quantification and disjoint type applications (rules T-TABS and T-TAPP)) are elaborated to regular universal quantification and type applications, respectively. Finally, the following lemma connects F_i^+ to F_{co}:

Lemma 2 (Elaboration soundness). *We have that:*

- *If* $A <: B \rightsquigarrow co$, *then* $co :: |A| \rhd |B|$.
- *If* $\Delta; \Gamma \vdash E \Rightarrow A \rightsquigarrow e$, *then* $|\Delta|; |\Gamma| \vdash e : |A|$.
- *If* $\Delta; \Gamma \vdash E \Leftarrow A \rightsquigarrow e$, *then* $|\Delta|; |\Gamma| \vdash e : |A|$.

4 Algorithmic System and Decidability

The subtyping relation in Fig. 4 is highly non-algorithmic due to the presence of a transitivity rule. This section presents an alternative algorithmic formulation. Our algorithm extends that of λ_i^+, which itself was inspired by Pierce's decision procedure [38], to handle disjoint quantifiers and the bottom type. We then prove that the algorithm is sound and complete with respect to declarative subtyping.

Additionally we prove that the subtyping and disjointness relations are decidable. Although the proofs of this fact are fairly straightforward, it is nonetheless remarkable since it contrasts with the subtyping relation for (full) $\mathsf{F}_{<:}$ [10], which is undecidable [40]. Thus while bounded quantification is infamous for its undecidability, disjoint quantification has the nicer property of being decidable.

4.1 Algorithmic Subtyping Rules

While Fig. 4 is a fine specification of how subtyping should behave, it cannot be read directly as a subtyping algorithm for two reasons: (1) the conclusions of rules S-REFL and S-TRANS overlap with the other rules, and (2) the premises of rule S-TRANS mention a type that does not appear in the conclusion. Simply dropping the two offending rules from the system is not possible without losing expressivity [29]. Thus we need a different approach. Following λ_i^+, we intend the algorithmic judgment $\mathcal{Q} \vdash A <: B$ to be equivalent to $A <: \mathcal{Q} \Rightarrow B$, where $\mathcal{Q}$ is a queue used to track record labels, domain types and disjointness constraints. The full rules of the algorithmic subtyping of F_i^+ are shown Fig. 9.

Definition 2 ($\mathcal{Q} ::= [\,] \mid l, \mathcal{Q} \mid B, \mathcal{Q} \mid \alpha * B, \mathcal{Q}$)**.** $\mathcal{Q} \Rightarrow A$ *is defined as follows:*

$$[\,] \Rightarrow A = A \qquad (B, \mathcal{Q}) \Rightarrow A = B \to (\mathcal{Q} \Rightarrow A)$$
$$(l, \mathcal{Q}) \Rightarrow A = \{l : \mathcal{Q} \Rightarrow A\} \qquad (\alpha * B, \mathcal{Q}) \Rightarrow A = \forall(\alpha * B).\, \mathcal{Q} \Rightarrow A$$

For brevity of the algorithm, we use metavariable c to mean type constants:

$$\text{Type Constants} \quad c ::= \mathsf{Int} \mid \bot \mid \alpha$$

The basic idea of $\mathcal{Q} \vdash A <: B$ is to perform a case analysis on B until it reaches type constants. We explain new rules regarding disjoint quantification and the bottom type. When a quantifier is encountered in B, rule A-FORALL pushes the type variables with its disjointness constraints onto $\mathcal{Q}$ and continue with the body. Correspondingly, in rule A-ALLCONST, when a quantifier is encountered in A, and the head of $\mathcal{Q}$ is a type variable, this variable is popped out and we continue with the body. Rule A-BOT is similar to its declarative counterpart. Two meta-functions $[\![\mathcal{Q}]\!]^{\top}$ and $[\![\mathcal{Q}]\!]^{\&}$ are meant to generate correct forms of coercions, and their definitions are shown in the appendix. For other algorithmic rules, we refer to λ_i^+ [5] for detailed explanations.

$\boxed{\mathcal{Q} \vdash A <: B \rightsquigarrow co}$ *(Algorithmic subtyping)*

$$\textsc{A-top}\quad \frac{}{\mathcal{Q} \vdash A <: \top \rightsquigarrow [\![\mathcal{Q}]\!]^{\top} \circ \mathsf{top}} \qquad \textsc{A-and}\quad \frac{\mathcal{Q} \vdash A <: B_1 \rightsquigarrow co_1 \qquad \mathcal{Q} \vdash A <: B_2 \rightsquigarrow co_2}{\mathcal{Q} \vdash A <: B_1 \,\&\, B_2 \rightsquigarrow [\![\mathcal{Q}]\!]^{\&} \circ \langle co_1, co_2 \rangle}$$

$$\textsc{A-arr}\quad \frac{\mathcal{Q}, B_1 \vdash A <: B_2 \rightsquigarrow co}{\mathcal{Q} \vdash A <: B_1 \to B_2 \rightsquigarrow co} \qquad \textsc{A-rcd}\quad \frac{\mathcal{Q}, l \vdash A <: B \rightsquigarrow co}{\mathcal{Q} \vdash A <: \{l : B\} \rightsquigarrow co}$$

$$\textsc{A-forall}\quad \frac{\mathcal{Q}, \alpha * B_1 \vdash A <: B_2 \rightsquigarrow co}{\mathcal{Q} \vdash A <: \forall(\alpha * B_1).\, B_2 \rightsquigarrow co} \qquad \textsc{A-const}\quad \frac{}{[\,] \vdash c <: c \rightsquigarrow \mathsf{id}} \qquad \textsc{A-bot}\quad \frac{}{\mathcal{Q} \vdash \bot <: c \rightsquigarrow \mathsf{bot}}$$

$$\textsc{A-arrConst}\quad \frac{[\,] \vdash A <: A_1 \rightsquigarrow co_1 \qquad \mathcal{Q} \vdash A_2 <: c \rightsquigarrow co_2}{A, \mathcal{Q} \vdash A_1 \to A_2 <: c \rightsquigarrow co_1 \to co_2} \qquad \textsc{A-rcdConst}\quad \frac{\mathcal{Q} \vdash A <: c \rightsquigarrow co}{l, \mathcal{Q} \vdash \{l : A\} <: c \rightsquigarrow co}$$

$$\textsc{A-andConst}\quad \frac{\mathcal{Q} \vdash A_i <: c \rightsquigarrow co \qquad i \in \{1, 2\}}{\mathcal{Q} \vdash A_1 \,\&\, A_2 <: c \rightsquigarrow co \circ \pi_i} \qquad \textsc{A-allConst}\quad \frac{[\,] \vdash A <: A_1 \qquad \mathcal{Q} \vdash A_2 <: c \rightsquigarrow co}{(\alpha * A, \mathcal{Q}) \vdash \forall(\alpha * A_1).\, A_2 <: c \rightsquigarrow co_{\forall}}$$

Fig. 9. Algorithmic subtyping

Correctness of the algorithm. We prove that the algorithm is sound and complete with respect to the specification. We refer the reader to our Coq formalization for more details. We only show the two major theorems:

Theorem 3 (Soundness). *If $\mathcal{Q} \vdash A <: B \rightsquigarrow co$ then $A <: \mathcal{Q} \Rightarrow B \rightsquigarrow co$.*

Theorem 4 (Completeness). *If $A <: B \rightsquigarrow co$, then $\exists co'.\ [\,] \vdash A <: B \rightsquigarrow co'$.*

4.2 Decidability

Moreover, we prove that our algorithmic type system is decidable. To see this, first notice that the bidirectional type system is syntax-directed, so we only need to show decidability of algorithmic subtyping and disjointness. The full (manual) proofs for decidability can be found in the appendix.

Lemma 3 (Decidability of algorithmic subtyping). *Given $\mathcal{Q}$, A and B, it is decidable whether there exists co, such that $\mathcal{Q} \vdash A <: B \rightsquigarrow co$.*

Lemma 4 (Decidability of disjointness checking). *Given Δ, A and B, it is decidable whether $\Delta \vdash A * B$.*

One interesting observation here is that although our disjointness quantification has a similar shape to bounded quantification $\forall(\alpha <: A).\, B$ in $\mathsf{F}_{<:}$ [10], subtyping for $\mathsf{F}_{<:}$ is undecidable [40]. In $\mathsf{F}_{<:}$, the subtyping relation between bounded quantification is:

$$\frac{\Delta \vdash A_2 <: A_1 \qquad \Delta, \alpha <: A_2 \vdash B_1 <: B_2}{\Delta \vdash \forall(\alpha <: A_1).\, B_1 <: \forall(\alpha <: A_2).\, B_2}\ \textsc{fsub-forall}$$

Compared with rule S-FORALL, both rules are contravariant on bounded/disjoint types, and covariant on the body. However, with bounded quantification it is fundamental to track the bounds in the environment, which complicates the design of the rules and makes subtyping undecidable with rule FSUB-FORALL. Decidability can be recovered by employing an invariant rule for bounded quantification (that is by forcing A_1 and A_2 to be identical). Disjoint quantification does not require such invariant rule for decidability.

5 Establishing Coherence for F_i^+

In this section, we establish the coherence property for F_i^+. The proof strategy mostly follows that of λ_i^+, but the construction of the heterogeneous logical relation is significantly more complicated. Firstly in Sect. 5.1 we discuss why adding BCD subtyping to disjoint polymorphism introduces significant complications. In Sect. 5.2, we discuss why a natural extension of System F's logical relation to deal with disjoint polymorphism fails. The technical difficulty is *well-foundedness*, stemming from the interaction between impredicativity and disjointness. Finally in Sect. 5.3, we present our (predicative) logical relation that is specially crafted to prove coherence for F_i^+.

5.1 The Challenge

Before we tackle the coherence of F_i^+, let us first consider how F_i (and its predecessor λ_i) enforces coherence. Its essentially syntactic approach is to make sure that there is at most one subtyping derivation for any two types. As an immediate consequence, the produced coercions are uniquely determined and thus the calculus is clearly coherent. Key to this approach is the invariant that the type system only produces *disjoint* intersection types. As we mentioned in Sect. 3, this invariant complicates the calculus and its metatheory, and leads to a weaker substitution lemma. Moreover, the syntactic coherence approach is incompatible with BCD subtyping, which leads to multiple subtyping derivations with different coercions and requires a more general substitution lemma. To accommodate BCD into λ_i, Bi et al. [5] have created the λ_i^+ calculus and developed a semantically-founded proof method based on logical relations. Because λ_i^+ does not feature polymorphism, the problem at hand is to incorporate support for polymorphism in this semantic approach to coherence, which turns out to be more challenging than is apparent.

$$
\begin{aligned}
(v_1, v_2) \in \mathcal{V}[\![\mathsf{Int}; \mathsf{Int}]\!] &\triangleq \exists i.\, v_1 = v_2 = i \\
(v_1, v_2) \in \mathcal{V}[\![\tau_1 \to \tau_2; \tau_1' \to \tau_2']\!] &\triangleq \forall (v, v') \in \mathcal{V}[\![\tau_1; \tau_1']\!].\, (v_1\, v, v_2\, v') \in \mathcal{E}[\![\tau_2; \tau_2']\!] \\
(\langle v_1, v_2\rangle, v_3) \in \mathcal{V}[\![\tau_1 \times \tau_2; \tau_3]\!] &\triangleq (v_1, v_3) \in \mathcal{V}[\![\tau_1; \tau_3]\!] \wedge (v_2, v_3) \in \mathcal{V}[\![\tau_2; \tau_3]\!] \\
(v_3, \langle v_1, v_2\rangle) \in \mathcal{V}[\![\tau_3; \tau_1 \times \tau_2]\!] &\triangleq (v_3, v_1) \in \mathcal{V}[\![\tau_3; \tau_1]\!] \wedge (v_3, v_2) \in \mathcal{V}[\![\tau_3; \tau_2]\!]
\end{aligned}
$$

Fig. 10. Selected cases from λ_i^+'s canonicity relation

5.2 Impredicativity and Disjointness at Odds

Figure 10 shows selected cases of *canonicity*, which is λ_i^+'s (heterogeneous) logical relation used in the coherence proof. The definition captures that two values v_1 and v_2 of types τ_1 and τ_2 are in $\mathcal{V}[\![\tau_1; \tau_2]\!]$ iff either the types are disjoint or the types are equal and the values are semantically equivalent. Because both alternatives entail coherence, canonicity is key to λ_i^+'s coherence proof.

Well-foundedness issues. For F_i^+, we need to extend canonicity with additional cases to account for universally quantified types. For reasons that will become clear in Sect. 5.3, the type indices become source types (rather than target types as in Fig. 10). A naive formulation of one case rule is:

$$
\begin{aligned}
&(v_1, v_2) \in \mathcal{V}[\![\forall(\alpha * A_1).\, B_1; \forall(\alpha * A_2).\, B_2]\!] \triangleq \\
&\qquad \forall C_1 * A_1, C_2 * A_2.\ (v_1 \,|C_1|, v_2 \,|C_2|) \in \mathcal{E}[\![[C_1/\alpha]B_1; [C_2/\alpha]B_2]\!]
\end{aligned}
$$

This case is problematic because it destroys the well-foundedness of λ_i^+'s logical relation, which is based on structural induction on the type indices. Indeed, the type $[C_1/\alpha]B_1$ may well be larger than $\forall(\alpha * A_1).\, B_1$.

However, System F's well-known parametricity logical relation [43] provides us with a means to avoid this problem. Rather than performing the type substitution immediately as in the above rule, we can defer it to a later point by adding it to an extra parameter ρ of the relation, which accumulates the deferred substitutions. This yields a modified rule where the type indices in the recursive occurrences are indeed smaller:

$$
\begin{aligned}
&(v_1, v_2) \in \mathcal{V}[\![\forall(\alpha * A_1).\, B_1; \forall(\alpha * A_2).\, B_2]\!]_\rho \triangleq \\
&\qquad \forall C_1 * A_1, C_2 * A_2. (v_1 \,|C_1|, v_2 \,|C_2|) \in \mathcal{E}[\![B_1; B_2]\!]_{\rho[\alpha \mapsto (C_1, C_2)]}
\end{aligned}
$$

Of course, the deferred substitution has to be performed eventually, to be precise when the type indices are type variables.

$$
(v_1, v_2) \in \mathcal{V}[\![\alpha; \alpha]\!]_\rho \triangleq (v_1, v_2) \in \mathcal{V}[\![\rho_1(\alpha); \rho_2(\alpha)]\!]_\emptyset
$$

Unfortunately, this way we have not only moved the type substitution to the type variable case, but also the ill-foundedness problem. Indeed, this problem is also present in System F. The standard solution is to not fix the relation R by which values at type α are related to $\mathcal{V}[\![\rho_1(\alpha); \rho_2(\alpha)]\!]$, but instead to make it a parameter that is tracked by ρ. This yields the following two rules for disjoint quantification and type variables:

$$(v_1, v_2) \in \mathcal{V}[\![\forall(\alpha * A_1).\, B_1; \forall(\alpha * A_2).\, B_2]\!]_\rho \triangleq \forall C_1 * A_1, C_2 * A_2, \mathsf{R} \subseteq C_1 \times C_2.$$
$$(v_1\,|C_1|, v_2\,|C_2|) \in \mathcal{E}[\![B_1; B_2]\!]_{\rho[\alpha \mapsto (C_1, C_2, \mathsf{R})]}$$
$$(v_1, v_2) \in \mathcal{V}[\![\alpha; \alpha]\!]_\rho \triangleq (v_1, v_2) \in \rho_{\mathsf{R}}(\alpha)$$

Now we have finally recovered the well-foundedness of the relation. It is again structurally inductive on the size of the type indexes.

Heterogeneous issues. We have not yet accounted for one major difference between the parametricity relation, from which we have borrowed ideas, and the canonicity relation, to which we have been adding. The former is homogeneous (i.e., the types of the two values is the same) and therefore has one type index, while the latter is heterogeneous (i.e., the two values may have different types) and therefore has two type indices. Thus we must also consider cases like $\mathcal{V}[\![\alpha; \mathsf{Int}]\!]$. A definition that seems to handle this case appropriately is:

$$(v_1, v_2) \in \mathcal{V}[\![\alpha; \mathsf{Int}]\!]_\rho \triangleq (v_1, v_2) \in \mathcal{V}[\![\rho_1(\alpha); \mathsf{Int}]\!]_\emptyset \tag{1}$$

Here is an example to motivate it. Let $E = \Lambda(\alpha * \top).\, ((\lambda x.\, x) : \alpha \,\&\, \mathsf{Int} \to \alpha \,\&\, \mathsf{Int})$. We expect that $E\,\mathsf{Int}\,1$ evaluates to $\langle 1, 1\rangle$. To prove that, we need to show $(1, 1) \in \mathcal{V}[\![\alpha; \mathsf{Int}]\!]_{[\alpha \mapsto (\mathsf{Int}, \mathsf{Int}, \mathsf{R})]}$. According to Eq. (1), this is indeed the case. However, we run into ill-foundedness issue again, because $\rho_1(\alpha)$ could be larger than α. Alas, this time the parametricity relation has no solution for us.

5.3 The Canonicity Relation for F_i^+

In light of the fact that substitution in the logical relation seems unavoidable in our setting, and that impredicativity is at odds with substitution, we turn to *predicativity*: we change rule T-TAPP to its predicative version:

$$\frac{\Delta; \Gamma \vdash E \Rightarrow \forall(\alpha * B).\, C \rightsquigarrow e \qquad \Delta \vdash t * B}{\Delta; \Gamma \vdash E\, t \Rightarrow [t/\alpha]C \rightsquigarrow e\,|t|}\ \textsc{T-TappMono}$$

where metavariable t ranges over monotypes (types minus disjoint quantification). We do not believe that predicativity is a severe restriction in practice, since many source languages (e.g., those based on the Hindley-Milner type system [24,32] like Haskell and OCaml) are themselves predicative and do not require the full generality of an impredicative core language.

Luckily, substitution with monotypes does not prevent well-foundedness. Figure 11 defines the *canonicity* relation for F_i^+. The canonicity relation is a family of binary relations over F_{co} values that are *heterogeneous*, i.e., indexed by two F_i^+ types. Two points are worth mentioning. (1) An apparent difference from λ_i^+'s logical relation is that our relation is now indexed by *source types*. The

$$
\begin{aligned}
(v_1, v_2) \in \mathcal{V}[\![\mathsf{Int}; \mathsf{Int}]\!] &\triangleq \exists i.\, v_1 = v_2 = i \\
(v_1, v_2) \in \mathcal{V}[\![\{l : A\}; \{l : B\}]\!] &\triangleq (v_1, v_2) \in \mathcal{V}[\![A; B]\!] \\
(v_1, v_2) \in \mathcal{V}[\![A_1 \to B_1; A_2 \to B_2]\!] &\triangleq \forall (v_2', v_1') \in \mathcal{V}[\![A_2; A_1]\!].\, (v_1\, v_1', v_2\, v_2') \in \mathcal{E}[\![B_1; B_2]\!] \\
(\langle v_1, v_2 \rangle, v_3) \in \mathcal{V}[\![A \,\&\, B; C]\!] &\triangleq (v_1, v_3) \in \mathcal{V}[\![A; C]\!] \wedge (v_2, v_3) \in \mathcal{V}[\![B; C]\!] \\
(v_3, \langle v_1, v_2 \rangle) \in \mathcal{V}[\![C; A \,\&\, B]\!] &\triangleq (v_3, v_1) \in \mathcal{V}[\![C; A]\!] \wedge (v_3, v_2) \in \mathcal{V}[\![C; B]\!] \\
(v_1, v_2) \in \mathcal{V}[\![\forall (\alpha * A_1).\, B_1; \forall (\alpha * A_2).\, B_2]\!] &\triangleq \forall \bullet \vdash t * A_1 \,\&\, A_2.\, (v_1\, |t|, v_2\, |t|) \in \mathcal{E}[\![[t/\alpha] B_1; [t/\alpha] B_2]\!] \\
(v_1, v_2) \in \mathcal{V}[\![A; B]\!] &\triangleq \mathsf{true} \quad \text{otherwise} \\
(e_1, e_2) \in \mathcal{E}[\![A; B]\!] &\triangleq \exists v_1, v_2.\, e_1 \longrightarrow^* v_1 \wedge e_2 \longrightarrow^* v_2 \ \wedge (v_1, v_2) \in \mathcal{V}[\![A; B]\!]
\end{aligned}
$$

$$
\rho \in \mathcal{D}[\![\Delta]\!] \triangleq \frac{}{\emptyset \in \mathcal{D}[\![\bullet]\!]} \qquad \frac{\rho \in \mathcal{D}[\![\Delta]\!] \qquad \bullet \vdash t * \rho(B)}{\rho[\alpha \mapsto t] \in \mathcal{D}[\![\Delta, \alpha * B]\!]}
$$

$$
(\gamma_1, \gamma_2) \in \mathcal{G}[\![\Gamma]\!]_\rho \triangleq \frac{}{(\emptyset, \emptyset) \in \mathcal{G}[\![\bullet]\!]_\rho} \qquad \frac{(\gamma_1, \gamma_2) \in \mathcal{G}[\![\Gamma]\!]_\rho \qquad (v_1, v_2) \in \mathcal{V}[\![\rho(A); \rho(A)]\!]}{(\gamma_1[x \mapsto v_1], \gamma_2[x \mapsto v_2]) \in \mathcal{G}[\![\Gamma, x : A]\!]_\rho}
$$

Fig. 11. The canonicity relation for F_i^+

reason is that the type translation function (Definition 1) discards disjointness constraints, which are crucial in our setting, whereas λ_i^+'s type translation does not have information loss. (2) Heterogeneity allows relating values of different types, and in particular values whose types are disjoint. The rationale behind the canonicity relation is to combine equality checking from traditional (homogeneous) logical relations with disjointness checking. It consists of two relations: the value relation $\mathcal{V}[\![A; B]\!]$ relates *closed* values; and the expression relation $\mathcal{E}[\![A; B]\!]$—defined in terms of the value relation—relates closed expressions.

The relation $\mathcal{V}[\![A; B]\!]$ is defined by induction on the structures of A and B. For integers, it requires the two values to be literally the same. For two records to behave the same, their fields must behave the same. For two functions to behave the same, they are required to produce outputs related at B_1 and B_2 when given related inputs at A_1 and A_2. For the next two cases regarding intersection types, the relation distributes over intersection constructor $\&$. Of particular interest is the case for disjoint quantification. Notice that it *does not* quantify over arbitrary relations, but directly substitutes α with monotype t in B_1 and B_2. This means that our canonicity relation *does not* entail parametricity. However, it suffices for our purposes to prove coherence. Another noticeable thing is that we keep the invariant that A and B are closed types throughout the relation, so we no longer need to consider type variables. This simplifies things a lot. Note that when one type is $\bot$, two values are vacuously related because there simply are no values of type $\bot$. We need to show that the relation is indeed well-founded:

Lemma 5 (Well-foundedness). *The canonicity relation of* F_i^+ *is well-founded.*

Proof. Let $|\cdot|_\forall$ and $|\cdot|_s$ be the number of $\forall$-quantifies and the size of types, respectively. Consider the measure $\langle |\cdot|_\forall, |\cdot|_s \rangle$, where $\langle \dots \rangle$ denotes lexicographic order. For the case of disjoint quantification, the number of $\forall$-quantifiers decreases. For the other cases, the measure of $|\cdot|_\forall$ does not increase, and the measure of $|\cdot|_s$ strictly decreases. □

5.4 Establishing Coherence

Logical equivalence. The canonicity relation can be lifted to open expressions in the standard way, i.e., by considering all possible interpretations of free type and term variables. The logical interpretations of type and term contexts are found in the bottom half of Fig. 11.

Definition 3 (Logical equivalence $\backsimeq_{log}$)

$$\Delta; \Gamma \vdash e_1 \backsimeq_{log} e_2 : A; B \triangleq |\Delta|; |\Gamma| \vdash e_1 : |A| \wedge |\Delta|; |\Gamma| \vdash e_2 : |B| \wedge$$
$$(\forall \rho, \gamma_1, \gamma_2.\ \rho \in \mathcal{D}[\![\Delta]\!] \wedge (\gamma_1, \gamma_2) \in \mathcal{G}[\![\Gamma]\!]_\rho \Longrightarrow (\gamma_1(\rho_1(e_1)), \gamma_2(\rho_2(e_2))) \in \mathcal{E}[\![\rho(A); \rho(B)]\!])$$

For conciseness, we write $\Delta; \Gamma \vdash e_1 \backsimeq_{log} e_2 : A$ to mean $\Delta; \Gamma \vdash e_1 \backsimeq_{log} e_2 : A; A$.

Contextual equivalence. Following λ_i^+, the notion of coherence is based on *contextual equivalence.* The intuition is that two programs are equivalent if we *cannot* tell them apart in any context. As usual, contextual equivalence is expressed using *expression contexts* ($\mathcal{C}$ and $\mathcal{D}$ denote F_i^+ and F_{co} expression contexts, respectively), Due to the bidirectional nature of the type system, the typing judgment of $\mathcal{C}$ features 4 different forms (full rules are in the appendix), e.g., $\mathcal{C} : (\Delta; \Gamma \Rightarrow A) \mapsto (\Delta'; \Gamma' \Rightarrow A') \rightsquigarrow \mathcal{D}$ reads if $\Delta; \Gamma \vdash E \Rightarrow A$ then $\Delta'; \Gamma' \vdash \mathcal{C}\{E\} \Rightarrow A'$. The judgment also generates a well-typed F_{co} context $\mathcal{D}$. The following two definitions capture the notion of contextual equivalence:

Definition 4 (Kleene Equality $\backsimeq$). *Two complete programs (i.e., closed terms of type* Int*), e and e', are Kleene equal, written $e \backsimeq e'$, iff there exists an integer i such that $e \longrightarrow^* i$ and $e' \longrightarrow^* i$.*

Definition 5 (Contextual Equivalence $\backsimeq_{ctx}$)

$$\Delta; \Gamma \vdash E_1 \backsimeq_{ctx} E_2 : A \triangleq \forall e_1, e_2.\ \Delta; \Gamma \vdash E_1 \Rightarrow A \rightsquigarrow e_1 \wedge \Delta; \Gamma \vdash E_2 \Rightarrow A \rightsquigarrow e_2 \wedge$$
$$(\forall \mathcal{C}, \mathcal{D}.\ \mathcal{C} : (\Delta; \Gamma \Rightarrow A) \mapsto (\bullet; \bullet \Rightarrow \mathsf{Int}) \rightsquigarrow \mathcal{D} \Longrightarrow \mathcal{D}\{e_1\} \backsimeq \mathcal{D}\{e_2\})$$

Coherence. For space reasons, we directly show the coherence statement of F_i^+. We need several technical lemmas such as compatibility lemmas, fundamental property, etc. The interested reader can refer to our Coq formalization.

Theorem 5 (Coherence). *We have that*

- *If $\Delta; \Gamma \vdash E \Rightarrow A$ then $\Delta; \Gamma \vdash E \backsimeq_{ctx} E : A$.*
- *If $\Delta; \Gamma \vdash E \Leftarrow A$ then $\Delta; \Gamma \vdash E \backsimeq_{ctx} E : A$.*

That is, coherence is a special case of Definition 5 where E_1 and E_2 are the same. At first glance, this appears underwhelming: of course E behaves the same as itself! The tricky part is that, if we expand it according to Definition 5, it is not E itself but all its translations e_1 and e_2 that behave the same!

6 Related Work

Coherence. In calculi featuring coercive subtyping, a semantics that interprets the subtyping judgment by introducing explicit coercions is typically defined on typing derivations rather than on typing judgments. A natural question that arises for such systems is whether the semantics is *coherent*, i.e., distinct typing derivations of the same typing judgment possess the same meaning. Since Reynolds [45] proved the coherence of a calculus with intersection types, many researchers have studied the problem of coherence in a variety of typed calculi. Two approaches are commonly found in the literature. The first approach is to find a normal form for a representation of the derivation and show that normal forms are unique for a given typing judgment [8,15,47]. However, this approach cannot be directly applied to Curry-style calculi (where the lambda abstractions are not type annotated). Biernacki and Polesiuk [6] considered the coherence problem of coercion semantics. Their criterion for coherence of the translation is *contextual equivalence* in the target calculus. Inspired by this approach, Bi et al. [5] proposed the canonicity relation to prove coherence for a calculus with disjoint intersection types and BCD subtyping. As we have shown in Sect. 5, constructing a suitable logical relation for F_i^+ is challenging. On the one hand, the original approach by Alpuim et al. [2] in F_i does not work any more due to the addition of BCD subtyping. On the other hand, simply combining System F's logical relation with λ_i^+'s canonicity relation does not work as expected, due to the issue of well-foundedness. To solve the problem, we employ immediate substitutions and a restriction to predicative instantiations.

BCD subtyping and decidability. The BCD type system was first introduced by Barendregt et al. [3] to characterize exactly the strongly normalizing terms. The BCD type system features a powerful subtyping relation, which serves as a base for our subtyping relation. The decidability of BCD subtyping has been shown in several works [27,38,41,51]. Laurent [28] formalized the relation in Coq in order to eliminate transitivity cuts from it, but his formalization does not deliver an algorithm. Only recently, Laurent [30] presented a general way of defining a BCD-like subtyping relation extended with generic contravariant/-covariant type constructors that enjoys the "sub-formula property". Our Coq formalization extends the approach used in λ_i^+, which follows a different idea based on Pierce's decision procedure [38], with parametric (disjoint) polymorphism and corresponding distributivity rules. More recently, Muehlboeck and Tate [34] presented a decidable algorithmic system (proved in Coq) with union and intersection types. Similar to F_i^+, their system also has distributive subtyping rules. They also discussed the addition of polymorphism, but left a Coq formalization for future work. In their work they regard intersections of disjoint types (e.g., $\mathsf{String} \,\&\, \mathsf{Int}$) as uninhabitable, which is different from our interpretation. As a consequence, coherence is a non-issue for them.

Intersection types, the merge operator and polymorphism. Forsythe [44] has intersection types and a merge-like operator. However to ensure coherence, various

	$\lambda_{,,}$ [16]	λ_i [36]	$\lambda_\wedge^\vee$ [7]	λ_i^+ [5]	F_i [2]	F_i^+
Disjointness	○	●	○	●	●	●
Unrestricted intersections	●	○	●	●	○	●
BCD subtyping	○	○	●	●	○	●
Polymorphism	○	○	○	○	●	●
Coherence	○	◑	○	●	◑	●
Bottom type	○	○	●	○	○	●

Fig. 12. Summary of intersection calculi (● = yes, ○ = no, ◑ = syntactic coherence)

restrictions were added to limit the use of merges. In Forsythe merges cannot contain more than one function. Castagna et al. [12] proposed a coherent calculus $\lambda\&$ to study overloaded functions. $\lambda\&$ has a special merge operator that works on functions only. Dunfield proposed a calculus [16] (which we call $\lambda_{,,}$) that shows significant expressiveness of type systems with unrestricted intersection types and an (unrestricted) merge operator. However, because of his unrestricted merge operator (allowing $1\,,,\,2$), his calculus lacks coherence. Blaauwbroek's $\lambda_\wedge^\vee$ [7] enriched $\lambda_{,,}$ with BCD subtyping and computational effects, but he did not address coherence. The coherence issue for a calculus similar to $\lambda_{,,}$ was first addressed in λ_i [36] with the notion of disjointness, but at the cost of dropping unrestricted intersections, and a strict notion of coherence (based on α-equivalence). Later Bi et al. [5] improved calculi with disjoint intersection types by removing several restrictions, adopted BCD subtyping and a semantic notion of coherence (based on contextual equivalence) proved using canonicity. The combination of intersection types, a merge operator and parametric polymorphism, while achieving coherence was first studied in F_i [2], which serves as a foundation for F_i^+. However, F_i suffered the same problems as λ_i. Additionally in F_i a bottom type is problematic due to interactions with disjoint polymorphism and the lack of unrestricted intersections. The issues can be illustrated with the well-typed F_i^+ expression $\Lambda(\alpha * \bot).\,\lambda x : \alpha.\, x\,,,\, x$. In this expression the type of $x\,,,\, x$ is $\alpha \,\&\, \alpha$. Such a merge does not violate disjointness because the only types that α can be instantiated with are top-like, and top-like types do not introduce incoherence. In F_i a type variable α can never be disjoint to another type that contains α, but (as the previous expression shows) the addition of a bottom type allows expressions where such (strict) condition does not hold. In this work, we removed those restrictions, extended BCD subtyping with polymorphism, and proposed a more powerful logical relation for proving coherence. Figure 12 summarizes the main differences between the aforementioned calculi.

There are also several other calculi with intersections and polymorphism. Pierce proposed $\mathsf{F}_\wedge$ [39], a calculus combining intersection types and bounded quantification. Pierce translates $\mathsf{F}_\wedge$ to System F extended with products, but he left coherence as a conjecture. More recently, Castagna et al. [14] proposed a polymorphic calculus with set-theoretic type connectives (intersections, unions, negations). But their calculus does not include a merge operator. Castagna and

Lanvin also proposed a gradual type system [13] with intersection and union types, but also without a merge operator.

Row polymorphism and bounded polymorphism. Row polymorphism was originally proposed by Wand [54] as a mechanism to enable type inference for a simple object-oriented language based on recursive records. These ideas were later adopted into type systems for extensible records [19,21,31]. Our merge operator can be seen as a generalization of record extension/concatenation, and selection is also built-in. In contrast to most record calculi, restriction is not a primitive operation in F_i^+, but can be simulated via subtyping. Disjoint quantification can simulate the *lacks* predicate often present in systems with row polymorphism. Recently Morris and McKinna presented a typed language [33], generalizing and abstracting existing systems of row types and row polymorphism. Alpuim et al. [2] informally studied the relationship between row polymorphism and disjoint polymorphism, but it would be interesting to study such relationship more formally. The work of Morris and McKinna may be interesting for such study in that it gives a general framework for row type systems.

Bounded quantification is currently the dominant mechanism in major mainstream object-oriented languages supporting both subtyping and polymorphism. $\mathsf{F}_{<:}$ [10] provides a simple model for bounded quantification, but type-checking in full $\mathsf{F}_{<:}$ is proved to be undecidable [40]. Pierce's thesis [39] discussed the relationship between calculi with simple polymorphism and intersection types and bounded quantification. He observed that there is a way to "encode" many forms of bounded quantification in a system with intersections and pure (unbounded) second-order polymorphism. That encoding can be easily adapted to F_i^+:

$$\forall(\alpha <: A).\, B \triangleq \forall(\alpha * \top).\, ([A \,\&\, \alpha/\alpha]B)$$

The idea is to replace bounded quantification by (unrestricted) universal quantification and all occurrences of α by $A \,\&\, \alpha$ in the body. Such an encoding seems to indicate that F_i^+ could be used as a decidable alternative to (full) $\mathsf{F}_{<:}$. It is worthwhile to note that this encoding does not work in F_i because $A \,\&\, \alpha$ is not well-formed (α is not disjoint to A). In other words, the encoding requires unrestricted intersections.

7 Conclusion and Future Work

We have proposed F_i^+, a type-safe and coherent calculus with disjoint intersection types, BCD subtyping and parametric polymorphism. F_i^+ improves the state-of-art of compositional designs, and enables the development of highly modular and reusable programs. One interesting and useful further extension would be implicit polymorphism. For that we want to combine Dunfield and Krishnaswami's approach [17] with our bidirectional type system. We would also like to study the parametricity of F_i^+. As we have seen in Sect. 5.2, it is not at all obvious how to extend the standard logical relation of System F to account for disjointness, and avoid potential circularity due to impredicativity. A promising solution is to use step-indexed logical relations [1].

Acknowledgments. We thank the anonymous reviewers and Yaoda Zhou for their helpful comments. This work has been sponsored by the Hong Kong Research Grant Council projects number 17210617 and 17258816, and by the Research Foundation - Flanders.

References

1. Ahmed, A.: Step-indexed syntactic logical relations for recursive and quantified types. In: Sestoft, P. (ed.) ESOP 2006. LNCS, vol. 3924, pp. 69–83. Springer, Heidelberg (2006). https://doi.org/10.1007/11693024_6
2. Alpuim, J., Oliveira, B.C.d.S., Shi, Z.: Disjoint polymorphism. In: Yang, H. (ed.) ESOP 2017. LNCS, vol. 10201, pp. 1–28. Springer, Heidelberg (2017). https://doi.org/10.1007/978-3-662-54434-1_1
3. Barendregt, H., Coppo, M., Dezani-Ciancaglini, M.: A filter lambda model and the completeness of type assignment. J. Symb. Logic **48**(04), 931–940 (1983)
4. Bi, X., Oliveira, B.C.d.S.: Typed first-class traits. In: European Conference on Object-Oriented Programming (ECOOP) (2018)
5. Bi, X., Oliveira, B.C.d.S., Schrijvers, T.: The essence of nested composition. In: European Conference on Object-Oriented Programming (ECOOP) (2018)
6. Biernacki, D., Polesiuk, P.: Logical relations for coherence of effect subtyping. In: International Conference on Typed Lambda Calculi and Applications (TLCA) (2015)
7. Blaauwbroek, L.: On the interaction between unrestricted union and intersection types and computational effects. Master's thesis, Technical University Eindhoven (2017)
8. Breazu-Tannen, V., Coquand, T., Gunter, C.A., Scedrov, A.: Inheritance as implicit coercion. Inf. Comput. **93**(1), 172–221 (1991)
9. Brent, R.P., Kung, H.T.: The chip complexity of binary arithmetic. In: Proceedings of the Twelfth Annual ACM Symposium on Theory of Computing, pp. 190–200 (1980)
10. Cardelli, L., Wegner, P.: On understanding types, data abstraction, and polymorphism. ACM Comput. Surv. **17**(4), 471–523 (1985)
11. Carette, J., Kiselyov, O., Shan, C.C.: Finally tagless, partially evaluated: tagless staged interpreters for simpler typed languages. J. Funct. Program. **19**(05), 509 (2009)
12. Castagna, G., Ghelli, G., Longo, G.: A calculus for overloaded functions with subtyping. In: Conference on LISP and Functional Programming (1992)
13. Castagna, G., Lanvin, V.: Gradual typing with union and intersection types. In: Proceedings of the ACM on Programming Languages, vol. 1, no. (ICFP), pp. 1–28 (2017)
14. Castagna, G., Nguyen, K., Xu, Z., Im, H., Lenglet, S., Padovani, L.: Polymorphic functions with set-theoretic types: part 1: syntax, semantics, and evaluation. In: Principles of Programming Languages (POPL) (2014)
15. Curien, P.L., Ghelli, G.: Coherence of subsumption, minimum typing and type-checking in $f_{\leq}$. Math. Struct. Comput. Sci. (MSCS) **2**(01), 55 (1992)
16. Dunfield, J.: Elaborating intersection and union types. J. Funct. Program. (JFP) **24**(2–3), 133–165 (2014)
17. Dunfield, J., Krishnaswami, N.R.: Complete and easy bidirectional typechecking for higher-rank polymorphism. In: International Conference on Functional Programming (ICFP) (2013)

18. Fokkinga, M.M.: Tupling and mutumorphisms. Squiggolist **1**(4) (1989)
19. Gaster, B.R., Jones, M.P.: A polymorphic type system for extensible records and variants. Technical report, University of Nottingham (1996)
20. Gibbons, J., Wu, N.: Folding domain-specific languages: deep and shallow embeddings (functional pearl). In: ICFP, pp. 339–347. ACM (2014)
21. Harper, R., Pierce, B.: A record calculus based on symmetric concatenation. In: Principles of Programming Languages (POPL) (1991)
22. Henglein, F.: Dynamic typing: syntax and proof theory. Sci. Comput. Program. **22**(3), 197–230 (1994)
23. Herman, D., Tomb, A., Flanagan, C.: Space-efficient gradual typing. High.-Order Symb. Comput. **23**(2), 167 (2010)
24. Hindley, R.: The principal type-scheme of an object in combinatory logic. Trans. Am. Math. Soc. **146**, 29–60 (1969)
25. Hinze, R.: An algebra of scans. In: Kozen, D. (ed.) MPC 2004. LNCS, vol. 3125, pp. 186–210. Springer, Heidelberg (2004). https://doi.org/10.1007/978-3-540-27764-4_11
26. Hofer, C., Ostermann, K., Rendel, T., Moors, A.: Polymorphic embedding of DSLs. In: International Conference on Generative Programming and Component Engineering (GPCE) (2008)
27. Kurata, T., Takahashi, M.: Decidable properties of intersection type systems. In: Dezani-Ciancaglini, M., Plotkin, G. (eds.) TLCA 1995. LNCS, vol. 902, pp. 297–311. Springer, Heidelberg (1995). https://doi.org/10.1007/BFb0014060
28. Laurent, O.: Intersection types with subtyping by means of cut elimination. Fundam. Inf. **121**(1–4), 203–226 (2012)
29. Laurent, O.: A syntactic introduction to intersection types (2012, unpublished note)
30. Laurent, O.: Intersection subtyping with constructors. In: Proceedings of the Ninth Workshop on Intersection Types and Related Systems (2018)
31. Leijen, D.: Extensible records with scoped labels. Trends Funct. Program. **5**, 297–312 (2005)
32. Milner, R.: A theory of type polymorphism in programming. J. Comput. Syst. Sci. **17**(3), 348–375 (1978)
33. Morris, J.G., McKinna, J.: Abstracting extensible data types. In: Principles of Programming Languages (POPL) (2019)
34. Muehlboeck, F., Tate, R.: Empowering union and intersection types with integrated subtyping. In: OOPSLA (2018)
35. Oliveira, B.C.d.S., Cook, W.R.: Extensibility for the masses. In: Noble, J. (ed.) ECOOP 2012. LNCS, vol. 7313, pp. 2–27. Springer, Heidelberg (2012). https://doi.org/10.1007/978-3-642-31057-7_2
36. Oliveira, B.C.d.S., Shi, Z., Alpuim, J.: Disjoint intersection types. In: International Conference on Functional Programming (ICFP) (2016)
37. Oliveira, B.C.d.S., van der Storm, T., Loh, A., Cook, W.R.: Feature-oriented programming with object algebras. In: Castagna, G. (ed.) ECOOP 2013. LNCS, vol. 7920, pp. 27–51. Springer, Heidelberg (2013). https://doi.org/10.1007/978-3-642-39038-8_2
38. Pierce, B.C.: A decision procedure for the subtype relation on intersection types with bounded variables. Technical report, Carnegie Mellon University (1989)
39. Pierce, B.C.: Programming with intersection types and bounded polymorphism. Ph.D. thesis, University of Pennsylvania (1991)
40. Pierce, B.C.: Bounded quantification is undecidable. Inf. Comput. **112**(1), 131–165 (1994)

41. Rehof, J., Urzyczyn, P.: Finite combinatory logic with intersection types. In: Ong, L. (ed.) TLCA 2011. LNCS, vol. 6690, pp. 169–183. Springer, Heidelberg (2011). https://doi.org/10.1007/978-3-642-21691-6_15
42. Rendel, T., Brachthäuser, J.I., Ostermann, K.: From object algebras to attribute grammars. In: Object-Oriented Programming, Systems Languages and Applications (OOPSLA) (2014)
43. Reynolds, J.C.: Types, abstraction and parametric polymorphism. In: Proceedings of the IFIP 9th World Computer Congress (1983)
44. Reynolds, J.C.: Preliminary design of the programming language Forsythe. Technical report, Carnegie Mellon University (1988)
45. Reynolds, J.C.: The coherence of languages with intersection types. In: Ito, T., Meyer, A.R. (eds.) TACS 1991. LNCS, vol. 526, pp. 675–700. Springer, Heidelberg (1991). https://doi.org/10.1007/3-540-54415-1_70
46. Oliveira, B.C.d.S., Hinze, R., Löh, A.: Extensible and modular generics for the masses. In: Revised Selected Papers from the Seventh Symposium on Trends in Functional Programming, TFP 2006, Nottingham, United Kingdom, 19–21 April 2006, pp. 199–216 (2006)
47. Schwinghammer, J.: Coherence of subsumption for monadic types. J. Funct. Program. (JFP) **19**(02), 157 (2008)
48. Scott, D.: Outline of a mathematical theory of computation. Oxford University Computing Laboratory, Programming Research Group (1970)
49. Scott, D.S., Strachey, C.: Toward a Mathematical Semantics for Computer Languages, vol. 1. Oxford University Computing Laboratory, Programming Research Group (1971)
50. Siek, J., Thiemann, P., Wadler, P.: Blame and coercion: together again for the first time. In: Conference on Programming Language Design and Implementation (PLDI) (2015)
51. Statman, R.: A finite model property for intersection types. Electron. Proc. Theor. Comput. Sci. **177**, 1–9 (2015)
52. Wadler, P., Blott, S.: How to make ad-hoc polymorphism less ad hoc. In: Proceedings of the 16th ACM SIGPLAN-SIGACT Symposium on Principles of Programming Languages, POPL 1989 (1989)
53. Wadler, P.: The expression problem. Java-Genericity Mailing List (1998)
54. Wand, M.: Complete type inference for simple objects. In: Symposium on Logic in Computer Science (LICS) (1987)
55. Zhang, W., Oliveira, B.C.d.S: Shallow EDLs and object-oriented programming. Program. J. (2019, to appear)

5

Asynchronous Timed Session Types from Duality to Time-Sensitive Processes

Laura Bocchi[1(✉)], Maurizio Murgia[1,4], Vasco Thudichum Vasconcelos[2], and Nobuko Yoshida[3]

[1] University of Kent, Canterbury, UK
l.bocchi@kent.ac.uk
[2] LASIGE, Faculty of Sciences, University of Lisbon, Lisbon, Portugal
[3] Imperial College London, London, UK
[4] University of Cagliari, Cagliari, Italy

Abstract. We present a behavioural typing system for a higher-order timed calculus using session types to model timed protocols. Behavioural typing ensures that processes in the calculus perform actions in the time-windows prescribed by their protocols. We introduce duality and subtyping for timed asynchronous session types. Our notion of duality allows typing a larger class of processes with respect to previous proposals. Subtyping is critical for the precision of our typing system, especially in the presence of session delegation. The composition of dual (timed asynchronous) types enjoys progress when using an urgent receive semantics, in which receive actions are executed as soon as the expected message is available. Our calculus increases the modelling power of extant calculi on timed sessions, adding a blocking receive primitive with timeout and a primitive that consumes an arbitrary amount of time in a given range.

Keywords: Session types · Timers · Duality · π-calculus

1 Introduction

Time is at the basis of many real-life protocols. These include common client-server interactions as for example, *"An SMTP server SHOULD have a timeout of at least 5 minutes while it is awaiting the next command from the sender"* [22]. By protocol, we intend application-level specifications of interaction patterns (via message passing) among distributed applications. An extensive literature offers theories and tools for formal analysis of timed protocols, modelled for instance as timed automata [3, 26, 34] or Message Sequence Charts [2]. These works allow to reason on the properties of *protocols*, defined as formal models. Recent work, based on session types, focus on the relationship between time-sensitive protocols, modelled as timed extensions of session types, and their implementations abstracted as *processes* in some timed calculus. The relationship between protocols and processes is given in terms of static behavioural typing [12,15] or run-time monitoring [6,7,30] of processes against types. Existing work on timed session types [7,12,15,30] is based on simple abstractions for processes which do not capture time sensitive primitives such as blocking (as well as non-blocking) receive primitives with timeout and time consuming actions with variable, yet bound, duration. This paper provides a theory of asynchronous timed session types for a calculus that features these two primitives. We focus on the asynchronous scenario, as modern distributed systems (e.g., web) are often based on asynchronous communications via FIFO channels [4,33]. The link between protocols and processes is given in terms of static behavioural typing, checking for punctuality of interactions with respect to protocols prescriptions. Unlike previous work on asynchronous timed session types [12], our type system can check processes against protocols that are *not wait-free*. In wait-free protocols, the time-windows for corresponding send and receive actions have an empty intersection. We illustrate wait-freedom using a protocol modelled as two timed session types, each owning a set of clocks (with no shared clocks between types).

$$S_{\mathsf{C}} = !\mathtt{Command}(x < 5, \{x\}).S'_{\mathsf{C}} \qquad S_{\mathsf{S}} = ?\mathtt{Command}(\mathrm{y} < 5, \{y\}).S'_{\mathsf{S}} \tag{1}$$

The protocol in (1) involves a client S_{C} with a clock x, and a server S_{S} with a clock y (with both x and y initially set to 0). Following the protocol, the client must send a message of type Command within 5 min, reset x, and continue as S'_{C}. Dually, the server must be ready to receive a command with a timeout of 5 min, reset y, and continue as S'_{S}. The model in (1) is *not wait-free*: the intersection of the time-windows for the send and receive actions is non-empty (the time-windows actually coincide). The protocol in (2), where the server must wait until after the client's deadline to read the message, is wait-free.

$$!\mathtt{Command}(x < 5, \{x\}).S''_{\mathsf{C}} \qquad ?\mathtt{Command}(\mathrm{y} = 5, \{y\}).S''_{\mathsf{S}} \tag{2}$$

Patterns like the one in (1) are common (e.g., the SMPT fragment mentioned at the beginning of this introduction) but, unfortunately, they are *not wait-free*, hence ruled out in previous work [12]. Arguably, (2) is an unpractical wait-free variant of (1): the client must always wait for at least 5 min to have the message read, no matter how early this message was sent. The definition of protocols for our typing system (which allows for *not wait-free* protocols) is based on a notion of *asynchronous timed duality*, and on a subtyping relation that provides accuracy of typing, especially in the case of channel passing.

Asynchronous timed duality. In the untimed scenario, each session type has one unique *dual* that is obtained by changing the polarities of the actions (send vs. receive, and selection vs. branching). For example, the dual of a session type S

that sends an integer and then receives a string is a session type $\overline{S}$ that receives an integer and then sends a string.

$$S = !\texttt{Int}.?\texttt{String} \qquad \overline{S} = ?\texttt{Int}.!\texttt{String}$$

Duality characterises well-behaved systems: the behaviour described by the composition of dual types has no communication mismatches (e.g., unexpected messages, or messages with values of unexpected types) nor deadlocks. In the timed scenario, this is no longer true. Consider a timed extension of session types (using the model of time in timed automata [3]), and of (untimed) duality so that dual send/receive actions have equivalent time constraints and resets. The example below shows a timed type S with its dual $\overline{S}$, where S owns clock x, and $\overline{S}$ owns clock y (with x and y initially set to 0):

$$S = !\texttt{Int}(x \leqslant 1, x).?\texttt{String}(x \leqslant 2) \qquad \overline{S} = ?\texttt{Int}(y \leqslant 1, y).!\texttt{String}(y \leqslant 2)$$

Here S sends an integer at any time satisfying $x \leqslant 1$, and then resets x. After that, S receives a string at any time satisfying $x \leqslant 2$. The timed dual of S is obtained by keeping the same time constraints (and renaming the clock—to make it clear that clocks are not shared). To illustrate our point, we use the semantics from timed session types [12], borrowed from Communicating Timed automata [23]. This semantics is *separated*, in the sense that only time actions may 'take time', while all other actions (e.g., communications) are instantaneous.[1] The aforementioned semantics allows for the following execution of $S \mid \overline{S}$:

$$\begin{array}{lll} S \mid \overline{S} \xrightarrow{0.4}\xrightarrow{\texttt{Int}} & ?\texttt{String}(x \leqslant 2) \mid \overline{S} & \text{(clocks values: } x = 0,\ y = 0.4) \\ \xrightarrow{0.6}\xrightarrow{\texttt{Int}} & ?\texttt{String}(x \leqslant 2) \mid !\texttt{String}(x \leqslant 2) & \text{(clocks values: } x = 0.6,\ y = 0) \\ \xrightarrow{2}\xrightarrow{!\texttt{String}} & ?\texttt{String}(x \leqslant 2) & \text{(clocks values: } x = 2.6,\ y = 2) \end{array}$$

where: (i) the system makes a time step of 0.4, then S sends the integer and resets x, yielding a state where $x = 0$ and $y = 0.4$; (ii) the system makes a time step of 0.6, then $\overline{S}$ receives the integer and resets y, yielding a state where $x = 0.6$ and $y = 0$; (iii) the system makes a time step of 2, then the continuation of $\overline{S}$ sends the string, when $y = 2$ and $x = 2.6$. In (iii), the string was sent too late: constraint $x \leqslant 2$ of the receiving endpoint is now unsatisfiable. The system cannot do any further legal step, and is stuck.

Urgent receive semantics. The example above shows that, in the timed asynchronous scenario, the straightforward extension of duality to the timed scenario does not necessarily characterise well-behaved communications. We argue, however, that the execution of $S \mid \overline{S}$, in particular the time reduction with label 0.6, does not reflect the semantics of most common receive primitives. In fact, most mainstream programming languages implement *urgent receive* semantics

[1] Separated semantics can describe situations where actions have an associated duration.

for receive actions. We call a semantics *urgent receive* when receive actions are executed as soon as the expected message is available, given that the guard of that action is satisfied. Conversely, *non-urgent receive* semantics allows receive actions to fire at any time satisfying the time constraint, as long as the message is in the queue. The aforementioned reduction with label 0.6 is permitted by non-urgent receive semantics such as the one in [23], since it defers the reception of the integer despite the integer being ready for reception and the guard ($y \leqslant 2$) being satisfied, but not by urgent receive semantics. Urgent receive semantics allows, instead, the following execution for $S \mid \overline{S}$:

$$\begin{array}{lll} S \mid \overline{S} \xrightarrow{0.4} \xrightarrow{!\texttt{int}} & ?\texttt{String}(x \leqslant 2) \mid \overline{S} & \text{(clocks values: } x = 0,\ y = 0.4) \\ \xrightarrow{?\texttt{int}} & ?\texttt{String}(x \leqslant 2) \mid !\texttt{String}(x \leqslant 2) & \text{(clocks values: } x = 0,\ y = 0) \\ \xrightarrow{2} \xrightarrow{!\texttt{String}} & ?\texttt{String}(x \leqslant 2) & \text{(clocks values: } x = 2,\ y = 2) \end{array}$$

If S sends the integer when $x = 0.4$, then $\overline{S}$ must receive the integer immediately, when $y = 0.4$. At this point, both endpoints reset their respective clocks, and the communication will continue in sync. Urgent receive primitives are common; some examples are the non-blocking `WaitFreeReadQueue.read()` and blocking `WaitFreeReadQueue.waitForData()` of Real-Time Java [13], and the receive primitives in Erlang and Golang. *Urgent receive semantics make interactions "more synchronous" but still as asynchronous as real-life programs.*

A calculus for timed asynchronous processes. Our calculus features two time-sensitive primitives. The first is a parametric receive operation $a^n(b).P$ on a channel a, with a timeout n that can be ∞ or any number in $\mathbf{R}_{\geqslant 0}$. The parametric receive captures a range of receive primitives: non-blocking ($n = 0$), blocking without timeout ($n = \infty$), or blocking with timeout ($n \in \mathbf{R}_{>0}$). The second primitive is a time-consuming action, $\mathtt{delay}(\delta).P$, where δ is a constraint expressing the time-window for the time consumed by that action. Delay processes model primitives like $\mathtt{Thread.sleep}(n)$ in real-time Java [13] or, more generally, any time-consuming action, with δ being an estimation of the delay of computation.

Processes in our calculus abstract implementations of protocols given as pairs of dual types. Consider the processes below.

$$P_C = \mathtt{delay}(x < 3).\,\overline{a}\,\mathtt{HELO}.P'_C \quad P_S = \mathtt{delay}(x = 5).\,a^0(b).P'_S \quad Q_S = a^5(b).Q'_S$$

Processes abiding the protocols in (2) could be as follows: P_C for the client S_C, and P_S for the server S_S. The client process P_C performs a time consuming action for up to 3 min, then sends command `HELO` to the server, and continues as P'_C. The server process P_S sleeps for exactly 5 min, receives the message immediately (without blocking), and continues as P'_S. A process for the protocol in (1) could, instead be the parallel composition of P_C, again for the client, and Q_S for the server. Process Q_S uses a blocking primitive with timeout; the server now blocks on the receive action with a timeout of 5 min, and continues as Q'_S as soon as a message is received. The blocking receive primitive with timeout is crucial to model processes typed against protocols one can express with asynchronous timed duality, in particular those that are not wait-free.

A type system for timed asynchronous processes. The relationship between types and processes in our calculus is given as a typing system. Well-typed processes are ensured to communicate at the times prescribed by their types. This result is given via Subject Reduction (Theorem 4), establishing that well-typedness is preserved by reduction. In our timed scenario, Subject Reduction holds under *receive liveness*, an assumption on the interaction structure of processes. This assumption is orthogonal to time. To characterise the interaction structures of a timed process we erase timing information from that processes (*time erasure*). Receive liveness requires that, whenever a time-erased processes is waiting for a message, the corresponding message is eventually provided by the rest of the system. While receive liveness is not needed for Subject Reduction in untimed systems [21], it is required for timed processes. This reflects the natural intuition that if an untimed-process violates progress, then its timed counterpart may miss deadlines. Notably, we can rely on existing behavioural checking techniques from the untimed setting to ensure receive liveness [17].

Receive liveness is not required for Subject Reduction in a related work on asynchronous timed session types [12]. The dissimilarity in the assumptions is only apparent; it derives from differences in the two semantics for processes. When our processes cannot proceed correctly (e.g., in case of missed deadlines) they reduce to a failed state, whereas the processes in [12] become stuck (indicating violation of progress).

Synopsis. In Sect. 2 we introduce the syntax and the formation rules for asynchronous timed session types. In Sect. 3, we give a modular Labelled Transition System (LTS) for types in isolation (Sect. 3.1) and for compositions of types (Sect. 3.3). The subtyping relation is given in Sect. 3.2 and motivated in Example 8, after introducing the typing rules. We introduce timed asynchronous duality and its properties in Sect. 4. Remarkably, the composition of dual timed asynchronous types enjoys progress when using an urgent receive semantics (Theorem 1). Section 5 presents a calculus for timed processes and Sect. 6 introduces its typing system. The properties of our typing system—Subject Reduction (Theorem 4) and Time Safety (Theorem 5)—are introduced in Sect. 7. Conclusions and related works are in Sect. 8. Proofs and additional material can be found in the online report [11].

2 Asynchronous Timed Session Types

Clocks and predicates. We use the model of time from timed automata [3]. Let $\mathbb{X}$ be a finite set of clocks, let $x_1, \ldots, x_n$ range over clocks, and let each clock take values in $\mathbf{R}_{\geqslant 0}$. Let $t_1, \ldots, t_n$ range over non-negative real numbers and $n_1, \ldots, n_n$ range over non-negative rationals. The set $\mathcal{G}(\mathbb{X})$ of predicates over $\mathbb{X}$ is defined by the following grammar.

$$\delta ::= \texttt{true} \mid x > n \mid x = n \mid x - y > n \mid x - y = n \mid \neg\delta \mid \delta_1 \wedge \delta_2 \quad \text{where } x, y \in \mathbb{X}$$

We derive false, $<$, $\geqslant$, $\leqslant$ in the standard way. Predicates in the form $x - y > n$ and $x - y = n$ are called *diagonal* predicates; in these cases we assume $x \neq y$. Notation $cn(\delta)$ stands for the set of clocks in δ.

Clock valuation and resets. A clock valuation $\nu : \mathbb{X} \mapsto \mathbf{R}_{\geqslant 0}$ returns the time of the clocks in $\mathbb{X}$. We write $\nu + t$ for the valuation mapping all $x \in \mathbb{X}$ to $\nu(x) + t$, ν_0 for the initial valuation (mapping all clocks to 0), and, more generally, ν_t for the valuation mapping all clocks to t. Let $\nu \models \delta$ denote that δ is satisfied by ν. A reset predicate λ over $\mathbb{X}$ is a subset of $\mathbb{X}$. When λ is $\varnothing$ then no reset occurs, otherwise the assignment for each $x \in \lambda$ is set to 0. We write $\nu[\lambda \mapsto 0]$ for the clock assignment that is like ν everywhere except that its assigns 0 to all clocks in λ.

Types. Timed session types, hereafter just types, have the following syntax:

$$T ::= (\delta, S) \mid \texttt{Nat} \mid \texttt{Bool} \mid \ldots$$

$$S ::= !T(\delta, \lambda).S \mid ?T(\delta, \lambda).S \mid \oplus\{\mathrm{l_i}(\delta_i, \lambda_i) : S_i\}_{i \in I} \mid \&\{\mathrm{l_i}(\delta_i, \lambda_i) : S_i\}_{i \in I} \mid \mu\alpha.S \mid \alpha \mid \texttt{end}$$

Sorts T include base types (Nat, Bool, etc.), and sessions (δ, S). Messages of type (δ, S) allow a participant involved in a session to delegate the remaining behaviour S; upon delegation the sender will no longer participate in the delegated session and receiver will execute the protocol described by S under any clock assignment satisfying δ. We denote the set of types with $\mathbb{T}$.

Type $!T(\delta, \lambda).S$ models a *send action* of a payload with sort T. The sending action is allowed at any time that satisfies the guard δ. The clocks in λ are reset upon sending. Type $?T(\delta, \lambda).S$ models the dual *receive action* of a payload with sort T. The receiving types require the endpoint to be ready to receive the message in the precise time window specified by the guard.

Type $\oplus\{\mathrm{l_i}(\delta_i, \lambda_i) : S_i\}_{i \in I}$ is a *select action*: the party chooses a branch $i \in I$, where I is a finite set of indices, selects the label l_i, and continues as prescribed by S_i. Each branch is annotated with a guard δ and reset λ. A branch j can be selected at any time allowed by δ_j. The dual type is $\&\{\mathrm{l_i}(\delta_i, \lambda_i) : S_i\}_{i \in I}$ for *branching actions*. Each branch is annotated with a guard and a reset. The endpoint must be ready to receive the label for j at any time allowed by δ_j (or until another branch is selected).

Recursive type $\mu\alpha.S$ associates a *type variable* α to a recursion body S. We assume that type variables are guarded in the standard way (i.e., they only occur under actions or branches). We let $\mathcal{A}$ denote the set of type variables.

Type end models successful termination.

2.1 Type Formation

The grammar for types allow to generate types that are not implementable in practice, as the one shown in Example 1.

Example 1 (Junk-types). Consider S in (3) under initial clock valuation ν_0.

$$S = ?T(x < 5, \varnothing).!T(x < 2, \varnothing).\mathtt{end} \tag{3}$$

The specified endpoint must be ready to receive a message in the time-window between 0 and 5 time units, as we evaluate $x < 5$ in ν_0. Assume that this receive action happens when $x = 3$, yielding a new state in which: (i) the clock valuation maps x to 3, and (ii) the endpoint must perform a send action while $x < 2$. Evidently, (ii) is no longer possible in the new clock valuation, as the $x < 2$ is now unsatisfiable. We could amend (3) in several ways: (a) by resetting x after the receive action; (b) by restricting the guard of the receive action (e.g., $x < 2$ instead of $x < 5$); or (c) by relaxing the guard of the send action. All these amendments would, however, yield a different type.

In the remainder of this section we introduce formation rules to rule out junk types as the one in Example 1 and characterise types that are well-formed. Intuitively, well-formed types allow, at any point, to perform some action in the present time or at some point in the future, unless the type is `end`.

Judgments. The formation rules for types are defined on judgments of the form

$$A;\ \delta \vdash S$$

where A is an environment assigning type variables to guards, and δ is a guard in $\mathcal{G}(\mathbb{X})$. A is used as an invariant to form recursive types. Guard δ collects the possible 'pasts' from which the next action in S could be executed (unless S is `end`). We use notation $\downarrow \delta$ (the past of δ) for a guard δ' such that $\nu \models \delta'$ if and only if $\exists t : \nu + t \models \delta$. For example, $\downarrow (1 \leqslant x \leqslant 2) = x \leqslant 2$ and $\downarrow (x \geqslant 3) = \mathtt{true}$. Similarly, we use the notation $\delta[\lambda \mapsto 0]$ to denote a guard in which all clocks in λ are reset. For example, $(x \leqslant 3 \wedge y \leqslant 2)[x \mapsto 0] = (x = 0 \wedge y \leqslant 2)$. We use the notation $\delta_1 \subseteq \delta_2$ whenever, for all ν, $\nu \models \delta_1 \implies \nu \models \delta_2$. The past and reset of a guard can be inferred algorithmically, and $\subseteq$ is decidable [8].

$$\frac{}{A;\ \mathtt{true} \vdash \mathtt{end}}\ [\mathtt{end}]$$

$$\frac{\square \in \{!, ?\} \qquad A;\ \gamma \vdash S \qquad \delta[\lambda \mapsto 0] \subseteq \gamma \qquad T \text{ base type}}{A;\ \downarrow \delta \vdash\ \square\, T(\delta, \lambda).S}\ [\mathtt{interact}]$$

$$\frac{\begin{array}{c}\square \in \{!, ?\} \qquad A;\ \gamma \vdash S \qquad \delta[\lambda \mapsto 0] \subseteq \gamma \quad T = (\delta', S') \\ \varnothing;\ \gamma' \vdash S' \quad \delta' \subseteq \gamma'\end{array}}{A;\ \downarrow \delta \vdash\ \square\, T(\delta, \lambda).S}\ [\mathtt{delegate}]$$

$$\frac{\square \in \{\oplus, \&\} \qquad \forall i \in I \quad A;\ \gamma_i \vdash S_i \quad \delta_i[\lambda_i \mapsto 0] \subseteq \gamma_i}{A;\ \downarrow \bigvee_{i \in I} \delta_i \vdash\ \square\, \{\mathrm{l}_i(\delta_i, \lambda_i) : S_i\}_{i \in I}}\ [\mathtt{choice}]$$

$$\frac{A, \alpha : \delta;\ \delta \vdash S}{A;\ \delta \vdash \mu\alpha.S}\ [\mathtt{rec}] \qquad \frac{}{A, \alpha : \delta;\ \delta \vdash \alpha}\ [\mathtt{var}]$$

Rule [end] states that the terminated type is well-formed against any A. The guard of the judgement is true since end is a final state (as end has no continuation, morally, the constraint of its continuation is always satisfiable). Rule [interact] ensures that the past of the current action δ entails the past of the subsequent action γ (considering resets if necessary): this rules out types in which the subsequent action can only be performed in the past. Rules [end] and [interact] are illustrated by the three examples below.

Example 2. The judgment below shows a type being *discarded* after an application of rule [interact] :

$$\varnothing;\ x \leqslant 3 \not\vdash\ ?\mathtt{Nat}(1 \leqslant x \leqslant 3, \varnothing).!\mathtt{Nat}(1 \leqslant x \leqslant 2, \varnothing).\mathtt{end} \tag{4}$$

The premise of [interact] would be $\delta \subseteq \downarrow \gamma$, which does not hold for $\delta = 1 \leqslant x \leqslant 3$ and $\downarrow \gamma = x \leqslant 2$. This means that guard $(1 \leqslant x \leqslant 3, \varnothing)$ of the first action may lead to a state in which guard $1 \leqslant x \leqslant 2$ for the subsequent action is unsatisfiable. If we amend the type in (4) by adding a reset in the first action, we obtain a well-formed type. We show its formation below, where for simplicity we omit obvious preconditions like Nat base type, etc.

$$\dfrac{\dfrac{\dfrac{}{\varnothing;\ \mathtt{true} \vdash \mathtt{end}}\,[\mathtt{end}] \qquad 1 \leqslant x \leqslant 2 \subseteq \mathtt{true}}{\varnothing;\ x \leqslant 2 \vdash !\mathtt{Nat}(1 \leqslant x \leqslant 2, \varnothing).\mathtt{end} \qquad x = 0 \subseteq x \leqslant 2}\,[\mathtt{interact}]}{\varnothing;\ x \leqslant 3 \vdash ?\mathtt{Nat}(1 \leqslant x \leqslant 3, \{x\}).!\mathtt{Nat}(1 \leqslant x \leqslant 2, \varnothing).\mathtt{end}}\,[\mathtt{interact}]$$

Rule [delegate] behaves as [interact] , with two additional premises on the delegated session: (1) S' needs to be well-formed, and (2) the guard of the next action in S' needs to be satisfiable with respect to δ'. Guard δ' is used to ensure a correspondence between the state of the delegating endpoint and that of the receiving endpoint. Rule [choice] is similar to [interact] but requires that there is at least one viable branch (this is accomplished by considering the weaker past $\downarrow \bigvee_{i \in I} \delta_i$) and checking each branch for formation. Rules [rec] and [var] are for recursive types and variables, respectively. In [rec] the guard δ can be easily computed by taking the past of the next action of the in S (or the disjunction if S is a branching or selection). An algorithm for deciding type formation can be found in [11].

Definition 1 (Well-formed types). *We say that S is well-formed against clock valuation ν if $\varnothing;\ \delta \vdash S$ and $\nu \models \delta$, for some guard δ. We say that S is well-formed if it is well formed against ν_0.*

We will tacitly assume types are well-formed, unless otherwise specified. The intuition of well-formedness is that if $A;\ \delta \vdash S$ then S can be run (using the types semantics given in Sect. 3) under any clock valuation ν such that $\nu \models \delta$. In the sequel, we take (well-formed) types equi-recursively [31].

3 Asynchronous Session Types Semantics and Subtyping

We give a compositional semantics of types. First, we focus on types in isolation from their environment and from their queues, which we call *simple type configurations*. Next we define subtyping for simple type configurations. Finally, we consider systems (i.e., composition of types communicating via queues).

$$\frac{\nu \models \delta}{(\nu, !T(\delta,\lambda)).S \xrightarrow{!T} (\nu[\lambda \mapsto 0], S)}\ [\text{snd}] \qquad \frac{\nu \models \delta}{(\nu, ?T(\delta,\lambda).S) \xrightarrow{?T} (\nu[\lambda \mapsto 0], S)}\ [\text{rcv}]$$

$$\frac{\nu \models \delta_j \qquad j \in I}{(\nu, \oplus\{\mathrm{l_i}(\delta_i,\lambda_i) : S_i\}_{i\in I}) \xrightarrow{!\mathrm{l_j}} (\nu[\lambda_j \mapsto 0], S_j)}\ [\text{sel}]$$

$$\frac{\nu \models \delta_j \qquad j \in I}{(\nu, \&\{\mathrm{l_i}(\delta,\lambda_i) : S_i\}_{i\in I}) \xrightarrow{?\mathrm{l_j}} (\nu[\lambda_j \mapsto 0], S_j)}\ [\text{bra}]$$

$$\frac{(\nu, S[\mu\mathtt{t}.S/\mathtt{t}]) \xrightarrow{\ell} (\nu',\ S')}{(\nu, \mu\mathtt{t}.S) \xrightarrow{\ell} (\nu', S')}\ [\text{rec}] \qquad (\nu, S) \xrightarrow{t} (\nu + t, S)\ [\text{time}]$$

Fig. 1. LTS for simple type configurations

3.1 Types in Isolation

The behaviour of *simple type configurations* is described by the Labelled Transition System (LTS) on pairs (ν, S) over $(\mathbb{V} \times \mathcal{S})$, where clock valuation ν gives the values of clocks in a specific state. The LTS is defined over the following labels

$$\ell ::= !m \mid ?m \mid t \mid \tau \qquad\qquad m ::= d \mid \mathrm{l}$$

Label $!m$ denotes an output action of message m and $?m$ an input action of m. A message m can be a sort T (that can be either a higher order message (δ, S) or base type), or a branching label l. The LTS for single types is defined as the least relation satisfying the rules in Fig. 1. Rules [snd], [rcv], [sel], and [bra] can only happen if the constraint of the next action is satisfied in the current clock valuation. Rule [rec] unfolds recursive types, and [time] always lets time elapse.

Let $\mathbf{s}$, $\mathbf{s}'$, $\mathbf{s}_i$ $(i \in \mathbb{N})$ range over simple type configurations (ν, S). We write $\mathbf{s} \xrightarrow{\ell}$ when there exists $\mathbf{s}'$ such that $\mathbf{s} \xrightarrow{\ell} \mathbf{s}'$, and write $\mathbf{s} \xrightarrow{t\,\ell}$ for $\mathbf{s} \xrightarrow{t}\xrightarrow{\ell}$.

3.2 Asynchronous Timed Subtyping

We define subtyping as a partial relation on simple type configurations. As in other subtyping relations for session types we consider send and receive actions dually [14,16,19]. Our subtyping relation is covariant on output actions and contra-variant on input actions, similarly to that of [14]. In this way, our subtyping $S <: S'$ captures the intuition that a process well-typed against S can be safely substituted with a process well-typed against S'. Definition 2, introduces a notation that is useful in the rest of this section.

Definition 2 (Future enabled send/receive). *Action ℓ is future enabled in* s *if* $\exists t : \mathsf{s} \xrightarrow{t\,\ell}$. *We write* $\mathsf{s} \overset{!}{\Rightarrow}$ *(resp.* $\mathsf{s} \overset{?}{\Rightarrow}$*) if there exists a sending action* $!m$ *(resp. a receiving action* $?m$*) that is future enabled in* s.

As common in session types, the communication structure does not allow for mixed choices: the grammar of types enforces choices to be either all input (branching actions), or output (selection actions). From this fact it follows that, given s, reductions $\mathsf{s} \overset{!}{\Rightarrow}$ and $\mathsf{s} \overset{?}{\Rightarrow}$ cannot hold simultaneously.

Definition 3 (Timed Type Simulation). *Fix* $\mathsf{s}_1 = (\nu_1, S_1)$ *and* $\mathsf{s}_2 = (\nu_2, S_2)$. *A relation* $\mathcal{R} \in (\mathbb{V} \times \mathcal{S})^2$ *is a* timed type simulation *if* $(\mathsf{s}_1, \mathsf{s}_2) \in \mathcal{R}$ *implies the following conditions:*

1. $S_1 = \mathtt{end}$ *implies* $S_2 = \mathtt{end}$
2. $\mathsf{s}_1 \xrightarrow{t\,!m_1} \mathsf{s}_1'$ *implies* $\exists \mathsf{s}_2', m_2 : \mathsf{s}_2 \xrightarrow{t\,!m_2} \mathsf{s}_2'$, $(m_2, m_1) \in \mathcal{S}, (\mathsf{s}_1', \mathsf{s}_2') \in \mathcal{R}$
3. $\mathsf{s}_2 \xrightarrow{t\,?m_2} \mathsf{s}_2'$ *implies* $\exists \mathsf{s}_1', m_1 : \mathsf{s}_1 \xrightarrow{t\,?m_1} \mathsf{s}_1'$, $(m_1, m_2) \in \mathcal{S}$, $(\mathsf{s}_1', \mathsf{s}_2') \in \mathcal{R}$
4. $\mathsf{s}_1 \overset{?}{\Rightarrow}$ *implies* $\mathsf{s}_2 \overset{?}{\Rightarrow}$ *and* $\mathsf{s}_2 \overset{!}{\Rightarrow}$ *implies* $\mathsf{s}_1 \overset{!}{\Rightarrow}$

where $\mathcal{S}$ *is the following extension of* $\mathcal{R}$ *to messages: (1)* $(T, T') \in \mathcal{S}$ *if* T *and* T' *are base types, and* T' *is a subtype of* T *by sorts subtyping, e.g.,* $(\mathtt{int}, \mathtt{nat}) \in \mathcal{S}$*; (2)* $(1, 1) \in \mathcal{S}$*; (3)* $((\delta_1, S_1), (\delta_2, S_2)) \in \mathcal{S}$, *if* $\forall \nu_1 \models \delta_1 \, \exists \nu_2 \models \delta_2 : ((\nu_1, S_1), (\nu_2, S_2)) \in \mathcal{R}$ *and* $\forall \nu_2 \models \delta_2 \, \exists \nu_1 \models \delta_1 : ((\nu_1, S_1), (\nu_2, S_2)) \in \mathcal{R}$.

Intuitively, if $(\mathsf{s}_1, \mathsf{s}_2) \in \mathcal{R}$ then any environment that can safely interact with s_2, can do so with s_1. We write that s_2 simulates s_1 whenever s_1 and s_2 are in a timed type simulation. Below, s_2 simulates s_1:

$$\mathsf{s}_1 = (\nu_0, !\mathtt{nat}(x < 5, \varnothing).\mathtt{end}) \quad \mathsf{s}_2 = (\nu_0, !\mathtt{int}(x \leqslant 10, \varnothing).\mathtt{end})$$

Conversely, s_1 does not simulate s_2 because of condition (2). Precisely, s_2 can make a transition $\mathsf{s}_2 \xrightarrow{10\,!\mathtt{int}}$ that cannot be matched by s_1 for two reasons: guard $x < 5$ is no longer satisfiable when $x = 10$, and $(\mathtt{nat}, \mathtt{int}) \notin \mathcal{S}$ since $\mathtt{int}$ is not a subtype of $\mathtt{nat}$. For receive actions, instead, we could substitute s with s' if s' had at least the receiving capabilities of s. Condition (4) in Definition 3 rules out relations that include, e.g., $((\nu, ?T(\mathtt{true}, \varnothing).\mathtt{end}), (\nu, !T(\mathtt{true}, \varnothing).\mathtt{end}))$.

Live simple type configurations. In our subtyping definition we are interested in simple type configurations that are not stuck. Consider the example below:

$$(\nu, !\mathtt{Int}(x \leqslant 10, \varnothing).\mathtt{end}) \tag{5}$$

The simple type configuration in (5) would not be stuck if $\nu = \nu_0$, but would be stuck for any $\nu = \nu'[x \mapsto 10]$. Definition 4 gives a formal definition of simple type configurations that are not stuck, i.e., that are *live*.

Definition 4 (Live simple type configuration). *A simple configuration* (ν, S) *is said* live *if:*

$$S = \mathtt{end} \quad \text{or } \exists t, \ell : (\nu, S) \xrightarrow{t \circ m} \qquad (\circ \in \{!, ?\})$$

Observe that for all well-formed S, (ν_0, S) is live.

Subtyping for simple type configurations. We can now define subtyping for simple type configurations and state its decidability.

Definition 5 (Subtyping). $\mathbf{s}_1$ *is a subtype of* $\mathbf{s}_2$*, written* $\mathbf{s}_1 <: \mathbf{s}_2$*, if there exists a timed type simulation* $\mathcal{R}$ on live simple type configurations *such that* $(\mathbf{s}_1, \mathbf{s}_2) \in \mathcal{R}$*. We write* $S_1 <: S_2$ *when* $(\nu_0, S_1) <: (\nu_0, S_2)$*. Abusing the notation, we write* $m <: m'$ *iff there exists* $\mathcal{S}$ *such that* $(m, m') \in \mathcal{S}$*.*

Subtyping has been shown to be decidable in the untimed setting [19] and in the timed first order setting [6]. In [6], decidability is shown through a reduction to model checking of timed automata networks. The result in [6] can be extended to higher-order messages using the techniques in [3], based on finite representations (called regions) of possibly infinite sets of clock valuations.

Proposition 1 (Decidability of subtyping). *Checking if* $(\delta_1, S_1) <: (\delta_2, S_2)$ *is decidable.*

3.3 Types with Queues, and Their Composition

As interactions are asynchronous, the behaviour of types must capture the states in which messages are in transit. To do this, we extend simple type configurations with queues. A *configuration* $\mathbf{S}$ is a triple $(\nu, S, \mathtt{M})$ where ν is clock valuation, S is a type and $\mathtt{M}$ a FIFO unbounded queue of the following form:

$$\mathtt{M} ::= \varnothing \mid m; \mathtt{M}$$

$\mathtt{M}$ contains the messages sent by the co-party of S and not yet received by S. We write $\mathtt{M}$ for $\mathtt{M}; \varnothing$, and call $(\nu, S, \mathtt{M})$ *initial* if $\nu = \nu_0$ and $\mathtt{M} = \varnothing$.

Composing types. Configurations are composed into *systems.* We denote $\mathbf{S} \mid \mathbf{S}'$ as the parallel composition of the two configurations $\mathbf{S}$ and $\mathbf{S}'$.

The labelled transition rules for systems are given in Fig. 2. Rule (snd) is for send actions. A send action can occur only if the time constraint of S is satisfied (by the premise, which uses either rule [snd] or [sel] in Fig. 1). Rule (que) models actions on queues. A queue is always ready to receive any message m. Rule (rcv) is for receive actions, where a message is read from the queue. A receiving action can only occur if the time constraint of S is satisfied (by the premise, which uses either rule [rcv] or [bra] in Fig. 1). The message is removed from the head of the queue of the receiving configuration. The third clause in the premise uses the notion of subtyping (Definition 3) for basic sorts, labels, and higher order messages. Rule (crcv) is the action of a configuration pulling a message of its queue. Rule (com) is for communication between a sending configuration and a buffer. Rule (ctime) lets time elapse in the same way for all configurations in a system. Rule (time) models time passing for single configurations. Time passing is subject to two constrains, expressed by the second and third conditions in the premise. Condition $(\nu, S) \overset{!}{\Rightarrow}$ requires the time action t to preserve the satisfiability of some send action. For example, in configuration

$$\frac{(\nu, S) \xrightarrow{!m} (\nu', S')}{(\nu, S, \mathtt{M}) \xrightarrow{!m} (\nu', S', \mathtt{M})}\ (\text{snd}) \qquad (\nu, S, \mathtt{M}) \xrightarrow{?m} (\nu, S, \mathtt{M}; m)\ (\text{que})$$

$$\frac{(\nu, S) \xrightarrow{?m'} (\nu', S') \quad m' <: m}{(\nu, S, m; \mathtt{M}) \xrightarrow{\tau} (\nu', S', \mathtt{M})}\ (\text{rcv}) \qquad \frac{\mathbf{S}_1 \xrightarrow{\tau} \mathbf{S}_1'}{\mathbf{S}_1 \mid \mathbf{S}_2 \xrightarrow{\tau} \mathbf{S}_1' \mid \mathbf{S}_2}\ (\text{crcv})$$

$$\frac{\mathbf{S}_1 \xrightarrow{!m} \mathbf{S}_1' \quad \mathbf{S}_2 \xrightarrow{?m} \mathbf{S}_2'}{\mathbf{S}_1 \mid \mathbf{S}_2 \xrightarrow{\tau} \mathbf{S}_1' \mid \mathbf{S}_2'}\ (\text{com}) \qquad \frac{\mathbf{S}_1 \xrightarrow{t} \mathbf{S}_1' \quad \mathbf{S}_2 \xrightarrow{t} \mathbf{S}_2'}{\mathbf{S}_1 \mid \mathbf{S}_2 \xrightarrow{t} \mathbf{S}_1' \mid \mathbf{S}_2'}\ (\text{ctime})$$

$$\frac{(\nu, S) \xrightarrow{t} (\nu', S) \qquad (\nu, S) \overset{!}{\Rightarrow} \text{ implies } (\nu', S) \overset{!}{\Rightarrow} \qquad \forall t' < t : (\nu + t', S, \mathtt{M}) \overset{\tau}{\not\rightarrow}}{(\nu, S, \mathtt{M}) \xrightarrow{t} (\nu', S, \mathtt{M})}\ (\text{time})$$

Fig. 2. LTS for systems. We omit the symmetric rules of (crcv), and (csnd).

$(\nu_0, !T(x < 2, \varnothing).S, \varnothing)$, a transition with label 2 would *not* preserve any send action (hence would not be allowed), while a transition with label 1.8 would be allowed by condition $(\nu, S) \overset{!}{\Rightarrow}$. Condition $\forall t' < t : (\nu + t', S, \mathtt{M}) \overset{\tau}{\not\rightarrow}$ in the premise of rule (time) checks that there is no ready message to be received in the queue. This is to model urgency: when a configuration is in a receiving state and a message is in the queue then the receiving action must happen without delay. For example, $(\nu_0, ?T(x < 2, \varnothing).S, \varnothing)$ can make a transition with label 1, but $(\nu_0, ?T(x < 2, \varnothing).S, m)$ cannot make any time transition. Below we show two examples of system executions. Example 3 illustrates a good communication, thanks to urgency. We also illustrate in Example 4 that without an urgent semantics the system in Example 3 gets stuck.

Example 3 (A good communication). Consider the following types:

$$S_1 = !T(x \leqslant 1, x).?T(x \leqslant 2).\mathtt{end} \qquad S_2 = ?T(y \leqslant 1, y).!T(y \leqslant 2).\mathtt{end}$$

System $(\nu[x \mapsto 0], S_1, \varnothing) \mid (\nu[x \mapsto 0], S_2, \varnothing)$ can make a time step with label 0.5 by (ctime), yielding the system in (6)

$$(\nu[x \mapsto 0.5], S_1, \varnothing) \mid (\nu[x \mapsto 0.5], S_2, \varnothing) \tag{6}$$

The system in (6) can move by a τ step thanks to (com): the left-hand side configuration makes a step with label $!T$ by (snd) while the right-hand side configuration makes a step $?T$ by (que), yielding system (7) below.

$$(\nu[x \mapsto 0], ?T(x \leqslant 2).\mathtt{end}, \varnothing) \mid (\nu[y \mapsto 0.5], S_2, T) \tag{7}$$

The right-hand side configuration in the system in (7) must *urgently* receive message T due to the third clause in the premise of rule (time). Hence, the only possible step forward for (7) is by (crcv) yielding the system in (8).

$$(\nu[x \mapsto 0], ?T(x \leqslant 2).\mathtt{end}, \varnothing) \mid (\nu[y \mapsto 0], !T(y \leqslant 2).\mathtt{end}, \varnothing) \tag{8}$$

Example 4 (In absence of urgency). Without urgency, the system in (7) from Example 3 may get stuck. Assume the third clause of rule (time) was removed: this would allow (7) to make a time step with label 0.5, followed by a step by (rcv) yielding the system in (9), where clock y is reset after the receive action.

$$(\nu[x \mapsto 0.5], ?T(x \leqslant 2).\texttt{end}, \varnothing) \mid (\nu[y \mapsto 0], !T(y \leqslant 2).\texttt{end}, \varnothing) \tag{9}$$

followed by a τ step by (com) reaching the following state:

$$(\nu[x \mapsto 2.5], ?T(x \leqslant 2).\texttt{end}, T) \mid (\nu[y \mapsto 0], \texttt{end}, \varnothing) \tag{10}$$

The message in the queue in (10) will never be received as the guard $x \leqslant 2$ is not satisfiable now or at any point in the future. This system is stuck. Instead, thanks to urgency, the clocks of the configurations of system (8) have been 'synchronised' after the receive action, preventing the system from getting stuck.

4 Timed Asynchronous Duality

We introduce a timed extension of duality. As in untimed duality, we let each send/select action be complemented by a corresponding receive/branching action. Moreover, we require time constraints and resets to match.

Definition 6 (Timed duality). *The dual type $\overline{S}$ of S is defined as follows:*

$$\overline{!T(\delta,\lambda).S} = ?T(\delta,\lambda).\overline{S} \qquad \overline{?T(\delta,\lambda).S} = !T(\delta,\lambda).\overline{S} \qquad \overline{\mu\alpha.S} = \mu\alpha.\overline{S}$$

$$\overline{\oplus\{\mathrm{l_i}(\delta_i,\lambda_i) : S_i\}_{i\in I}} = \&\{\mathrm{l_i}(\delta_i,\lambda_i) : \overline{S_i}\}_{i\in I} \qquad \overline{\alpha} = \alpha$$

$$\overline{\&\{\mathrm{l_i}(\delta_i,\lambda_i) : S_i\}_{i\in I}} = \oplus\{\mathrm{l_i}(\delta_i,\lambda_i) : \overline{S_i}\}_{i\in I} \qquad \overline{\texttt{end}} = \texttt{end}$$

Duality with urgent receive semantics enjoys the following properties: systems with dual types fulfil progress (Theorem 1); behaviour (resp. progress) of a system is preserved by the substitution of a type with a subtype (Theorem 2) (resp. Theorem 3). A system enjoys progress if it reaches states that are either final or that allow further communications, possibly after a delay. Recall that we assume types to be well-formed (cf. Definition 1): Theorems 1, 2, and 3 rely on this assumption.

Definition 7 (Type progress). *We say that a system $(\nu, S, \texttt{M})$ is a* success *if $S = \texttt{end}$ and $\texttt{M} = \varnothing$. We say that $\mathbf{S}_1 \mid \mathbf{S}_2$ satisfies* progress *if:*

$$\mathbf{S}_1 \mid \mathbf{S}_2 \longrightarrow^* \mathbf{S}'_1 \mid \mathbf{S}'_2 \quad \Longrightarrow \quad \mathbf{S}'_1 \textit{ and } \mathbf{S}'_2 \textit{ are success or } \exists t : \mathbf{S}'_1 \mid \mathbf{S}'_2 \xrightarrow{t\,\tau}$$

Theorem 1 (Duality progress). *System $(\nu_0, S, \varnothing) \mid (\nu_0, \overline{S}, \varnothing)$ enjoys progress.*

We show that subtyping does not introduce new behaviour, via the usual notion of timed simulation [1]. Let $\mathbf{c}, \mathbf{c}_1, \mathbf{c}_2$ range over systems. Fix $\mathbf{c}_1 = (\nu^1_1, S^1_1, \texttt{M}^1_1) \mid (\nu^1_2, S^1_2, \texttt{M}^1_2)$, and $\mathbf{c}_2 = (\nu^2_1, S^2_1, \texttt{M}^2_1) \mid (\nu^2_2, S^2_2, \texttt{M}^2_2)$. We say that a binary relation over systems preserves end if: $S^i_1 = \texttt{end} \wedge \texttt{M}^i_1 = \varnothing$ iff $S^i_2 = \texttt{end} \wedge \texttt{M}^i_2 = \varnothing$ for all $i \in \{1, 2\}$. Write $\mathbf{c}_1 \lesssim \mathbf{c}_2$ if $(\mathbf{c}_1, \mathbf{c}_2)$ are in a timed simulation that preserves end.

Theorem 2 (Safe substitution). *If* $S' <: \overline{S}$, *then* $(\nu_0, S, \varnothing) \mid (\nu_0, S', \varnothing) \lesssim (\nu_0, S, \varnothing) \mid (\nu_0, \overline{S}, \varnothing)$.

Theorem 3 (Progressing substitution). *If* $S' <: \overline{S}$, *then* $(\nu_0, S, \varnothing) \mid (\nu_0, S', \varnothing)$ *satisfies progress.*

5 A Calculus for Asynchronous Timed Processes

We introduce our asynchronous calculus for timed processes. The calculus abstracts implementations that execute one or more sessions. We let $P, P', Q, \ldots$ range over processes, X range over process variables, and define $n \in \mathbb{R}_{\geqslant 0} \cup \{\infty\}$. We use the notation $\boldsymbol{a}$ for ordered sequences of channels or variables.

$$
\begin{array}{rlllr}
P ::= & \overline{a}\,v.P & \mid & \texttt{delay}(\delta).\,P & \text{(time-consuming)} \\
\mid & a \triangleleft \mathrm{l}.\,P & \mid & a^n(b).\,P & \\
\mid & \texttt{if } v \texttt{ then } P \texttt{ else } P & \mid & a^n \triangleright \{\mathrm{l}_i : P_i\}_{i \in I} & \\
\mid & P \mid P & \mid & \texttt{failed} & \text{(run-time)} \\
\mid & 0 & \mid & \texttt{delay}(t).\,P & \\
\mid & \texttt{def } D \texttt{ in } P & & & \\
\mid & X\langle \boldsymbol{a}\,;\,\boldsymbol{a}\rangle & & D ::= X(\boldsymbol{a}\,;\,\boldsymbol{a}) = P & \\
\mid & (\nu ab)P & & & \\
\mid & ab : h & & h ::= \varnothing \mid h \cdot v \mid h \cdot a &
\end{array}
$$

$\overline{a}\,v.P$ sends a value v on channel a and continues as P. Similarly, $a \triangleleft \mathrm{l}.\,P$ sends a label l on channel a and continue as P. Process `if` v `then` P `else` Q behaves as either P or Q depending on the boolean value v. Process $P \mid Q$ is for parallel composition of P and Q, and 0 is the idle process. `def` D `in` P is the standard recursive process: D is a declaration, and P is a process that may contain recursive calls. In recursive calls $X\langle \boldsymbol{a}\,;\,\boldsymbol{a}\rangle$ the first list of parameters has to be instantiated with values of ground types, while the second with channels. Recursive calls are instantiated with equations $X(\boldsymbol{a}\,;\,\boldsymbol{a})$ in D. Process $(\nu ab)P$ is for scope restriction of endpoints a and b. Process $ab : h$ is a queue with name ab (colloquially used to indicate that it contains messages in transit from a to b) and content h. (νab) binds endpoints a and b, and queues ab and ba in P.

There are two kind of time-consuming processes: those performing a time-consuming action (e.g., method invocation, sleep), and those waiting to receive a message. We model the first kind of processes with $\texttt{delay}(\delta).\,P$, and the second kind of processes with $a^n(b).\,P$ (receive) and $a^n \triangleright \{\mathrm{l}_i : P_i\}_{i \in I}$ (branching). In $\texttt{delay}(\delta).\,P$, δ is a constraints as those defined for types, but on one single clock x. The name of the clock here is immaterial: clock x is used as a syntactic tool to define intervals for the time-consuming (delay) action. In this sense, assume x is bound in $\texttt{delay}(\delta).\,P$. Process $\texttt{delay}(\delta).\,P$ consumes any amount of time t such that t is a solution of δ. For example $\texttt{delay}(x \leqslant 3).\,P$ consumes any value between 0 to 3 time units, then behaves as P. Process $a^n(b).\,P$ receive a message on channel a, instantiates b and continue as P. Parameter n models different receive primitives: non-blocking ($n = 0$), blocking ($n = \infty$), and blocking with timeout ($n \in \mathbb{R}^{\geqslant 0}$). If $n \in \mathbb{R}^{\geqslant 0}$ and no message is in the queue, the process waits n time units before moving into a failed state. If n is set to ∞ the process models a blocking primitive without timeout. Branching process $a^n \triangleright \{l_i : P_i\}_{i \in I}$ is similar, but receives a label l_i and continues as P_i.

Run-time processes are not written by programmers and only appear upon execution. Process `failed` is the process that has violated a time constraint. We say that P is a *failed state* if it has `failed` as a syntactic sub-term. Process $\mathtt{delay}(t).\,P$ delays for exactly t time units.

Well-formed processes. Sessions are modelled as processes of the following form

$$(\nu ab)(P \mid ab : h \mid ba : h')$$

where P is the process for endpoints a and b, ab is the queue for messages from a to b, and ba is the queues for messages from b to a. A process can have more than one ongoing session. For each, we expect that all necessary queues are present and well-placed. We ensure that queues are well-placed via a well-formedness property for processes (see [11] for an inductive definition). Well-formedness rules out processes of the following form:

$$(\nu ab)\ (a^n(c).\,(ba : h' \mid P) \mid Q \mid ab : h) \tag{11}$$

The process in (11) in not well-formed since queue ba for communications to endpoint a is not usable as it is in the continuation of the receive action. Well-formedness of processes is necessary to our safety results. We check well-formedness orthogonally to the typing system for the sake of simpler typing rules. While well-formedness ensures the absence of misplaced queues, the presence of an appropriate pair of queues for every session is ensured by the typing rules.

Session creation. Usually well-formedness is ensured by construction, as sessions are created by a specific (synchronous) reduction rule [10,21]. This kind of session creation is cumbersome in the timed setting as it allows delays that are not captured by protocols, hence well-typed processes may miss deadlines. Other work on timed session types [12] avoids this problem by requiring that all session creations occur before any delay action. Our calculus allows session to be created at any point, even after delays. In (12) a session with endpoints c and d is created after a send action (assume P includes the queues for this new session).

$$(\nu ab)\,(\overline{a}\,v.\mathtt{delay}(x \leqslant 3).\,(\nu cd)(P) \mid Q \mid ab : h \mid ba : h') \tag{12}$$

A process like the one in (12) may be thought as a dynamic session creation that happens synchronously (as in [10,21]), but assuming that all participants are ready to engage without delays. Our approach yields a simplification to the calculus (syntax and reduction rules) and, yet, a more general treatment of session initiation than the work in [12].

$$\frac{P \rightharpoonup P'}{P \longrightarrow P'} \qquad \frac{P \rightsquigarrow P'}{P \longrightarrow P'} \qquad \texttt{[Red1/Red2]}$$

$$\overline{a}\, v.P \mid ab : h \;\rightharpoonup\; P \mid ab : h \cdot v \qquad \texttt{[Send]}$$

$$a^n(c).\, P \mid ba : v \cdot h \;\rightharpoonup\; P[v/c] \mid ba : h \qquad \texttt{[Rcv]}$$

$$a \lhd \mathrm{l}.\, P \mid ab : h \;\rightharpoonup\; P \mid ab : h \cdot \mathtt{l} \qquad \texttt{[Sel]}$$

$$a^n \rhd \{\mathrm{l}_i : P_i\}_{i \in I} \mid ba : \mathtt{l}_j \cdot h \;\rightharpoonup\; P_j \mid ba : h \qquad (j \in I) \qquad \texttt{[Bra]}$$

$$\frac{\models \delta[t/x]}{\mathtt{delay}(\delta).\, P \;\rightharpoonup\; \mathtt{delay}(t).\, P} \qquad \texttt{[Det]}$$

$$\mathtt{if\ true\ then}\ P\ \mathtt{else}\ Q \;\rightharpoonup\; P \qquad \texttt{[IfT]}$$

$$\frac{P \rightharpoonup P'}{P \mid Q \rightharpoonup P' \mid Q} \qquad \frac{P \rightharpoonup P'}{\mathtt{def}\ D\ \mathtt{in}\ P \rightharpoonup \mathtt{def}\ D\ \mathtt{in}\ P'} \qquad \texttt{[Par/Def]}$$

$$\mathtt{def}\ X(\boldsymbol{a}' \,;\, \boldsymbol{b}') = P'\ \mathtt{in}\ X\langle \boldsymbol{v} \,;\, \boldsymbol{b}\rangle \mid Q \;\rightharpoonup\; \mathtt{def}\ X(\boldsymbol{a}' \,;\, \boldsymbol{b}') = P'\ \mathtt{in}\ P'[\boldsymbol{v}, \boldsymbol{b}/\boldsymbol{a}', \boldsymbol{b}'] \mid Q \qquad \texttt{[Rec]}$$

$$\frac{P \equiv P' \quad P' \rightharpoonup Q' \quad Q' \equiv Q}{P \rightharpoonup Q} \qquad \frac{P \rightharpoonup P'}{(\nu ab)P \rightharpoonup (\nu ab)P'} \qquad \texttt{[AStr/AScope]}$$

$$\frac{P \equiv P' \quad P' \rightsquigarrow Q' \quad Q' \equiv Q}{P \rightsquigarrow Q} \qquad P \rightsquigarrow \Phi_t(P) \qquad \texttt{[TStr/Delay]}$$

Fig. 3. Reduction for processes (rule [IfF], symmetric for [IfT] is omitted).

$$\Phi_t(0) = 0 \qquad \Phi_t(ab : h) = ab : h \qquad \Phi_t(\mathtt{failed}) = \mathtt{failed}$$

$$\Phi_t(P_1 \mid P_2) = \Phi_t(P_1) \mid \Phi_t(P_2),\ \text{if}\ \mathtt{Wait}(P_i) \cap \mathtt{NEQueue}(P_j) = \emptyset,\ i \neq j \in \{1, 2\}$$

$$\Phi_t(\mathtt{delay}(t').\, P) = \mathtt{delay}(t' - t).\, P \quad \text{if}\ t' \geqslant t$$

$$\Phi_t(a^{t'}(a').\, P) = \begin{cases} a^{t'-t}(a').\, P & \text{if}\ t' \geqslant t \\ \mathtt{failed} & \text{otherwise} \end{cases}$$

$$\Phi_t(a^{\infty}(a').\, P) = a^{\infty}(a').\, P$$

$$\Phi_t((\nu ab)P) = (\nu ab)\Phi_t(P)$$

$$\Phi_t(\mathtt{def}\ D\ \mathtt{in}\ P) = \mathtt{def}\ D\ \mathtt{in}\ \Phi_t(P)$$

Fig. 4. Time-passing function $\Phi_t(P)$. Rule for $a^{t'} \rhd \{\mathrm{l}_i : P_i\}_{i \in I}$ is omitted for brevity. $\phi_t(P)$ is undefined in the remaining cases.

Reduction for processes. Processes are considered modulo structural equivalence, denoted by $\equiv$, and defined by adding the following rule for delays to the standard ones [28]: $\texttt{delay}(0).\, P \equiv P$. Reduction rules for processes are given in Fig. 3. A reduction step $\longrightarrow$ can happen because of either an instantaneous step $\rightharpoonup$ by [Red1] or time-consuming step $\rightsquigarrow$ by [Red2]. Rules [Send], [Rcv], [Sel], and [Bra] are the usual asynchronous communication rules. Rule [Det] models the random occurrence of a precise delay t, with t being a solution of δ. The other untimed rules, [IfT], [Par], [Def], [Rec], [AStr], and [AScope] are standard. Note that rule [Par] does not allow time passing, which is handled by rule [Delay]. Rule [TStr] is the timed version of [AStr]. Rule [Delay] applies a *time-passing* function Φ_t (defined in Fig. 4) which distributes the delay t across all the parts of a process. $\Phi_t(P)$ is a partial function: it is undefined if P can immediately make an urgent action, such as evaluation of expressions or output actions. If $\Phi_t(P)$ is defined, it returns the process resulting from letting t time units elapse in P. $\Phi_t(P)$ may return a failed state, if delay t makes a deadline in P expire. The definition of $\Phi_t(P_1 \mid P_2)$ relies on two auxiliary functions: $\texttt{Wait}(P)$ and $\texttt{NEQueue}(P)$ (see [11] for the full definition). $\texttt{Wait}(P)$ returns the set of channels on which P (or some syntactic sub-term of P) is waiting to receive a message/label. $\texttt{NEQueue}(P)$ returns the set of endpoints with a non-empty inbound queue. For example, $\texttt{Wait}(a^t(b).\, Q) = \texttt{Wait}(a^t \rhd \{l_i : P_i\}_{i\in I}) = \{a\}$ and $\texttt{NEQueue}(ba : h) = \{a\}$ given that $h \neq \varnothing$. $\Phi_t(P_1 \mid P_2)$ is defined only if no urgent action could immediately happen in $P_1 \mid P_2$. For example, $\Phi_t(P_1 \mid P_2)$ is undefined for $P_1 = a^t(b).\, Q$ and $P_2 = ba : v$.

In the rest of this section we show the reductions of two processes: one with urgent actions (Example 5), and one to a failed state (Example 6). We omit processes that are immaterial for the illustration (e.g., unused queues).

Example 5 (Urgency and undefined Φ_t). We show the reduction of process $P = (\nu ab)(\overline{a}\,\text{'Hi'}.Q \mid ab : \varnothing \mid b^{10}(c).\, P')$ that has an urgent action. Process P can make the following reduction by [Send]:

$$P \rightharpoonup (\nu ab)(Q \mid ab : \text{'Hi'} \mid b^{10}(c).\, P')$$

At this point, to apply rule [Delay], say with $t = 5$, we need to apply the time-passing function as shown below:

$$\Phi_5((\nu ab)(\overline{a}\,\text{'Hi'}.Q \mid ab : \text{'Hi'} \mid b^{10}(c).\, P')) = (\nu ab)(\overline{a}\,\text{'Hi'}.Q \mid \Phi_5(ab : \text{'Hi'} \mid b^{10}(c).\, P'))$$

which is undefined. $\Phi_5(ab : \varnothing \mid b^{10}(c).\, P')$ is undefined because $\texttt{Wait}(b^{10}(c).\, P) \cap \texttt{NEQueue}(ab : \text{'Hi'}) = \{b\} \neq \varnothing$. Since $\Phi_5(P')$ is undefined. Instead, the message in queue ab can be received by rule [Rcv]:

$$(\nu ab)(Q \mid ab : \text{'Hi'} \mid b^{10}(c).\, P') \rightharpoonup (\nu ab)(Q \mid ab : \varnothing \mid P[\text{'Hi'}/c])$$

Example 6 (An execution with failure). We show a reduction to a failing state of a process with a non-blocking receive action (expecting a message immediately) composed with another process that sends a message after a delay.

$$\begin{array}{lll} & \mathtt{delay}(x=3).\,\overline{a}\,\text{`Hi'}.Q \mid ab:\varnothing \mid b^0(c).\,P & \text{apply [Det]} \\ \rightharpoonup & \mathtt{delay}(3).\,\overline{a}\,\text{`Hi'}.Q \mid ab:\varnothing \mid b^0(c).\,P = P' & \text{apply [Delay] with } t=3 \\ \rightharpoonup & \Phi_3(P') & \end{array}$$

The application of the time-passing function to P' yields a failing state (a message is not received in time) as shown below, where the second equality holds since $\mathtt{Wait}(b^0(c).\,P) \cap \mathtt{NEQueue}(ab:\varnothing) = \varnothing$:

$$\begin{array}{l} \Phi_3(\mathtt{delay}(3).\,\overline{a}\,\text{`Hi'}.Q \mid b^0(c).\,P \mid ab:\varnothing) = \\ \Phi_3(\mathtt{delay}(3).\,\overline{a}\,\text{`Hi'}.Q) \mid \Phi_3(b^0(c).\,P \mid \Phi_3(ab:\varnothing)) = \\ \mathtt{delay}(0).\,\overline{a}\,\text{`Hi'}.Q \mid \mathtt{failed} \mid ab:\varnothing \end{array}$$

6 Typing for Asynchronous Timed Processes

We validate programs against specifications using judgements of the form $\Gamma \vdash P \rhd \Delta$. Environments are defined as follows:

$$\begin{array}{ll} \Delta ::= \varnothing \mid \Delta, a:(\nu, S) \mid \Delta, ab:\mathtt{M} & \Theta ::= \varnothing \mid \Theta \cup \{\Delta\} \\ \Gamma ::= \varnothing \mid \Gamma, a:T \mid \Gamma, X:(\boldsymbol{T};\Theta) & \end{array}$$

Environment Δ is a session environment, used to keep track of the ongoing sessions. When $\Delta(a) = (\nu, S)$ it means that the process being validated is acting as a role in session a specified by S, and ν is the clock valuation describing a (virtual) time in which the next action in S may be executed. We write $\mathrm{dom}(\Delta)$ for the set of variables and channels in Δ. Environment Γ maps variables a to sorts T and process variables X to pairs $(\boldsymbol{T};\Theta)$, where $\boldsymbol{T}$ is a vector of sorts and Θ is a set of session environments. The mapping of process variable is used to type recursive processes: $\boldsymbol{T}$ is used to ensure well-typed instantiation of the recursion parameters, and Θ is used to model the set of possible scenarios when a new iteration begins.

Notation, assumptions, and auxiliary definitions. We write $\Delta + t$ for the session environment obtained by incrementing all clock valuations in the codomain of Δ by t.

Definition 8. *We define the disjoint union $A \uplus B$ of sets of clocks A and B as:*

$$A \uplus B = \{in_l(x) \mid x \in A\} \cup \{in_r(x) \mid x \in B\}$$

where in_l and in_r are one to one endofunctions on clocks and, for all $x \in A$ and $y \in B$, $in_l(x) \neq in_r(y)$. With an abuse of notation, we define the disjoint union of clock valuations ν_1, ν_2, in symbols $\nu_1 \uplus \nu_2$, as a clock valuation satisfying:

$$\nu_1 \uplus \nu_2(in_l(x)) = \nu_1(x) \qquad \nu_1 \uplus \nu_2(in_r(x)) = \nu_2(x)$$

We use the symbol $\biguplus$ for the iterate disjoint union.

For a configuration (ν, S) we define $\texttt{val}((\nu, \texttt{S})) = \nu$, and $\texttt{type}((\nu, \texttt{S})) = S$. We overload function val to session environments Δ as follows:

$$\texttt{val}(\Delta) = \biguplus_{a \in \text{dom}(\Delta)} \texttt{val}(\Delta(a))$$

We require Θ to satisfy the following three conditions:

1. If $\Delta \in \Theta$ and $\Delta(a) = (\nu, S)$, then S is well-formed (Definition 1) against ν;
2. For all $\Delta_1 \in \Theta$, $\Delta_2 \in \Theta$: $\texttt{type}(\Delta_1(a)) = S$ iff $\texttt{type}(\Delta_2(a)) = S$;
3. There is guard δ such that:

$$\{\nu \mid \nu \models \delta\} = \bigcup_{\Delta \in \Theta} \texttt{val}(\Delta).$$

The last condition ensures that Θ is finitely representable, and is key for decidability of type checking.

Example 7. We show some examples of Θ that do or do not satisfy the last requirement above. Let $S_1 = !T(x \leqslant 2).\texttt{end}$ and $S_2 = !T(y \leqslant 2).\texttt{end}$, and let:

$$\begin{aligned}
\Theta_1 &= \{\Delta \mid \Delta(a) = (\nu_1, S_1) \wedge \Delta(b) = (\nu_2, S_2) \wedge \nu_1(x) \leqslant 2 \wedge \nu_1(x) = \nu_2(y)\};\\
\Theta_2 &= \{\Delta \mid \Delta(a) = (\nu_1, S_1) \wedge \Delta(b) = (\nu_2, S_2) \wedge \nu_1(x) \leqslant \sqrt{2} \wedge \nu_1(x) = \nu_2(y)\};\\
\Theta_3 &= \{\Delta \mid \Delta(a) = (\nu_1, S_1) \wedge \Delta(b) = (\nu_2, S_2) \wedge \nu_1(x) + \nu_2(y) = 2\}.
\end{aligned}$$

We have that Θ_1 satisfies condition (3): let $\delta_1 = x \leqslant 2 \wedge y - x = 0$. It is easy to see that $\{\nu \mid \nu \models \delta_1\} = \bigcup_{\Delta \in \Theta} \texttt{val}(\Delta)$. For Θ_2, a candidate proposition would be $\delta_2 = x \leqslant \sqrt{2} \wedge y - x = 0$. However, δ_2 can not be derived with the syntax of propositions, as $\sqrt{2}$ is irrational. Indeed, Θ_2 does not satisfy the condition. For Θ_3, let $\delta_3 = x + y = 2$. Again, δ_3 is not a guard, as additive constraints in the form $x + y = n$ are not allowed. Indeed, also Θ_3 does not satisfy the condition.

In the following, we write $\boldsymbol{a} : \boldsymbol{T}$ for $a_1 : T_1, \ldots, a_n : T_n$ when $\boldsymbol{a} = a_1, \ldots, a_n$ and $\boldsymbol{T} = T_1, \ldots, T_n$ (assuming $\boldsymbol{a}$ and $\boldsymbol{T}$ have the same number of elements). Similarly for $\boldsymbol{b} : (\boldsymbol{\nu}, \boldsymbol{S})$. In the typing rules, we use a few auxiliary definitions: Definition 9 (t-reading Δ) checks if any ongoing sessions in a Δ can perform an input action within a given timespan, and Definition 10 (Compatibility of configurations) extends the notion of duality to systems that are not in an initial state.

Definition 9 (t-reading Δ). *Session environment Δ is t-reading if there exist some $a \in \text{dom}(\Delta)$, $t' < t$ and m such that: $\Delta(a) = (\nu, S) \wedge (\nu + t', S) \xrightarrow{?m}$.*

Namely, Δ is t-reading if any of the open sessions in the mapping prescribe a read action within the time-frame between ν and $\nu + t$. Definition 9 is used in the typing rules for time-consuming processes – [Vrcv], [Drcv], and [Del$t$] – to 'disallow' derivations when a (urgent) receive may happen.

Definition 10 (Compatibility of configurations). *Configuration $(\nu_1, S_1, \texttt{M}_1)$ is compatible with $(\nu_2, S_2, \texttt{M}_2)$, written $(\nu_1, S_1, \texttt{M}_1) \bot (\nu_2, S_2, \texttt{M}_2)$, if:*

1. $\mathtt{M}_1 = \varnothing \vee \mathtt{M}_2 = \varnothing$,
2. $\forall i \neq j \in \{1,2\} : \mathtt{M}_i = m;\mathtt{M}_i' \Rightarrow \exists \nu_i', S_i', m' : (\nu_i, S_i) \xrightarrow{?m'} (\nu_i', S_i') \wedge m <: m' \wedge (\nu_i', S_i', \mathtt{M}_i') \bot (\nu_j, S_j, \mathtt{M}_j)$,
3. $\mathtt{M}_1 = \varnothing \wedge \mathtt{M}_2 = \varnothing \Rightarrow \nu_1 = \nu_2 \wedge S_1 = \overline{S_2}$.

By condition (3) initial configurations are compatible when they include dual types, i.e., $(\nu_0, S, \varnothing)\bot(\nu_0, \overline{S}, \varnothing)$. By condition (2) two configurations may temporarily misalign as execution proceeds: one may have read a message from its queue, while the other has not, as long as the former is ready to receive it immediately. Thanks to the particular shape of type's interactions, initial configurations – of the form $(\nu_0, S, \varnothing)\bot(\nu_0, \overline{S}, \varnothing)$ – will only reach systems, say $(\nu_1, S_1, \mathtt{M}_1)\bot(\nu_2, S_2, \mathtt{M}_2)$, in which at least one between $\mathtt{M}_1$ and $\mathtt{M}_2$ is empty. Condition (1) requires compatible configurations to satisfy this basic property.

Typing rules. The typing rules are given in Fig. 5. Rule [Vrcv] is for input processes. The first premise consists of two conditions requiring the time-span $[\nu, \nu + n]$ in which the process can receive the message to *coincide* with δ:

- $\nu + t \models \delta \Rightarrow t \leqslant n$ rules out processes that are not ready to receive a message when prescribed by the type.
- $t \leqslant n \Rightarrow \nu + t \models \delta$ requires that $a^n(b).P$ can read only at times that satisfy the type prescription δ.[2]

The second premise of [Vrcv] requires the continuation P to be well-typed against the continuation of the type, for all possible session environments where the virtual time is somewhere between $[\nu, \nu + n]$, where the virtual valuation ν in the mapping of session a is reset according to λ. Rule [Drcv], for processes receiving delegated sessions, is like [Vrcv] except: (a) the continuation P is typed against a session environment *extended with the received session* S', and (b) the clock valuation ν' of the receiving session must satisfy δ'. Recall that by formation rules (Sect. 2.1) S' is well-formed against all ν' that satisfy δ'.

Rule [Vsend] is for output processes. Send actions are instantaneous, hence the type current ν needs to satisfy δ. As customary, the continuation of the process needs to be well-typed against the continuation of the type (with ν being reset according to λ, and Γ extended with information on the sort of b). [Dsend] for delegation is similar but: (a) the delegated session is removed from the session environment (the process can no longer engage in the delegated session), and (b) valuation ν' of the delegated session must satisfy guard δ'.

Rule [Delδ] checks that P is well-typed against all possible solutions of δ. Rule [Del$t$] shifts the virtual valuations in the session environment of t. This is as the corresponding rule in [12] but with the addition of the check that Δ is not t-reading, needed because of urgent semantics.

Rule [Res] is for processes with scopes.

---

2 While not necessary for our safety results, this constraint simplifies our theory. Timing variations between types and programs are all handled in one place: rule [Subt].

Rule [Rec] is for recursive processes. The rule is as usual [21] except that we use a set of session environments Θ (instead of a single Δ) to capture a set of possible scenarios in which a recursion instance may start, which may have different clock valuations. Rule [Var] is also as expected except for the use of Θ.

Rules [Par] and [Subt] straightforward.

Example 8 (Typing with subtyping). Subtyping substantially increases the power of our type system, in particular in the presence of channel passing. Intuitively, without subtyping, the type of any higher-order send action should be an equality constraint (e.g., $x = 1$) rather than more general timeout (e.g., $x < 1$). We illustrate our point using P defined below:

$$P = (\nu a_1 b_1)(\nu a_2 b_2)(P_1 \mid P_2 \mid P_3 \mid Q) \qquad P_1 = \mathtt{delay}(x \leqslant 1).\, \overline{a_1}\, a_2$$
$$P_2 = b_1^1(c).\, c^2(d) \qquad P_3 = \mathtt{delay}(1 \leqslant x \wedge x \leqslant 2).\, \overline{b_2}\, \mathtt{true}$$

where Q contains empty queues of the involved endpoints. Intuitively, P proceeds as follows: (1) P_1 sends channel a_2 to P_2 within one time unit, and terminates; (2) P_2 reads the message as soon as it arrives, and listens for a message across the received channel (a_2) for two time units; (3) P_3 sends value $\mathtt{true}$ through channel b_2 at a time in between 1 and 2, unaware that now she is communicating with P_2, and then terminates; (4) P_2 reads the message immediately and terminates. See below for one possible reduction:

$$\begin{aligned} P &\longrightarrow^* (\nu a_1 b_1)(\nu a_2 b_2)(\overline{a_1}\, a_2 \mid b_1^0(c).\, c^2(d) \mid \mathtt{delay}(0 \leqslant x \wedge x \leqslant 1).\, \overline{b_2}\, \mathtt{true}) \mid Q) \\ &\longrightarrow^* (\nu a_1 b_1)(\nu a_2 b_2)(0 \mid a_2^2(d) \mid \mathtt{delay}(0.5).\, \overline{b_2}\, \mathtt{true} \mid Q) \\ &\longrightarrow (\nu a_1 b_1)(\nu a_2 b_2)(0 \mid a_2^{1.5}(d) \mid \overline{b_2}\, \mathtt{true} \mid Q) \\ &\longrightarrow^* (\nu a_1 b_1)(\nu a_2 b_2)(0 \mid 0 \mid 0 \mid Q) \end{aligned}$$

Although P executes correctly, the involved processes are well-typed against types that are not dual:

$$\vdash\ P_1 \rhd a_1 : (\nu_0, S_1), a_2 : (\nu_0, S_2) \qquad \vdash\ P_2 \rhd b_1 : (\nu_0, S_1') \qquad \vdash\ P_3 \rhd b_2 : (\nu_0, \overline{S_2})$$

for $S_1 = !(y \leqslant 1, S_2)(x \leqslant 1)$, $S_2 = ?\mathtt{Bool}(1 \leqslant y \wedge y \leqslant 2)$, $S_1' = ?(y = 0, S_2')(x \leqslant 1)$. In order to type-check P, we need to apply rule [Res], requiring endpoints of the same session to have dual types. But clearly: $S_1' \neq \overline{S_1}$. Without subtyping, P would not be well-typed. By subtyping, however, $(y \leqslant 1, S_2) <: (y = 0, S_2')$ with $S_2' = ?\mathtt{Bool}(y \leqslant 2).\mathtt{end}$, and then $S_1' <: \overline{S_1'}$. Thanks to the subtyping rule [subt] we can derive $\vdash\ P_2 \rhd b_1 :\ (\nu_0, \overline{S_1})$ and, in turn, $\vdash\ P \rhd \emptyset$.

7 Subject Reduction and Time Safety

The main properties of our typing system are Subject Reduction and Time Safety. Time Safety ensures that the execution of well-typed processes will only

$$\frac{\begin{array}{c}\forall t: \quad \nu + t \models \delta \iff t \leqslant n \\ \forall t \leqslant n: \quad \Gamma, b : T \;\vdash\; P \rhd \Delta + t, a : (\nu + t[\lambda \mapsto 0],\ S) \quad \Delta \text{ not } t\text{-reading}\end{array}}{\Gamma \;\vdash\; a^n(b).\, P \rhd \Delta, a : (\nu,\ ?T(\delta, \lambda).S)} \;[\mathtt{Vrcv}]$$

$$\frac{\begin{array}{c}\forall t: \quad \nu + t \models \delta \iff t \leqslant n \quad T = (\delta', S') \quad \nu' \models \delta' \\ \forall t \leqslant n: \quad \Gamma \;\vdash\; P \rhd \Delta + t, a : (\nu + t[\lambda \mapsto 0],\ S), b : (\nu',\ S') \quad \Delta \text{ not } t\text{-reading}\end{array}}{\Gamma \;\vdash\; a^n(b).\, P \rhd \Delta, a : (\nu,\ ?T(\delta, \lambda).S)} \;[\mathtt{Drcv}]$$

$$\frac{\Gamma \;\vdash\; b : T \quad \nu \models \delta \quad \Gamma \;\vdash\; P \rhd \Delta, a : (\nu\,[\lambda \mapsto 0],\ S)}{\Gamma \;\vdash\; \overline{a}\, b.P \rhd \Delta, a : (\nu,\ !T(\delta, \lambda).S)} \;[\mathtt{Vsend}]$$

$$\frac{T = (\delta', S') \quad \nu' \models \delta' \quad \nu \models \delta \quad \Gamma \;\vdash\; P \rhd \Delta, a : (\nu\,[\lambda \mapsto 0],\ S)}{\Gamma \;\vdash\; \overline{a}\, b.P \rhd \Delta, a : (\nu,\ !T(\delta, \lambda).S), b : (\nu',\ S')} \;[\mathtt{Dsend}]$$

$$\frac{\forall t \in \delta : \Gamma \;\vdash\; \mathtt{delay}(t).\, P \rhd \Delta}{\Gamma \;\vdash\; \mathtt{delay}(\delta).\, P \rhd \Delta} \qquad \frac{\Gamma \;\vdash\; P \rhd \Delta + t \quad \Delta \text{ not } t\text{-reading}}{\Gamma \;\vdash\; \mathtt{delay}(t).\, P \rhd \Delta} \;[\mathtt{Del}\delta/\mathtt{Del}t]$$

$$\frac{(\nu_1, S_1, \mathtt{M}_1) \bot (\nu_2, S_2, \mathtt{M}_2) \quad \Gamma \;\vdash\; P \rhd \Delta,\ a : (\nu_1,\ S_1),\ b : (\nu_2,\ S_2),\ ba : \mathtt{M}_1,\ ab : \mathtt{M}_2}{\Gamma \;\vdash\; (\nu ab) P \rhd \Delta} \;[\mathtt{Res}]$$

$$\frac{\Delta \in \Theta \quad \forall i: \;\; \Gamma \;\vdash\; \boldsymbol{v}_i : \boldsymbol{T}_i}{\Gamma, X : \boldsymbol{T}; \Theta \;\vdash\; X\langle \boldsymbol{v}\,;\, \boldsymbol{b} \rangle \rhd \Delta} \qquad \frac{\Gamma \;\vdash\; P \rhd \Delta_1 \quad \Gamma \;\vdash\; Q \rhd \Delta_2}{\Gamma \;\vdash\; P \mid Q \rhd \Delta_1, \Delta_2} \;[\mathtt{Var}/\mathtt{Par}]$$

$$\frac{\forall (\boldsymbol{\nu}, \boldsymbol{S}) \in \Theta: \;\; \Gamma, \boldsymbol{a} : \boldsymbol{T}, X : \boldsymbol{T}; \Theta \;\vdash\; P \rhd \boldsymbol{b} : (\boldsymbol{\nu}, \boldsymbol{S}) \quad \Gamma, X : \boldsymbol{T}; \Theta \;\vdash\; Q \rhd \Delta}{\Gamma \;\vdash\; \mathtt{def}\ X(\boldsymbol{a}\,;\,\boldsymbol{b}) = P\ \mathtt{in}\ Q \rhd \Delta} \;[\mathtt{Rec}]$$

$$\frac{\Gamma \vdash P \rhd \Delta' \qquad \Delta' <: \Delta}{\Gamma \vdash P \rhd \Delta} \qquad \frac{\Gamma \vdash P \rhd \Delta}{\Gamma \vdash P \rhd \Delta, a : (\nu,\ \mathtt{end})} \;[\mathtt{Subt}/\mathtt{Weak}]$$

Fig. 5. Selected typing rules for processes

reach *fail-free* states. Recall, P is fail-free when none of its sub-terms is the process `failed`. Time Safety builds on a condition that is not related with time, but with the structure of the process interactions. If an untimed process gets stuck due to mismatches in its communication structure, a timed process with the same communication structure may move to a failed state. Consider P below:

$$\begin{array}{ll} P = (\nu ab)(\nu cd)\, Q & R = ab : \varnothing \mid ba : \varnothing \mid cd : \varnothing \mid dc : \varnothing \\ Q = a^5(e).\, \overline{d}\, e.0 \mid c^5(e).\, \overline{b}\, e.0 \mid R & \end{array} \tag{13}$$

P is well-typed: $\varnothing \;\vdash\; P \rhd a : (\nu_0, S), b : (\nu_0, \overline{S}), c : (\nu_0, S), d : (\nu_0, \overline{S})$ with $S = ?\mathtt{Int}(x \leqslant 5, \varnothing).\mathtt{end}$. However, P can only make time steps, and when, overall, more than 5 time units elapse (e.g., 6 in the reduction below) P reaches a failed state due to a circular dependency between actions of sessions (νab) and (νcd):

$$P \;\longrightarrow\; \Phi_6(Q) = (\nu ab)(\nu cd)\, (\mathtt{failed} \mid \mathtt{failed} \mid R)$$

Our typing system does not check against such circularities across different interleaved sessions. This is common in work on untimed [21] and timed [12] session types. However, in the untimed scenario, progress for interleaved sessions can be guaranteed by means of additional checks on processes [17]. Time Safety builds on the results in [17] by using an assumption (receive liveness) on the underneath structure of the timed processes. This assumptions is formally captured in Definition 11, which is based on an untimed variant of our calculus.

The untimed calculus. We define untimed processes, denoted by $\hat{P}$, as processes obtained from the grammar given for timed processes (Sect. 5) without delays and failed processes. In untimed processes, time annotations of branching/receive processes are immaterial, hence omitted in the rest of the paper.

Given a (timed) process P, one can obtain its untimed counter-part by *erasing* delays and failed processes; we denoted the result of such erasure on P by $\texttt{erase}(P)$. The semantics of untimed processes is defined as the one for timed processes (Sect. 5) except that reduction rules [Delay], [TStr], and [Red2], are removed. Abusing the notation, we write $\hat{P} \longrightarrow \hat{P}'$ when an untimed process $\hat{P}$ moves to a state $\hat{P}'$ using the semantics for untimed processes. The definitions of $\texttt{Wait}(\hat{P})$ and $\texttt{NEQueue}(\hat{P})$ can be derived from the definitions for timed processes in the straightforward way.

Definition 11 (receive liveness) formalises our assumption on the interaction structures of a process.

Definition 11 (Receive liveness). *$\hat{P}$ is said to satisfy receive liveness (or is* live, *for short) if, for all $\hat{P}'$ such that $\hat{P} \longrightarrow^* \hat{P}'$:*

$$\hat{P}' \equiv (\nu ab)\hat{Q} \wedge a \in \texttt{Wait}(\hat{Q}) \implies \exists \hat{Q}' : \hat{Q} \longrightarrow^* \hat{Q}' \wedge a \in \texttt{NEQueue}(\hat{Q}')$$

In any reachable state $\hat{P}'$ of a live untimed process $\hat{P}$, if any endpoint a in $\hat{P}'$ is waiting to receive a message ($a \in \texttt{Wait}(\hat{Q})$), then the overall process is able to reach a state $\hat{Q}'$ where a can perform the receive action ($a \in \texttt{NEQueue}(\hat{Q}')$).

Consider process P in (13). The untimed process $\texttt{erase}(P)$ is not live because $\texttt{Wait}(\texttt{erase}(P)) = \{a, c\}$ and $a, c \notin \texttt{NEQueue}(\texttt{erase}(P))$, since $\texttt{NEQueue}(\texttt{erase}(P))$ is the empty set. Syntactically, $\texttt{erase}(P)$ is as P, but it does not have the same behaviour. P can only make time steps, reaching a failed process, while $\texttt{erase}(P)$ is stuck, as untimed processes only make communication steps.

Properties. Time safety relies on Subject Reduction Theorem 4, which establishes a relation (preserved by reduction) of well-typed processes and their types.

Theorem 4 (Subject reduction for closed systems). *Let* $\texttt{erase}(P)$ *be live. If $\emptyset \vdash P \rhd \emptyset$ and $P \longrightarrow P'$ then $\emptyset \vdash P' \rhd \emptyset$.*

Note that Subject Reduction assumes $\texttt{erase}(P)$ to be live. For instance, the example of P in (13) is well-typed, but $\texttt{erase}(P)$ is not live. The process can reduce to a failed state (as illustrated earlier in this section) that cannot be typed (failed processes are not well-typed). Time Safety establishes that well-typed processes only reduce to fail-free states.

Theorem 5 (Time safety). *If* $\texttt{erase}(P)$ *is live,* $\vdash P \rhd \emptyset$ *and* $P \longrightarrow^* P'$, *then* P' *is fail-free.*

Typing is decidable if one uses processes annotated with the following information: (1) scope restrictions $(\nu ab : S)P$ are annotated with the type S of the session for endpoint a (the type of b is implicitly assumed to be $\overline{S}$ and both endpoints are type checked in the initial clock valuation ν_0); (2) receive actions $a^n(b : T).\,P$ are annotated with the type T of the received message; (3) recursion $X(\boldsymbol{a} : \boldsymbol{T}\,;\, \boldsymbol{a} : \boldsymbol{S}, \delta) = P$ are annotated with types for each parameter, and a guard modelling the state of the clocks. We call annotated programs those annotated processes derived without using productions marked as run-time (i.e., $\texttt{failed}$ and $\texttt{delay}(t).\,P$), and where n in $a^n(b : T).\,P$ ranges over $\mathbb{Q}_{\geqslant 0} \cup \{\infty\}$.

Proposition 2. *Type checking for annotated programs is decidable.*

8 Conclusion and Related Work

We introduced duality and subtyping relations for asynchronous timed session types. Unlike for untimed and timed synchronous [6] dualities, the composition of dual types does not enjoy progress in general. Compositions of asynchronous timed dual types enjoy progress *when using an urgent receive semantics.* We propose a behavioural typing system for a timed calculus that features non-blocking and blocking receive primitives (with and without timeout), and time consuming primitives of arbitrary but constrained delays. The main properties of the typing system are Subject Reduction and Time Safety; both results rely on an assumption (receive liveness) of the underneath interaction structure of processes. In related work on timed session types [12], receive liveness is not required for Subject Reduction; this is because the processes in [12] block (rather than reaching a failed state) whenever they cannot progress correctly, hence e.g., missed deadline are regarded as progress violations. By explicitly capturing failures, our calculus paves the way for future work on combining static checking with run-time instrumentation to prevent or handle failures.

Asynchronous timed session types have been introduced in [12], in a multiparty setting, together with a timed π-calculus, and a type system. The direct extension of session types with time introduces unfeasible executions (i.e., types may get stuck), as we have shown in Example 1. [12] features a notion of feasibility for choreographies, which ensures that types enjoy progress. We ensure progress of types by formation and duality. The semantics of types in [12] is different from ours in that receive actions are not urgent. The work in [12] gives one extra condition on types (wait-freedom), because feasible types may still yield undesirable executions in well-typed processes. Thanks to our duality, subtyping, and calculus (in particular the blocking receive primitive with timeout) this condition is unnecessary in this work. As a result, our typing system allows for types that are *not wait-free.* By dropping wait-freedom, we can type a class of common real-world protocols in which processes may be ready to receive messages even before the final deadline of the corresponding senders. Remarkably,

SMTP mentioned in the introduction is *not wait-free*. For some other aspects, our work is less general than the one in [12], as we consider binary sessions rather than multiparty sessions. A theory of timed multiparty asynchronous protocols that encompasses the protocols in [12] and those considered here is an interesting future direction. The work in [6] introduces a theory of synchronous timed session types, based on a decidable notion of compatibility, called *compliance*, that ensures progress of types, and is equivalent to synchronous timed duality and subtyping in a precise sense [6]. Our duality and subtyping are similar to those in [6], but apply to the asynchronous scenario. The work in [15] introduces a typed calculus based on temporal session types. The temporal modalities in [15] can be used as a discrete model of time. Timed session types, thanks to clocks and resets, are able to model complex timed dependencies that temporal session types do not seem able to capture. Other work studies models for asynchronous timed interactions, e.g., Communicating Timed Automata [23] (CTA), timed Message Sequence Charts [2], but not their relationships with processes. The work in [5] introduces a refinement for CTA, and presents a notion of urgency similar to the one used in this paper, preliminary studied also in [29].

Several timed calculi have been introduced outside the context of behavioural types. The work in [32] extends the π- calculus with time primitives inspired in CTA and is closer, in principle, to our types than our processes. Another timed extension of the π-calculus with time-consuming actions has been applied to the analysis the active times of processes [18]. Some works focus on specific aspects of timed behaviour, such as timeouts [9], transactions [24, 27], and services [25]. Our calculus does not feature exception handlers, nor timed transactions. Our focus in on detecting time violations via static typing, so that a process only moves to fail-free states.

The calculi in [7, 12, 15] have been used in combination with session types. The calculus in [12] features a non-blocking receive primitive similar to our $a^0(b).\,P$, but that never fails (i.e., time is not allowed to flow if a process tries to read from an empty buffer—possibly leading to a stuck process rather than a failed state). The calculus in [7] features a blocking receive primitive without timeout, equivalent to our $a^\infty(b).\,P$. The calculus in [15], seems able to encode a non-blocking receive primitive like the one of [12] and a blocking receive primitive without timeout like our $a^\infty(b).\,P$. None of these works features blocking receive primitives with timeouts. Furthermore, existing works feature [7, 12] or can encode [15] only precise delays, equivalent to $\texttt{delay}(x = n).\,P$. Such punctual predictions are often difficult to achieve. Arbitrary but constrained delays are closer abstractions of time-consuming programming primitives (and possibly, of predictions one can derive by cost analysis, e.g., [20]).

As to applications, timed session types have been used for run-time monitoring [7, 30] and static checking [12]. A promising future direction is that of integrating static typing with run-time verification and enforcement, towards a theory of hybrid timed session types. In this context, extending our calculus with exception handlers [9, 24, 27] could allow an extension of the typing system, that introduces run-time instrumentation to handle unexpected time failures.

References

1. Aceto, L., Ingólfsdóttir, A., Larsen, K.G., Srba, J.: Reactive Systems: Modelling, Specification and Verification. Cambridge University Press, Cambridge (2007). https://doi.org/10.1017/CBO9780511814105
2. Akshay, S., Gastin, P., Mukund, M., Kumar, K.N.: Model checking time-constrained scenario-based specifications. In: FSTTCS. LIPIcs, vol. 8, pp. 204–215. Schloss Dagstuhl - Leibniz-Zentrum fuer Informatik (2010). https://doi.org/10.4230/LIPIcs.FSTTCS.2010.204
3. Alur, R., Dill, D.L.: A theory of timed automata. TCS **126**, 183–235 (1994)
4. Advanced Message Queuing Protocols (AMQP). https://www.amqp.org/
5. Bartoletti, M., Bocchi, L., Murgia, M.: Progress-preserving refinements of CTA. In: CONCUR. LIPIcs, vol. 118, pp. 40:1–40:19. Schloss Dagstuhl-Leibniz-Zentrum fuer Informatik (2018). https://doi.org/10.4230/LIPIcs.CONCUR.2018.40
6. Bartoletti, M., Cimoli, T., Murgia, M.: Timed session types. Log. Methods Comput. Sci. **13**(4) (2017). https://doi.org/10.23638/LMCS-13(4:25)2017
7. Bartoletti, M., Cimoli, T., Murgia, M., Podda, A.S., Pompianu, L.: A contract-oriented middleware. In: Braga, C., Ölveczky, P.C. (eds.) FACS 2015. LNCS, vol. 9539, pp. 86–104. Springer, Cham (2016). https://doi.org/10.1007/978-3-319-28934-2_5
8. Bengtsson, J., Yi, W.: Timed automata: semantics, algorithms and tools. In: Desel, J., Reisig, W., Rozenberg, G. (eds.) ACPN 2003. LNCS, vol. 3098, pp. 87–124. Springer, Heidelberg (2004). https://doi.org/10.1007/978-3-540-27755-2_3
9. Berger, M., Yoshida, N.: Timed, distributed, probabilistic, typed processes. In: Shao, Z. (ed.) APLAS 2007. LNCS, vol. 4807, pp. 158–174. Springer, Heidelberg (2007). https://doi.org/10.1007/978-3-540-76637-7_11
10. Bettini, L., Coppo, M., D'Antoni, L., De Luca, M., Dezani-Ciancaglini, M., Yoshida, N.: Global progress in dynamically interleaved multiparty sessions. In: van Breugel, F., Chechik, M. (eds.) CONCUR 2008. LNCS, vol. 5201, pp. 418–433. Springer, Heidelberg (2008). https://doi.org/10.1007/978-3-540-85361-9_33
11. Bocchi, L., Murgia, M., Vasconcelos, V., Yoshida, N.: Asynchronous timed session types: from duality to time-sensitive processes (2018). https://www.cs.kent.ac.uk/people/staff/lb514/tstp.html
12. Bocchi, L., Yang, W., Yoshida, N.: Timed multiparty session types. In: Baldan, P., Gorla, D. (eds.) CONCUR 2014. LNCS, vol. 8704, pp. 419–434. Springer, Heidelberg (2014). https://doi.org/10.1007/978-3-662-44584-6_29
13. Bruno, E.J., Bollella, G.: Real-Time Java Programming: With Java RTS, 1st edn. Prentice Hall PTR, Upper Saddle River (2009)
14. Chen, T.C., Dezani-Ciancaglini, M., Yoshida, N.: On the preciseness of subtyping in session types. In: PPDP, pp. 135–146. ACM (2014). https://doi.org/10.1145/2643135.2643138
15. Das, A., Hoffmann, J., Pfenning, F.: Parallel complexity analysis with temporal session types. Proc. ACM Program. Lang. **2**(ICFP), 91:1–91:30 (2018). https://doi.org/10.1145/3236786
16. Demangeon, R., Honda, K.: Full abstraction in a subtyped pi-calculus with linear types. In: Katoen, J.-P., König, B. (eds.) CONCUR 2011. LNCS, vol. 6901, pp. 280–296. Springer, Heidelberg (2011). https://doi.org/10.1007/978-3-642-23217-6_19
17. Dezani-Ciancaglini, M., de'Liguoro, U., Yoshida, N.: On progress for structured communications. In: Barthe, G., Fournet, C. (eds.) TGC 2007. LNCS, vol. 4912, pp.

257–275. Springer, Heidelberg (2008). https://doi.org/10.1007/978-3-540-78663-4_18
18. Fischer, M., Förster, S., Windisch, A., Monjau, D., Balser, B.: A new time extension to π-calculus based on time consuming transition semanticss. In: Grimm, C. (ed.) Languages for System Specification, pp. 271–283. Springer, Boston (2004). https://doi.org/10.1007/1-4020-7991-5_17
19. Gay, S.J., Hole, M.: Subtyping for session types in the pi calculus. Acta Inf. **42**(2–3), 191–225 (2005). https://doi.org/10.1007/s00236-005-0177-z
20. Hoffmann, J., Shao, Z.: Automatic static cost analysis for parallel programs. In: Vitek, J. (ed.) ESOP 2015. LNCS, vol. 9032, pp. 132–157. Springer, Heidelberg (2015). https://doi.org/10.1007/978-3-662-46669-8_6
21. Honda, K., Yoshida, N., Carbone, M.: Multiparty asynchronous session types. In: POPL, pp. 273–284. ACM (2008)
22. Klensin, J.: Simple mail transfer protocol. RFC 5321, October 2008. https://tools.ietf.org/html/rfc5321
23. Krcal, P., Yi, W.: Communicating timed automata: the more synchronous, the more difficult to verify. In: Ball, T., Jones, R.B. (eds.) CAV 2006. LNCS, vol. 4144, pp. 249–262. Springer, Heidelberg (2006). https://doi.org/10.1007/11817963_24
24. Laneve, C., Zavattaro, G.: Foundations of web transactions. In: Sassone, V. (ed.) FoSSaCS 2005. LNCS, vol. 3441, pp. 282–298. Springer, Heidelberg (2005). https://doi.org/10.1007/978-3-540-31982-5_18
25. Lapadula, A., Pugliese, R., Tiezzi, F.: CWS: a timed service-oriented calculus. In: Jones, C.B., Liu, Z., Woodcock, J. (eds.) ICTAC 2007. LNCS, vol. 4711, pp. 275–290. Springer, Heidelberg (2007). https://doi.org/10.1007/978-3-540-75292-9_19
26. Larsen, K.G., Pettersson, P., Yi, W.: Uppaal in a nutshell. Int. J. Softw. Tools Technolo. Transf. **1**, 134–152 (1997)
27. López, H.A., Pérez, J.A.: Time and exceptional behavior in multiparty structured interactions. In: Carbone, M., Petit, J.-M. (eds.) WS-FM 2011. LNCS, vol. 7176, pp. 48–63. Springer, Heidelberg (2012). https://doi.org/10.1007/978-3-642-29834-9_5
28. Milner, R.: Communicating and Mobile Systems: The π-calculus. Cambridge University Press, New York (1999)
29. Murgia, M.: On urgency in asynchronous timed session types. In: ICE. EPTCS, vol. 279, pp. 85–94 (2018). https://doi.org/10.4204/EPTCS.279.9
30. Neykova, R., Bocchi, L., Yoshida, N.: Timed runtime monitoring for multiparty conversations. Formal Asp. Comput. **29**(5), 877–910 (2017). https://doi.org/10.1007/s00165-017-0420-8
31. Pierce, B.C.: Types and Programming Languages. MIT Press, Cambridge (2002)
32. Saeedloei, N., Gupta, G.: Timed π-calculus. In: Abadi, M., Lluch Lafuente, A. (eds.) TGC 2013. LNCS, vol. 8358, pp. 119–135. Springer, Cham (2014). https://doi.org/10.1007/978-3-319-05119-2_8
33. Vinoski, S.: Advanced message queuing protocol. IEEE Internet Comput. **10**(6), 87–89 (2006). https://doi.org/10.1109/MIC.2006.116
34. Yovine, S.: Kronos: a verification tool for real-time systems. (Kronos user's manual release 2.2). Int. J. Softw. Tools Technol. Transf. **1**, 123–133 (1997)

6

Semi-automated Reasoning About Non-determinism in C Expressions

Dan Frumin[1(✉)], Léon Gondelman[1], and Robbert Krebbers[2]

[1] Radboud University, Nijmegen, The Netherlands
{dfrumin,lgg}@cs.ru.nl
[2] Delft University of Technology, Delft, The Netherlands
mail@robbertkrebbers.nl

Abstract. Research into C verification often ignores that the C standard leaves the evaluation order of expressions unspecified, and assigns undefined behavior to write-write or read-write conflicts in subexpressions—so called "sequence point violations". These aspects should be accounted for in verification because C compilers exploit them.

We present a verification condition generator (vcgen) that enables one to semi-automatically prove the absence of undefined behavior in a given C program for *any* evaluation order. The key novelty of our approach is a symbolic execution algorithm that computes a *frame* at the same time as a *postcondition*. The frame is used to automatically determine how resources should be distributed among subexpressions.

We prove correctness of our vcgen with respect to a new monadic definitional semantics of a subset of C. This semantics is modular and gives a concise account of non-determinism in C.

We have implemented our vcgen as a tactic in the Coq interactive theorem prover, and have proved correctness of it using a separation logic for the new monadic definitional semantics of a subset of C

1 Introduction

The ISO C standard [22]—the official specification of the C language—leaves many parts of the language semantics either *unspecified* (*e.g.*, the order of evaluation of expressions), or *undefined* (*e.g.*, dereferencing a NULL pointer or integer overflow). In case of undefined behavior a program may do literally anything, *e.g.*, it may crash, or it may produce an arbitrary result and side-effects. Therefore, to establish the correctness of a C program, one needs to ensure that the program has no undefined behavior for *all* possible choices of non-determinism due to unspecified behavior.

In this paper we focus on the undefined and unspecified behaviors related to C's expression semantics, which have been ignored by most existing verification tools, but are crucial for establishing the correctness of realistic C programs. The C standard does not require subexpressions to be evaluated in a specific order (*e.g.*, from left to right), but rather allows them to be evaluated in *any* order.

Moreover, an expression has undefined behavior when there is a conflicting write-write or read-write access to the same location between two *sequence points* [22, 6.5p2] (so called "sequence point violation"). Sequence points occur *e.g.*, at the end of a full expression (`;`), before and after each function call, and after the first operand of a conditional expression (`- ? - : -`) has been evaluated [22, Annex C]. Let us illustrate this by means of the following example:

```
int main() {
  int x; int y = (x = 3) + (x = 4);
  printf("%d␣%d\n", x, y);
}
```

Due to the unspecified evaluation order, one would naively expect this program to print either "3 7" or "4 7", depending on which assignment to `x` was evaluated first. But this program exhibits undefined behavior due to a sequence point violation: there are two conflicting writes to the variable `x`. Indeed, when compiled with GCC (version 8.2.0), the program in fact prints "4 8", which does not correspond to the expected results of any of the evaluation orders.

One may expect that these programs can be easily ruled out statically using some form of static analysis, but this is not the case. Contrary to the simple program above, one can access the values of arbitrary pointers, making it impossible to statically establish the absence of write-write or read-write conflicts. Besides, one should not merely establish the absence of undefined behavior due to conflicting accesses to the same locations, but one should also establish that there are no other forms of undefined behavior (*e.g.*, that no NULL pointers are dereferenced) for *any evaluation order*.

To deal with this issue, Krebbers [29,30] developed a program logic based on Concurrent Separation Logic (CSL) [46] for establishing the absence of undefined behavior in C programs in the presence of non-determinism. To get an impression of how his logic works, let us consider the rule for the addition operator:

$$\frac{\{P_1\}\, \mathsf{e}_1\, \{\Psi_1\} \qquad \{P_2\}\, \mathsf{e}_2\, \{\Psi_2\} \qquad \forall \mathrm{v}_1\, \mathrm{v}_2.\, \Psi_1\, \mathrm{v}_1 * \Psi_2\, \mathrm{v}_2 \vdash \Phi\, (\mathrm{v}_1 + \mathrm{v}_2)}{\{P_1 * P_2\}\, \mathsf{e}_1 + \mathsf{e}_2\, \{\Phi\}}$$

This rule is much like the rule for parallel composition in CSL—the precondition should be separated into two parts P_1 and P_2 describing the resources needed for proving the Hoare triples of both operands. Crucially, since P_1 and P_2 describe disjoint resources as expressed by the *separating conjunction* $*$, it is guaranteed that e_1 and e_2 do not interfere with each other, and hence cannot cause sequence point violations. The purpose of the rule's last premise is to ensure that for all possible return values v_1 and v_2, the postconditions Ψ_1 and Ψ_2 of both operands can be combined into the postcondition Φ of the whole expression.

Krebbers's logic [29,30] has some limitations that impact its usability:

- The rules are not algorithmic, and hence it is not clear how they could be implemented as part of an automated or interactive tool.
- It is difficult to extend the logic with new features. Soundness was proven with respect to a monolithic and ad-hoc model of separation logic.

In this paper we address both of these problems.

We present a new algorithm for symbolic execution in separation logic. Contrary to ordinary symbolic execution in separation logic [5], our symbolic executor takes an expression and a precondition as its input, and computes not only the postcondition, but also simultaneously computes a *frame* that describes the resources that have *not* been used to prove the postcondition. The frame is used to infer the pre- and postconditions of adjacent subexpressions. For example, in $\mathsf{e}_1 + \mathsf{e}_2$, we use the frame of e_1 to symbolically execute e_2.

In order to enable semi-automated reasoning about C programs, we integrate our symbolic executor into a *verification condition generator (vcgen).* Our vcgen does not merely turn programs into proof goals, but constructs the proof goals only as long as it can discharge goals automatically using our symbolic executor. When an attempt to use the symbolic executor fails, our vcgen will return a new goal, from which the vcgen can be called back again after the user helped out. This approach is useful when integrated into an interactive theorem prover.

We prove soundness of the symbolic executor and verification condition generator with respect to a refined version of the separation logic by Krebbers [29,30]. Our new logic has been developed on top of the Iris framework [24–26,33], and thereby inherits all advanced features of Iris (like its expressive support for ghost state and invariants), without having to model these explicitly. To make our new logic better suited for proving the correctness of the symbolic executor and verification condition generator, our new logic comes with a weakest precondition connective instead of Hoare triples as in Krebbers's original logic.

To streamline the soundness proof of our new program logic, we give a new *monadic definitional translation* of a subset of C relevant for non-determinism and sequence points into an ML-style functional language with concurrency. Contrary to the direct style operational semantics for a subset of C by Krebbers [29,30], our approach leads to a semantics that is both easier to understand, and easier to extend with additional language features.

We have mechanized our whole development in the Coq interactive theorem prover. The symbolic executor and verification condition generator are defined as computable functions in Coq, and have been integrated into tactics in the Iris Proof Mode/MoSeL framework [32,34]. To obtain end-to-end correctness, we mechanized the proofs of soundness of our symbolic executor and verification condition generator with respect to our new separation logic and new monadic definitional semantics for a subset of C. The Coq development is available at [18].

Contributions. We describe an approach to semi-automatically prove the absence of undefined behavior in a given C program for *any* evaluation order. While doing so, we make the following contributions:

- We define λMC: a small C-style language with a semantics by a monadic translation into an ML-style functional language with concurrency (Sect. 2);
- We present a separation logic with weakest preconditions for λMC based on the separation logic for non-determinism in C by Krebbers [29,30] (Sect. 3);

- We prove soundness of our separation logic with weakest preconditions by giving a modular model using the Iris framework [24–26,33] (Sect. 4);
- We present a new symbolic executor that not only computes the postcondition of a C expression, but also a *frame*, used to determine how resources should be distributed among subexpressions (Sect. 5);
- On top of our symbolic executor, we define a verification condition generator that enables semi-automated proofs using an interactive theorem prover (Sect. 6);
- We demonstrate that our approach can be implemented and proved sound using Coq for a superset of the λMC language considered in this paper (Sect. 7).

2 λMC: A Monadic Definitional Semantics of C

In this section we describe a small C-style language called λMC, which features non-determinism in expressions. We define its semantics by translation into a ML-style functional language with concurrency called HeapLang.

We briefly describe the λMC source language (Sect. 2.1) and the HeapLang target language (Sect. 2.2) of the translation. Then we describe the translation scheme itself (Sect. 2.3). We explain in several steps how to exploit concurrency and monadic programming to give a concise and clear definitional semantics.

2.1 The Source Language λMC

The syntax of our source language called λMC is as follows:

$$
\begin{aligned}
\mathtt{v} \in \mathsf{val} &::= \mathtt{z} \mid \mathtt{f} \mid \mathtt{l} \mid \mathtt{NULL} \mid (\mathtt{v}_1, \mathtt{v}_2) \mid () && (\mathtt{z} \in \mathbb{Z},\ \mathtt{l} \in \mathsf{Loc}) \\
\mathtt{e} \in \mathsf{expr} &::= \mathtt{v} \mid \mathtt{x} \mid (\mathtt{e}_1, \mathtt{e}_2) \mid \mathtt{e.1} \mid \mathtt{e.2} \mid \mathtt{e}_1 \circledcirc \mathtt{e}_2 \mid && (\circledcirc \in \{+, -, \dots\}) \\
&\quad\ \mathtt{x} \leftarrow \mathtt{e}_1 \,;\, \mathtt{e}_2 \mid \mathtt{if(e_1)\{e_2\}\{e_3\}} \mid \mathtt{while(e_1)\{e_2\}} \mid \mathtt{e_1(e_2)} \mid \\
&\quad\ \mathtt{alloc(e)} \mid \mathtt{*e} \mid \mathtt{e}_1 = \mathtt{e}_2 \mid \mathtt{free(e)}
\end{aligned}
$$

The values include integers, NULL pointers, concrete locations l, function pointers f, structs with two fields (tuples), and the unit value () (for functions without return value). There is a global list of function definitions, where each definition is of the form f(x){e}. Most of the expression constructs resemble standard C notation, with some exceptions. We do not differentiate between expressions and statements to keep our language uniform. As such, if-then-else and sequencing constructs are not duplicated for both expressions and statements. Moreover, we do not differentiate between *lvalues* and *rvalues* [22, 6.3.2.1]. Hence, there is no address operator &, and, similarly to ML, the load (*e) and assignment ($\mathtt{e}_1 = \mathtt{e}_2$) operators take a reference as their first argument.

The *sequenced bind* operator $\mathtt{x} \leftarrow \mathtt{e}_1\,;\mathtt{e}_2$ generalizes the normal sequencing operator $\mathtt{e}_1\,;\mathtt{e}_2$ of C by binding the result of $\mathtt{e}_1$ to the variable $\mathtt{x}$ in $\mathtt{e}_2$. As such, $\mathtt{x} \leftarrow \mathtt{e}_1\,;\mathtt{e}_2$ can be thought of as the declaration of an immutable local variable $\mathtt{x}$. We omit mutable local variables for now, but these can be easily added as an extension to our method, as shown in Sect. 7. We write $\mathtt{e}_1\,;\mathtt{e}_2$ for a sequenced bind $\_ \leftarrow \mathtt{e}_1\,;\mathtt{e}_2$ in which we do not care about the return value of $\mathtt{e}_1$.

To focus on the key topics of the paper—non-determinism and the sequence point restriction—we take a minimalistic approach and omit most other features of C. Notably, we omit non-local control (return, break, continue, and goto). Our memory model is simplified; it only supports structs with two fields (tuples), but no arrays, unions, or machine integers. In Sect. 7 we show that some of these features (arrays, pointer arithmetic, and mutable local variables) can be incorporated.

2.2 The Target Language HeapLang

The target language of our definitional semantics of λMC is an ML-style functional language with concurrency primitives and a call-by-value semantics. This language, called HeapLang, is included as part of the Iris Coq development [21]. The syntax is as follows:

$$
\begin{aligned}
v \in \mathit{Val} &::= z \mid \mathtt{true} \mid \mathtt{false} \mid \mathtt{rec}\, f\ x = e \mid \ell \mid () \mid \ldots \qquad (z \in \mathbb{Z}, \ell \in \mathit{Loc})\\
e \in \mathit{Expr} &::= v \mid x \mid e_1\ e_2 \mid \mathtt{ref}(e) \mid \,!_{\mathsf{HL}}\, e \mid e_1 :=_{\mathsf{HL}} e_2 \mid \mathtt{assert}(e) \mid \\
&\qquad e_1 \mid\mid_{\mathsf{HL}} e_2 \mid \mathtt{newmutex} \mid \mathtt{acquire} \mid \mathtt{release} \mid \ldots
\end{aligned}
$$

The language contains some concurrency primitives that we will use to model non-determinism in λMC. Those primitives are $(\mid\mid_{\mathsf{HL}})$, `newmutex`, `acquire`, and `release`. The first primitive is the parallel composition operator, which executes expressions e_1 and e_2 in parallel, and returns a tuple of their results. The expression `newmutex` () creates a new mutex. If *lk* is a mutex that was created this way, then `acquire` *lk* tries to acquire it and blocks until no other thread is using *lk*. An acquired mutex can be released using `release` *lk*.

2.3 The Monadic Definitional Semantics of λMC

We now give the semantics of λMC by translation into HeapLang. The translation is carried out in several stages, each iteration implementing and illustrating a specific aspect of C. First, we model non-determinism in expressions by concurrency, parallelizing execution of subexpressions (step 1). After that, we add checks for sequence point violations in the translation of the assignment and dereferencing operations (step 2). Finally, we add function calls and demonstrate how the translation can be simplified using a monadic notation (step 3).

Step 1: Non-determinism via Parallel Composition. We model the unspecified evaluation order in binary expressions like $\mathtt{e}_1 + \mathtt{e}_2$ and $\mathtt{e}_1 = \mathtt{e}_2$ by executing the subexpressions in parallel using the $(||_{\mathsf{HL}})$ operator:

$$\begin{aligned}
[\![\mathtt{e}_1 + \mathtt{e}_2]\!] &\triangleq \mathtt{let}\ (v_1, v_2) = [\![\mathtt{e}_1]\!] \ ||_{\mathsf{HL}}\ [\![\mathtt{e}_2]\!]\ \mathtt{in}\ v_1 +_{\mathsf{HL}} v_2 \\
[\![\mathtt{e}_1 = \mathtt{e}_2]\!] &\triangleq \mathtt{let}\ (v_1, v_2) = [\![\mathtt{e}_1]\!] \ ||_{\mathsf{HL}}\ [\![\mathtt{e}_2]\!]\ \mathtt{in} \\
&\quad \mathtt{match}\, v_1\, \mathtt{with} \\
&\quad \mid \mathsf{None} \to \mathtt{assert(false)} \quad \texttt{(* NULL pointer *)} \\
&\quad \mid \mathsf{Some}\ l \to \mathtt{match}\ !_{\mathsf{HL}}\, l\, \mathtt{with} \\
&\qquad\qquad\qquad \mid \mathsf{None} \to \mathtt{assert(false)} \quad \texttt{(* Use after free *)} \\
&\qquad\qquad\qquad \mid \mathsf{Some}\ _ \to l :=_{\mathsf{HL}} \mathsf{Some}\ v_2;\ v_2
\end{aligned}$$

Since our memory model is simple, the value interpretation is straightforward:

$$[\![\mathtt{z}]\!]_{val} \triangleq \mathtt{z} \quad (\text{if } \mathtt{z} \in \mathbb{Z}) \qquad\qquad [\![\mathtt{NULL}]\!]_{val} \triangleq \mathsf{None}$$

$$[\![\mathtt{(v_1, v_2)}]\!]_{val} \triangleq ([\![\mathtt{v_1}]\!]_{val}, [\![\mathtt{v_2}]\!]_{val}) \qquad [\![\mathtt{()}]\!]_{val} \triangleq () \qquad [\![\mathtt{l}]\!]_{val} \triangleq \mathsf{Some}\ \mathtt{l}$$

The only interesting case is the translation of locations. Since there is no concept of a `NULL` pointer in HeapLang, we use the option type to distinguish `NULL` pointers from concrete locations (`l`). The interpretation of assignments thus contains a pattern match to check that no `NULL` pointers are dereferenced. A similar check is performed in the interpretation of the load operation (`*e`). Moreover, each location contains an option to distinguish freed from active locations.

Step 2: Sequence Points. So far we have not accounted for undefined behavior due to sequence point violations. For instance, the program `(x = 3) + (x = 4)` gets translated into a HeapLang expression that updates the value of the location `x` non-deterministically to either 3 or 4, and returns 7. However, in C, the behavior of this program is *undefined*, as it exhibits a sequence point violation: there is a write conflict for the location `x`.

To give a semantics for sequence point violations, we follow the approach by Norrish [44], Ellison and Rosu [17], and Krebbers [29,30]. We keep track of a set of locations that have been written to since the last sequence point. We refer to this set as the *environment* of our translation, and represent it using a global variable *env* of the type `mset` *Loc*. Because our target language HeapLang is concurrent, all updates to the environment *env* must be executed *atomically*, *i.e.*, inside a critical section, which we enforce by employing a global mutex *lk*. The interpretation of assignments $\mathtt{e}_1 = \mathtt{e}_2$ now becomes:

$$
\begin{aligned}
\texttt{ret}\, e &\triangleq \lambda\,\_\,\_.\, e \\
e_1 \mid\mid e_2 &\triangleq \lambda\, env\, lk.\, (e_1\ env\ lk) \mid\mid_{\mathsf{HL}} (e_2\ env\ lk) \\
x \leftarrow e_1;\, e_2 &\triangleq \lambda\, env\, lk.\ \texttt{let}\, x = e_1\ env\ lk\ \texttt{in}\, e_2\ env\ lk \\
\texttt{atomic\_env}\, e &\triangleq \lambda\, env\, lk.\, \texttt{acquire}\ lk; \texttt{let}\, a = e\ env\ \texttt{in}\,\texttt{release}\ lk; a \\
\texttt{atomic}\, e &\triangleq \lambda\, env\, lk.\, \texttt{acquire}\ lk; \texttt{let}\, a = e\ env\ (\texttt{newmutex}\ ())\ \texttt{in}\,\texttt{release}\ lk; a \\
\texttt{run}(e) &\triangleq e\ (\texttt{mset\_create}\ ())\ (\texttt{newmutex}\ ())
\end{aligned}
$$

Fig. 1. The monadic combinators.

$$
\begin{aligned}
[\![\mathtt{e}_1 = \mathtt{e}_2]\!] \triangleq\ & \texttt{let}\ (v_1, v_2) = [\![\mathtt{e}_1]\!] \mid\mid_{\mathsf{HL}} [\![\mathtt{e}_2]\!]\ \texttt{in} \\
& \texttt{acquire}\ lk; \\
& \texttt{match}\, v_1\, \texttt{with} \\
& \quad \mid \texttt{None} \rightarrow \texttt{assert(false)} \qquad \texttt{(* NULL pointer *)} \\
& \quad \mid \texttt{Some}\ l \rightarrow \\
& \qquad \texttt{assert}(\neg\texttt{mset\_member}\ l\ env);\ \texttt{(* Seq. point violation *)} \\
& \qquad \texttt{match}\ !_{\mathsf{HL}}\, l\, \texttt{with} \\
& \qquad\ \mid \texttt{None} \rightarrow \texttt{assert(false)}\quad \texttt{(* Use after free *)} \\
& \qquad\ \mid \texttt{Some}\ \_ \rightarrow \texttt{mset\_add}\ l\ env;\ l :=_{\mathsf{HL}} \texttt{Some}\ v_2; \\
& \texttt{release}\ lk;\ v_2
\end{aligned}
$$

Whenever we assign to (or read from) a location l, we check if the location l is not already present in the environment *env*. If the location l is present, then it was already written to since the last sequence point. Hence, accessing the location constitutes undefined behavior (see the `assert` in the interpretation of assignments above). In the interpretation of assignments, we furthermore insert the location l into the environment *env*.

In order to make sure that one can access a variable again after a sequence point, we define the *sequenced bind* operator $\mathtt{x} \leftarrow \mathtt{e}_1\,;\mathtt{e}_2$ as follows:

$$[\![\mathtt{x} \leftarrow \mathtt{e}_1\,; \mathtt{e}_2]\!] \triangleq \texttt{let}\ x = [\![\mathtt{e}_1]\!]\ \texttt{in}\,\texttt{acquire}\ lk;\ \texttt{mset\_clear}\ env;\ \texttt{release}\ lk;\ [\![\mathtt{e}_2]\!]$$

After we finished executing the expression $\mathtt{e}_1$, we clear the environment *env*, so that all locations are accessible in $\mathtt{e}_2$ again.

Step 3: Non-interleaved Function Calls. As the final step, we present the correct translation scheme for function calls. Unlike the other expressions, function calls are not interleaved during the execution of subexpressions [22, 6.5.2.2p10]. For instance, in the program `f() + g()` the possible orders of execution are: either all the instructions in `f()` followed by all the instructions in `g()`, or all the instructions in `g()` followed by all the instructions in `f()`.

$$
\begin{aligned}
[\![\mathtt{e}_1 + \mathtt{e}_2]\!] &\triangleq (v_1, v_2) \leftarrow [\![\mathtt{e}_1]\!] \mid\mid [\![\mathtt{e}_2]\!];\ \mathtt{ret}\,(v_1 +_{\mathsf{HL}} v_2)\\
[\![\mathtt{e}_1 = \mathtt{e}_2]\!] &\triangleq (v_1, v_2) \leftarrow [\![\mathtt{e}_1]\!] \mid\mid [\![\mathtt{e}_2]\!];\\
&\qquad \mathtt{atomic\_env}\,(\lambda\, env.\\
&\qquad\quad \mathtt{match}\, v_1\, \mathtt{with}\\
&\qquad\quad \mid \mathtt{None} \rightarrow \mathtt{assert(false)} \qquad \mathtt{(*\ NULL\ pointer\ *)}\\
&\qquad\quad \mid \mathtt{Some}\ l \rightarrow\\
&\qquad\qquad \mathtt{assert}(\neg\mathtt{mset\_member}\ l\ env);\ \mathtt{(*\ Seq.\ point\ violation\ *)}\\
&\qquad\qquad \mathtt{match}\ !_{\mathsf{HL}}\, l\ \mathtt{with}\\
&\qquad\qquad \mid \mathtt{None} \rightarrow \mathtt{assert(false)} \quad \mathtt{(*\ Use\ after\ free\ *)}\\
&\qquad\qquad \mid \mathtt{Some}\ \_ \rightarrow \mathtt{mset\_add}\ l\ env;\ l :=_{\mathsf{HL}} \mathtt{Some}\ v_2;\ \mathtt{ret}\, v_2)\\
[\![\mathtt{x} \leftarrow \mathtt{e}_1\, ;\mathtt{e}_2]\!] &\triangleq x \leftarrow [\![\mathtt{e}_1]\!];\ \_ \leftarrow (\mathtt{atomic\_env\ mset\_clear});\ [\![\mathtt{e}_2]\!]\\
[\![\mathtt{e}_1\,(\mathtt{e}_2)]\!] &\triangleq (f, a) \leftarrow [\![\mathtt{e}_1]\!] \mid\mid [\![\mathtt{e}_2]\!];\ \mathtt{atomic}\,(\mathtt{atomic\_env\ mset\_clear};\, f\ a)\\
[\![\mathtt{f\,(x)\{e\}}]\!] &\triangleq \mathtt{let\ rec\,f\ x} = v \leftarrow [\![\mathtt{e}]\!];\ \_ \leftarrow (\mathtt{atomic\_env\ mset\_clear});\ \mathtt{ret}\, v
\end{aligned}
$$

Fig. 2. Selected clauses from the monadic definitional semantics.

To model this, we execute each function call *atomically*. In the previous step we used a global mutex for guarding the access to the environment. We could use that mutex for function calls too. However, reusing a single mutex for entering each critical section would not work because a body of a function may contain invocations of other functions. To that extent, we use multiple mutexes to reflect the hierarchical structure of function calls.

To handle multiple mutexes, each C expression is interpreted as a HeapLang function that receives a mutex and returns its result. That is, each C expression is modeled by a monadic expression in the *reader monad* $M(A) \triangleq \mathtt{mset}\ Loc \rightarrow \mathtt{mutex} \rightarrow A$. For consistency's sake, we now also use the monad to thread through the reference to the environment ($\mathtt{mset}\ Loc$), instead of using a global variable *env* as we did in the previous step.

We use a small set of monadic combinators, shown in Fig. 1, to build the translation in a more abstract way. The return and bind operators are standard for the reader monad. The parallel operator runs two monadic expressions concurrently, propagating the environment and the mutex. The `atomic` combinator invokes a monadic expression with a fresh mutex. The `atomic_env` combinator atomically executes its body with the current environment as an argument. The `run` function executes the monadic computation by instantiating it with a fresh mutex and a new environment. Selected clauses for the translation are presented in Fig. 2. The translation of the binary operations remains virtually unchanged, except for the usage of monadic parallel composition instead of the standard one. The translation for the assignment and the sequenced bind uses the `atomic_env` combinator for querying and updating the environment. We also have to adapt our translation of values, by wrapping it in `ret`: $[\![\mathtt{v}]\!] \triangleq \mathtt{ret}\ [\![\mathtt{v}]\!]_{val}$.

A global function definition `f(x){e}` is translated as a top level let-binding. A function call is then just an atomically executed function invocation in HeapLang, modulo the fact that the function pointer and the arguments are computed in parallel. In addition, sequence points occur at the beginning of each function call and at the end of each function body [22, Annex C], and we reflect that in our translation by clearing the environment at appropriate places.

Our semantics by translation can easily be extended to cover other features of C, *e.g.*, a more advanced memory model (see Sect. 7). However the fragment presented here already illustrates the challenges that non-determinism and sequence point violations pose for verification. In the next section we describe a logic for reasoning about the semantics by translation given in this section.

3 Separation Logic with Weakest Preconditions for λMC

In this section we present a separation logic with weakest precondition propositions for reasoning about λMC programs. The logic tackles the main features of our semantics—non-determinism in expressions evaluation and sequence point violations. We will discuss the high-level rules of the logic pertaining to C connectives by going through a series of small examples.

The logic presented here is similar to the separation logic by Krebbers [29], but it is given in a weakest precondition style, and moreover, it is constructed *synthetically* on top of the separation logic framework Iris [24–26, 33], whereas the logic by Krebbers [29] is interpreted directly in a bespoke model.

The following grammar defines the formulas of the logic:

$$P, Q \in \mathsf{Prop} ::= \mathsf{True} \mid \mathsf{False} \mid \forall x.\, P \mid \exists x.\, P \mid \mathrm{v}_1 = \mathrm{v}_2 \mid \mathtt{l} \overset{q}{\mapsto}_{\xi} v \mid \qquad (q \in (0,1])$$
$$P * Q \mid P \mathrel{-\!\!*} Q \mid \mathsf{wp}\, e\, \{\Phi\} \mid \ldots \qquad (\xi \in \{L, U\})$$

Most of the connectives are commonplace in separation logic, with the exception of the modified points-to connective, which we describe in this section.

As is common, Hoare triples $\{P\}\, \mathsf{e}\, \{\Phi\}$ are syntactic sugar for $P \vdash \mathsf{wp}\ \mathsf{e}\ \{\Phi\}$. The weakest precondition connective $\mathsf{wp}\ \mathsf{e}\ \{\Phi\}$ states that the program e is safe (the program has defined behavior), and if e terminates to a value v, then v satisfies the predicate Φ. We write $\mathsf{wp}\ \mathsf{e}\ \{\mathrm{v}.\, \Phi\ \mathrm{v}\}$ for $\mathsf{wp}\ \mathsf{e}\ \{\lambda \mathrm{v}.\, \Phi\ \mathrm{v}\}$.

Contrary to the paper by Krebbers [29], we use weakest preconditions instead of Hoare triples throughout this paper. There are several reasons for doing so:

1. We do not have to manipulate the preconditions explicitly, *e.g.*, by applying the consequence rule to the precondition.
2. The soundness of our symbolic executor (Theorem 5.1) can be stated more concisely using weakest precondition propositions.
3. It is more convenient to integrate weakest preconditions into the Iris Proof Mode/MoSeL framework in Coq that we use for our implementation (Sect. 7).

A selection of rules is presented in Fig. 3. Each inference rule $\dfrac{P_1 \ \ldots\ P_n}{Q}$ in this paper should be read as the entailment $P_1 * \ldots * P_n \vdash Q$. We now explain and motivate the rules of our logic.

$$\text{WP-VALUE}\quad \frac{\Phi\ \mathtt{v}}{\mathsf{wp}\ \mathtt{v}\ \{\Phi\}} \qquad \text{WP-WAND}\quad \frac{\mathsf{wp}\ \mathtt{e}\ \{\Phi\} \qquad (\forall \mathtt{v}.\ \Phi\ \mathtt{v} \mathrel{-\!\!*} \Psi\ \mathtt{v})}{\mathsf{wp}\ \mathtt{e}\ \{\Psi\}} \qquad \text{WP-SEQ}\quad \frac{\mathsf{wp}\ \mathtt{e}_1\ \{\mathtt{v}.\ \mathbb{U}(\mathsf{wp}\ \mathtt{e}_2[\mathtt{v}/\mathtt{x}]\ \{\Phi\})\}}{\mathsf{wp}\ (\mathtt{x} \leftarrow \mathtt{e}_1\,;\mathtt{e}_2)\ \{\Phi\}}$$

$$\text{WP-BIN-OP}\quad \frac{\mathsf{wp}\ \mathtt{e}_1\ \{\Psi_1\} \qquad \mathsf{wp}\ \mathtt{e}_2\ \{\Psi_2\} \qquad (\forall \mathtt{w}_1 \mathtt{w}_2.\ \Psi_1\ \mathtt{w}_1 * \Psi_2\ \mathtt{w}_2 \mathrel{-\!\!*} \Phi(\mathtt{w}_1\ [\![\circledcirc]\!]\ \mathtt{w}_2))}{\mathsf{wp}\ (\mathtt{e}_1 \circledcirc \mathtt{e}_2)\ \{\Phi\}}$$

$$\text{WP-LOAD}\quad \frac{\mathsf{wp}\ \mathtt{e}\ \left\{\mathtt{l}.\ \exists \mathtt{w}\ q.\ \mathtt{l} \overset{q}{\mapsto}_U \mathtt{w} * (\mathtt{l} \overset{q}{\mapsto}_U \mathtt{w} \mathrel{-\!\!*} \Phi\ \mathtt{w})\right\}}{\mathsf{wp}\ (*\mathtt{e})\ \{\Phi\}} \qquad \text{WP-ALLOC}\quad \frac{\mathsf{wp}\ \mathtt{e}\ \{\mathtt{v}.\ \forall \mathtt{l}.\ \mathtt{l} \mapsto_U \mathtt{v} \mathrel{-\!\!*} \Phi\ \mathtt{l}\}}{\mathsf{wp}\ \mathtt{alloc(e)}\ \{\Phi\}}$$

$$\text{WP-STORE}\quad \frac{\begin{array}{c}\mathsf{wp}\ \mathtt{e}_1\ \{\Psi_1\} \qquad \mathsf{wp}\ \mathtt{e}_2\ \{\Psi_2\} \\ (\forall \mathtt{l}\ \mathtt{w}.\ \Psi_1\ \mathtt{l} * \Psi_2\ \mathtt{w} \mathrel{-\!\!*} \exists \mathtt{v}.\ \mathtt{l} \mapsto_U \mathtt{v} * (\mathtt{l} \mapsto_L \mathtt{w} \mathrel{-\!\!*} \Phi\ \mathtt{w}))\end{array}}{\mathsf{wp}\ (\mathtt{e}_1 = \mathtt{e}_2)\ \{\Phi\}} \qquad \text{WP-FREE}\quad \frac{\mathsf{wp}\ \mathtt{e}\ \{\mathtt{l}.\ \exists \mathtt{v}.\ \mathtt{l} \mapsto_U \mathtt{v} * \Phi\ ()\}}{\mathsf{wp}\ \mathtt{free(e)}\ \{\Phi\}}$$

$$\text{MAPSTO-SPLIT}\quad \mathtt{l} \overset{q_1}{\mapsto}_{\xi_1} \mathtt{v} * \mathtt{l} \overset{q_2}{\mapsto}_{\xi_2} \mathtt{v} \dashv\vdash \mathtt{l} \overset{q_1+q_2}{\longmapsto}_{\xi_1 \vee \xi_2} \mathtt{v} \qquad \text{MAPSTO-VALUES-AGREE}\quad \frac{\mathtt{l} \overset{q_1}{\mapsto}_{\xi_1} \mathtt{v}_1 \qquad \mathtt{l} \overset{q_2}{\mapsto}_{\xi_2} \mathtt{v}_2}{\mathtt{v}_1 = \mathtt{v}_2}$$

$$\text{U-UNLOCK}\quad \frac{\mathtt{l} \overset{q}{\mapsto}_L \mathtt{v}}{\mathbb{U}(\mathtt{l} \overset{q}{\mapsto}_U \mathtt{v})} \qquad \text{U-MONO}\quad \frac{P \mathrel{-\!\!*} Q}{\mathbb{U}P \mathrel{-\!\!*} \mathbb{U}Q} \qquad \text{U-INTRO}\quad \frac{P}{\mathbb{U}P} \qquad \text{U-SEP}\quad \frac{\mathbb{U}P * \mathbb{U}Q}{\mathbb{U}(P * Q)}$$

Fig. 3. Selected rules for weakest preconditions.

Non-determinism. In the introduction (Sect. 1) we have already shown the rule for addition from Krebbers's logic [29], which was written using Hoare triples. Using weakest preconditions, the corresponding rule (WP-BIN-OP) is:

$$\frac{\mathsf{wp}\ \mathtt{e}_1\ \{\Psi_1\} \qquad \mathsf{wp}\ \mathtt{e}_2\ \{\Psi_2\} \qquad (\forall \mathtt{w}_1 \mathtt{w}_2.\ \Psi_1\ \mathtt{w}_1 * \Psi_2\ \mathtt{w}_2 \mathrel{-\!\!*} \Phi(\mathtt{w}_1\ [\![\circledcirc]\!]\ \mathtt{w}_2))}{\mathsf{wp}\ (\mathtt{e}_1 \circledcirc \mathtt{e}_2)\ \{\Phi\}}$$

This rule closely resembles the usual rule for parallel composition in ordinary concurrent separation logic [46]. This should not be surprising, as we have given a definitional semantics to binary operators using the parallel composition operator. It is important to note that the premises WP-BIN-OP are combined using the *separating conjunction* $*$. This ensures that the weakest preconditions $\mathsf{wp}\ \mathtt{e}_1\ \{\Psi_1\}$ and $\mathsf{wp}\ \mathtt{e}_2\ \{\Psi_2\}$ for the subexpressions $\mathtt{e}_1$ and $\mathtt{e}_2$ are verified with respect to disjoint resources. As such they do not interfere with each other, and can be evaluated in parallel without causing sequence point violations.

To see how one can use the rule WP-BIN-OP, let us verify $P \vdash \mathsf{wp}\ (\mathtt{e}_1 + \mathtt{e}_2)\ \{\Phi\}$. That is, we want to show that $(\mathtt{e}_1 + \mathtt{e}_2)$ satisfies the postcondition Φ assuming the precondition P. This goal can be proven by separating the precondition P into disjoint parts $P_1 * P_2 * R \dashv\vdash P$. Then using WP-BIN-OP the goal can be reduced to proving $P_i \vdash \mathsf{wp}\ \mathsf{e}_i\ \{\Psi_i\}$ for $i \in \{0,1\}$, and $R * \Psi_1\ \mathtt{w}_1 * \Psi_2\ \mathtt{w}_2 \vdash \Phi(\mathtt{w}_1\ [\![\circledcirc]\!]\ \mathtt{w}_2)$ for any return values $\mathtt{w}_i$ of the expressions e_i.

Fractional Permissions. Separation logic includes the *points-to connective* $\mathtt{l} \mapsto \mathtt{v}$, which asserts unique ownership of a location $\mathtt{l}$ with value $\mathtt{v}$. This connective is used to specify the behavior of stateful operations, which becomes apparent in the following proposed rule for load:

$$\frac{\mathsf{wp}\ \mathsf{e}\ \{\mathtt{l}.\ \exists \mathtt{w}.\ \mathtt{l} \mapsto \mathtt{w} * (\mathtt{l} \mapsto \mathtt{w} \mathrel{-\!\!*} \Phi\ \mathtt{w})\}}{\mathsf{wp}\ (*\mathsf{e})\ \{\Phi\}}$$

In order to verify $*\mathsf{e}$ we first make sure that e evaluates to a location $\mathtt{l}$, and then we need to provide the points-to connective $\mathtt{l} \mapsto \mathtt{w}$ for some value stored at the location. This rule, together with WP-VALUE, allows for verification of simple programs like $\mathtt{l} \mapsto \mathtt{v} \vdash \mathsf{wp}\ (*\mathtt{l})\ \{\mathtt{w}.\ \mathtt{w} = \mathtt{v} * \mathtt{l} \mapsto \mathtt{v}\}$.

However, the rule above is too weak. Suppose that we wish to verify the program $*\mathtt{l} + *\mathtt{l}$ from the precondition $\mathtt{l} \mapsto \mathtt{v}$. According to WP-BIN-OP, we have to separate the proposition $\mathtt{l} \mapsto \mathtt{v}$ into two disjoint parts, each used to verify the load operation. In order to enable sharing of points-to connectives we use *fractional permissions* [7,8]. In separation logic with fractional permissions each points-to connective is annotated with a fraction $q \in (0,1]$, and the resources can be split in accordance with those fractions:

$$\mathtt{l} \overset{q_1+q_2}{\longmapsto} \mathtt{v} \dashv\vdash \mathtt{l} \overset{q_1}{\longmapsto} \mathtt{v} * \mathtt{l} \overset{q_2}{\longmapsto} \mathtt{v}.$$

A connective $\mathtt{l} \overset{1}{\mapsto} \mathtt{v}$ provides a unique ownership of the location, and we refer to it as a *write permission*. A points-to connective with $q \leq 1$ provides shared ownership of the location, referred to as a *read permission*. By convention, we write $\mathtt{l} \mapsto \mathtt{v}$ to denote the write permission $\mathtt{l} \overset{1}{\mapsto} \mathtt{v}$.

With fractional permissions at hand, we can relax the proposed load rule, by allowing to dereference a location even if we only have a read permission:

$$\frac{\mathsf{wp}\ \mathsf{e} \left\{\mathtt{l}.\ \exists \mathtt{w}\, q.\ \mathtt{l} \overset{q}{\mapsto} \mathtt{w} * (\mathtt{l} \overset{q}{\mapsto} \mathtt{w} \mathrel{-\!\!*} \Phi\ \mathtt{w})\right\}}{\mathsf{wp}\ (*\mathsf{e})\ \{\Phi\}}$$

This corresponds to the intuition that multiple subexpressions can safely dereference the same location, but not write to them.

Using the rule above we can verify $\mathtt{l} \mapsto 1 \vdash \mathsf{wp}\ (*\mathtt{l} + *\mathtt{l})\ \{\mathtt{v}.\ \mathtt{v} = 2 * \mathtt{l} \mapsto 1\}$ by splitting the assumption into $\mathtt{l} \overset{0.5}{\longmapsto} 1 * \mathtt{l} \overset{0.5}{\longmapsto} 1$ and first applying WP-BIN-OP with Ψ_1 and Ψ_2 being $\lambda \mathtt{v}.\ (\mathtt{v} = 1) * \mathtt{l} \overset{0.5}{\longmapsto} 1$. Then we apply WP-LOAD on both subgoals. After that, we can use MAPSTO-SPLIT to prove the remaining formula:

$$(\mathtt{v}_1 = 1) * \mathtt{l} \overset{0.5}{\longmapsto} 1 * (\mathtt{v}_2 = 1) * \mathtt{l} \overset{0.5}{\longmapsto} 1 \ \vdash\ (\mathtt{v}_1 + \mathtt{v}_2 = 2) * \mathtt{l} \mapsto 1.$$

The Assignment Operator. The second main operation that accesses the heap is the assignment operator $\mathsf{e}_1 = \mathsf{e}_2$. The arguments on the both sides of the assignment are evaluated in parallel, and a points-to connective is required to perform an update to the heap. A naive version of the assignment rule can be obtained by combining the binary operation rule and the load rule:

$$\frac{\mathsf{wp}\ \mathsf{e}_1\ \{\Psi_1\} \qquad \mathsf{wp}\ \mathsf{e}_2\ \{\Psi_2\} \qquad (\forall \mathtt{l}\ \mathtt{w}.\ \Psi_1\ \mathtt{l} * \Psi_2\ \mathtt{w} \twoheadrightarrow \exists \mathtt{v}.\ \mathtt{l} \mapsto \mathtt{v} * (\mathtt{l} \mapsto \mathtt{w} \twoheadrightarrow \Phi\ \mathtt{w}))}{\mathsf{wp}\ (\mathsf{e}_1 = \mathsf{e}_2)\ \{\Phi\}}$$

The write permission $\mathtt{l} \mapsto \mathtt{v}$ can be obtained by combining the resources of both sides of the assignment. This allows us to verify programs like $\mathtt{l} = *\mathtt{l} + *\mathtt{l}$.

However, the rule above is unsound, because it fails to account for sequence point violations. We could use the rule above to prove safety of undefined programs, *e.g.*, the program $\mathtt{l} = (\mathtt{l} = 3)$.

To account for sequence point violations we decorate the points-to connectives $\mathtt{l} \overset{q}{\mapsto}_{\xi} \mathtt{v}$ with *access levels* $\xi \in \{L, U\}$. These have the following semantics: we can read from and write to a location that is unlocked (U), and the location becomes locked (L) once someone writes to it. Proposition $\mathtt{l} \overset{q}{\mapsto}_U \mathtt{v}$ (resp. $\mathtt{l} \overset{q}{\mapsto}_L \mathtt{v}$) asserts ownership of the unlocked (resp. locked) location $\mathtt{l}$. We refer to such propositions as *lockable points-to connectives.* Using lockable points-to connectives we can formulate the correct assignment rule:

$$\frac{\mathsf{wp}\ \mathsf{e}_1\ \{\Psi_1\} \qquad \mathsf{wp}\ \mathsf{e}_2\ \{\Psi_2\} \qquad (\forall \mathtt{l}\ \mathtt{w}.\ \Psi_1\ \mathtt{l} * \Psi_2\ \mathtt{w} \twoheadrightarrow \exists \mathtt{v}.\ \mathtt{l} \mapsto \mathtt{v} * (\mathtt{l} \mapsto_L \mathtt{w} \twoheadrightarrow \Phi\ \mathtt{w}))}{\mathsf{wp}\ (\mathsf{e}_1 = \mathsf{e}_2)\ \{\Phi\}}$$

The set $\{L, U\}$ has a lattice structure with $L \leq U$, and the levels can be combined with a join operation, see MAPSTO-SPLIT. By convention, $\mathtt{l} \overset{q}{\mapsto} \mathtt{v}$ denotes $\mathtt{l} \overset{q}{\mapsto}_U \mathtt{v}$.

The Unlocking Modality. As locations become locked after using the assignment rule, we wish to unlock them in order to perform further heap operations. For instance, in the expression $\mathtt{l} = 4\,; *\mathtt{l}$ the location $\mathtt{l}$ becomes unlocked after the sequence point ";" between the store and the dereferencing operations. To reflect this in the logic, we use the rule WP-SEQ which features the *unlocking modality* $\mathbb{U}$ (which is called the unlocking assertion in [29, Definition 5.6]):

$$\frac{\mathsf{wp}\ \mathsf{e}_1\ \{\_.\ \mathbb{U}(\mathsf{wp}\ \mathsf{e}_2\ \{\Phi\})\}}{\mathsf{wp}\ (\mathsf{e}_1\,;\mathsf{e}_2)\ \{\Phi\}}$$

Intuitively, $\mathbb{U}P$ states that P holds, after unlocking all locations. The rules of $\mathbb{U}$ in Fig. 3 allow one to turn $(P_1 * \ldots * P_m) * (\mathtt{l}_1 \mapsto_L \mathtt{v}_1 * \ldots * \mathtt{l}_m \mapsto_L \mathtt{v}_m) \vdash \mathbb{U}Q$ into $(P_1 * \ldots * P_m) * (\mathtt{l}_1 \mapsto_U \mathtt{v}_1 * \ldots * \mathtt{l}_m \mapsto_U \mathtt{v}_m) \vdash Q$. This is done by applying either U-UNLOCK or U-INTRO to each premise; then collecting all premises into one formula under $\mathbb{U}$ by U-SEP; and finally, applying U-MONO to the whole sequent.

4 Soundness of Weakest Preconditions for λMC

In this section we prove adequacy of the separation logic with weakest preconditions for λMC as presented in Sect. 3. We do this by giving a model using the Iris framework that is structured in a similar way as the translation that we gave in Sect. 2. This translation consisted of three layers: the target HeapLang language, the monadic combinators, and the λMC operations themselves. In the model, each corresponding layer abstracts from the details of the previous layer, in such a way that we never have to break the abstraction of a layer. At the end, putting all of this together, we get the following adequacy statement:

Theorem 4.1 (Adequacy of Weakest Preconditions). *If* $\mathsf{wp}\ \mathsf{e}\ \{\Phi\}$ *is derivable, then* e *has no undefined behavior for any evaluation order. In other words,* run(e) *does not assert false.*

The proof of the adequacy theorem closely follows the layered structure, by combining the correctness of the monadic run combinator with adequacy of HeapLang in Iris [25, Theorem 6]. The rest of this section is organized as:

1. Because our translation targets HeapLang, we start by recalling the separation logic with weakest preconditions, for HeapLang part of Iris (Sect. 4.1).
2. On top of the logic for HeapLang, we define a notion of weakest preconditions $\mathsf{wp}_{\mathsf{mon}}\ e\ \{\Phi\}$ for expressions e built from our monadic combinators (Sect. 4.2).
3. Next, we define the lockable points-to connective $\ell \overset{q}{\mapsto}_{\xi} v$ using Iris's machinery for custom ghost state (Sect. 4.3).
4. Finally, we define weakest preconditions for λMC by combining the weakest preconditions for monadic expressions with our translation scheme (Sect. 4.4).

4.1 Weakest Preconditions for HeapLang

We recall the most essential Iris connectives for reasoning about HeapLang programs: $\mathsf{wp}_{\mathsf{HL}}\ e\ \{\Phi\}$ and $\ell \mapsto_{\mathsf{HL}} v$, which are the HeapLang weakest precondition proposition and the HeapLang points-to connective, respectively. Other Iris connectives are described in [6, Section 8.1] or [25,33]. An example rule is the store rule for HeapLang, shown in Fig. 4. The rule requires a points-to connective $\ell \mapsto_{\mathsf{HL}} v$, and the user receives the updated points-to connective $\ell \mapsto_{\mathsf{HL}} w$ back for proving $\Phi\ ()$. Note that the rule is formulated for a concrete location ℓ and a value w, instead of arbitrary expressions. This does not limit the expressive power; since the evaluation order in HeapLang is deterministic[1], arbitrary expressions can be handled using the WP_{HL}-BIND rule. Using this rule, one can bind an expression e in an arbitrary evaluation context K. We can thus use the WP_{HL}-BIND rule twice to derive a more general store rule for HeapLang:

$$\frac{\mathsf{wp}_{\mathsf{HL}}\ e_2\ \{w.\ \mathsf{wp}_{\mathsf{HL}}\ e_1\ \{\ell.\ (\exists v.\ \ell \mapsto_{\mathsf{HL}} v) * (\ell \mapsto_{\mathsf{HL}} w \mathrel{-\!\!*} \Phi\ ())\}\}}{\mathsf{wp}_{\mathsf{HL}}\ (e_1 :=_{\mathsf{HL}} e_2)\ \{\Phi\}}$$

[1] And right-to-left, although our monadic translation does not rely on that.

$$(\ell \mapsto_{\mathsf{HL}} v) * (\ell \mapsto_{\mathsf{HL}} v \mathrel{-\!\!*} \Phi\, v) \vdash \mathsf{wp}_{\mathsf{HL}}\ !_{\mathsf{HL}}\, \ell \,\{\Phi\}$$

$$(\ell \mapsto_{\mathsf{HL}} v) * (\ell \mapsto_{\mathsf{HL}} w \mathrel{-\!\!*} \Phi\, ()) \vdash \mathsf{wp}_{\mathsf{HL}}\ \ell :=_{\mathsf{HL}} w \,\{\Phi\}$$

WPHL-BIND

$$\frac{\mathsf{wp}_{\mathsf{HL}}\ e\,\{v.\,\mathsf{wp}_{\mathsf{HL}}\ K[\,v\,]\,\{\Phi\}\}}{\mathsf{wp}_{\mathsf{HL}}\ K[\,e\,]\,\{\Phi\}}$$

$$R * (\forall \gamma\ lk.\ \mathsf{is\_mutex}(\gamma, lk, R) \mathrel{-\!\!*} \Phi\ lk) \vdash \mathsf{wp}_{\mathsf{HL}}\ \texttt{newmutex}\ ()\,\{\Phi\}$$

$$\mathsf{is\_mutex}(\gamma, lk, R) * (R * \mathsf{locked}(\gamma) \mathrel{-\!\!*} \Phi\, ()) \vdash \mathsf{wp}_{\mathsf{HL}}\ \texttt{acquire}\ lk\,\{\Phi\}$$

$$\mathsf{is\_mutex}(\gamma, lk, R) * R * \mathsf{locked}(\gamma) * \Phi\, () \vdash \mathsf{wp}_{\mathsf{HL}}\ \texttt{release}\ lk\,\{\Phi\}$$

$$\mathsf{is\_mutex}(\gamma, lk, R) * \mathsf{is\_mutex}(\gamma, lk, R) \dashv\vdash \mathsf{is\_mutex}(\gamma, lk, R) \qquad \text{(ISMUTEX-DUPL)}$$

Fig. 4. Selected $\mathsf{wp}_{\mathsf{HL}}$ rules.

To verify the monadic combinators and the translation of λMC operations in the upcoming Sects. 4.2 and 4.4, we need the specifications for all the functions that we use, including those on mutable sets and mutexes. The rules for mutable sets are standard, and thus omitted. They involve the usual abstract predicate $\mathsf{is\_mset}(s, X)$ stating that the reference s represents a set with contents X. The rules for mutexes are presented in Fig. 4. When a new mutex is created, a user gets access to a proposition $\mathsf{is\_mutex}(\gamma, lk, R)$, which states that the value lk is a mutex containing the resources R. This proposition can be duplicated freely (ISMUTEX-DUPL). A thread can acquire the mutex and receive the resources contained in it. In addition, the thread receives a token $\mathsf{locked}(\gamma)$ meaning that it has entered the critical section. When a thread leaves the critical section and releases the mutex, it has to give up both the token and the resources R.

4.2 Weakest Preconditions for Monadic Expressions

As a next step, we define a weakest precondition proposition $\mathsf{wp}_{\mathsf{mon}}\ e\,\{\Phi\}$ for a monadic expression e. The definition is constructed in the ambient logic, and it encapsulates the monadic operations in a separate layer. Due to that, we are able to carry out proofs of high-level specifications without breaking the abstraction (Sect. 4.4). The specifications for selected monadic operations in terms of $\mathsf{wp}_{\mathsf{mon}}$ are presented in Fig. 5. We define the weakest precondition for a monadic expression e as follows:

$$\mathsf{wp}_{\mathsf{mon}}\ e\,\{\Phi\} \triangleq \mathsf{wp}_{\mathsf{HL}}\ e \left\{ \begin{array}{c} g.\ \forall \gamma\ env\ lk.\ \mathsf{is\_mutex}(\gamma, lk, \mathsf{env\_inv}(env)) \mathrel{-\!\!*} \\ \mathsf{wp}_{\mathsf{HL}}\ (g\ env\ lk)\,\{\Phi\} \end{array} \right\}$$

The idea is that we first reduce e to a monadic value g. To perform this reduction we have the outermost $\mathsf{wp}_{\mathsf{HL}}$ connective in the definition of $\mathsf{wp}_{\mathsf{mon}}$. This monadic value is then evaluated with an arbitrary environment and an arbitrary mutex. Note that we universally quantify over any mutex lk to support nested locking in `atomic`. This definition is parameterized by an *environment invariant* $\mathsf{env\_inv}(env)$, which describes the resources accessible in the critical sections. We show how to define $\mathsf{env\_inv}$ in the next subsection.

WP-RET
$$\frac{\mathsf{wp}_{\mathsf{HL}}\ e\ \{\Phi\}}{\mathsf{wp}_{\mathsf{mon}}\ (\mathtt{ret}\ e)\ \{\Phi\}}$$

WP-BIND
$$\frac{\mathsf{wp}_{\mathsf{mon}}\ e_1\ \{v.\, \mathsf{wp}_{\mathsf{mon}}\ e_2[v/x]\ \{\Phi\}\}}{\mathsf{wp}_{\mathsf{mon}}\ (x \leftarrow e_1;\ e_2)\ \{\Phi\}}$$

WP-PAR
$$\frac{\mathsf{wp}_{\mathsf{mon}}\ e_1\ \{\Psi_1\} \qquad \mathsf{wp}_{\mathsf{mon}}\ e_2\ \{\Psi_2\} \qquad (\forall w_1 w_2.\, \Psi_1\ w_1 * \Psi_2\ w_2 \twoheadrightarrow \Phi\ (w_1, w_2))}{\mathsf{wp}_{\mathsf{mon}}\ (e_1 \mid\mid e_2)\ \{\Phi\}}$$

WP-ATOMIC-ENV
$$\frac{\forall \mathit{env}.\, \mathsf{env\_inv}(\mathit{env}) \twoheadrightarrow \mathsf{wp}_{\mathsf{HL}}\ (v\ \mathit{env})\ \{w.\, \mathsf{env\_inv}(\mathit{env}) * \Phi\ w\}}{\mathsf{wp}_{\mathsf{mon}}\ (\mathtt{atomic\_env}\ v)\ \{\Phi\}}$$

Fig. 5. Selected monadic $\mathsf{wp}_{\mathsf{mon}}$ rules.

Using this definition we derive the monadic rules in Fig. 5. In a monad, the expression evaluation order is made explicit via the bind operation $x \leftarrow e_1;\ e_2$. To that extent, contrary to HeapLang, we no longer have a rule like WP$_{\text{HL}}$-BIND, which allows to bind an expression in a general evaluation context. Instead, we have the rule WP-BIND, which reflects that the only evaluation context we have is the monadic bind $x \leftarrow [\bullet];\ e$.

4.3 Modeling the Heap

The monadic rules in Fig. 5 are expressive enough to derive some of the λMC-level rules, but we are still missing one crucial part: handling of the heap. In order to do that, we need to define lockable points-to connectives $\mathtt{l} \overset{q}{\mapsto}_{\xi} \mathtt{v}$ in such a way that they are linked to the HeapLang points-to connectives $\ell \mapsto_{\mathsf{HL}} v$.

The key idea is the following. The environment invariant env_inv of monadic weakest preconditions will track *all* HeapLang points-to connectives $\ell \mapsto_{\mathsf{HL}} v$ that have ever been allocated at the λMC level. Via Iris ghost state, we then connect this knowledge to the lockable points-to connectives $\mathtt{l} \overset{q}{\mapsto}_{\xi} \mathtt{v}$. We refer to the construction that allows us to carry this out as the *lockable heap*. Note that the description of lockable heap is fairly technical and requires an understanding of the ghost state mechanism in Iris.

A lockable heap is a map $\sigma : \mathit{Loc} \xrightarrow{\text{fin}} \{L, U\} \times \mathit{Val}$ that keeps track of the access levels and values associated with the locations. The connective $\mathsf{full\_heap}(\sigma)$ asserts the ownership of all the locations present in the domain of σ. Specifically, it asserts $\ell \mapsto_{\mathsf{HL}} v$ for each $\{\ell \leftarrow (\xi, v)\} \in \sigma$. The connective $\ell \overset{q}{\mapsto}_{\xi} v$ then states that $\{\ell \leftarrow (\xi, v)\}$ is part of the global lockable heap, and it asserts this with the fractional permission q. We treat the lockable heap as an opaque abstraction, whose exact implementation via Iris ghost state is described in the Coq formalization [18]. The main interface for the locking heap are the rules in Fig. 6. The rule HEAP-ALLOC states that we can turn a HeapLang points-to connective $\ell \mapsto_{\mathsf{HL}} v$ into $\ell \mapsto_{\xi} v$ by changing the lockable heap σ accordingly. The

$$\frac{\ell \mapsto_{\mathsf{HL}} v \qquad \mathsf{full\_heap}(\sigma)}{\Rrightarrow \ell \mapsto_U v * \mathsf{full\_heap}(\sigma\,[\ell \leftarrow (U,v)])}\ \text{HEAP-ALLOC}$$

$$\frac{\ell \mapsto_U v \qquad \mathsf{full\_heap}(\sigma)}{\Rrightarrow \sigma(\ell) = (U,v) * \ell \mapsto_{\mathsf{HL}} v * (\forall v'\,\xi'.\,\ell \mapsto_{\mathsf{HL}} v' \Rrightarrow\!\!* \ \ell \mapsto_{\xi'} v' * \mathsf{full\_heap}(\sigma\,[\ell \leftarrow (\xi',v')]))}\ \text{HEAP-UPD}$$

Fig. 6. Selected rules of the lockable heap construction.

rule HEAP-UPD states that given $\ell \mapsto_\xi v$, we can temporarily get a HeapLang points-to connective $\ell \mapsto_{\mathsf{HL}} v$ out of the locking heap and update its value.

The environment invariant $\mathsf{env\_inv}(env)$ in the definition of $\mathsf{wp}_{\mathsf{mon}}$ ties the contents of the lockable heap to the contents of the environment env:

$$\mathsf{env\_inv}(env) \triangleq \exists \sigma\, X.\ \mathsf{is\_set}(env, X) * \mathsf{full\_heap}(\sigma) * (\forall \ell \in X. \exists v.\, \sigma(\ell) = (L, v))$$

The first conjunct states that $X : \wp^{\mathrm{fin}}(Loc)$ is a set of locked locations, according to the environment env. The second conjunct asserts ownership of the global lockable heap σ. Finally, the last conjunct states that the contents of env agrees with the lockable heap: every location that is in X is locked according to σ.

The Unlocking Modality. The unlocking modality is defined in the logic as:

$$\mathbb{U} P \triangleq \exists S.\, (\mathop{\Huge *}_{(\mathtt{l},\mathtt{v},q)\in S} \mathtt{l} \overset{q}{\mapsto}_L \mathtt{v}) * ((\mathop{\Huge *}_{(\mathtt{l},\mathtt{v},q)\in S} \mathtt{l} \overset{q}{\mapsto}_U \mathtt{v}) \mathrel{-\!\!*} P)$$

Here S is a finite multiset of tuples containing locations, values, and fractions. The update modality accumulates the locked locations, waiting for them to be unlocked at a sequence point.

4.4 Deriving the λMC Rules

To model weakest preconditions for λMC (Fig. 3) we compose the construction we have just defined with the translation of Sect. 2 $\mathsf{wp}\ \mathsf{e}\ \{\Phi\} \triangleq \mathsf{wp}_{\mathsf{mon}}\ [\![\mathsf{e}]\!]\ \{\Phi'\}$. Here, Φ' is the obvious lifting of Φ from λMC values to HeapLang values. Using the rules from Figs. 5 and 6 we derive the high-level λMC rules without unfolding the definition of the monadic $\mathsf{wp}_{\mathsf{mon}}$.

Example 4.2. Consider the rule WP-STORE for assignments $\mathsf{e}_1 = \mathsf{e}_2$. Using WP-BIND and WP-PAR, the soundness of WP-STORE can be reduced to verifying the assignment with e_1 being $\mathtt{l}$, e_2 being $\mathtt{v}'$, under the assumption $\mathtt{l} \mapsto_U \mathtt{v}$. We use WP-ATOMIC-ENV to turn our goal into a HeapLang weakest precondition proposition and to gain access an environment env, and to the proposition $\mathsf{env\_inv}(env)$, from which we extract the lockable heap σ. We then use HEAP-UPD to get access to the underlying HeapLang location and obtain that l is not locked according to σ. Due to the environment invariant, we obtain that l is not in *env*, which allows us to prove the assert for sequence point violation in the interpretation of the assignment. Finally, we perform the physical update of the location.

5 A Symbolic Executor for λMC

In order to turn our program logic into an automated procedure, it is important to have rules for weakest preconditions that have an algorithmic form. However, the rules for binary operators in our separation logic for λMC do not have such a form. Take for example the rule WP-BIN-OP for binary operators $e_1 \circledcirc e_2$. This rule cannot be applied in an algorithmic manner. To use the rule one should supply the postconditions for e_1 and e_2, and frame the resources from the context into two disjoint parts. This is generally impossible to do automatically.

To address this problem, we first describe how the rules for binary operators can be transformed into algorithmic rules by exploiting the notion of *symbolic execution* [5] (Sect. 5.1). We then show how to implement these algorithmic rules as part of an automated symbolic execution procedure (Sect. 5.2).

5.1 Rules for Symbolic Execution

We say that we can *symbolically execute* an expression e using a *precondition* P, if we can find a *symbolic execution tuple* (w, Q, R) consisting of a *return value* w, a *postcondition* Q, and a *frame* R satisfying:

$$P \vdash \mathsf{wp}\ e\ \{v.\ v = w * Q\} * R$$

This specification is much like that of ordinary symbolic execution in separation logic [5], but there is important difference. Apart from computing the postcondition Q and the return value w, there is also the frame R, which describes the resources that are *not used* for proving e. For instance, if the precondition P is $P' * l \overset{q}{\mapsto} w$ and e is a load operation $*l$, then we can symbolically execute e with the postcondition Q being $l \overset{q/2}{\longmapsto} w$, and the frame R being $P' * l \overset{q/2}{\longmapsto} w$. Clearly, P' is not needed for proving the load, so it can be moved into the frame. More interestingly, since loading the contents of l requires a read permission $l \overset{p}{\mapsto} w$, with $p \in (0, 1]$, we can split the hypothesis $l \overset{q}{\mapsto} w$ into two halves and move one into the frame. Below we will see why that matters.

If we can symbolically execute one of the operands of a binary expression $e_1 \circledcirc e_2$, say e_1 in P, and find a symbolic execution tuple (w_1, Q, R), then we can use the following admissible rule:

$$\frac{R \vdash \mathsf{wp}\ e_2\ \{w_2.\ Q \twoheadrightarrow \Phi\ (w_1\ [\![\circledcirc]\!]\ w_2)\}}{P \vdash \mathsf{wp}\ (e_1 \circledcirc e_2)\ \{\Phi\}}$$

This rule has a much more algorithmic flavor than the rule WP-BIN-OP. Applying the above rule now boils down to finding such a tuple (w, Q, R), instead of having to infer postconditions for both operands, as we need to do to apply WP-BIN-OP.

For instance, given an expression $(*\mathtt{l}) \circledcirc \mathsf{e}_2$ and a precondition $P' * \mathtt{l} \overset{q}{\mapsto} \mathtt{v}$, we can derive the following rule:

$$\frac{P' * \mathtt{l} \overset{q/2}{\longmapsto} \mathtt{v} \vdash \mathsf{wp}\ \mathsf{e}_2 \left\{ \mathtt{w}_2.\ \mathtt{l} \overset{q/2}{\longmapsto} \mathtt{v} \mathrel{-\!\!*} \Phi\ (\mathtt{v}\ [\![\circledcirc]\!]\ \mathtt{w}_2) \right\}}{P' * \mathtt{l} \overset{q}{\mapsto} \mathtt{v} \vdash \mathsf{wp}\ (*\mathtt{l} \circledcirc \mathsf{e}_2)\ \{\Phi\}}$$

This rule matches the intuition that only a fraction of the permission $\mathtt{l} \overset{q}{\mapsto} \mathtt{v}$ is needed to prove a load $*\mathtt{l}$, so that the remaining half of the permission can be used to prove the correctness of e_2 (which may contain other loads of $\mathtt{l}$).

5.2 An Algorithm for Symbolic Execution

For an arbitrary expression e and a proposition P, it is unlikely that one can find such a symbolic execution tuple $(\mathtt{w}, Q, R)$ automatically. However, for a certain class of C expressions that appear in actual programs we can compute a choice of such a tuple. To illustrate our approach, we will define such an algorithm for a small subset $\overline{\mathsf{expr}}$ of C expressions described by the following grammar:

$$\bar{\mathsf{e}} \in \overline{\mathsf{expr}} ::= \mathsf{v} \mid *\bar{\mathsf{e}} \mid \bar{\mathsf{e}}_1 = \bar{\mathsf{e}}_2 \mid \bar{\mathsf{e}}_1 \circledcirc \bar{\mathsf{e}}_2.$$

We keep this subset small to ease presentation. In Sect. 7 we explain how to extend the algorithm to cover the sequenced bind operator $\mathtt{x} \leftarrow \bar{\mathsf{e}}_1 ; \bar{\mathsf{e}}_2$.

Moreover, to implement symbolic execution, we cannot manipulate arbitrary separation logic propositions. We thus restrict to *symbolic heaps* ($m \in \mathsf{sheap}$), which are defined as finite partial functions $\mathsf{Loc} \overset{\text{fin}}{\rightharpoonup} (\{L, U\} \times (0, 1] \times \mathsf{val})$ representing a collection of points-to propositions:

$$[\![m]\!] \triangleq \mathop{\LARGE *}_{\substack{\mathtt{l} \in \mathrm{dom}(m) \\ m(\mathtt{l}) = (\xi, \mathtt{q}, \mathtt{v})}} \mathtt{l} \overset{q}{\mapsto}_{\xi} \mathtt{v}.$$

We use the following operations on symbolic heaps:

- $m[\mathtt{l} \mapsto (\xi, q, \mathtt{v})]$ sets the entry $m(\mathtt{l})$ to $(\xi, q, \mathtt{v})$;
- $m \setminus \{\mathtt{l} \mapsto \_\}$ removes the entry $m(\mathtt{l})$ from m;
- $m_1 \sqcup m_2$ merges the symbolic heaps m_1 and m_2 in such a way that for each $\mathtt{l} \in \mathrm{dom}(m_1) \cup \mathrm{dom}(m_2)$, we have:

$$(m_1 \sqcup m_2)(\mathtt{l}) = \begin{cases} m_i(\mathtt{l}) & \text{if } \mathtt{l} \in \mathrm{dom}(m_i) \text{ and } \mathtt{l} \notin \mathrm{dom}(m_j) \\ (\xi \vee \xi', q + q', \mathtt{v}) & \text{if } m_1(\mathtt{l}) = (\xi, q, \mathtt{v}) \text{ and } m_2(\mathtt{l}) = (\xi', q', \_). \end{cases}$$

With this representation of propositions, we define the symbolic execution algorithm as a partial function $\mathsf{forward} : (\mathsf{sheap} \times \mathsf{expr}) \rightarrow (\mathsf{val} \times \mathsf{sheap} \times \mathsf{sheap})$, which satisfies the specification stated in Sect. 5.1, *i.e.*, for which the following holds:

Theorem 5.1. *Given an expression* e *and an symbolic heap* m, *if* $\mathsf{forward}(m, \mathsf{e})$ *returns a tuple* $(\mathtt{w}, m_1^o, m_1)$, *then* $[\![m]\!] \vdash \mathsf{wp}\ \mathsf{e}\ \{\mathtt{v}.\ \mathtt{v} = \mathtt{w} * [\![m_1^o]\!]\} * [\![m_1]\!]$.

The definition of the algorithm is shown in Fig. 7. Given a tuple $(m, \mathtt{e})$, a call to $\mathsf{forward}\,(m, \mathtt{e})$ either returns a tuple $(\mathtt{v}, m^o, m')$ or fails, which either happens when $\mathtt{e} \notin \overline{\mathsf{expr}}$ or when one of intermediate steps of computation fails. In the latter cases, we write $\mathsf{forward}\,(m, \mathtt{e}) = \bot$.

The algorithm proceeds by case analysis on the expression e. In each case, the expected output is described by the equation $\mathsf{forward}\,(m, \mathtt{e}) = (\mathtt{v}, m^o, m')$. The results of the intermediate computations appear on separate lines under the clause "**where** ...". If one of the corresponding equations does not hold, *e.g.*, a recursive call fails, then the failure is propagated. Let us now explain the case for the assignment operator.

If e is an assignment operator $\mathtt{e}_1 = \mathtt{e}_2$, we first evaluate $\mathtt{e}_1$ and then $\mathtt{e}_2$. Fixing the order of symbolic execution from left to right does not compromise the non-determinism underlying the C semantics of binary operators. Indeed, when $\mathsf{forward}\,(m, \mathtt{e}_1) = (\mathtt{v}_1, m_1^o, m_1)$, we evaluate the expression $\mathtt{e}_2$, using the frame m_1, *i.e.*, only the resources of m that remain after the execution of $\mathtt{e}_1$. When $\mathsf{forward}\,(m, \mathtt{e}_1) = (\mathtt{l}, m_1^o, m_1)$, with $\mathtt{l} \in \mathsf{Loc}$, and $\mathsf{forward}\,(m_1, \mathtt{e}_2) = (\mathtt{v}_2, m_2^o, m_2)$, the function $\mathsf{delete\_full\_2}\,(\mathtt{l}, m_2, m_1^o \sqcup m_2^o)$ checks whether $(m_2 \sqcup m_1^o \sqcup m_2^o)(\mathtt{l})$

$$\mathsf{forward}\,(m, \mathtt{v}) \triangleq (\mathtt{v}, \varnothing, m)$$

$$\begin{aligned} \mathsf{forward}\,(m, \mathtt{e}_1 \circledcirc \mathtt{e}_2) &\triangleq (\mathtt{v}_1 \; [\![\circledcirc]\!] \; \mathtt{v}_2, m_1^o \sqcup m_2^o, m_2) \\ \textbf{where}\ (\mathtt{v}_1, m_1^o, m_1) &= \mathsf{forward}\,(m, \mathtt{e}_1) \\ (\mathtt{v}_2, m_2^o, m_2) &= \mathsf{forward}\,(m_1, \mathtt{e}_2) \end{aligned}$$

$$\begin{aligned} \mathsf{forward}\,(m, {*}\mathtt{e}_1) &\triangleq (\mathtt{w}, m_2^o \sqcup \{\mathtt{l} \mapsto (U, q, \mathtt{w})\}, m_2) \\ \textbf{where}\quad (\mathtt{l}, m_1^o, m_1) &= \mathsf{forward}\,(m, \mathtt{e}_1) \qquad \text{provided } \mathtt{l} \in \mathsf{Loc} \\ (m_2, m_2^o, q, \mathtt{w}) &= \mathsf{delete\_frac\_2}\,(\mathtt{l}, m_1, m_1^o) \end{aligned}$$

$$\begin{aligned} \mathsf{forward}\,(m, \mathtt{e}_1 = \mathtt{e}_2) &\triangleq (\mathtt{v}_2, m_3^o \sqcup \{\mathtt{l} \mapsto (L, 1, \mathtt{v}_2)\}, m_3) \\ \textbf{where}\quad (\mathtt{l}, m_1^o, m_1) &= \mathsf{forward}\,(m, \mathtt{e}_1) \qquad \text{provided } \mathtt{l} \in \mathsf{Loc} \\ (\mathtt{v}_2, m_2^o, m_2) &= \mathsf{forward}\,(m_1, \mathtt{e}_2) \\ (m_3, m_3^o) &= \mathsf{delete\_full\_2}\,(\mathtt{l}, m_2, m_1^o \sqcup m_2^o) \end{aligned}$$

$$\mathsf{forward}\,(m, \mathtt{e}) \triangleq \bot \qquad \text{if } \mathtt{e} \notin \overline{\mathsf{expr}}$$

Auxiliary functions:

$$\mathsf{delete\_frac\_2}\,(\mathtt{l}, m_1, m_2) \triangleq \begin{cases} (m_1\,[\mathtt{l} \mapsto (U, q/2, \mathtt{v})], m_2, q/2, \mathtt{v}) & \text{if } m_1(\mathtt{l}) = (U, q, \mathtt{v}) \\ (m_1, m_2\,[\mathtt{l} \mapsto (U, q/2, \mathtt{v})], q/2, \mathtt{v}) & \text{if } m_1(\mathtt{l}) \neq (U, \_, \_), \\ & \quad m_2(\mathtt{l}) = (U, q, \mathtt{v}) \\ \bot & \text{otherwise} \end{cases}$$

$$\begin{aligned} \mathsf{delete\_full\_2}\,(\mathtt{l}, m_1, m_2) &\triangleq (m_1 \setminus \{\mathtt{l} \mapsto \_\}, m_2 \setminus \{\mathtt{l} \mapsto \_\}) \\ \textbf{where}\ (U, 1, \_) &= (m_1 \sqcup m_2)(\mathtt{l}) \end{aligned}$$

Fig. 7. The definition of the symbolic executor.

contains the write permission $\mathtt{l} \mapsto_U \_$. If this holds, it removes the location $\mathtt{l}$, so that the write permission is now consumed. Finally, we merge $\{\mathtt{l} \mapsto (L, 1, \mathtt{v}_2)\}$ with the output heap m_3^o, so that after assignment, the write permission $\mathtt{l} \mapsto_L \mathtt{v}_2$ is given back in a locked state.

6 A Verification Condition Generator for λMC

To establish correctness of programs, we need to prove goals $P \vdash \mathsf{wp}\ \mathsf{e}\ \{\Phi\}$. To prove such a goal, one has to repeatedly apply the rules for weakest preconditions, intertwined with logical reasoning. In this section we will automate this process for λMC by means of a *verification condition generator* (vcgen).

As a first attempt to define a vcgen, one could try to recurse over the expression e and apply the rules in Fig. 3 eagerly. This would turn the goal into a separation logic proposition that subsequently should be solved. However, as we pointed out in Sect. 5.1, the resulting separation logic proposition will be very difficult to prove—either interactively or automatically—due to the existentially quantified postconditions that appear because of uses of the rules for binary operators (*e.g.,* WP-BIN-OP). We then proposed alternative rules that avoid the need for existential quantifiers. These rules look like:

$$\frac{R \vdash \mathsf{wp}\ \mathsf{e}_2\ \{\mathsf{v}_2.\ Q \mathrel{-\!\!*} \Phi\ (\mathsf{v}_1\ [\![\circledcirc]\!]\ \mathsf{v}_2)\}}{P \vdash \mathsf{wp}\ (\mathsf{e}_1 \circledcirc \mathsf{e}_2)\ \{\Phi\}}$$

To use this rule, the crux is to symbolically execute e_1 with precondition P into a symbolic execution triple (v_1, Q, R), which we alluded could be automatically computed by means of the symbolic executor if $\mathsf{e}_1 \in \overline{\mathsf{expr}}$ (Sect. 5.2).

We can only use the symbolic executor if P is of the shape $[\![m]\!]$ for a symbolic heap m. However, in actual program verification, the precondition P is hardly ever of that shape. In addition to a series of points-to connectives (as described by a symbolic heap), we may have arbitrary propositions of separation logic, such as pure facts, abstract predicates, nested Hoare triples, Iris ghost state, *etc.* These propositions may be needed to prove intermediate verification conditions, *e.g.,* for function calls. As such, to effectively apply the above rule, we need to separate our precondition P into two parts: a symbolic heap $[\![m]\!]$ and a remainder P'. Assuming $\mathsf{forward}(m, \mathsf{e}_1) = (\mathsf{v}_1, m_1^o, m_1)$, we may then use the following rule:

$$\frac{P' * [\![m_1]\!] \vdash \mathsf{wp}\ \mathsf{e}_2\ \{\mathsf{v}_2.\ [\![m_1^o]\!] \mathrel{-\!\!*} \Phi\ (\mathsf{v}_1\ [\![\circledcirc]\!]\ \mathsf{v}_2)\}}{P' * [\![m]\!] \vdash \mathsf{wp}\ (\mathsf{e}_1 \circledcirc \mathsf{e}_2)\ \{\Phi\}}$$

It is important to notice that by applying this rule, the remainder P' remains in our precondition as is, but the symbolic heap is changed from $[\![m]\!]$ into $[\![m_1]\!]$, *i.e.,* into the frame that we obtained by symbolically executing e_1.

It should come as no surprise that we can automate this process, by applying rules, such as the one we have given above, recursively, and threading through symbolic heaps. Formally, we do this by defining the vcgen as a total function: $\mathsf{vcg} : (\mathsf{sheap} \times \mathsf{expr} \times (\mathsf{sheap} \to \mathsf{val} \to \mathsf{Prop})) \to \mathsf{Prop}$ where Prop is the type of propositions of our logic. The definition of vcg is given in Fig. 8. Before explaining the details, let us state its correctness theorem:

Theorem 6.1. *Given an expression* e*, a symbolic heap* m*, and a postcondition* Φ*, the following statement holds:*

$$\frac{P' \vdash \mathsf{vcg}\,(m, \mathsf{e}, \lambda m'\,\mathtt{v}.\,[\![m']\!] \mathrel{-\!\!*} \Phi\,\mathtt{v})}{P' * [\![m]\!] \vdash \mathsf{wp}\;\mathsf{e}\;\{\Phi\}}$$

This theorem reflects the general shape of the rules we previously described. We start off with a goal $P' * [\![m]\!] \vdash \mathsf{wp}\;\mathsf{e}\;\{\Phi\}$, and after using the vcgen, we should prove that the generated goal follows from P'. It is important to note that the continuation in the vcgen is not only parameterized by the return value, but also by a symbolic heap corresponding to the resources that remain. To get these resources back, the vcgen is initiated with the continuation $\lambda m'\,\mathtt{v}.\,[\![m']\!] \mathrel{-\!\!*} \Phi\,\mathtt{v}$.

Most clauses of the definition of the vcgen (Fig. 8) follow the approach we described so far. For unary expressions like load we generate a condition that corresponds to the weakest precondition rule. For binary expressions, we symbolically execute either operand, and proceed recursively in the other. There are a number of important bells and whistles that we will discuss now.

Sequencing. In the case of sequenced binds $\mathtt{x} \leftarrow \mathsf{e}_1\,;\mathsf{e}_2$, we recursively compute the verification condition for e_1 with the continuation:

$$\lambda m'\,\mathtt{v}.\,\mathbb{U}\;(\mathsf{vcg}(\mathsf{unlock}(m'), \mathsf{e}_2\,[\mathtt{v}/\mathtt{x}], \mathcal{K}))\,.$$

Due to a sequence point, all locations modified by e_1 will be in the unlocked state after it is finished executing. Therefore, in the recursive call to e_2 we unlock all locations in the symbolic heap (*c.f.* $\mathsf{unlock}(m')$), and we include a $\mathbb{U}$ modality in the continuation. The $\mathbb{U}$ modality is crucial so that the resources that are not given to the vcgen (the remainder P' in Theorem 6.1) can also be unlocked.

Handling Failure. In the case of binary operators $\mathsf{e}_1 \circledcirc \mathsf{e}_2$, it could be that the symbolic executor fails on both e_1 and e_2, because neither of the arguments were of the right shape (*i.e.*, not an element of $\overline{\mathsf{expr}}$), or the required resources were not present in the symbolic heap. In this case the vcgen generates the goal of the form $[\![m]\!] \mathrel{-\!\!*} \mathsf{wp}\;(\mathsf{e}_1 \circledcirc \mathsf{e}_2)\;\{\mathcal{K}_{\mathtt{ret}}\}$ where $\mathcal{K}_{\mathtt{ret}} \triangleq \lambda\mathtt{w}.\,\exists m'.\,[\![m']\!] * \mathcal{K}\;m'\,\mathtt{w}$. What appears here is that the current symbolic heap $[\![m]\!]$ is given back to the user, which they can use to prove the weakest precondition of $e_1 \circledcirc e_2$ by hand. Through the postcondition $\exists m'.\,[\![m']\!] * \mathcal{K}\;m'\,\mathtt{w}$ the user can resume the vcgen, by choosing a new symbolic heap m' and invoking the continuation $\mathcal{K}\,m'\,\mathtt{w}$.

For assignments $\mathsf{e}_1 = \mathsf{e}_2$ we have a similar situation. Symbolic execution of both e_1 and e_2 may fail, and then we generate a goal similar to the one for binary operators. If the location $\mathtt{l}$ that we wish to assign to is not in the symbolic heap, we use the continuation $[\![m]\!] \mathrel{-\!\!*} \exists\mathtt{w}.\,\mathtt{l} \mapsto_U \mathtt{w} * (\mathtt{l} \mapsto_L \mathtt{v} \mathrel{-\!\!*} \mathcal{K}_{\mathtt{ret}}\;\mathtt{v})$. As before, the user gets back the current symbolic heap $[\![m]\!]$, and could resume the vcgen through the postcondition $\mathcal{K}_{\mathtt{ret}}\;\mathtt{v}$ by picking a new symbolic heap.

$$\mathsf{vcg}(m, \mathtt{v}, \mathcal{K}) \triangleq \mathcal{K}\; m\, \mathtt{v}$$

$$\mathsf{vcg}(m, \mathsf{e}_1 \circledcirc \mathsf{e}_2, \mathcal{K}) \triangleq$$

$$\begin{cases} \mathsf{vcg}(m_2, \mathsf{e}_2, \lambda m'\, \mathtt{v}_2.\, \mathcal{K}\;(m' \sqcup m^o)\,(\mathtt{v}_1 \circledcirc \mathtt{v}_2)) & \text{if } \mathsf{forward}(m, \mathsf{e}_1) = (\mathtt{v}_1, m^o, m_2) \\ \mathsf{vcg}(m_1, \mathsf{e}_1, \lambda m'\, \mathtt{v}_1.\, \mathcal{K}\;(m' \sqcup m^o)\,(\mathtt{v}_1 \circledcirc \mathtt{v}_2)) & \text{if } \mathsf{forward}(m, \mathsf{e}_1) = \bot \text{ and} \\ & \quad \mathsf{forward}(m, \mathsf{e}_2) = (\mathtt{v}_2, m^o, m_1) \\ [\![m]\!] \mathrel{-\!\!*} \mathsf{wp}\;(\mathsf{e}_1 \circledcirc \mathsf{e}_2)\;\{\mathcal{K}_{\mathtt{ret}}\} & \text{otherwise} \end{cases}$$

$$\mathsf{vcg}(m, *\mathsf{e}, \mathcal{K}) \triangleq \mathsf{vcg}(m, \mathsf{e}, \mathcal{K}')$$

$$\textbf{with } \mathcal{K}' \triangleq \lambda m\, \mathtt{l}.\; \begin{cases} \mathcal{K}\; m\, \mathtt{w} & \text{if } \mathtt{l} \in \mathsf{Loc} \text{ and } m(\mathtt{l}) = (U, q, \mathtt{w}) \\ [\![m]\!] \mathrel{-\!\!*} \exists \mathtt{w}\; q.\, \mathtt{l} \overset{q}{\mapsto}_U \mathtt{w} * (\mathtt{l} \overset{q}{\mapsto}_U \mathtt{w} \mathrel{-\!\!*} \mathcal{K}_{\mathtt{ret}}\; \mathtt{w}) & \text{otherwise} \end{cases}$$

$$\mathsf{vcg}(m, \mathsf{e}_1 = \mathsf{e}_2, \mathcal{K}) \triangleq$$

$$\begin{cases} \mathsf{vcg}(m_2, \mathsf{e}_2, \lambda m'\, \mathtt{v}.\, \mathcal{K}'\;(m' \sqcup m^o)(\mathtt{l}, \mathtt{v})) & \text{if } \mathsf{forward}(m, \mathsf{e}_1) = (\mathtt{l}, m^o, m_2) \\ \mathsf{vcg}(m_1, \mathsf{e}_1, \lambda m'\, \mathtt{l}.\, \mathcal{K}'\;(m' \sqcup m^o)(\mathtt{l}, \mathtt{v})) & \text{if } \mathsf{forward}(m, \mathsf{e}_1) = \bot \text{ and} \\ & \quad \mathsf{forward}(m, \mathsf{e}_2) = (\mathtt{v}, m^o, m_1) \\ [\![m]\!] \mathrel{-\!\!*} \mathsf{wp}\;(\mathsf{e}_1 = \mathsf{e}_2)\;\{\mathcal{K}_{\mathtt{ret}}\} & \text{otherwise} \end{cases}$$

$$\textbf{with } \mathcal{K}' \triangleq \lambda m\;(\mathtt{l}, \mathtt{v}).$$

$$\begin{cases} \mathcal{K}\;(m' \sqcup \{\mathtt{l} \mapsto (L, 1, \mathtt{v})\})\,\mathtt{v} & \text{if } \mathtt{l} \in \mathsf{Loc} \text{ and } \mathsf{delete\_full}(\mathtt{l}, m) = m' \\ [\![m]\!] \mathrel{-\!\!*} \exists \mathtt{w}.\, \mathtt{l} \mapsto_U \mathtt{w} * (\mathtt{l} \mapsto_L \mathtt{v} \mathrel{-\!\!*} \mathcal{K}_{\mathtt{ret}}\; \mathtt{v}) & \text{otherwise} \end{cases}$$

$$\mathsf{vcg}(m, \mathtt{x} \leftarrow \mathsf{e}_1\, ; \mathsf{e}_2, \mathcal{K}) \triangleq \mathsf{vcg}(m, \mathsf{e}_1, \lambda m'\, \mathtt{v}.\, \mathbb{U}\; (\mathsf{vcg}(\mathsf{unlock}(m'), \mathsf{e}_2[\mathtt{v}/\mathtt{x}], \mathcal{K})))$$

Auxiliary functions:

$$\mathcal{K}_{\mathtt{ret}} : \mathsf{val} \to \mathsf{Prop} \triangleq \lambda \mathtt{w}.\, (\exists m'.\, [\![m']\!] * \mathcal{K}\; m'\, \mathtt{w}) \qquad \mathsf{unlock}(m) \triangleq \bigsqcup_{\substack{\mathtt{l} \in \mathrm{dom}(m) \\ m(\mathtt{l}) = (\_, q, \mathtt{v})}} \{\mathtt{l} \mapsto (U, q, \mathtt{v})\}$$

Fig. 8. Selected cases of the verification condition generator.

7 Discussion

Extensions of the Language. The memory model that we have presented in this paper was purposely oversimplified. In Coq, the memory model for λMC additionally supports mutable local variables, arrays, and pointer arithmetic. Adding support for these features was relatively easy and required only local changes to the definitional semantics and the separation logic.

For implementing mutable local variables, we tag each location with a Boolean that keeps track of whether it is an allocated or a local variable. That way, we can forbid deallocating local variables using the `free(−)` operator.

Our extended memory model is block/offset-based like CompCert's memory model [38]. Pointers are not simply represented as locations, but as pairs (ℓ, i), where ℓ is a HeapLang reference to a memory block containing a list of values, and i is an offset into that block. The points-to connectives of our separation logic then correspondingly range over block/offset-based pointers.

Symbolic Execution of Sequence Points. We adapt our forward algorithm to handle sequenced bind operators $\mathtt{x} \leftarrow \mathsf{e}_1 \,;\mathsf{e}_2$. The subtlety lies in supporting nested sequenced binds. For example, in an expression $(\mathtt{x} \leftarrow \mathsf{e}_1 \,;\mathsf{e}_2) + \mathsf{e}_3$ the postcondition of e_1 can be used (along with the frame) for the symbolic execution of e_2, but it cannot be used for the symbolic execution of e_3. In order to solve this, our forward algorithm takes a *stack* of symbolic heaps as an input, and returns a *stack* of symbolic heaps (of the same length) as a frame. All the cases shown in Fig. 7 are easily adapted w.r.t. this modification, and the following definition captures the case for the sequence point bind:

$$\begin{aligned}
&\mathsf{forward}(\vec{m}, \mathtt{x} \leftarrow \mathsf{e}_1 \,; \mathsf{e}_2) \triangleq (\mathtt{v}_2, m_2^o \sqcup m', \vec{m_2})\\
&\quad \textbf{where}\ \ (\mathtt{v}_1, m_1^o, \vec{m_1}) \qquad\quad = \mathsf{forward}(\vec{m}, \mathsf{e}_1)\\
&\qquad\qquad\ \ (\mathtt{v}_2, m_2^o, m' :: \vec{m_2}) = \mathsf{forward}(\mathsf{unlock}(m_1^o) :: \vec{m_1}, \mathsf{e}_2\,[\mathtt{v}_1/\mathtt{x}])
\end{aligned}$$

Shared Resource Invariants. As in Krebbers's logic [29], the rules for binary operators in Fig. 3 require the resources to be separated into disjoint parts for the subexpressions. If both sides of a binary operator are function calls, then they can only share read permissions despite that both function calls are executed atomically. Following Krebbers, we address this limitation by adding a shared resource invariant R to our weakest preconditions and add the following rules:

$$\frac{R_1 \qquad \mathsf{wp}_{R_1 * R_2}\, \mathsf{e}\, \{\mathtt{v}.\ R_1 \mathrel{-\!\!*} \Phi\, \mathtt{v}\}}{\mathsf{wp}_{R_2}\, \mathsf{e}\, \{\Phi\}} \qquad \frac{\begin{array}{c}\mathtt{f(x)\{e\}}\ \text{defined}\\ R \mathrel{-\!\!*} \mathbb{U}(\mathsf{wp}_{\mathsf{True}}\, \mathsf{e}\,[\mathtt{x}/\mathtt{v}]\ \{\mathtt{w}.\ R * \Phi\, \mathtt{w}\})\end{array}}{\mathsf{wp}_R\, \mathtt{f(v)}\ \{\Phi\}}$$

To temporarily transfer resources into the invariant, one can use the first rule. Because function calls are not interleaved, one can use the last rule to gain access to the shared resource invariant for the duration of the function call.

Our handling of shared resource invariants generalizes the treatment by Krebbers: using custom ghost state in Iris we can endow the resource invariant with a protocol. This allows us to verify examples that were previously impossible [29]:

```
int f(int *p, int y) { return (*p = y); }
int main() { int x; f(&x, 3) + f(&x, 4); return x; }
```

Krebbers could only prove that `main` returns 0, 3 or 4, whereas we can prove it returns 3 or 4 by combining resource invariants with Iris's ghost state.

Implementation in Coq. In the Coq development [18] we have:

- Defined λMC with the extensions described above, as well as the monadic combinators, as a shallow embedding on top of Iris's HeapLang [21,25].
- Modeled the separation logic for λMC and the monadic combinators as a shallow embedding on top of the Iris's program logic for HeapLang.

- Implemented the symbolic executor and vcgen as computable Coq functions, and proved their soundness w.r.t. our separation logic.
- Turned the verification condition generator into a tactic that integrates into the Iris Proof Mode/MoSeL framework [32,34].

This last point allowed us to leverage the existing machinery for separation logic proofs in Coq. Firstly, we get basic building blocks for implementing the vcgen tactic for free. Secondly, when the vcgen is unable to solve the goal, one can use the Iris Proof Mode/MoSeL tactics to help out in a convenient manner.

To implement the symbolic executor and vcgen, we had to reify the terms and values of λMC. To see why reification is needed, consider the data type for symbolic heaps, which uses locations as keys. In proofs, those locations appear as universally quantified variables. To compute using these, we need to reify them into some symbolic representation. We have implemented the reification mechanism using type classes, following Spitters and van der Weegen [47].

With all the mechanics in place, our vcgen is able to significantly aid us. Consider the following program that copies the contents of one array into another:

```
int arraycopy(int *p, int *q, int n) {
  int pend = p + n;
  while (p < pend) { *(p++) = *(q++); }
}
```

We proved $\{\mathtt{p} \mapsto \vec{x} * \mathtt{q} \mapsto \vec{y} * (|\vec{x}| = |\vec{y}| = n)\}\mathtt{arraycopy(p,q,n)}\{\mathtt{p} \mapsto \vec{y} * \mathtt{q} \mapsto \vec{y}\}$ in 11 lines of Coq code. The vcgen can automatically process the program up until the while loop. At that point, the user has to manually perform an induction on the array, providing a suitable induction hypothesis. The vcgen is then able to discharge the base case automatically. In the inductive case, it will automatically process the program until the next iteration of the while loop, where the user has to apply the induction hypothesis.

8 Related Work

C Semantics. There has been a considerable body of work on formal semantics for the C language, including several large projects that aimed to formalize substantial subsets of C [17,20,30,37,41,44], and projects that focused on specific aspects like its memory model [10,13,27,28,31,38,40,41], weak memory concurrency [4,36,43], non-local control flow [35], verified compilation [37,48], *etc.*

The focus of this paper—non-determinism in C expressions—has been treated formally a number of times, notably by Norrish [44], Ellison and Rosu [17], Krebbers [31], and Memarian *et al.* [41]. The first three have in common that they model the sequence point restriction by keeping track of the locations that have been written to. The treatment of sequence points in our definitional semantics is closely inspired by the work of Ellison and Rosu [17], which resembles closely what is in the C standard. Krebbers [31] used a more restrictive version of the semantics by Ellison and Rosu—he assigned undefined behavior in some corner cases to ease the soundness theorem of his logic. We directly proved soundness of the logic w.r.t. the more faithful model by Ellison and Rosu.

Memarian *et al.* [41] give a semantics to C by elaboration into a language they call Core. Unspecified evaluation order in Core is modeled using an unseq operation, which is similar to our $||_{\mathsf{HL}}$ operation. Compared to our translation, Core is much closer to C (it has function calls, memory operations, *etc.* as primitives, while we model them with monadic combinators), and supports concurrency.

Reasoning Tools and Program Logics for C. Apart from formalizing the semantics of C, there have been many efforts to create reasoning tools for the C language in one way or another. There are standalone tools, like VeriFast [23], VCC [12], and the Jessie plugin of Frama-C [42], and there are tools built on top of general purpose proof assistants like VST [1,10] in Coq, or AutoCorres [19] in Isabelle/HOL. Although, admittedly, all of these tools cover larger subsets of C than we do, as far as we know, they all ignore non-determinism in expressions.

There are a few exceptions. Norrish proved confluence for a certain class of C expressions [45]. Such a confluence result may be used to justify proofs in a tool that does not have an underlying non-deterministic semantics.

Another exception is the separation logic for non-determinism in C by Krebbers [29]. Our work is inspired by his, but there are several notable differences:

- We have proved soundness with respect to a definitional semantics for a subset of C. We believe that this approach is more modular, since the semantics can be specified at a higher level of abstraction.
- We have built our logic on top of the Iris framework. This makes the development more modular (since we can use all the features as well as the Coq infrastructure of Iris) and more expressive (as shown in Sect. 7).
- There was no automation like our vcgen, so one had to subdivide resources between subexpressions manually all the time. Also, there was not even tactical support for carrying out proofs manually. Our logic is redesigned to get such support from the Iris Proof Mode/MoSeL framework.

To handle missing features of C as part of our vcgen, we plan to explore approaches by other verification projects in proof assistants. A notable example of such a project is VST, which supports machine arithmetic [16] and data types like structs and unions [10] as part of its tactics for symbolic execution.

Separation Logic and Symbolic Execution. In their seminal work, Berdine *et al.* [5] demonstrate the application of symbolic execution to automated reasoning in separation logic. In their setting, frame inference is used to perform symbolic execution of function calls. The frame has to be computed when the call site has more resources than needed to invoke a function. In our setting we compute frames for subexpressions, which, unlike functions, do not have predefined specifications. Due to that, we have to perform frame inference simultaneously with symbolic execution. The symbolic execution algorithm of Berdine *et al.* can handle inductive predicates, and can be extended with shape analysis [15]. We do not support such features, and leave them to future work.

Caper [14] is a tool for automated reasoning in concurrent separation logic, and it also deals with non-determinism, although the nature of non-determinism in Caper is different. Non-determinism in Caper arises due to branching on unknown conditionals and due to multiple possible ways to apply ghost state related rules (rules pertaining to abstract regions and guards). The former cause is tackled by considering sets of symbolic execution traces, and the latter is resolved by employing heuristics based on bi-abduction [9]. Applications of abductive reasoning to our approach to symbolic execution are left for future work.

Recently, Bannister *et al.* [2, 3] proposed a new separation logic connective for performing forwards reasoning whilst avoiding frame inference. This approach, however, is aimed at sequential deterministic programs, focusing on a notion of partial correctness that allows for failed executions. Another approach to verification of sequential stateful programs is based on characteristic formulae [11]. A stateful program is transformed into a higher-order logic predicate, implicitly encoding the frame rule. The resulting formula is then proved by a user in Coq.

When implementing a vcgen in a proof assistant (see *e.g.*, [10, 39]) it is common to let the vcgen return a new goal when it gets stuck, from which the user can help out and call back the vcgen. The novelty of our work is that this approach is applied to operations that are called in parallel.

Acknowledgments. We are grateful to Gregory Malecha and the anonymous reviewers and for their comments and suggestions. This work was supported by the Netherlands Organisation for Scientific Research (NWO), project numbers STW.14319 (first and second author) and 016.Veni.192.259 (third author).

References

1. Appel, A.W. (ed.): Program Logics for Certified Compilers. Cambridge University Press, New York (2014)
2. Bannister, C., Höfner, P.: False failure: creating failure models for separation logic. In: Desharnais, J., Guttmann, W., Joosten, S. (eds.) RAMiCS 2018. LNCS, vol. 11194, pp. 263–279. Springer, Cham (2018). https://doi.org/10.1007/978-3-030-02149-8_16
3. Bannister, C., Höfner, P., Klein, G.: Backwards and forwards with separation logic. In: Avigad, J., Mahboubi, A. (eds.) ITP 2018. LNCS, vol. 10895, pp. 68–87. Springer, Cham (2018). https://doi.org/10.1007/978-3-319-94821-8_5
4. Batty, M., Owens, S., Sarkar, S., Sewell, P., Weber, T.: Mathematizing C++ concurrency. In: POPL, pp. 55–66 (2011)
5. Berdine, J., Calcagno, C., O'Hearn, P.W.: Symbolic execution with separation logic. In: Yi, K. (ed.) APLAS 2005. LNCS, vol. 3780, pp. 52–68. Springer, Heidelberg (2005). https://doi.org/10.1007/11575467_5
6. Birkedal, L., Bizjak, A.: Lecture Notes on Iris: Higher-Order Concurrent Separation Logic, August 2018. https://iris-project.org/tutorial-material.html
7. Bornat, R., Calcagno, C., O'Hearn, P.W., Parkinson, M.J.: Permission accounting in separation logic. In: POPL, pp. 259–270 (2005)
8. Boyland, J.: Checking interference with fractional permissions. In: Cousot, R. (ed.) SAS 2003. LNCS, vol. 2694, pp. 55–72. Springer, Heidelberg (2003). https://doi.org/10.1007/3-540-44898-5_4
9. Calcagno, C., Distefano, D., O'Hearn, P.W., Yang, H.: Compositional shape analysis by means of bi-abduction. J. ACM **58**(6), 26:1–26:66 (2011)
10. Cao, Q., Beringer, L., Gruetter, S., Dodds, J., Appel, A.W.: VST-Floyd: a separation logic tool to verify correctness of C programs. JAR **61**(1–4), 367–422 (2018)

11. Charguéraud, A.: Characteristic formulae for the verification of imperative programs. SIGPLAN Not. **46**(9), 418–430 (2011)
12. Cohen, E., et al.: VCC: a practical system for verifying concurrent C. In: Berghofer, S., Nipkow, T., Urban, C., Wenzel, M. (eds.) TPHOLs 2009. LNCS, vol. 5674, pp. 23–42. Springer, Heidelberg (2009). https://doi.org/10.1007/978-3-642-03359-9_2
13. Cohen, E., Moskal, M., Tobies, S., Schulte, W.: A precise yet efficient memory model for C. ENTCS **254**, 85–103 (2009)
14. Dinsdale-Young, T., da Rocha Pinto, P., Andersen, K.J., Birkedal, L.: Caper - automatic verification for fine-grained concurrency. In: Yang, H. (ed.) ESOP 2017. LNCS, vol. 10201, pp. 420–447. Springer, Heidelberg (2017). https://doi.org/10.1007/978-3-662-54434-1_16
15. Distefano, D., O'Hearn, P.W., Yang, H.: A local shape analysis based on separation logic. In: Hermanns, H., Palsberg, J. (eds.) TACAS 2006. LNCS, vol. 3920, pp. 287–302. Springer, Heidelberg (2006). https://doi.org/10.1007/11691372_19
16. Dodds, J., Appel, A.W.: Mostly sound type system improves a foundational program verifier. In: Gonthier, G., Norrish, M. (eds.) CPP 2013. LNCS, vol. 8307, pp. 17–32. Springer, Cham (2013). https://doi.org/10.1007/978-3-319-03545-1_2
17. Ellison, C., Rosu, G.: An executable formal semantics of C with applications. In: POPL, pp. 533–544 (2012)
18. Frumin, D., Gondelman, L., Krebbers, R.: Semi-automated reasoning about non-determinism in C expressions: Coq development, February 2019. https://cs.ru.nl/~dfrumin/wpc/
19. Greenaway, D., Lim, J., Andronick, J., Klein, G.: Don't sweat the small stuff: formal verification of C code without the pain. In: PLDI, pp. 429–439 (2014)
20. Hathhorn, C., Ellison, C., Roşu, G.: Defining the undefinedness of C. In: PLDI, pp. 336–345 (2015)
21. Iris: Iris Project, November 2018. https://iris-project.org/
22. ISO: ISO/IEC 9899–2011: Programming Languages - C. ISO Working Group 14 (2012)
23. Jacobs, B., Smans, J., Piessens, F.: A quick tour of the VeriFast program verifier. In: Ueda, K. (ed.) APLAS 2010. LNCS, vol. 6461, pp. 304–311. Springer, Heidelberg (2010). https://doi.org/10.1007/978-3-642-17164-2_21
24. Jung, R., Krebbers, R., Birkedal, L., Dreyer, D.: Higher-order ghost state. In: ICFP, pp. 256–269 (2016)
25. Jung, R., Krebbers, R., Jourdan, J.H., Bizjak, A., Birkedal, L., Dreyer, D.: Iris from the ground up: a modular foundation for higher-order concurrent separation logic. J. Funct. Program. **28**, e20 (2018). https://doi.org/10.1017/S0956796818000151
26. Jung, R., et al.: Iris: monoids and invariants as an orthogonal basis for concurrent reasoning. In: POPL, pp. 637–650 (2015)
27. Kang, J., Hur, C., Mansky, W., Garbuzov, D., Zdancewic, S., Vafeiadis, V.: A formal C memory model supporting integer-pointer casts. In: POPL, pp. 326–335 (2015)
28. Krebbers, R.: Aliasing restrictions of C11 formalized in Coq. In: Gonthier, G., Norrish, M. (eds.) CPP 2013. LNCS, vol. 8307, pp. 50–65. Springer, Cham (2013). https://doi.org/10.1007/978-3-319-03545-1_4
29. Krebbers, R.: An operational and axiomatic semantics for non-determinism and sequence points in C. In: POPL, pp. 101–112 (2014)
30. Krebbers, R.: The C standard formalized in Coq. Ph.D. thesis, Radboud University Nijmegen (2015)
31. Krebbers, R.: A formal C memory model for separation logic. JAR **57**(4), 319–387 (2016)

32. Krebbers, R., et al.: MoSeL: a general, extensible modal framework for interactive proofs in separation logic. PACMPL **2**(ICFP), 77:1–77:30 (2018)
33. Krebbers, R., Jung, R., Bizjak, A., Jourdan, J.-H., Dreyer, D., Birkedal, L.: The Essence of higher-order concurrent separation logic. In: Yang, H. (ed.) ESOP 2017. LNCS, vol. 10201, pp. 696–723. Springer, Heidelberg (2017). https://doi.org/10.1007/978-3-662-54434-1_26
34. Krebbers, R., Timany, A., Birkedal, L.: Interactive proofs in higher-order concurrent separation logic. In: POPL, pp. 205–217 (2017)
35. Krebbers, R., Wiedijk, F.: Separation logic for non-local control flow and block scope variables. In: Pfenning, F. (ed.) FoSSaCS 2013. LNCS, vol. 7794, pp. 257–272. Springer, Heidelberg (2013). https://doi.org/10.1007/978-3-642-37075-5_17
36. Lahav, O., Vafeiadis, V., Kang, J., Hur, C., Dreyer, D.: Repairing Sequential Consistency in C/C++11. In: PLDI, pp. 618–632 (2017)
37. Leroy, X.: Formal verification of a realistic compiler. CACM **52**(7), 107–115 (2009)
38. Leroy, X., Blazy, S.: Formal verification of a C-like memory model and its uses for verifying program transformations. JAR **41**(1), 1–31 (2008)
39. Malecha, G.: Extensible proof engineering in intensional type theory. Ph.D. thesis, Harvard University (2014)
40. Memarian, K., et al.: Exploring C semantics and pointer provenance. PACMPL **3**(POPL), 67:1–67:32 (2019)
41. Memarian, K., et al.: Into the depths of C: elaborating the De Facto Standards. In: PLDI, pp. 1–15 (2016)
42. Moy, Y., Marché, C.: The Jessie Plugin for Deduction Verification in Frama-C, Tutorial and Reference Manual (2011)
43. Nienhuis, K., Memarian, K., Sewell, P.: An operational semantics for C/C++11 concurrency. In: OOPSLA, pp. 111–128 (2016)
44. Norrish, M.: C Formalised in HOL. Ph.D. thesis, University of Cambridge (1998)
45. Norrish, M.: Deterministic expressions in C. In: Swierstra, S.D. (ed.) ESOP 1999. LNCS, vol. 1576, pp. 147–161. Springer, Heidelberg (1999). https://doi.org/10.1007/3-540-49099-X_10
46. O'Hearn, P.W.: Resources, concurrency, and local reasoning. Theor. Comput. Sci. **375**(1), 271–307 (2007). Festschrift for John C. Reynolds's 70th birthday
47. Spitters, B., Van der Weegen, E.: Type classes for mathematics in type theory. Math. Struct. Comput. Sci. **21**(4), 795–825 (2011)
48. Stewart, G., Beringer, L., Cuellar, S., Appel, A.W.: Compositional CompCert. In: POPL, pp. 275–287 (2015)

7

Probabilistic Programming Inference via Intensional Semantics

Simon Castellan[1] and Hugo Paquet[2(✉)]

[1] Imperial College London, London, UK
simon.castellan@phis.me
[2] University of Cambridge, Cambridge, UK
hugo.paquet@cl.cam.ac.uk

Abstract. We define a new denotational semantics for a first-order probabilistic programming language in terms of *probabilistic event structures*. This semantics is *intensional*, meaning that the interpretation of a program contains information about its behaviour throughout execution, rather than a simple distribution on return values. In particular, occurrences of sampling and conditioning are recorded as explicit events, partially ordered according to the data dependencies between the corresponding statements in the program.

This interpretation is *adequate*: we show that the usual measure-theoretic semantics of a program can be recovered from its event structure representation. Moreover it can be leveraged for MCMC inference: we prove correct a version of single-site Metropolis-Hastings with *incremental recomputation*, in which the proposal kernel takes into account the semantic information in order to avoid performing some of the redundant sampling.

Keywords: Probabilistic programming · Denotational semantics · Event structures · Bayesian inference

1 Introduction

Probabilistic programming languages [8] were put forward as promising tools for practitioners of Bayesian statistics. By extending traditional programming languages with primitives for sampling and conditioning, they allow the user to express a wide class of statistical models, and provide a simple interface for encoding inference problems. Although the subject of active research, it is still notoriously difficult to design inference methods for probabilistic programs which perform well for the full class of expressible models.

One popular inference technique, proposed by Wingate et al. [21], involves adapting well-known *Monte-Carlo Markov chain* methods from statistics to probabilistic programs, by manipulating *program traces*. One such method is the Metropolis-Hastings algorithm, which relies on a key *proposal* step: given a program trace x (a sequence $x_1, \ldots, x_n$ of random choices with their likelihood), a proposal for the *next* trace sample is generated by choosing $i \in \{1, \ldots, n\}$ uniformly, resampling x_i, and then continuing to execute the program, only performing additional sampling for those random choices not appearing in x. The variables already present in x are not resampled: only their likelihood is updated according to the new value of x_i. Likewise, some conditioning statements must be re-evaluated in case the corresponding weight is affected by the change to x_i.

Observe that there is some redundancy in this process, since the updating process above will only affect variables and observations when their density directly depends on the value of x_i. This may significantly affect performance: to solve an inference problem one must usually perform a large number of proposal steps. To overcome this problem, some recent implementations, notably [12,25], make use of *incremental recomputation*, whereby some of the redundancy can be avoided via a form of static analysis. However, as pointed out by Kiselyov [13], establishing the correctness of such implementations is tricky.

Here we address this by introducing a theoretical framework in which to reason about data dependencies in probabilistic programs. Specifically, our first contribution is to define a *denotational semantics* for a first-order probabilistic language, in terms of graph-like structures called *event structures* [22]. In event structures, computational events are partially ordered according to the dependencies between them; additionally they can be equipped with quantitative information to represent probabilistic processes [16,23]. This semantics is *intensional*, unlike most existing semantics for probabilistic programs, in which the interpretation of a program resembles a probability distribution on output values. We relate our approach to a measure-theoretic semantics [18] through an *adequacy* result.

Our second contribution is the design of a Metropolis-Hastings algorithm which exploits the event structure representation of the program at hand. Some of the redundancy in the proposal step of the algorithm is avoided by taking into account the extra dependency information given by the semantics. We provide a proof of correctness for this algorithm, and argue that an implementation is realistically achievable: we show in particular that all graph structures involved and the associated quantitative information admit a finite, concrete representation.

Outline of the Paper. In Sect. 2 we give a short introduction to probabilistic programming. We define our main language of study and its measure-theoretic semantics. In Sect. 3.1, we introduce MCMC methods and the Metropolis-Hastings algorithm in the context of probabilistic programming. We then motivate the need for intensional semantics in order to capture data dependency. In Sect. 4 we define our interpretation of programs and prove adequacy. In Sect. 5 we define an updated version of the algorithm, and prove its correctness. We conclude in Sect. 6.

The proofs of the statements are detailed in the technical report [4].

2 Probabilistic Programming

In this section we motivate the need for capturing data dependency in probabilistic programs. Let us start with a brief introduction to probabilistic programming – a more comprehensive account can be found in [8].

2.1 Conditioning and Posterior Distribution

Let us introduce the problem of inference in probabilistic programming from the point of view of programming language theory.

We consider a first-order programming language enriched with a real number type $\mathbb{R}$ and a primitive `sample` for drawing random values from a given family of standard probability distributions. The language is idealised—but it is assumed that an implementation of the language comprises built-in sampling procedures for those standard distributions. Thus, repeatedly running the program `sample Uniform` $(0, 1)$ returns a sequence of values approaching the true uniform distribution on $[0, 1]$.

Via other constructs in the language, standard distributions can be combined, as shown in the following example program of type $\mathbb{R}$:

```
let x = sample Uniform(0, 1) in
let y = sample Gaussian(x, 2) in
x + y
```

Here the output will follow a probability distribution built out of the usual uniform and Gaussian distributions. Many probabilistic programming languages will offer more general programming constructs: conditionals, recursion, higher-order functions, data types, *etc.*, enabling a wide range of distributions to be expressed in this way. Such a program is sometimes called a *generative model.*

Conditioning. The process of conditioning involves rescaling the distribution associated with a generative model, so as to reflect some bias. Going back to the example above, say we have made some external measurement indicating that $y = 0$, but we would like to account for possible noise in the measurement using another Gaussian. To express this we modify the program as follows:

```
let x = sample Uniform (0, 1) in
let y = sample Gaussian (x, 2) in
observe y (Gaussian (0, 0.01));
x + y;
```

The purpose of the `observe` statement is to increase the occurrence of executions in which y is close to 0; the original distribution, known as the **prior**, must be updated accordingly. The probabilistic weight of each execution is multiplied by an appropriate *score*, namely the **likelihood** of the current value of y in the Gaussian distribution with parameters $(0, 0.01)$. (This is known as a *soft constraint.* Conditioning via *hard constraints*, *i.e.* only giving a nonzero score to executions where y is exactly 0, is not practically feasible.)

The language studied here does not have an `observe` construct, but instead an explicit `score` primitive; this appears already in [18,19]. So the third line in the program above would instead be `score(pdf-Gaussian (0, 0.01) (y))` where `pdf-Gaussian (0, 0.01)` is the *density* function of the Gaussian distribution. The resulting distribution is not necessarily normalised. We obtain the **posterior** distribution by computing the normalising constant, following Bayes' rule:

$$\text{posterior} \propto \text{likelihood} \times \text{prior}.$$

This process is known as Bayesian inference and has ubiquitous applications. The difficulty lies in computing the normalising constant, which is usually obtained as an integral. Below we discuss *approximate* methods for sampling from the posterior distribution; they do not rely on this normalising step.

Measure Theory. Because this work makes heavy use of probability theory, we start with a brief account of measure theory. A standard textbook for this is [1]. Recall that a **measurable space** is a set X equipped with a **σ-algebra** Σ_X: a set of subsets of X containing $\emptyset$ and closed under complements and countable unions. Elements of Σ_X are called **measurable sets**. A **measure** on X is a function $\mu : \Sigma_X \to [0, \infty]$, such that $\mu(\emptyset) = 0$ and, for any countable family $\{U_i\}_{i \in I}$ of measurable sets, $\mu(\bigcup_{i \in I} U_i) = \sum_{i \in I} \mu(U_i)$.

An important example is that of the set $\mathbb{R}$ of real numbers, whose σ-algebra $\Sigma_\mathbb{R}$ is generated by the intervals $[a, b)$, for $a, b \in \mathbb{R}$ (in other words, it is the smallest σ-algebra containing those intervals). The **Lebesgue measure** on $(\mathbb{R}, \Sigma_\mathbb{R})$ is the (unique) measure λ assigning $b - a$ to every interval $[a, b)$ (with $a \leq b$).

Given measurable spaces (X, Σ_X) and (Y, Σ_Y), a function $f : X \to Y$ is **measurable** if for every $U \in \Sigma_Y$, $f^{-1}U \in \Sigma_X$. A measurable function $f : X \to [0, \infty]$ can be *integrated*: given $U \in \Sigma_X$ the **integral** $\int_U f \, d\lambda$ is a well-defined element of $[0, \infty]$; indeed the map $\mu : U \mapsto \int_U f d\lambda$ is a measure on X, and f is said to be a **density** for μ. The precise definition of the integral is standard but slightly more involved; we omit it.

We identify the following important classes of measures: a measure μ on (X, Σ_X) is a **probability measure** if $\mu(X) = 1$. It is **finite** if $\mu(X) < \infty$, and it is **s-finite** if $\mu = \sum_{i \in I} \mu_i$, a pointwise, countable sum of finite measures.

We recall the usual product and coproduct constructions for measurable spaces and measures. If $\{X_i\}_{i \in I}$ is a countable family of measurable spaces, their **product** $\prod_{i \in I} X_i$ and **coproduct** $\coprod_{i \in I} X_i = \bigcup_{i \in I} \{i\} \times X_i$ as sets can be turned into measurable spaces, where:

- $\Sigma_{\prod_{i \in I} X_i}$ is generated by $\{\prod_{i \in I} U_i \mid U_i \in \Sigma_{X_i} \text{ for all } i\}$, and
- $\Sigma_{\coprod_{i \in I} X_i}$ is generated by $\{\{i\} \times U_i \mid i \in I \text{ and } U_i \in \Sigma_{X_i}\}$.

The measurable spaces in this paper all belong to a well-behaved subclass: call (X, Σ_X) a **standard Borel space** if it either countable and discrete (*i.e.* all $U \subseteq X$ are in Σ_X), or measurably isomorphic to $(\mathbb{R}, \Sigma_\mathbb{R})$. Note that standard Borel spaces are closed under countable products and coproducts, and that in a standard Borel space all singletons are measurable.

2.2 A First-Order Probabilistic Programming Language

We consider a first-order, call-by-value language $\mathcal{L}$ with types

$$A, B ::= 1 \mid \mathbb{R} \mid \coprod_{i \in I} A_i \mid \prod_{i \in I} A_i$$

where I ranges over nonempty countable sets. The types denote measurable spaces in a natural way: $[\![1]\!]$ is the singleton space, and $[\![\mathbb{R}]\!] = (\mathbb{R}, \Sigma_{\mathbb{R}})$. Products and coproducts are interpreted via the corresponding measure-theoretic constructions: $[\![\prod_{i\in I} A_i]\!] = \prod_{i\in I}[\![A_i]\!]$ and $[\![\coprod_{i\in I} A_i]\!] = \coprod_{i\in I}[\![A_i]\!] = \bigcup_{i\in I}\{i\} \times [\![A_i]\!]$. Moreover, each measurable space $[\![A]\!]$ has a canonical measure $\mu_{[\![A]\!]} : \Sigma_{[\![A]\!]} \to \mathbb{R}$, induced from the Lebesgue measure on $\mathbb{R}$ and the Dirac measure on $[\![1]\!]$ via standard product and coproduct measure constructions.

The terms of $\mathcal{L}$ are given by the following grammar:

$$\begin{aligned} M, N ::= &\ () \mid M; N \mid f \mid \texttt{let}\ a\ \texttt{=}\ M\ \texttt{in}\ N \mid x \\ &\mid (M_i)_{i\in I} \mid \texttt{case}\ M\ \texttt{of}\ \{(i, x) \Rightarrow N_i\}_{i\in I} \\ &\mid \texttt{sample}\ d\ \texttt{(}M\texttt{)} \mid \texttt{score}\ M \end{aligned}$$

and we use standard syntactic sugar to manipulate integers and booleans: $\mathbb{B} = 1 + 1$, $\mathbb{N} = \sum_{i\in\omega} 1$, and constants are given by the appropriate injections. Conditionals and sequencing can be expressed in the usual way: $\texttt{if}\ M\ \texttt{then}\ N_1\ \texttt{else}\ N_2 = \texttt{case}\ M\ \texttt{of}\ \{(i, \_) \Rightarrow N_i\}_{i\in\{1,2\}}$, and $M; N = \texttt{let}\ a\ \texttt{=}\ M\ \texttt{in}\ N$, where a does not occur in N. In the grammar above:

- f ranges over measurable functions $[\![A]\!] \to [\![B]\!]$, where A and B are types;
- d ranges over a family of *parametric distributions* over the reals, *i.e.* measurable functions $\mathbb{R}^n \times \mathbb{R} \to \mathbb{R}$, for some $n \in \mathbb{N}$, such that for every $\mathbf{r} \in \mathbb{R}^n$, $\int d(\mathbf{r}, -) = 1$. For the purposes of this paper we ignore all issues related to invalid parameters, arising from *e.g.* a call to `gaussian` with standard deviation $\sigma = 0$. (An implementation could, say, choose to behave according to an alternative distribution in this case.)

The typing rules are as follows:

$$\frac{\Gamma \vdash M : A \qquad \Gamma, a : A \vdash N : B}{\Gamma \vdash \texttt{let}\ a\ \texttt{=}\ M\ \texttt{in}\ N : B} \qquad \frac{\Gamma \vdash M : \mathbb{R}^n \qquad d : \mathbb{R}^n \times \mathbb{R} \to \mathbb{R}}{\Gamma \vdash \texttt{sample}\ d\ \texttt{(}M\texttt{)} : \mathbb{R}}$$

$$\frac{\Gamma \vdash M : \mathbb{R}}{\Gamma \vdash \texttt{score}\ M : 1} \qquad \frac{}{\Gamma, a : A \vdash a : A} \qquad \frac{}{\Gamma \vdash () : \mathbf{1}}$$

$$\frac{\Gamma \vdash M : \sum_{i\in I} A_i \qquad \Gamma, x : A_i \vdash N_i : C}{\Gamma \vdash \texttt{case}\ M\ \texttt{of}\ \{(i, x) \Rightarrow N_i\}_{i\in I} : C} \qquad \frac{\Gamma \vdash M_i : A_i}{\Gamma \vdash (M_i)_{i\in I} : \prod_{i\in I} A_i}$$

$$\frac{f : [\![A]\!] \to [\![B]\!]\ \text{measurable} \qquad \Gamma \vdash M : A}{\Gamma \vdash f\ M : B}$$

Among the measurable functions f, we point out the following of interest:

- The usual product projections $\pi_i : [\![\prod_{i\in I} A_i]\!] \to [\![A_i]\!]$ and coproduct injections $\iota_i : [\![A_i]\!] \to [\![\coprod_{i\in I} A_i]\!]$;
- The operators $+, \times : \mathbb{R}^2 \to \mathbb{R}$,
- The tests, eg. $\geq 0 : [\![\mathbb{R}]\!] \to [\![\mathbb{B}]\!]$,
- The constant functions $1 \to A$ of the form $() \mapsto a$ for some $a \in [\![A]\!]$.

Examples for d include $\texttt{uniform} : \mathbb{R}^2 \times \mathbb{R} \to \mathbb{R}$, $\texttt{gaussian} : \mathbb{R}^2 \times \mathbb{R} \to \mathbb{R}$, ...

2.3 Measure-Theoretic Semantics of Programs

We now define a semantics of probabilistic programs using the measure-theoretic concept of *kernel*, which we define shortly. The content of this section is not new: using kernels as semantics for probabilistic was originally proposed in [14], while the (more recent) treatment of conditioning (`score`) via *s-finite* kernels is due to Staton [18]. Intuitively, kernels provide a semantics of open terms $\Gamma \vdash M : A$ as measures on $[\![A]\!]$ varying according to the values of variables in Γ.

Formally, a **kernel** from (X, Σ_X) to (Y, Σ_Y) is a function $k : X \times \Sigma_Y \to [0, \infty]$ such that for each $x \in X$, $k(x, -)$ is a measure, and for each $U \in \Sigma_Y$, $k(-, U)$ is measurable. (Here the σ-algebra $\Sigma_{[0,\infty]}$ is the restriction of that of $\mathbb{R}+\{\infty\}$.) We say k is **finite** (resp. **probabilistic**) if each $k(x, -)$ is a finite (resp. probability) measure, and it **s-finite** if it is a countable pointwise sum $\sum_{i\in I} k_i$ of finite kernels. We write $k : X \rightsquigarrow Y$ when k is an s-finite kernel from X to Y.

A term $\Gamma \vdash M : A$ will denote an s-finite kernel $[\![M]\!] : [\![\Gamma]\!] \rightsquigarrow [\![A]\!]$, where the context $\Gamma = x_1 : A_1, \ldots, x_n : A_n$ denotes the product of its components: $[\![\Gamma]\!] = [\![A_1]\!] \times \cdots \times [\![A_n]\!]$.

Notice that any measurable function $f : X \to Y$ can be seen as a *deterministic* kernel $f^\dagger : X \rightsquigarrow Y$. Given two s-finite kernels $k : A \rightsquigarrow B$ and $l : A \times B \rightsquigarrow C$, we define their composition $l \circ k : A \rightsquigarrow C$:

$$(l \circ k)(a, X) = \int_{b\in B} l((a, b), C) \times k(a, \mathrm{d}b).$$

Staton [18] proved that $l \circ k$ is a s-finite kernel.

The interpretation of terms is defined by induction:

- $[\![()]\!]$ is the lifting of $[\![\Gamma]\!] \to 1 : x \mapsto ()$.
- $[\![\texttt{let}\ a\ \texttt{=}\ M\ \texttt{in}\ N]\!]$ is $[\![N]\!] \circ [\![M]\!]$
- $[\![f\, M]\!] = f^\dagger \circ [\![M]\!]$
- $[\![a]\!](x, X) = \delta_x(X)$, the Dirac distribution $\delta_x(X) = 1$ if $x \in X$ and zero otherwise.
- $[\![\texttt{sample}\ d\ \texttt{(}M\texttt{)}]\!] = \texttt{sam} \circ [\![M]\!]$ where $\texttt{sam}_d : \mathbb{R}^n \rightsquigarrow \mathbb{R}$ is given by $\texttt{sam}_d(\mathbf{r}, X) = \int_{x\in X} d(\mathbf{r}, x)\mathrm{d}x$.
- $[\![\texttt{score}\ M]\!] = \texttt{sco} \circ [\![M]\!]$ where $\texttt{sco} : [\![R]\!] \to [\![1]\!]$ is $\texttt{sco}(r, X) = r \cdot \delta_{()}(X)$.
- $[\![(M_i)_{i\in I}]\!](\gamma, \prod_{i\in I} X_i) = \prod_{i\in I} [\![M_i]\!](\gamma, X_i)$: this is well-defined since the $\prod X_i$ generate the measurable sets of the product space.

$[\![\texttt{case } M \texttt{ of } \{(i,x) \Rightarrow N_i\}_{i\in I}]\!] = \texttt{coprod} \circ [\![M]\!]$ where $\texttt{coprod} : \Gamma \times [\![\coprod_{i\in I} A_i]\!] \rightsquigarrow [\![B]\!]$ maps $(\gamma, \{i\} \times X)$ to $[\![N_i]\!](\gamma, X)$.

We observe that when M is a program making no use of conditioning (*i.e.* a generative model), the kernel $[\![M]\!]$ is probabilistic:

Lemma 1. *For $\Gamma \vdash M : A$ without scores, $[\![M]\!](\gamma, [\![A]\!]) = 1$ for each $\gamma \in [\![\Gamma]\!]$.*

2.4 Exact Inference

Note that a kernel $1 \rightsquigarrow [\![A]\!]$ is the same as a measure on $[\![A]\!]$. Given a closed program $\vdash M : A$, the measure $[\![M]\!]$ is a combination of the prior (occurrences of `sample`) and the likelihood (`score`). Because `score` can be called on arbitrary arguments, it may be the case that the measure of the total space (that is, the coefficient $[\![M]\!]([\![A]\!])$, often called the *model evidence*) is 0 or ∞.

Whenever this is *not* the case, $[\![M]\!]$ can be normalised to a probability measure, the posterior distribution. For every $U \in \Sigma_{[\![A]\!]}$,

$$\text{norm}[\![M]\!](U) = \frac{[\![M]\!](U)}{[\![M]\!]([\![A]\!])}.$$

However, in many cases, this computation is intractable. Thus the goal of *approximate inference* is to approach $\text{norm}[\![M]\!]$, the *true posterior*, using a well-chosen sequence of samples.

3 Approximate Inference via Intensional Semantics

3.1 An Introduction to Approximate Inference

In this section we describe the Metropolis-Hastings (MH) algorithm for approximate inference in the context of probabilistic programming. Metropolis-Hastings is a generic algorithm to sample from a probability distribution D on a measurable state space $\mathbb{X}$, of which we know the density $d : \mathbb{X} \to \mathbb{R}$ up to some normalising constant.

MH is part of a family of inference algorithms called *Monte-Carlo Markov chain*, in which the posterior distribution is approximated by a series of samples generated using a Markov chain.

Formally, the MH algorithm defines a Markov chain M on the state space $\mathbb{X}$, that is a probabilistic kernel $M : \mathbb{X} \rightsquigarrow \mathbb{X}$. The correctness of the MH algorithm is expressed in terms of convergence. It says that for almost all $x \in \mathbb{X}$, the distribution $M^n(x, \cdot)$ converges to D as n goes to infinity, where M^n is the n-iteration of M: $M \circ \ldots \circ M$. Intuitively, this means that iterated sampling from M gets closer to D with the number of iterations.

The MH algorithm is itself parametrised by a Markov chain, referred to as the **proposal kernel** $P : \mathbb{X} \rightsquigarrow \mathbb{X}$: for each sampled value $x \in \mathbb{X}$, a proposed value for the next sample is drawn according to $P(x, \cdot)$. Note that correctness only holds under certain assumptions on P.

The MH algorithm assumes that we know how to sample from P, and that its density is known, ie. there is a function $p : \mathbb{X}^2 \to \mathbb{R}$ such that $p(x, \cdot)$ is the density of the distribution $P(x, \cdot)$,

The MH Algorithm. On an input state x, the MH algorithm samples from $P(x, \cdot)$ and gets a new sample x'. It then compares the likelihood of x and x' by computing an acceptance ratio $\alpha(x, x')$ which says whether the return state is x' or x. In pseudo-code, for an input state $x \in \mathbb{X}$:

1. Sample a new state x' from the distribution $P(x, \cdot)$
2. Compute the acceptance ratio of x' with respect to x:

$$\alpha(x, x') = \min\left(1, \frac{d(x') \times p(x, x')}{d(x) \times p(x', x)}\right)$$

3. With probability $\alpha(x, x')$, return the new sample x', otherwise return the input state x.

The formula for $\alpha(x, x')$ is known as the Hastings acceptance ratio and is key to the correctness of the algorithm.

Very little is assumed of P, which makes the algorithm very flexible; but of course the convergence rate may vary depending on the choice of P. We give a more formal description of MH in Sect. 5.2.

Single-Site MH and Incremental Recomputation. To apply this algorithm to probabilistic programming, we need a proposal kernel. Given a program M, the execution traces of M form a measurable set $\mathbb{X}_M$. In this setting the proposal is given by a kernel $\mathbb{X}_M \rightsquigarrow \mathbb{X}_M$.

A widely adopted choice of proposal is the *single-site proposal kernel* which, given a trace $x \in \mathbb{X}_M$, generates a new trace x' as follows:

1. Select uniformly one of the random choices s encountered in x.
2. Sample a new value for this instruction.
3. Re-execute the program M from that point onwards and with this new value for s, only ever resampling a variable when the corresponding instruction did not already appear in x.

Observe that there is some redundancy in this process: in the final step, the entire program has to be explored even though only a subset of the random choices will be re-evaluated. Some implementations of Trace MH for probabilistic programming make use of *incremental recomputation*.

We propose in this paper to statically compile a program M to an *event structure* G_M which makes explicit the probabilistic dependences between events, thus avoiding unnecessary sampling.

3.2 Capturing Probabilistic Dependencies Using Event Structures

Consider the program depicted in Fig. 1 in which we are interested in learning the parameters μ and σ of a Gaussian distribution from which we have observed two data points, say v_1 and v_2. For $i = 1, 2$ the function $f_i : \mathbb{R} \to \mathbb{R}$ expresses a soft constraint; it can be understood as indicating how much the sampled value of $\mathtt{x}i$ matches the observed value v_i.

A *trace* of this program will be of the form

$$\mathsf{Sam}\,\mu \cdot \mathsf{Sam}\,\sigma \cdot \mathsf{Sam}\,x_1 \cdot \mathsf{Sam}\,x_2 \cdot \mathsf{Sco}\,(f_1\,x_1) \cdot \mathsf{Sco}\,(f_2\,x_2) \cdot \mathsf{Rtn}\,(\mu, \sigma),$$

for some μ, σ, x_1, and $x_2 \in \mathbb{R}$ corresponding to sampled values for variables `mu`, `sigma`, `x1` and `x2`.

```
let mu = sample uniform (150, 200) in
let sigma = sample uniform (1, 50) in
let x1 = sample gaussian (mu, sigma) in
let x2 = sample gaussian (mu, sigma) in
score (f1 x1); score (f2 x2);
(mu, sigma)
```

Fig. 1. A simple probabilistic program

A proposal step following the single-site kernel may choose to resample μ; then it must run through the entire trace, checking for potential dependencies to μ, though in this case none of the other variables need to be resampled.

So we argue that viewing a program as tree of traces is not most appropriate in this context: we propose instead to compile a program into a partially ordered structure reflecting the probabilistic dependencies.

With our approach, the example above would yield the partial order displayed below on the right-hand side. The nodes on the first line corresponds to the sample for μ and σ, and those on the second line to x_1 and x_2. This provides an accurate account of the probabilistic dependencies: whenever $e \leq e'$ (where $\leq$ is the reflexive, transitive closure of $\rightarrowtriangle$), it is the case that e' depends on e.

According to this representation of the program, a trace is no longer a linear order, but instead another partial order, similar to the previous one only annotated with a specific value for each variable. This is displayed below, on the left-hand side; note that the order $\leq$ is drawn top to bottom. There is an obvious erasure map from the trace (left) to the graph (right); this will be important later on.

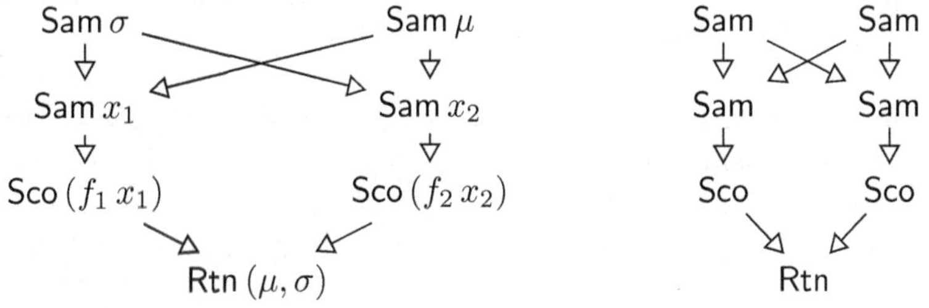

Conflict and Control Flow. We have seen that a partial order can be used to faithfully represent the data dependency in the program; it is however not sufficient to accurately describe the control flow. In particular, computational events may live in different *branches* of a conditional statement, as in the following example:

```
let x = sample uniform (0, 5) in
if x ≥ 2 then sample gaussian (3, 1)
else sample uniform (2, 4)
```

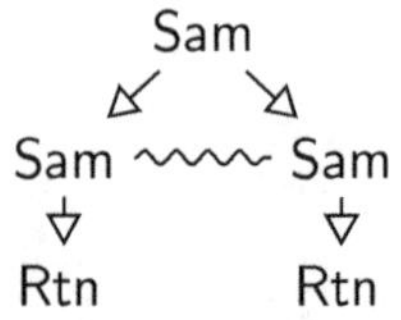

The last two samples are independent, but also *incompatible*: in any given trace only one of them will occur. An example of a trace for this program is Sam 1 · Sam 3 · Rtn 3.

We represent this information by enriching the partial order with a conflict relation, indicating when two actions are in different branches of a conditional statement. The resulting structure is depicted on the right. Combining partial order and conflict in this way can be conveniently formalised using **event structures** [22]:

Definition 1. *An* ***event structure*** *is a tuple* $(E, \leq, \#)$ *where* $(E, \leq)$ *is a partially ordered set and* $\#$ *is an irreflexive, binary relation on* E *such that*

- *for every* $e \in E$*, the set* $[e] = \{e' \in E \mid e' \leq e\}$ *is finite, and*
- *if* $e\#e'$ *and* $e' \leq e''$*, then* $e\#e''$*.*

From the partial order $\leq$, we extract **immediate causality** $\rightarrowtriangle$: $e \rightarrowtriangle e'$ when $e < e'$ with no events in between; and from the conflict relation, we extract **minimal conflict** $\sim\!\sim$: $e \sim\!\sim e'$ when $e\#e'$ and there are no other conflicts in $[e] \cup [e']$. In pictures we draw $\rightarrowtriangle$ and $\sim\!\sim$ rather than $\leq$ and $\#$.

A subset $x \subseteq E$ is a **configuration** of E if it is down-closed (if $e' \leq e \in x$ then $e' \in x$) and conflict-free (if $e, e' \in x$ then $\neg(e\#e')$). So in this framework, configurations correspond to exactly to *partial* executions traces of E.

The configuration $[e]$ is the **causal history** of e; we also write $[e)$ for $[e] \setminus \{e\}$. We write $\mathscr{C}(E)$ for the set of all finite configurations of E, a partial order under inclusion. A configuration x is **maximal** if it is maximal in $\mathscr{C}(E)$: for every $x' \in \mathscr{C}(E)$, if $x \subseteq x'$ then $x = x'$. We use the notation $x \overset{e}{-\!\!\!\subset} x'$ when $x' = x \cup \{e\}$, and in that case we say x' **covers** x.

An event structure is **confusion-free** if minimal conflict is transitive, and if any two events e, e' in minimal conflict satisfy $[e) = [e')$.

Compositionality. In order to give semantics to the language in a compositional manner, we must consider arbitrary *open* programs, *i.e.* with free parameters. Therefore we also represent each call to a parameter a as a *read* event, marked Rd a . For instance the program $x + y$ with two real parameters will become the event structure

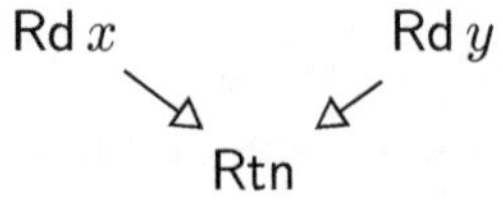

Note that the read actions on x and y are independent in the program (no order is specified), and the event structure respects this independence.

Our dependency graphs are event structures where each event carries information about the syntactic operation it comes from, a **label**, which depends on the typing context of the program:

$$\mathscr{L}^{\mathtt{static}}_{\Gamma \vdash B} ::= \mathsf{Rd}\, a \mid \mathsf{Rtn} \mid \mathsf{Sam} \mid \mathsf{Sco}\,,$$

where a ranges over variables $a : A$ in Γ.

Definition 2. *A* ***dependency graph*** *over $\Gamma \vdash B$ is an event structure G along with a labelling map $\mathsf{lbl} : G \to \mathscr{L}^{static}_{\Gamma \vdash B}$ where any two events $s, s' \in G$ labelled Rtn are in conflict, and all maximal configurations of G are of the form $[r]$ for $r \in G$ a return event.*

The condition on return events ensures that in any configuration of G there is at most one return event. Events of G are called static events.

We use dependency graphs as a causal representation of programs, reflecting the dependency between different parts of the program. In what follows we enrich this representation with runtime information in order to keep track of the dataflow of the program (in Sect. 3.3), and the associated distributions (in Sect. 3.4).

3.3 Runtime Values and Dataflow Graphs

We have seen how data dependency can be captured by representing a program P as a dependency graph G_P. But observe that this graph does not give any runtime information about the data in P; every event $s \in G_P$ only carries a label $\mathsf{lbl}(s)$ indicating the class of action it belongs to. (For an event labelled $\mathsf{Rd}\, a$, G does not specify the value at a; whereas at runtime this will be filled by an element of $[\![A]\!]$ where A is the type of a.)

To each label, we can associate a measurable space of possible runtime values:

$$\mathscr{Q}(\mathsf{Rd}\, b) = [\![\Gamma(b)]\!] \qquad \mathscr{Q}(\mathsf{Rtn}) = [\![A]\!] \qquad \mathscr{Q}(\mathsf{Sam}) = (\mathbb{R}, \Sigma_{\mathbb{R}}) \qquad \mathscr{Q}(\mathsf{Sco}) = (\mathbb{R}, \Sigma_{\mathbb{R}}).$$

Then, in a particular execution, an event $s \in G_P$ has a value in $\mathscr{Q}(\mathsf{lbl}(s))$, and can be instead labelled by the following expanded set:

$$\mathscr{L}^{\mathtt{run}}_{\Gamma \vdash B} ::= \mathsf{Rd}\, a\, v \mid \mathsf{Rtn}\, v \mid \mathsf{Sam}\, r \mid \mathsf{Sco}\, r$$

where r ranges over real numbers; in $\mathsf{Rd}\, a\, v$, $a : A \in \Gamma$ and $v \in [\![A]\!]$; and in $\mathsf{Rtn}\, v$, v ranges over elements of $[\![B]\!]$. Notice that there is an obvious forgetful map $\alpha : \mathscr{L}^{\mathtt{run}}_{\Gamma \vdash A} \to \mathscr{L}^{\mathtt{static}}_{\Gamma \vdash A}$, discarding the runtime value. This runtime value can be extracted from a label in $\mathscr{L}^{\mathtt{run}}_{\Gamma \vdash B}$ as follows:

$$\mathbf{q}(\mathsf{Rd}\, b\, v) = v \qquad \mathbf{q}(\mathsf{Rtn}\, v) = v \qquad \mathbf{q}(\mathsf{Sam}\, r) = r \qquad \mathbf{q}(\mathsf{Sco}\, r) = r.$$

In particular, we have $\mathbf{q}(\ell) \in \mathscr{Q}(\alpha(\ell))$.

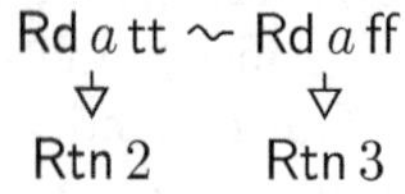

Such runtime events organise themselves in an event structure E_P, labelled over $\mathscr{L}^{\text{run}}_{\Gamma \vdash B}$, the **runtime graph** of P. Runtime graphs are in general uncountable, and so difficult to represent pictorially. It can be done in some simple, finite cases: the graph for `if` a `then 2 else 3` is depicted on the right. Recall that in dependency graphs conflict was used to represent conditional branches; here instead conflict is used to keep disjoint the possible outcomes of the same static event. (Necessarily, this static event must be a sample or a read, since other actions (return, score) are deterministic.)

Intuitively one can project runtime events to static events by erasing the runtime information; this suggests the existence of a function $\pi_P : E_P \to G_P$. This function will turn out to satisfy the axioms of a *rigid map of event structures*:

Definition 3. *Given event structures* $(E, \leq_E, \#_E)$ *and* $(G, \leq_G, \#_G)$ *a function* $\pi : E \to G$ *is a* ***rigid map*** *if*

- *it preserves configurations: for every* $x \in \mathscr{C}(E)$, $\pi x \in \mathscr{C}(G)$
- *it is* locally injective*: for every* $x \in \mathscr{C}(E)$ *and* $e, e' \in x$, *if* $\pi(e) = \pi(e')$ *then* $e = e'$.
- *it preserves dependency: if* $e \leq_E e'$ *then* $\pi(e) \leq_G \pi(e')$.

In general π is not injective, since many runtime events may correspond to the same static event – in that case however the axioms will require them to be in conflict. The last condition in the definition ensures that all causal dependencies come from G.

Given $x \in \mathscr{C}(G_P)$ we define the possible runtime values for x as the set $\mathscr{Q}(x)$ of functions mapping $s \in x$ to a runtime value in $\mathscr{Q}(\mathsf{lbl}(s))$; in other words $\mathscr{Q}(x) = \prod_{s \in x} \mathscr{Q}(\mathsf{lbl}(s))$. A configuration x' of E_P can be viewed as a trace over $\pi_P\, x'$; hence $\pi_P^{-1}\{x\} := \{x' \in \mathscr{C}(E_P) \mid \pi_P x' = x\}$ is the set of traces of P over x. We can now define dataflow graphs:

Definition 4. *A* ***dataflow graph*** *on* $\Gamma \vdash B$ *is a triple* $\mathbf{S} = (E_S, G_S, \pi_S : E_S \to G_S)$ *with* G_S *a dependency graph and* E_S *a runtime graph, such that:*

- π_S *is a rigid map and* $\mathit{lbl} \circ \pi_S = \alpha \circ \mathit{lbl} : E_S \to \mathscr{L}^{\mathtt{static}}_{\Gamma \vdash B}$
- *for each* $x \in \mathscr{C}(G_S)$, *the following function is injective*

$$
\begin{aligned}
q_x : \pi_S^{-1}\{x\} &\to \mathscr{Q}(x) \\
x' &\mapsto (s \mapsto \mathbf{q}(\mathit{lbl}(s)))
\end{aligned}
$$

- *if* $e, e' \in E_S$ *with* $e \rightsquigarrow e'$ *then* $\pi e = \pi e'$, *and moreover* e *and* e' *are either both sample or both read events.*

As mentioned above, maximal configurations of E_P correspond to total traces of P, and will be the states of the Markov chain in Sect. 5. By the second axiom, they can be seen as pairs $(x \in \mathscr{C}(G_S), q \in \mathscr{Q}(x))$. Because of the third axiom, E_S is always confusion-free.

Measurable Fibres. Rigid maps are convenient in this context because, they allow for reasoning about program traces by organising them as *fibres*. The key property we rely on is the following:

Lemma 2. *If $\pi : E \to G$ is a rigid map of event structures, then the induced map $\pi : \mathscr{C}(E) \to \mathscr{C}(G)$ is a* discrete fibration*: that is, for every $y \in \mathscr{C}(E)$, if $x \subseteq \pi y$ for some $x \in \mathscr{C}(G)$, then there is a unique $y' \in \mathscr{C}(E)$ such that $y' \subseteq y$ and $\pi y' = x$.*

This enables an essential feature of our approach: given a configuration x of the dataflow graph G, the fibre $\pi^{-1}\{x\}$ over it contains all the (possibly partial) program traces over x, *i.e.* those whose path through the program corresponds to that of x. Additionally the lemma implies that every pair of configurations $x, x' \in \mathscr{C}(G)$ such that $x \subseteq x'$ induces a **restriction map** $r_{x,x'} : \pi^{-1}\{x'\} \to \pi^{-1}\{x\}$, whose action on a program trace over x' is to return its *prefix* over x.

Although there is no measure-theoretic structure in the definition of dataflow graphs, we can recover it: for every $x \in \mathscr{C}(G_S)$, the fibre $\pi_S^{-1}\{x\}$ can be equipped with the σ-algebra induced from $\Sigma_{\mathscr{Q}(x)}$ via q_x; it is generated by sets $q_x^{-1}U$ for $U \in \Sigma_{\mathscr{Q}(x)}$.

It is easy to check that this makes the restriction map $r_{x,x'} : \pi_S^{-1}\{x'\} \to \pi_S^{-1}\{x\}$ measurable for each pair x, x' of configurations with $x \subseteq x'$. (Note that this makes **S** a *measurable event structure* in the sense of [16].) Moreover, the map $q_{x,s} : \pi_S^{-1}\{x\} \to \mathscr{Q}(\mathsf{lbl}(s))$ for $s \in x \in \mathscr{C}(G_S)$, mapping $x' \in \pi_S^{-1}\{x\}$ to $\mathbf{q}(\mathsf{lbl}(s'))$ for s' the unique antecedent by π_S of s in x', is also measurable.

We will also make use of the following result:

Lemma 3. *Consider a dataflow* **S** *and $x, y, z \in \mathscr{C}(G_S)$ with $x \subseteq y$, $x \subseteq z$, and $y \cup z \in \mathscr{C}(G_S)$. If $y \cap z = x$, then the space $\pi_S^{-1}\{y \cup z\}$ is isomorphic to the set*

$$\{(u_y, u_z) \in \pi_S^{-1}\{y\} \times \pi_S^{-1}\{z\} \mid r_{x,y}(u_y) = r_{x,z}(u_z)\},$$

with σ-algebra generated by sets of the form $\{(u_y, u_z) \in X_y \times X_z \mid X_y \in \Sigma_{\pi_S^{-1}\{y\}}, X_z \in \Sigma_{\pi_S^{-1}\{z\}}$ and $r_{x,y}(u_y) = r_{x,z}(u_z)\}$.

(For the reader with knowledge of category theory, this says exactly that the diagram

$$\begin{array}{ccc}
\pi_S^{-1}\{y \cup z\} & \xrightarrow{r_{y,y\cup z}} & \pi_S^{-1}\{y\} \\
{\scriptstyle r_{z,y\cup z}}\downarrow & & \downarrow{\scriptstyle r_{x,y}} \\
\pi_S^{-1}\{z\} & \xrightarrow[r_{x,z}]{} & \pi_S^{-1}\{x\}
\end{array}$$

is a pullback in the category of measurable spaces.)

3.4 Quantitative Dataflow Graphs

We can finally introduce the last bit of information we need about programs in order to perform inference: the probabilistic information. So far, in a dataflow graph, we know when the program is sampling, but not from which distribution. This is resolved by adding for each sample event s in the dependency graph a kernel $k_s : \pi^{-1}\{[s)\} \rightsquigarrow \pi^{-1}\{[s]\}$. Given a trace x over $[s)$, k_s specifies a probability distribution according to which x will be extended to a trace over $[s]$. This distribution must of course have support contained in the set $r^{-1}_{[s),[s]}\{x\}$ of traces over $[s]$ of which x is a prefix; this is the meaning of the technical condition in the definition below.

Definition 5. *A* ***quantitative dataflow graph*** *is a tuple* $\mathbf{S} = (E_S, G_S, \pi : E_S \to G_S, (k^S_s))$ *where for each sample event* $s \in G_S$, k^S_s *is a kernel* $\pi^{-1}\{[s)\} \rightsquigarrow \pi^{-1}\{[s]\}$ *satisfying for all* $x \in \pi^{-1}\{[s)\}$,

$$k^S_s(x, \pi^{-1}\{[s]\} \setminus r^{-1}_{[s),[s]}\{x\}) = 0.$$

This axiom stipulates that any extension $x' \in \pi^{-1}_S\{[s]\}$ of $x \in \pi^{-1}_S\{[s)\}$ drawn by k_s must contain x; in effect k_s only samples the runtime value for s.

From Graphs to Kernels. We show how to collapse a quantitative dataflow graph $\mathbf{S}$ on $\Gamma \vdash B$ to a kernel $[\![\Gamma]\!] \rightsquigarrow [\![B]\!]$. First, we extend the kernel family on sampling events $(k^S_s : \pi^{-1}\{[s)\} \rightsquigarrow \pi^{-1}\{[s]\})$ to a family $(k^{S[\gamma]}_s : \pi^{-1}\{[s)\} \rightsquigarrow \pi^{-1}\{[s]\})$ defined on *all* events $s \in S$, parametrised by the value of the environment $\gamma \in [\![\Gamma]\!]$. To define $k^{S[\gamma]}_s(x, \cdot)$ it is enough to specify its value on the generating set for $\Sigma_{\pi^{-1}\{[s]\}}$. As we have seen this contains elements of the form $q^{-1}_{[s]}(U)$ with $U \in \Sigma_{\mathcal{Q}([s])}$. We distinguish the following cases corresponding to the nature of s:

- If s is a sample event, $k^{S[\gamma]}_s = k^S_s$
- If s is a read on $a : A$, any $x \in \pi^{-1}[s)$ has runtime information $q_{[s)}(x)$ in $\mathcal{Q}([s))$ which can be extended to $\mathcal{Q}([s])$ by mapping s to $\gamma(a)$:

$$k^{S[\gamma]}_s(x, q^{-1}_{[s]}U) = \delta_{q_{[s)}(x)[s:=\gamma(a)]}(U)$$

- If s is a return or a score event: any $x \in \pi^{-1}\{[s)\}$ has at most one extension to $o(x) \in \pi^{-1}\{[s]\}$ (because return and score events cannot be involved in a minimal conflict): $k^{S[\gamma]}_s(x, q^{-1}_{[s]}(U)) = \delta_{q_{[s]}(o(x))}(U)$. If $o(x)$ does not exist, we let $k^{S[\gamma]}_s(x, X) = 0$.

We can now define a kernel $k^{S[\gamma]}_{x,s} : \pi^{-1}\{x\} \rightsquigarrow \pi^{-1}\{x'\}$ for every atomic extension $x \stackrel{s}{\longrightarrow\!\!\subset} x'$ in G_S, ie. when $x' \setminus x = \{s\}$, as follows:

$$k^{S[\gamma]}_{x,s}(y, U) = k_s(r_{[s),x}(y), \{w \in \pi^{-1}_S\{[s]\} \mid (y, w) \in U\}).$$

The second argument to k_s above is always measurable, by a standard measure-theoretic argument based on Lemma 3, as $x \cap [s] = [s)$.

From this definition we derive:

Lemma 4. *If* $x \stackrel{s_1}{\longrightarrow\!\!\subset} x_1$ *and* $x \stackrel{s_2}{\longrightarrow\!\!\subset} x_2$ *are concurrent extensions of* x *(*i.e. s_1 *and* s_2 *are not in conflict), then* $k^{S[\gamma]}_{x_1,s_2} \circ k^{S[\gamma]}_{x,s_1} = k^{S[\gamma]}_{x_2,s_1} \circ k^{S[\gamma]}_{x,s_2}$.

Given a configuration $x \in \mathscr{C}(G_S)$ and a covering chain $\emptyset \overset{s_1}{-\!\!\subset} x_1 \ldots \overset{s_n}{-\!\!\subset} x_n = x$, we can finally define a measure on $\pi^{-1}\{x\}$:

$$\mu_x^{S[\gamma]} = k_{x_{n-1},s_n}^{S[\gamma]} \circ \ldots \circ k_{\emptyset,s_1}^{S[\gamma]}(*, \cdot),$$

where $*$ is the only trace over $\emptyset$. The particular covering chain used does not matter by the previous lemma. Using this, we can define the kernel of a quantitative dataflow graph $\mathbf{S}$ as follows:

$$\mathsf{kernel}(\mathbf{S})(\gamma, X) = \sum_{r \in G_S, \mathsf{lbl}(r) = \mathsf{Rtn}} \mu_{[r]}^{S[\gamma]}(q_{[r],r}^{-1}(X)),$$

where the measurable map $q_{[r],r} : \pi^{-1}\{r\} \to [\![B]\!]$ looks up the runtime value of r in an element of the fibre over $[r]$ (defined in Sect. 3.3).

Lemma 5. *kernel*$(\mathbf{S})$ *is an s-finite kernel* $[\![\Gamma]\!] \rightsquigarrow [\![B]\!]$.

4 Programs as Labelled Event Structures

We now detail our interpretation of programs as quantitative dataflow graphs. Our interpretation is given by induction, similarly to the measure-theoretic interpretation given in Sect. 2.3, in which composition of kernels plays a central role. In Sect. 4.1, we discuss how to compose quantitative dataflow graphs, and in Sect. 4.2, we define our interpretation.

4.1 Composition of Probablistic Event Structures

Consider two quantitative dataflow graphs, S on $\Gamma \vdash A$, and T on $\Gamma, a : A \vdash B$ where a does not occur in Γ. In what follows we show how they can be composed to form a quantitative dataflow graph $T \odot^a S$ on $\Gamma \vdash B$.

Unlike in the kernel model of Sect. 2.3, we will need two notions of composition. The first one is akin to the usual sequential composition: actions in T must wait on S to return before they can proceed. The second is closer to parallel composition: actions on T which do not depend on a read of the variable a can be executed in parallel with S. The latter composition is used to interpret the let construct. In `let` a `=` M `in` N, we want all the probabilistic actions or reads on other variables which do not depend on the value of a to be in parallel with M. However, in a program such as `case` M `of` $\{(i, x) \Rightarrow N_i\}_{i \in I}$ we do not want any actions of N_i to start before the selected branch is known, *i.e.* before the return value of M is known.

By way of illustration, consider the following simple example, in which we only consider runtime graphs, ignoring the rest of the structure for now. Suppose S and T are given by

S =
Rd b tt
Rd b ff
Rtn ff
Rtn tt
T =
Sam r
Rd a tt
Rd a ff
Rtn ((), tt)
Rtn ((), ff)

The graph S can be seen to correspond to the program if b then ff else tt and T to the pairing (sample d (0), a) for any d. Here S is a runtime graph on $b : \mathbb{B} \vdash \mathbb{B}$ and T on $a : \mathbb{B}, b : \mathbb{B} \vdash \mathbb{B}$.

Both notions of compositions are displayed in the diagram below. The sequential composition (left) corresponds to

$$\text{if } b \text{ then } (\text{sample } d \ (0), \text{ff}) \text{ else } (\text{sample } d \ (0), \text{tt})$$

and the parallel composition to (sample d (0), if b then ff else tt):

$$T \odot_{\text{seq}}^a S = \begin{pmatrix} \text{Rd } b\,\text{tt} \sim \text{Rd } b\,\text{ff} \\ \Downarrow \qquad \Downarrow \\ \text{Sam } r \quad \text{Sam } r \\ \Downarrow \qquad \Downarrow \\ \text{Rtn ff} \quad \text{Rtn tt} \end{pmatrix} \qquad T \odot_{\text{par}}^a S = \begin{pmatrix} \text{Sam } r \quad \text{Rd } b\,\text{tt} \sim \text{Rd } b\,\text{ff} \\ \searrow \quad \Downarrow \qquad \Downarrow \\ \text{Rtn ff} \quad \text{Rtn tt} \end{pmatrix}$$

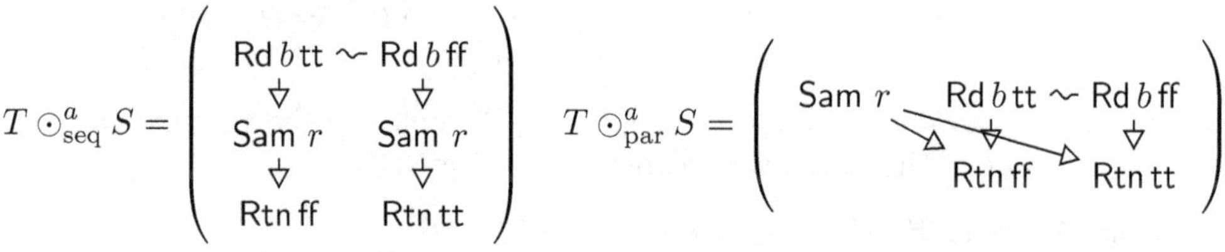

Composition of Runtime and Dependency Graphs. Let us now define both composition operators at the level of the event structures. Through the bijection $\mathscr{L}_{\Gamma \vdash B}^{\text{static}} \simeq \mathscr{L}_{\Gamma' \vdash 1}^{\text{run}}$ where $\Gamma'(a) = 1$ for all $a \in \text{dom}(\Gamma)$, we will see dependency graphs and runtime graphs as the same kind of objects, event structures labelled over $\mathscr{L}_{\Gamma \vdash A}^{\text{run}}$.

The two compositions $S \odot_{\text{par}}^a T$ and $S \odot_{\text{seq}}^a T$ are two instances of the same construction, parametrised by a set of labels $D \subseteq \mathscr{L}_{\Gamma,a:A \vdash B}^{\text{run}}$. Informally, D specifies which events of T are to depend on the return value of S in the resulting composition graph. It is natural to assume in particular that D contains all reads on a, and all return events.

Sequential and parallel composition are instances of this construction where D is set to one of the following:

$$D_{\text{seq}}^{\Gamma,a:A \vdash B} = \mathscr{L}_{\Gamma,a:A \vdash B}^{\text{run}} \qquad\qquad D_{\text{par}}^{\Gamma,a:A \vdash B} = \{\text{Rd } a\,v, \text{Rtn } v \in \mathscr{L}_{\Gamma,a:A \vdash B}^{\text{run}}\}.$$

We proceed to describe the construction for an abstract D. Let T be an event structure labelled by $\mathscr{L}_{\Gamma,a:A \vdash B}^{\text{run}}$ and S labelled by $\mathscr{L}_{\Gamma \vdash A}^{\text{run}}$. A configuration $x \in \mathscr{C}(S)$ is a **justification** of $y \in \mathscr{C}(T)$ when

1. if $\text{lbl}(y)$ intersects D, then x contains a return event
2. for all $t \in y$ with label $\text{Rd } a\,v$, there exists an event $s \in x$ labelled $\text{Rtn } v$.

In particular if $\text{lbl}(y)$ does not intersect D, then any configuration of S is a justification of y. A **minimal justification** of y is a justification that admits no proper subset which is also a justification of y. We now define the event structure $S \cdot_D T$ as follows:

- *Events:* $S \cup \{(x,t) \mid x \in \mathscr{C}(S), t \in T, x \text{ minimal justification for } [t]\}$;
- *Causality:* $\leq_S \ \cup \ \{(x,t),(x',t') \mid x \subseteq x' \wedge t \leq t'\} \ \cup \ \{s,(x,t) \mid s \in x\}$;
- *Conflict:* the symmetric closure of

$$\#_S \cup \{(x,t),(x',t') \mid x \cup x' \notin \mathscr{C}(T) \vee t \#_B t'\}$$
$$\cup \{s,(x,t) \mid \{s\} \cup x \notin \mathscr{C}(S)\}.$$

Lemma 6. *$S \cdot_D T$ is an event structure, and the following is an order-isomorphism:*

$$\langle\cdot,\cdot\rangle : \{(x,y) \in \mathscr{C}(S) \times \mathscr{C}(T) \mid x \textit{ is a justification of } y\} \cong \mathscr{C}(S \cdot_D T).$$

This event structure is not quite what we want, since it still contains return events from S and reads on a from T. To remove them, we use the following general construction. Given a Σ-labelled event structure E and $V \subseteq E$ a set of visible events, its **projection** $E \downarrow V$ has events V and causality, conflict and labelling inherited from E. Thus the composition of S and T is:

$$S \odot_D^a T := S \cdot_D T \downarrow (\{s \in S \mid\ s \text{ not a return}\} \cup \{(x,t) \mid\ t \text{ not a read on } a\}).$$

As a result $S \odot_D^a T$ is labelled over $\mathscr{L}^{\mathtt{run}}_{\Gamma \vdash B}$ as needed.

Dataflow Information. We now explain how this construction lifts to dataflow graphs. Consider dataflow graphs $S = (E_S, G_S, \pi_S : E_S \to G_S)$ on $\Gamma \vdash A$ and $T = (E_T, G_T, \pi_T : E_T \to E_T)$ on $\Gamma, a : A \vdash B$. Given $D \subseteq \mathscr{L}^{\mathtt{static}}_{\Gamma, a:A \vdash B}$ we define

$$E_{S \cdot_D T} = E_S \cdot_{\alpha^{-1}D} E_T \qquad G_{S \cdot_D T} = G_S \cdot_D G_T$$
$$E_{S \odot_D^a T} = E_S \odot^a_{\alpha^{-1}D} E_T \qquad G_{S \odot_D^a T} = G_S \odot_D^a G_T$$

Lemma 7. *The maps π_S and π_T extend to rigid maps*

$$\pi_{S \cdot_D T} : E_{S \cdot_{\alpha^{-1}D} T} \to G_{S \cdot_D T}$$
$$\pi_{S \odot_D^a T} : E_{S \odot^a_{\alpha^{-1}D} T} \to G_{S \odot_D^a T}$$

Moreover, if $\langle x, y\rangle \in \mathscr{C}(E_{S \cdot_D T})$, $\langle \pi_S\, x, \pi_T\, y\rangle$ is a well-defined configuration of $G_{S \cdot_D T}$. As a result, for $\langle x, y\rangle \in \mathscr{C}(G_{S \cdot_D T})$, we have a injection $\varphi_{x,y} : \pi^{-1}\{\langle x, y\rangle\} \to \pi^{-1}\{x\} \times \pi^{-1}\{y\}$ making the following diagram commute:

$$\begin{array}{ccc} \pi^{-1}\{\langle x,y\rangle\} & \xrightarrow{\varphi_{x,y}} & \pi^{-1}\{x\} \times \pi^{-1}\{y\} \\ q_{\langle x,y\rangle}\downarrow & & \downarrow q_x \times q_y \\ \mathscr{Q}(\langle x,y\rangle) & \xrightarrow[\cong]{} & \mathscr{Q}(x) \times \mathscr{Q}(y) \end{array}$$

In particular, $\varphi_{x,y}$ is measurable and induces the σ-algebra on $\pi^{-1}\{\langle x, y\rangle\}$. We write φ_x for the map $\varphi_{x,\emptyset}$, an isomorphism.

Adding Probability. At this point we have defined all the components of dataflow graphs $S \odot_D^a T$ and $S \cdot_D T$. We proceed to make them quantitative.

Observe first that each sampling event of $G_{S \cdot_D T}$ (or equivalently of $G_{S \odot_D^a T}$ – sampling events are never hidden) corresponds either to a sampling event of G_S, or to an event (x, t) where t is a sampling event of G_T. We consider both cases to define a family of kernels $(k_s^{S \cdot_D T})$ between the fibres of $S \cdot_D T$. This will in turn induce a family $(k_s^{S \odot_D^a T})$ on $S \odot_D^a T$.

– If s is a sample event of G_S, we use the isomorphisms $\varphi_{[s)}$ and $\varphi_{[s]}$ of Lemma 7 to define:

$$k_s^{S\odot_D^a T}(v, X) = k_s^S(\varphi_{[s)}^{-1} v, \varphi_{[s]}^{-1} X).$$

– If s corresponds to (x, t) for t a sample event of G_T, then for every $X_x \in \Sigma_{\pi_S^{-1}\{x\}}$ and $X_t \in \Sigma_{\pi_T^{-1}\{[t)\}}$ we define

$$k_{(x,t)}^{S\odot_D^a T}(\langle x', y' \rangle, \varphi_{x,[t]}^{-1}(X_x \times X_t)) = \delta_{x'}(X_x) \times k_t^T(y', X_t).$$

By Lemma 7, the sets $\varphi_{x,[t]}^{-1}(X_x \times X_t)$ form a basis for $\Sigma_{\pi^{-1}\{\langle x,[t)\rangle\}}$, so that this definition determines the entire kernel.

So we have defined a kernel $k_s^{S\cdot_D T}$ for each sample event s of $G_{S\cdot_D T}$. We move to the composition $(S \odot_D^a T)$. Recall that the *causal history* of a configuration $z \in \mathscr{C}(G_{S\odot_D^a T})$ is the set $[z]$, a configuration of $G_{S\cdot_D T}$. We see that hiding does not affect the fibre structure:

Lemma 8. *For any $z \in \mathscr{C}(G_{S\odot_D^a T})$, there is a measurable isomorphism ψ_z : $\pi_{S\odot_D^a T}^{-1}\{z\} \cong \pi_{S\cdot_D T}^{-1}\{[z]\}$.*

Using this result and the fact that $G_{S\odot_D^a T} \subseteq G_{S\cdot_D T}$, we may define for each s:

$$k_s^{S\odot_D^a T}(v, X) = k_s^{S\cdot_D T}(\psi_{[s)}(v), \psi_{[s]} X).$$

We conclude:

Lemma 9. *$S \odot_D^a T := (G_{S\odot_D^a T}, E_{S\odot_D^a T}, \pi_{S\odot_D^a T}, (k_s^{S\odot_D^a T}))$ is a quantitative dataflow graph on $\Gamma \vdash B$.*

Multicomposition. By chaining this composition, we can compose on several variables at once. Given quantitative dataflow graphs S_i on $\Gamma \vdash A_i$ and T on $\Gamma, a_1 : A_1, \ldots, a_n : A_n \vdash A$ we define

$$(S_i) \odot_{\text{par}}^{(a_i)} T := S_1 \odot_{\text{par}}^{a_1} (\ldots \odot_{\text{par}}^{a_n} T)$$
$$(S_i) \odot_{\text{seq}}^{(a_i)} T := S_1 \odot_{\text{seq}}^{a_1} (\ldots \odot_{\text{seq}}^{a_n} T)$$

4.2 Interpretation of Programs

We now describe how to interpret programs of our language using quantitative dataflow graphs. To do so we follow the same pattern as for the measure-theoretical interpretation given in Sect. 2.3.

Interpretation of Functions. Given a measurable function $f : [\![A]\!] \to [\![B]\!]$, we define the quantitative dataflow graph

$$S_f^a = \left(\sum_{v \in [\![A]\!]} \begin{array}{c} \mathsf{Rd}\, a\, v \\ \downarrow \\ \mathsf{Rtn}\, (f\, v) \end{array} \quad \to \quad \begin{array}{c} \mathsf{Rd}\, a \\ \downarrow \\ \mathsf{Rtn} \end{array} \right).$$

We then define $[\![f\, M]\!]_{\mathcal{G}}$ as $[\![M]\!]_{\mathcal{G}} \odot_{\text{par}}^a S_f^a$ where a is chosen so as not to occur free in M.

Probablistic Actions. In order to interpret scoring and sampling primitives, we need the following two quantitative dataflow graphs:

$$\texttt{score} = \left(\sum_{r \in \mathbb{R}} \begin{array}{c} \mathsf{Rd}\, a\, r \\ \downarrow \\ \mathsf{Sco}\, r \\ \downarrow \\ \mathsf{Rtn}\, () \end{array} \rightarrow \begin{array}{c} \mathsf{Rd}\, a \\ \downarrow \\ \mathsf{Sco} \\ \downarrow \\ \mathsf{Rtn} \end{array} \right) \qquad \texttt{sample}_d = \left(\sum_{\mathbf{r} \in \mathbb{R}^n} \begin{array}{c} \mathsf{Rd}\, a\, \mathbf{r} \\ \downarrow \\ \mathsf{Sam}\, s \\ \downarrow \\ \mathsf{Rtn}\, () \end{array} \rightarrow \begin{array}{c} \mathsf{Rd}\, a \\ \downarrow \\ \mathsf{Sam} \\ \downarrow \\ \mathsf{Rtn} \end{array}, k_{\mathsf{Sam}} \right)$$

and we define k_{Sam} by integrating the density function d; here we identify $\mathscr{Q}(\{\mathsf{Rd}\, a\, , \mathsf{Sam}\})$ and $\pi^{-1}\{\{\mathsf{Rd}\, a\, , \mathsf{Sam}\}\}$:

$$k_{\mathsf{Sam}}(\{\mathsf{Rd}\, a\, \mathbf{r}\}, U) = \int_{q \in U, q(\mathsf{Rd}\, a) = \mathbf{r}} d(\mathbf{r}, q(\mathsf{Sam}))\mathrm{d}\lambda.$$

We can now interpret scoring and sampling constructs:

$$[\![\texttt{score}\ M]\!]_{\mathcal{G}} = [\![M]\!]_{\mathcal{G}} \odot^{a}_{\mathrm{par}} \texttt{score} \qquad [\![\texttt{sample}\ d\ (M)]\!]_{\mathcal{G}} = [\![M]\!]_{\mathcal{G}} \odot^{a}_{\mathrm{par}} \texttt{sample}_d.$$

Interpretation of Tuples and Variables. Given a family $(a_i)_{i \in I}$, we define the dataflow graph $\texttt{tuple}_{(a_i : A_i)}$ on $a_1 : A_1, \ldots, a_n : A_n \vdash A_1 \times \ldots \times A_n$ as follows. Its set of events is the disjoint union

$$\bigcup_{i \in I, v \in [\![A_i]\!]} \mathsf{Rd}\, a_i\, v + \bigcup_{\mathbf{v} \in [\![A_1 \times \ldots \times A_n]\!]} \mathsf{Rtn}\, \mathbf{v}$$

where the conflict is induced by $\mathsf{Rd}\, a_i\, v \sim\!\sim \mathsf{Rd}\, a_i\, v'$ for $v \neq v'$; and causality contains all the pairs $\mathsf{Rd}\, a_i\, v \twoheadrightarrow \mathsf{Rtn}\, (v_1, \ldots, v_n)$ where $v_i = v$. Then we form a quantitative dataflow graph $\texttt{Tuple}_{(a_i : A_i)}$, whose dependency graph is $\texttt{tuple}_{(a_i : 1)}$ (up to the bijection $\mathscr{L}^{\texttt{run}}_{\Gamma \vdash A} \simeq \mathscr{L}^{\texttt{static}}_{\Gamma' \vdash 1}$ where $\Gamma'(a) = 1$ for $a \in \mathrm{dom}(\Gamma)$); and the runtime graph is $\texttt{tuple}_{(a_i : A_i)}$, along with the obvious rigid map between them.

We then define the semantics of $(M_1, \ldots, M_n)$:

$$[\![(M_1, \ldots, M_n)]\!]_{\mathcal{G}} = ([\![M_i]\!]_{\mathcal{G}})_i \odot^{(a_i)}_{\mathrm{par}} \texttt{Tuple}_{\mathtt{a_i : A_i}},$$

where the a_i are chosen free in all of the M_j. This construction is also useful to interpret variables:

$$[\![a]\!]_{\mathcal{G}} = \texttt{Tuple}_{a : A} \qquad \text{where } \Gamma \vdash a : A.$$

Interpretation of Pattern Matching. Consider now a term of the form $\mathsf{case}\, M$ of $\{(i, a) \Rightarrow N_i\}_{i \in i}$. By induction, we have that $[\![N_i]\!]_{\mathcal{G}}$ is a quantitative dataflow graph on $\Gamma, a : A_i \vdash B$. Let us write $[\![N_i]\!]^{*}_{\mathcal{G}}$ for the quantitative dataflow graph on $\Gamma, a : (\sum_{i \in I} A_i) \vdash B$ obtained by relabelling events of the form $\mathsf{Rd}\, a\, v$ to $\mathsf{Rd}\, a\, (i, v)$, and sequentially precomposing with $\texttt{Tuple}_{a : \sum_{i \in I} A_i}$. This ensures that minimal events in $[\![N_i]\!]^*_{\mathcal{G}}$ are reads on a. We then build the quantitative dataflow graph $\sum_{i\in I}[\![N_i]\!]^*_{\mathcal{G}}$ on $\Gamma, a : \sum_{i\in I} A_i \vdash B$. This can be composed with $[\![M]\!]_{\mathcal{G}}$:

$$[\![\texttt{case } M \texttt{ of } \{(i,a) \Rightarrow N_i\}_{i\in I}]\!]_{\mathcal{G}} = [\![M]\!]_{\mathcal{G}} \odot^a_{\mathrm{seq}} \left(\sum_{i\in I}[\![N_i]\!]^*_{\mathcal{G}}\right).$$

It is crucial here that one uses *sequential* composition: none of the branches must be evaluated until the outcome of M is known.

Adequacy of Composition. We now prove that our interpretation is adequate with respect to the measure-theoretic semantics described in Sect. 2.3. Given any subset $D \subseteq \mathscr{L}^{\texttt{static}}_{\Gamma,a:A\vdash B}$ containing returns and reads on a, we show that the composition $S \odot^a_D T$ does implement the composition of kernels:

Theorem 1. *For S a quantitative dataflow graph on $\Gamma \vdash A$ and T on $\Gamma, a : A \vdash B$, we have*

$$\mathsf{kernel}(S \odot^a_D T) = \mathsf{kernel}(T) \circ \mathsf{kernel}(S) : [\![\Gamma]\!] \to [\![B]\!].$$

From this result, we can deduce that the semantics in terms of quantitative dataflow graphs is adequate with respect to the measure-theoretic semantics:

Theorem 2. *For every term $\Gamma \vdash M : A$, $\mathsf{kernel}([\![M]\!]_{\mathcal{G}}) = [\![M]\!]$.*

5 An Inference Algorithm

In this section, we exploit the intensional semantics defined above and define a Metropolis-Hastings inference algorithm. We start, in Sect. 5.1, by giving a concrete presentation of those quantitative dataflow graphs arising as the interpretation of probabilistic programs; we argue this makes them well-suited for manipulation by an algorithm. Then, in Sect. 5.2, we give a more formal introduction to the Metropolis-Hastings sampling methods than that given in Sect. 3. Finally, in Sect. 5.3, we build the proposal kernel on which our implementation relies, and conclude.

5.1 A Concrete Presentation of Probabilistic Dataflow Graphs

Quantitative dataflow graphs as presented in the previous sections are not easy to handle inside of an algorithm: among other things, the runtime graph has an uncountable set of events. In this section we show that some dataflow graphs, in particular those needed for modelling programs, admit a finite representation.

Recovering Fibres. Consider a dataflow graph $\mathbf{S} = (E_S, G_S, \pi_S)$ on $\Gamma \vdash B$. It follows from Lemma 3 that the fibre structure of $\mathbf{S}$ is completely determined by the spaces $\pi_S^{-1}\{[s]\}$, for $s \in G_S$, so we focus on trying to give a simplified representation for those spaces.

First, let us notice that if s is a return or score event, given $x \in \pi^{-1}\{x\}$, the value $q_x(s)$ is determined by $q|_{[s)}$. In other words the map $\pi^{-1}\{[s]\} \to \mathscr{Q}([s))$ is an injection. This is due to the fact that minimal conflict in E_S cannot involve return or score events. As a result, E_S induces a partial function $o_s^S : \mathscr{Q}([s)) \rightharpoonup \mathscr{Q}(\mathsf{lbl}(s))$, called the **outcome function**. It is defined as follows:

$$o_s^S(q) = \begin{cases} q_{[s]}(x')(s) & \text{if there exists } x' \in \pi^{-1}\{x'\}, q_{[s]}(x')|_{[s)} = q, \\ \text{undefined} & \text{otherwise.} \end{cases}$$

Note that x' must be unique by the remark above since its projection to $\mathscr{Q}([s))$ is determined by q. The function o^S is partial, because it might be the case that the event s occurs conditionally on the runtime value on $[s)$.

In fact this structure is all we need in order to describe a dataflow graph:

Lemma 10. *Given G_S a dependency graph on $\Gamma \vdash B$, and partial functions $(o_s) : \mathscr{Q}([s)) \rightharpoonup \mathscr{Q}(\mathsf{lbl}(s))$ for score and return events of S. There exists a dataflow graph $(E_S, G_S, \pi_S : E_S \to G_S)$ whose outcome functions coincide with the o_s. Moreover, there is an order-isomorphism*

$$\mathscr{C}(E_S) \cong \{(x, q) \mid x \in \mathscr{C}(G_S), q \in \mathscr{Q}(x), \forall s \in x, o_s(q|_{[s)}) = q(s)\}.$$

Adding Probabilities. To add probabilities, we simply equip each sample event s of G_S with a density function $d_s : \mathscr{Q}([s)) \times \mathbb{R} \rightharpoonup \mathbb{R}$.

Definition 6. *A **concrete quantitative dataflow graph** is a tuple $(G_S, (o_s : \mathscr{Q}([s)) \rightharpoonup \mathscr{Q}(\mathsf{lbl}(s))), (d_s : \mathscr{Q}([s)) \times \mathbb{R} \rightharpoonup \mathbb{R})_{s \in sample(G_S)})$ where $d_s(x, \cdot)$ is normalised.*

Lemma 11. *Any concrete quantitative dataflow graph $\mathcal{S}$ unfolds to a quantitative dataflow graph* `unfold` $\mathcal{S}$.

We see now that the quantitative dataflow graphs arising as the interpretation of a program must be the unfolding of a concrete quantitative dataflow graph:

Lemma 12. *For any concrete quantitative dataflow graphs $\mathcal{S}$ on $\Gamma \vdash A$ and $\mathcal{T}$ on $\Gamma, a : A \vdash B$,* `unfold` $\mathcal{S} \odot_D^a \mathcal{T}$`unfold` $\mathcal{T}$ *is the unfolding of a concrete quantitative dataflow graph. It follows that for any program $\Gamma \vdash M : B$, $[\![M]\!]_{\mathcal{G}}$ is the unfolding of a concrete quantitative dataflow graph.*

5.2 Metropolis-Hastings

Recall that the Metropolis-Hastings algorithm is used to sample from a density function $d : \mathbb{A} \to \mathbb{R}$ which may not be normalised. Here $\mathbb{A}$ is a measurable *state space*, equipped with a measure λ. The algorithm works by building a Markov chain whose stationary distribution is D, the probability distribution obtained from d after normalisation:

$$\forall X \in \Sigma_{\mathbb{A}}, D(X) = \frac{\int_{x \in X} d(x)}{\int_{x \in \mathbb{A}} d(x)}.$$

Our presentation and reasoning in the rest of this section are inspired by the work of Borgström et al. [2].

Preliminaries on Markov Chains. A Markov chain on a measurable state space $\mathbb{A}$ is a probability kernel $k : \mathbb{A} \rightsquigarrow \mathbb{A}$, viewed as a transition function: given a state $x \in \mathbb{A}$, the distribution $k(x, \cdot)$ is the distribution from which a next sample state will be drawn. Usually, each $k(x, \cdot)$ comes with a procedure for sampling: we will treat this as a probabilistic program $M(x)$ whose output is the next state. Given an initial state $x \in \mathbb{A}$ and a natural number $n \in \mathbb{N}$, we have a distribution $k^n(x, \cdot)$ on $\mathbb{A}$ obtained by iterating k n times. We say that the Markov chain k has **limit** the distribution μ on $\mathbb{A}$ when

$$\lim_{n \to \infty} ||k^n(x, \cdot) - \mu|| = 0 \qquad \text{where } ||\mu_1 - \mu_2|| = \sup_{A \in \Sigma_{\mathbb{A}}} \mu_1(A) - \mu_2(A).$$

For the purposes of this paper, we call a Markov chain $k : \mathbb{A} \to \mathbb{A}$ **computable** when there exists a type A such that $[\![A]\!] = \mathbb{A}$ (up to iso) and an expression *without scores* $x : A \vdash K : A$ such that $[\![K]\!] = k$. (Recall that programs without conditioning denote probabilistic kernels, and are easily sampled from, since all standard distributions in the language are assumed to come with a built-in sampler.)

We will use terms of our language to describe computable Markov chains language, taking mild liberties with syntax. We assume in particular that programs may call each other as subroutines (this can be done via substitutions), and that manipulating finite structures is computable and thus representable in the language.

The Metropolis-Hastings Algorithm. Recall that we wish to sample from a distribution with un-normalised density $d : \mathbb{A} \to \mathbb{R}$; d is assumed to be computable. The Markov chain defined by the Metropolis-Hastings algorithm has two parameters: a computable Markov chain $x : A \vdash P : A$, the *proposal kernel*, and a measurable, computable function $p : \mathbb{A}^2 \to \mathbb{R}$ representing the kernel $[\![P]\!]$, *i.e.*

$$[\![P]\!](x, X') = \int_{x' \in X'} p(x, x')\, d\lambda(x').$$

The Markov-chain $\mathtt{MH}(P, p, d)$ is defined as

$$\begin{aligned}\mathtt{MH}(P,p,d)(x) := \;& \mathtt{let}\ x' \ \mathtt{=}\ P(x)\ \mathtt{in} \\ & \mathtt{let}\ \alpha\ \mathtt{=}\ \min\left(1, \frac{d(x') \times p(x,x')}{d(x) \times p(x',x)}\right)\ \mathtt{in} \\ & \mathtt{let}\ u\ \mathtt{=}\ \mathtt{sample\ uniform}\ (0,1)\ \mathtt{in} \\ & \mathtt{if}\ u < \alpha\ \mathtt{then}\ x'\ \mathtt{else}\ x\end{aligned}$$

In words, the Markov chain works as follows: given a start state x, it generates a proposal for the next state x' using P. It then computes an *acceptance ratio* α, which is the probability with which the new sample will be *accepted*: the return state will then either be the original x or x', accordingly.

Assuming P and p satisfy a number of conditions, the algorithm is correct:

Theorem 3. *Assume that P and p satisfies the following properties:*

1. ***Strong irreducibility:*** *There exists $n \in \mathbb{N}$ such that for all $x \in \mathbb{A}$ and $X \in \Sigma_{\mathbb{A}}$ such that $D(X) \neq \emptyset$ and $d(x) > 0$, there exists $n \in \mathbb{N}$ such that $[\![P]\!]^n(x, X) > 0$.*
2. *$[\![P]\!](x, X') = \int_{x' \in X'} p(x, x')$.*
3. *If $d(x) > 0$ and $p(x, y) > 0$ then $d(y) > 0$.*
4. *If $d(x) > 0$ and $d(y) > 0$, then $p(x, y) > 0$ iff $p(y, x) > 0$.*

Then, the limit of MH(P, p, d) *for any initial state $x \in \mathbb{A}$ with $d(x) > 0$ is equal to D, the distribution obtained after normalising d.*

5.3 Our Proposal Kernel

Consider a closed program $\vdash M : A$ in which every measurable function is a computable one. Then, its interpretation as a concrete quantitative dataflow graph is computable, and we write $\mathcal{S}$ for the quantitative dataflow graph whose unfolding is $[\![M]\!]_{\mathcal{G}}$. Moreover, because M is closed, its measure-theoretic semantics gives a measure $[\![M]\!]$ on $[\![A]\!]$. Assume that norm$([\![M]\!])$ is well-defined: it is a probability distribution on $[\![A]\!]$. We describe how a Metropolis-Hastings algorithm may be used to sample from it, by reducing this problem to that of sampling from configurations of $E_{\mathcal{S}}$ according to the following density:

$$d_{\mathcal{S}}(x, q) := \left(\prod_{s \in \mathsf{sample}(x)} d_s(q(s)) \right) \left(\prod_{s \in \mathsf{score}(x)} q(s) \right).$$

Lemma 10 induces a natural measure on $\mathscr{C}(E_{\mathcal{S}})$. We have:

Lemma 13. *For all $X \in \Sigma_{\mathscr{C}(E_{\mathcal{S}})}$, $\mu^{\mathcal{S}}(X) = \int_{y \in X} d_{\mathcal{S}}(y) \mathrm{d}y$.*

Note that $d_{\mathcal{S}}(x, q)$ is easy to compute, but it is not normalised. Computing the normalising factor is in general intractable, but the Metropolis-Hastings algorithm does not require the density to be normalised.

Let us write $\mu^{\mathcal{S}}_{\text{norm}}(X) = \frac{\mu^{\mathcal{S}}(X)}{\mu^{\mathcal{S}}(\mathscr{C}(E_{\mathcal{S}}))}$ for the normalised distribution. By adequacy, we have for all $X \in \Sigma_{[\![A]\!]}$:

$$\text{norm}[\![M]\!](X) = \mu^{\mathcal{S}}_{\text{norm}}(\texttt{result}^{-1}(X)).$$

where $\texttt{result} : \max \mathscr{C}(E_{\mathcal{S}}) \rightharpoonup [\![A]\!]$ maps a maximal configuration of $E_{\mathcal{S}}$ to its return value, if any. This says that sampling from norm$[\![M]\!]$ amounts to sampling from $\mu^{\mathcal{S}}_{\text{norm}}$ and only keeping the return value.

Accordingly, we focus on designing a Metropolis-Hastings algorithm for sampling values in $\mathscr{C}(E_{\mathcal{S}})$ following the (unnormalised) density $d_{\mathcal{S}}$. We start by defining a proposal kernel for this algorithm.

To avoid overburdening the notation, we will no longer distinguish between a type and its denotation. Since G_S is finite, it can be represented by a type, and so can $\mathscr{C}(G_S)$. Moreover, $\mathscr{C}(E_S)$ is a subset of $\sum_{x\in\mathscr{C}(G_S)}\mathscr{Q}(x)$ which is also representable as the type of pairs $(x \in \mathscr{C}(G_S), q \in \mathscr{Q}(x))$. Operations on G_S and related objects are all computable and measurable so we can directly use them in the syntax. In particular, we will make use of the function $\texttt{ext} : \mathscr{C}(E_S) \to G_S{+}1$ which for each configuration $(x, q) \in \mathscr{C}(E_S)$ returns $(1, \mathfrak{s})$ if there exists $x \overset{s}{\longrightarrow\!\!\subset}$ with $o_s(q|_{[s)})$ defined, and $(2, *)$ if (x, q) is maximal.

Informally, for $(x, q) \in \mathscr{C}(E_S)$, the algorithm is:

- Pick a sample event $s \in x$, randomly over the set of sample events of x.
- Construct $x_0 := x \setminus \{s' \in x \mid s' \geq s\} \cup \{s\} \in \mathscr{C}(G_S)$.
- Return a maximal extension (x', q') of $(x_0, q|_{x_0})$ by only resampling the sample events of x' which are not in x.

The last step follows the single-site MH principle: sample events in $x \cap x'$ have already been evaluated in x, and are not updated. However, events which are in $x' \setminus x$ belong to conditional branches not explored in x; they must be sampled.

We start by formalising the last step of the algorithm. We give a probabilistic program complete which has three parameters: the original configuration (x, q), the current modification (x_0, q_0) and returns a possible maximal extension:

$$
\begin{array}{l}
\texttt{complete}(x, q, x_0, q_0) = \texttt{case ext}(x_0, q_0)\ \texttt{of} \\
\quad (2, ()) \Rightarrow (x_0, q_0) \\
\quad (1, s) \Rightarrow \\
\qquad \texttt{if } s \texttt{ is a return or a score event then} \\
\qquad\quad \texttt{complete}(x, v, x_0 \cup \{s\}, q_0[s := o_s(q_0)]) \\
\qquad \texttt{else if } s \in x \\
\qquad\qquad \texttt{complete}(x, q, x_0 \cup \{s\}, q_0[s := q(s)]) \\
\qquad \texttt{else} \\
\qquad\qquad \texttt{complete}(x, q, x_0 \cup \{s\}, q_0[s := \texttt{sample } d\ (q_0)])
\end{array}
$$

The program starts by trying to extend (x_0, q_0) by calling ext. If (x_0, q_0) is already maximal, we directly return it. Otherwise, we get an event s. To extend the quantitative information, there are three cases:

- if s is not a sample event, ie. since S is closed it must be a return or a score event, we use the function o_s.
- if s is a sample event occurring in x, we use the value in q
- if s is a sample event not occurring in x, we sample a value for it.

This program is recursive, but because G_S is finite, there is a static bound on the number of recursive calls; thus this program can be unfolded to a program expressible in our language. We can now define the proposal kernel:

$P_S(x, q) =$
  let s = sample uniformly over sample events in x in
  let r = sample d_s $(q_{|}[s])$ in
  let x_0 = $x \setminus \{s' \geq s \mid s' \in x\}$ in
  complete$(x, q, x_0, q[s := r])$

We now need to compute the density for P_S to be able to apply Metropolis-Hastings. Given $(x, q), (x', q') \in \mathscr{C}(E_S)$, we define:

$$p_S((x,q),(x',q')) = \sum_{s \in \text{sample}(x)} \left(\frac{q_s(v'|_{[s)})}{|\text{sample}(x)|} \times \prod_{s' \in \text{sample}(x' \setminus x)} q_{s'}(v|_{[s')}) \right).$$

Theorem 4. *The Markov chain P_S and density p satisfy the hypothesis of Theorem 3, as a result for any $(x, q) \in \mathscr{C}(E_S)$ the distribution $[\![MH(d_S, P_S, p_S)^n]\!]((x, q), \cdot)$ tends to μ^P_{norm} as n goes to infinity.*

One can thus sample from norm($[\![M]\!]$) using the algorithm above, keeping only the return value of the obtained configuration.

Let us re-state the key advantage of our approach: having access to the data dependency information, complete requires fewer steps in general, because at each proposal step only a portion of the graph needs exploring.

6 Conclusion

Related Work. There are numerous approaches to the semantics of programs with random choice. Among those concerned with statistical applications of probabilistic programming are Staton et al. [18,19], Ehrhard et al. [7], and Dahlqvist et al. [6]. A game semantics model was announced in [15].

The work of Scibior et al. [17] was influential in suggesting a denotational approach for proving correctness of inference, in the framework of quasi-Borel spaces [9]. It is not clear however how one could reason about data dependencies in this framework, because of the absence of explicit causal information.

Hur et al. [11] gives a proof of correctness for Trace MCMC using new forms of operational semantics for probabilistic programs. This method is extended to higher-order programs with *soft constraints* in Borgström et al. [2]. However, these approaches do not consider incremental recomputation.

To the best of our knowledge, this is the first work addressing formal correctness of incremental recomputation in MCMC. However, methods exist which take advantage of data dependency information to improve the performance of each proposal step in "naive" Trace MCMC. We mention in particular the work on *slicing* by Hur et al. [10]; other approaches include [5, 24]. In the present work we claim no immediate improvement in performance over these techniques, but only a mathematical framework for reasoning about the structures involved.

It is worth remarking that our event structure representation is reminiscent of *graphical model* representation made explicit in some languages. Indeed, for a first-order language such as the one of this paper, Bayesian networks can directly be used as a semantics, see [20]. We claim that the alternative view offered by event structures will allow for an easier extension to higher-order programs, using ideas from game semantics.

Perspectives. This is the start of an investigation into intensional semantics for probabilistic programs. Note that the framework of event structures is very flexible and the semantics presented here is by no means the only possible one. Additionally, though the present work only treats the case of a first-order language, we believe that building on recent advances in probabilistic concurrent game semantics [3, 16] (from which the present work draws much inspiration), we can extend the techniques of this paper to arbitrary higher-order probabilistic programs with recursion.

Acknowledgements. We thank the anonymous referees for helpful comments and suggestions. We also thank Ohad Kammar for suggesting the idea of using causal structures for reasoning about data dependency in this context. This work has been partially sponsored by: EPSRC EP/K034413/1, EP/K011715/1, EP/L00058X/1, EP/N027833/1, EP/N028201/1, and an EPSRC PhD studentship.

References

1. Billingsley, P.: Probability and Measure. John Wiley & Sons, New York (2008)
2. Borgström, J., Lago, U.D., Gordon, A.D., Szymczak, M.: A lambda-calculus foundation for universal probabilistic programming. In: ACM SIGPLAN Notices, vol. 51, pp. 33–46. ACM (2016)
3. Castellan, S., Clairambault, P., Paquet, H., Winskel, G.: The concurrent game semantics of probabilistic PCF. In: 2018 33rd Annual ACM/IEEE Symposium on Logic in Computer Science (LICS). ACM/IEEE (2018)
4. Castellan, S., Paquet, H.: Probabilistic programming inference via intensional semantics. Technical report (2019). http://iso.mor.phis.me/publis/esop19.pdf
5. Chen, Y., Mansinghka, V., Ghahramani, Z.: Sublinear approximate inference for probabilistic programs. stat, 1050:6 (2014)
6. Dahlqvist, F., Danos, V., Garnier, I., Silva, A.: Borel kernels and their approximation, categorically. arXiv preprint arXiv:1803.02651 (2018)
7. Ehrhard, T., Pagani, M., Tasson, C.: Measurable cones and stable, measurable functions: a model for probabilistic higher-order programming, vol. 2, pp. 59:1–59:28 (2018)
8. Gordon, A.D., Henzinger, T.A., Nori, A.V., Rajamani, S.K.: Probabilistic programming. In: Proceedings of the on Future of Software Engineering, pp. 167–181. ACM (2014)
9. Heunen, C., Kammar, O., Staton, S., Yang, H.: A convenient category for higher-order probability theory. In: LICS 2017, Reykjavik, pp. 1–12 (2017)

10. Hur, C.-K., Nori, A.V., Rajamani, S.K., Samuel, S. Slicing probabilistic programs. In: ACM SIGPLAN Notices, vol. 49, pp. 133–144. ACM (2014)
11. Hur, C.-K., Nori, A.V., Rajamani, S.K., Samuel, S.: A provably correct sampler for probabilistic programs. In: LIPIcs-Leibniz International Proceedings in Informatics, vol. 45. Schloss Dagstuhl-Leibniz-Zentrum fuer Informatik (2015)
12. Kiselyov, O.: Probabilistic programming language and its incremental evaluation. In: Igarashi, A. (ed.) APLAS 2016. LNCS, vol. 10017, pp. 357–376. Springer, Cham (2016). https://doi.org/10.1007/978-3-319-47958-3_19
13. Kiselyov, O.: Problems of the lightweight implementation of probabilistic programming. In: Proceedings of Workshop on Probabilistic Programming Semantics (2016)
14. Kozen, D.: Semantics of probabilistic programs. J. Comput. Syst. Sci. **22**(3), 328–350 (1981)
15. Ong, L., Vákár, M.: S-finite kernels and game semantics for probabilistic programming. In: POPL 2018 Workshop on Probabilistic Programming Semantics (PPS) (2018)
16. Paquet, H., Winskel, G.: Continuous probability distributions in concurrent games. Electr. Notes Theor. Comput. Sci. **341**, 321–344 (2018)
17. Ścibior, A., et al.: Denotational validation of higher-order Bayesian inference. In: Proceedings of the ACM on Programming Languages, vol. 2(POPL), p. 60 (2017)
18. Staton, S.: Commutative semantics for probabilistic programming. In: Yang, H. (ed.) ESOP 2017. LNCS, vol. 10201, pp. 855–879. Springer, Heidelberg (2017). https://doi.org/10.1007/978-3-662-54434-1_32
19. Staton, S., Yang, H., Wood, F.D., Heunen, C., Kammar, O.: Semantics for probabilistic programming: higher-order functions, continuous distributions, and soft constraints. In: Proceedings of LICS 2016, New York, NY, USA, July 5–8, 2016, pp. 525–534 (2016)
20. van de Meent, J.-W., Paige, B., Yang, H., Wood, F.: An introduction to probabilistic programming. arXiv preprint arXiv:1809.10756 (2018)
21. Wingate, D., Stuhlmüller, A., Goodman, N.: Lightweight implementations of probabilistic programming languages via transformational compilation. In: Proceedings of the Fourteenth International Conference on Artificial Intelligence and Statistics, pp. 770–778 (2011)
22. Winskel, G.: Event structures. In: Brauer, W., Reisig, W., Rozenberg, G. (eds.) ACPN 1986. LNCS, vol. 255, pp. 325–392. Springer, Heidelberg (1987). https://doi.org/10.1007/3-540-17906-2_31
23. Winskel, G.: Distributed probabilistic and quantum strategies. Electr. Notes Theor. Comput. Sci. **298**, 403–425 (2013)
24. Wu, Y., Li, L., Russell, S., Bodik, R.: Swift: compiled inference for probabilistic programming languages. arXiv preprint arXiv:1606.09242 (2016)
25. Yang, L., Hanrahan, P., Goodman, N.: Generating efficient MCMC kernels from probabilistic programs. In: Artificial Intelligence and Statistics, pp. 1068–1076 (2014)

8

A Process Algebra for Link Layer Protocols

Rob van Glabbeek[1,2(✉)], Peter Höfner[1,2], and Michael Markl[1,3]

[1] Data61, CSIRO, Sydney, Australia
rvg@cs.stanford.edu
[2] Computer Science and Engineering, University of New South Wales, Sydney, Australia
[3] Institut für Informatik, Universität Augsburg, Augsburg, Germany

Abstract. We propose a process algebra for link layer protocols, featuring a unique mechanism for modelling frame collisions. We also formalise suitable liveness properties for link layer protocols specified in this framework. To show applicability we model and analyse two versions of the Carrier-Sense Multiple Access with Collision Avoidance (CSMA/CA) protocol. Our analysis confirms the hidden station problem for the version without virtual carrier sensing. However, we show that the version with virtual carrier sensing not only overcomes this problem, but also the exposed station problem with probability 1. Yet the protocol cannot guarantee packet delivery, not even with probability 1.

1 Introduction

The (data) link layer is the 2nd layer of the ISO/OSI model of computer networking [18]. Amongst others, it is responsible for the transfer of data between adjacent nodes in Wide Area Networks (WANs) and Local Area Networks (LANs).

Examples of link layer protocols are Ethernet for LANs [16], the Point-to-Point Protocol [24] and the High-Level Data Link Control protocol (e.g. [14]). Part of this layer are also multiple access protocols such as the Carrier-Sense Multiple Access with Collision Detection (CSMA/CD) protocol for re-transmission in Ethernet bus networks and hub networks, or the Carrier-Sense Multiple Access with Collision Avoidance (CSMA/CA) protocol [17,19] in wireless networks.

One of the unique characteristics of the link layer is that when devices attempt to use a medium simultaneously, *collisions of messages* occur. So, any modelling language and formal analysis of layer-2 protocols has to support such collisions. Moreover, some protocols are of probabilistic nature: CSMA/CA for example chooses time slots probabilistically with discrete uniform distribution.

As we are not aware of any formal framework with primitives for modelling data collisions, this paper introduces a process algebra for modelling and analysing link layer protocols. In Sect. 2 we present an algebra featuring a unique mechanism for modelling collisions, 'hard-wired' in the semantics. It is the non-probabilistic fragment of the Algebra for Link Layer protocols (ALL), which we introduce in Sect. 3. In Sect. 4 we formulate *packet delivery*, a liveness property that ideally ought to hold for link layer protocols, either outright, or with a high probability. In Sect. 5 we use this framework to formally model and analyse the CSMA/CA protocol.

Our analysis confirms the hidden station problem for the version of CSMA/CA without virtual carrier sensing (Sect. 5.2). However, we also show that the version with virtual carrier sensing overcomes not only this problem, but also the exposed station problem with probability 1. Yet the protocol cannot guarantee packet delivery, not even with probability 1.

2 A Non-probabilistic Subalgebra

In this section we propose a timed process algebra that can model the collision of link layer messages, called *frames*.[1] It can be used for link layer protocols that do not feature probabilistic choice, and is inspired by the (Timed) Algebra for Wireless Networks ((T-)AWN) [2,12,13], a process algebra suitable for modelling and analysing protocols on layers 3 (network) and 4 (transport) of the OSI model.

The process algebra models a (wired or wireless) network as an encapsulated parallel composition of network nodes. Due to the nature of the protocols under consideration, on each node exactly one sequential process is running. The algebra features a discrete model of time, where each sequential process maintains a local variable `now` holding its local clock value—an integer. We employ only one clock for each sequential process. All sequential processes in a network synchronise in taking time steps, and at each time step all local clocks advance by one unit. Since this means that all clocks are in sync and do not run at different speeds it is clear that we do not consider the problem of clock shift. For the rest, the variable `now` behaves like any other variable maintained by a process: its value can be read when evaluating guards, thereby making progress time-dependant, and any value can be assigned to it, thereby resetting the local clock. Network nodes communicate with their direct neighbours—those nodes that are in transmission range. The algebra provides a mobility option that allows nodes to move in or out of transmission range. The encapsulation of the entire network inhibits communications between network nodes and the outside world, with the exception of the receipt and delivery of data packets from or to clients (the higher OSI layers).

2.1 A Language for Sequential Processes

The internal state of a process is determined, in part, by the values of certain data variables that are maintained by that process. To this end, we assume a data structure with several types, variables ranging over these types, operators and predicates. Predicate logic yields terms (or *data expressions*) and formulas

[1] As it is the nonprobabilistic fragment of a forthcoming algebra we do not name it.

to denote data values and statements about them. Our data structure always contains the types TIME, DATA, MSG, CHUNK, ID and $\mathscr{P}$(ID) of discrete *time values*, which we take to be integers, *network layer data*, *messages*, *chunks* of messages that take one time unit to transmit, *node identifiers* and *sets of node identifiers*. We further assume that there are variables now of type TIME and rfr of type CHUNK. In addition, we assume a set of *process names*. Each process name X comes with a *defining equation*

$$X(\mathtt{var}_1,\ldots,\mathtt{var}_n) \stackrel{def}{=} P,$$

in which $n \in \mathbb{N}$, $\mathtt{var}_i$ are variables and P is a *sequential process expression* defined by the grammar below. It may contain the variables $\mathtt{var}_i$ as well as X. However, all occurrences of data variables in P have to be *bound*.[2] The choice of the underlying data structure and the process names with their defining equations can be tailored to any particular application of our language.

The *sequential process expressions* are given by the following grammar:

$$P ::= X(exp_1,\ldots,exp_n) \mid [\varphi]P \mid [\![\mathtt{var} := exp]\!]P \mid \alpha.P \mid P+P$$
$$\alpha ::= \mathbf{transmit}(ms) \mid \mathbf{newpkt}(\mathtt{data},\mathtt{dest}) \mid \mathbf{deliver}(\mathtt{data})$$

Here X is a process name, exp_i a data expression of the same type as $\mathtt{var}_i$, φ a data formula, $\mathtt{var} := exp$ an assignment of a data expression exp to a variable var of the same type, ms a data expression of type MSG, and data, dest data variables of types DATA, ID respectively.

Given a valuation of the data variables by concrete data values, the sequential process $[\varphi]P$ acts as P if φ evaluates to true, and deadlocks if φ evaluates to false. In case φ contains free variables that are not yet interpreted as data values, values are assigned to these variables in any way that satisfies φ, if possible. The process $[\![\mathtt{var} := exp]\!]P$ acts as P, but under an updated valuation of the data variable var. The process $P+Q$ may act either as P or as Q, depending on which of the two processes is able to act at all. In a context where both are able to act, it is not specified how the choice is made. The process $\alpha.P$ first performs the action α and subsequently acts as P. The above behaviour is identical to AWN, and many other standard process algebras. The action **transmit**(ms) transmits (the data value bound to the expression) ms to all other network nodes within transmission range. The action **newpkt**(data, dest) models the injection by the network layer of a data packet data to be transmitted to a destination dest. Technically, data and dest are variables that will be bound to the obtained values upon receipt of a **newpkt**. Data is delivered to the network layer by **deliver**(data). In contrast to AWN, we do not have a primitive for

[2] An occurrence of a data variable in P is *bound* if it is one of the variables $\mathtt{var}_i$, one of the two special variables now or rfr, a variable var occurring in a subexpression $[\![\mathtt{var} := exp]\!]Q$, an occurrence in a subexpression $[\varphi]Q$ of a variable occurring free in φ, or a variable data or dest occurring in a subexpression **newpkt**(data, dest).Q. Here Q is an arbitrary sequential process expression.

receiving messages from neighbouring nodes, because our processes are *always* listening to neighbouring nodes, in parallel with anything else they do.

As in AWN, the internal state of a sequential process described by an expression P is determined by P, together with a *valuation* ξ associating values $\xi(\mathtt{var})$ to variables var maintained by this process. Valuations naturally extend to ξ-*closed* expressions—those in which all variables are either bound or in the domain of ξ. We denote the valuation that assigns the value v to the variable var, and agrees with ξ on all other variables, by $\xi[\mathtt{var} := v]$. The valuation $\xi_{|S}$ agrees with ξ on all variables $\mathtt{var} \in S$ and is undefined otherwise. Moreover we use $\xi[\mathtt{var}{+}{+}]$ as an abbreviation for $\xi[\mathtt{var} := \xi(\mathtt{var}) + 1]$, for suitable types.

To capture the durational nature of transmitting a message between network nodes, we model a message as a sequence of *chunks*, each of which takes one time unit to transmit. The function $\mathtt{dur}: \mathtt{MSG} \to \mathtt{TIME}_{>0}$ calculates the amount of time steps needed for a sending a message, i.e. it calculates the number of chunks. We employ the internal data type $\mathtt{CHUNK} := \{m{:}c \mid m \in \mathtt{MSG}, 1 \leq c \leq \mathtt{dur}(m)\} \cup \{\underline{\mathtt{conflict}}, \underline{\mathtt{idle}}\}$. The chunk $m{:}c$ indicates the cth fragment of a message m. Data conflicts—junk transmitted via the medium—is modelled by the special chunk conflict, and the absence of an incoming chunk is modelled by idle.

Our process algebra maintains a variable rfr of type CHUNK, storing the fragment of the current message received so far.

As a value of this variable, $m{:}c$ indicates that the first c chunks of message m have been received in order; conflict indicates that the last incoming chunk was not the expected (next) part of a message in progress, and idle indicates that the channel was idle during the last time step. The table on the right, with $*$ a wild card, shows how the value of rfr evolves upon receiving a new chunk *ch*.

rfr	*ch*	rfr $\star$ *ch*
$*$	conflict	conflict
$*$	idle	idle
$*$	$m{:}1$	$m{:}1$
$m{:}c$	$m{:}c{+}1$	$m{:}c{+}1$
rfr	$m{:}c{+}1$	conflict if $rfr \neq m{:}c$

Specifications may refer to the data type CHUNK only through the Boolean functions NEW—having a single argument *msg* of type MSG—and IDLE, defined by $\text{NEW}(msg) := (\mathtt{rfr} = (msg : \mathtt{dur}(msg))$ and $\text{IDLE} := (\mathtt{rfr} = \underline{\mathtt{idle}})$. A guard $[\text{NEW}(msg)]$ evaluates to true iff a new message *msg* has just been received; $[\text{IDLE}]$ evaluates to true iff in the last time slice the medium was idle.

The structural operational semantics of Table 1 describes how one internal state can evolve into another by performing an *action*. The set Act of actions consists of **transmit**$(m{:}c, ch)$, **wait**(ch), **newpkt**$(d, dest)$, **deliver**(d), and internal actions τ, for each choice of $m \in \mathtt{MSG}$, $c \in \{1, \ldots, \mathtt{dur}(m)\}$, $ch \in \mathtt{CHUNK}$, $d \in \mathtt{DATA}$ and $dest \in \mathtt{ID}$, where the first two actions are time consuming. On every time-consuming action, each process receives a chunk *ch* and updates the variable rfr accordingly; moreover, the variable now is incremented on all process expressions in a (complete) network synchronously.

Besides the special variables now and rfr, the formal semantics employs an internal variable $\mathtt{cntr} \in \mathbb{N}$ that enumerates the chunks of split messages and is

Table 1. Structural operational semantics for sequential process expressions

(1)	$\xi, \mathbf{transmit}(ms).P \xrightarrow{\mathbf{transmit}(\xi(ms):\mathtt{c+},ch)} \xi\begin{bmatrix}\mathtt{cntr}\,\text{++}\\ \mathtt{rfr} := \mathtt{rfr} \star ch\\ \mathtt{now}\,\text{++}\end{bmatrix}, \mathbf{transmit}(\xi(ms)).P$	(if $\mathtt{c+} < \mathbf{dur}(\xi(ms))$) $(\forall ch \in \mathtt{CHUNK})$
(2)	$\xi, \mathbf{transmit}(ms).P \xrightarrow{\mathbf{transmit}(\xi(ms):\mathtt{c+},ch)} \xi\begin{bmatrix}\mathtt{cntr} := 0\\ \mathtt{rfr} := \mathtt{rfr} \star ch\\ \mathtt{now}\,\text{++}\end{bmatrix}, P$	(if $\mathtt{c+} = \mathbf{dur}(\xi(ms))$) $(\forall ch \in \mathtt{CHUNK})$
(3)	$\xi, \mathbf{newpkt}(\mathrm{data}, \mathrm{dest}).P \xrightarrow{\mathbf{newpkt}(d,dest)} \xi\begin{bmatrix}\mathtt{data} := d\\ \mathtt{dest} := dest\end{bmatrix}, P$	$(\forall d \in \mathtt{DATA},\ dest \in \mathtt{ID})$
(4)	$\xi, \mathbf{newpkt}(\mathrm{data}, \mathrm{dest}).P \xrightarrow{\mathbf{wait}(ch)} \xi\begin{bmatrix}\mathtt{rfr} := \mathtt{rfr} \star ch\\ \mathtt{now}\,\text{++}\end{bmatrix}, \mathbf{newpkt}(\mathrm{data}, \mathrm{dest}).P$	$(\forall ch \in \mathtt{CHUNK})$
(5)	$\xi, \mathbf{deliver}(\mathrm{data}).P \xrightarrow{\mathbf{deliver}(\xi(\mathtt{data}))} \xi, P$	
(6)	$\xi, [\![\mathbf{var} := exp]\!]P \xrightarrow{\tau} \xi[\mathtt{var} := \xi(exp)], P$	
(7)	$\dfrac{\xi_{\vert \mathtt{RO}}[\mathtt{var}_i := \xi(exp_i)]_{i=1}^{n}, P \xrightarrow{a} \zeta, P'}{\xi, X(exp_1, \ldots, exp_n) \xrightarrow{a} \zeta, P'}\ (X(\mathtt{var}_1, \ldots, \mathtt{var}_n) \stackrel{def}{=} P)$	$(\forall a \in \mathrm{Act} - \{\mathbf{wait}(ch) \mid ch \in \mathtt{CHUNK}\})$
(8)	$\dfrac{\xi_{\vert \mathtt{RO}}[\mathtt{var}_i := \xi(exp_i)]_{i=1}^{n}, P \xrightarrow{\mathbf{wait}(ch)} \zeta, P'}{\xi, X(exp_1, \ldots, exp_n) \xrightarrow{\mathbf{wait}(ch)} \xi\begin{bmatrix}\mathtt{rfr} := \mathtt{rfr} \star ch\\ \mathtt{now}\,\text{++}\end{bmatrix}, X(exp_1, \ldots, exp_n)}\ (X(\mathtt{var}_1, \ldots, \mathtt{var}_n) \stackrel{def}{=} P)$	$(\forall ch \in \mathtt{CHUNK})$
(9)	$\xi, P \xrightarrow{\mathbf{wait}(ch)} \xi\begin{bmatrix}\mathtt{rfr} := \mathtt{rfr} \star ch\\ \mathtt{now}\,\text{++}\end{bmatrix}, P$	(if $\xi(P)\uparrow$) $(\forall ch \in \mathtt{CHUNK})$
(10)	$\dfrac{\xi, P \xrightarrow{a} \zeta, P'}{\xi, P + Q \xrightarrow{a} \zeta, P'} \quad \dfrac{\xi, Q \xrightarrow{a} \zeta, Q'}{\xi, P + Q \xrightarrow{a} \zeta, Q'}$	$(\forall a \in \mathrm{Act} - \{\mathbf{wait}(ch) \mid ch \in \mathtt{CHUNK}\})$
(11)	$\dfrac{\xi, P \xrightarrow{\mathbf{wait}(ch)} \zeta, P' \quad \xi, Q \xrightarrow{\mathbf{wait}(ch)} \zeta', Q'}{\xi, P + Q \xrightarrow{\mathbf{wait}(ch)} \zeta, P' + Q'}$	$(\forall ch \in \mathtt{CHUNK})$
(12)	$\dfrac{\xi \xrightarrow{\varphi} \zeta}{\xi, [\varphi]P \xrightarrow{\tau} \zeta, P} \quad \dfrac{\xi \stackrel{\varphi}{\not\rightarrow}}{\xi, [\varphi]P \xrightarrow{\mathbf{wait}(ch)} \xi\begin{bmatrix}\mathtt{rfr} := \mathtt{rfr} \star ch\\ \mathtt{now}\,\text{++}\end{bmatrix}, [\varphi]P}$	$(\forall ch \in \mathtt{CHUNK})$

used to identify which chunk needs to be sent next. The variables `now`, `rfr` and `cntr` are not meant to be changed by ALL specifications, e.g. by using assignments. We call them read-only and collect them in the set $\mathtt{RO} = \{\mathtt{now}, \mathtt{rfr}, \mathtt{cntr}\}$.

Let us have a closer look at the rules of Table 1.

The first two rules describe the sending of a message *ms*. Remember that $\mathtt{dur}(ms)$ calculates the time needed to send *ms*. The counter `cntr` keeps track of the time passed already. The action $\mathbf{transmit}(m{:}c, ch)$ occurs when the node transmits the fragment $m{:}c$; simultaneously, it receives the fragment *ch*.[3] The counter `cntr` is 0 before a message is sent, and is incremented before the transmission of each chunk. So, each chunk sent has the form $\xi(ms){:}\xi(\mathtt{cntr}){+}1$. To ease readability we abbreviate $\xi(\mathtt{cntr}){+}1$ by `c+`. In case the (already incremented) counter `c+` is strictly smaller than the number of chunks needed to send $\xi(ms)$, another **transmit**-action is needed (Rule 1); if the last fragment has been sent ($\mathtt{c+} = \mathtt{dur}(\xi(ms))$) the process can continue to act as P (Rule 2).

The actions $\mathbf{newpkt}(d, dest)$ and $\mathbf{deliver}(d)$ are instantaneous and model the submission of data d from the network layer, destined for *dest*, and the delivery of data d to the network layer, respectively. The process $\mathbf{newpkt}(d, dest).P$ has also the possibility to wait, namely if no network layer instruction arrives.

Rule 6 defines a rule for assignment in a straightforward fashion; only the valuation of the variable `var` is updated.

In Rules 7 and 8, which define recursion, $\xi_{|\mathtt{RO}}[\mathtt{var}_i := \xi(exp_i)]_{i=1}^{n}$ is the valuation that *only* assigns the values $\xi(exp_i)$ to the variables $\mathtt{var}_i$, for $i = 1, \ldots, n$, and maintains the values of the variables `now`, `rfr` and `cntr`. These rules state that a defined process X has the same transitions as the body p of its defining equation. In case of a **wait**-transition, the sequential process does not progress, and accordingly the recursion is not yet unfolded.

Most transition rules so far feature statements of the form $\xi(exp)$ where *exp* is a data expression. The application of the rule depends on $\xi(exp)$ being defined. Rule 9 covers all cases where the above rules cannot be applied since at least one data expression in an action α is not defined. A state ξ, P is *unvalued*, denoted by $\xi(p)\!\uparrow$, if P has the form $\mathbf{transmit}(ms).P$, $\mathbf{deliver}(\mathtt{data}).P$, $[\![\mathtt{var} := exp]\!]P$ or $X(exp_1, \ldots, exp_n)$ with either $\xi(ms)$ or $\xi(\mathtt{data})$ or $\xi(exp)$ or some $\xi(exp_i)$ undefined. From such a state the process can merely wait.

A process $P + Q$ can wait *only* if both P and Q can do the same; if either P or Q can achieve 'proper' progress, the choice process $P + Q$ always chooses progress over waiting. A simple induction shows that if $\xi, P \xrightarrow{\mathbf{wait}(ch)} \zeta, P'$ and $\xi, Q \xrightarrow{\mathbf{wait}(ch)} \zeta', Q'$ then $P = P'$, $Q = Q'$ and $\zeta = \zeta'$.

The first rule of (12), describing the semantics of guards $[\varphi]$, is taken from AWN. Here $\xi \xrightarrow{\varphi} \zeta$ says that ζ is an extension of ξ, i.e. a valuation that agrees with ξ on all variables on which ξ is defined, and evaluates other variables occurring free in φ, such that the formula φ holds under ζ. All variables not free in φ and not evaluated by ξ are also not evaluated by ζ. Its negation $\xi \stackrel{\varphi}{\not\rightarrow}$ says

[3] Normally, a node is in its own transmission range. In that case the received chunk *ch* will be either the chunk $m{:}c$ it is transmitting itself, or <u>`conflict`</u> in case some other node within transmission range is transmitting as well.

that no such extension exists, and thus, that φ is false in the current state, no matter how we interpret the variables whose values are still undefined. If that is the case, the process $[\varphi]p$ will idle by performing the action $\mathbf{wait}(ch)$.

2.2 A Language for Node Expressions

We model network nodes in the context of a (wireless) network by *node expressions* of the form

$$id{:}(\xi, P){:}R\,.$$

Here $id \in \texttt{ID}$ is the *address* of the node, P is a sequential process expression with a valuation ξ, and $R \in \mathscr{P}(\texttt{ID})$ is the *range* of the node, defined as the set of nodes within transmission range of *id*. Unlike AWN, the process algebra does not offer a parallel operator for combining sequential processes; such an operator is not needed due to the nature of link layer protocols.

In the semantics of this layer it is crucial to handle frame collisions. The idea is that all chunks sent are recorded, together with the respective recipient. In case a node receives more than one chunk at a time, a conflict is raised, as it is impossible to send two or more messages via the same medium at the same time.

The formal semantics for node expressions, presented in Table 2, uses transition labels $\mathbf{traffic}(\mathcal{T},\mathcal{R})$, $id{:}\,\mathbf{deliver}(d)$, $id{:}\,\mathbf{newpkt}(d, id')$, $\mathbf{connect}(id, id')$, $\mathbf{disconnect}(id, id')$ and τ, with partial functions $\mathcal{T},\mathcal{R}\colon \texttt{ID} \rightharpoonup \texttt{CHUNK}$, $id, id' \in \texttt{ID}$, and $d \in \texttt{DATA}$.

Table 2. Structural operational semantics for node expressions

$$\frac{P \xrightarrow{\mathbf{wait}(\underline{\texttt{idle}})} P'}{id{:}P{:}R \xrightarrow{\mathbf{traffic}(\emptyset,\emptyset)} id{:}P'{:}R} \qquad \frac{P \xrightarrow{\mathbf{transmit}(m:c,\underline{\texttt{idle}})} P'}{id{:}P{:}R \xrightarrow{\mathbf{traffic}(\{(r,\,m:c)\,|\,r\in R\},\emptyset)} id{:}P'{:}R}$$

$$\frac{P \xrightarrow{\mathbf{wait}(ch)} \quad (ch \neq \underline{\texttt{idle}})}{id{:}P{:}R \xrightarrow{\mathbf{traffic}(\emptyset,\{(id,\,ch)\})} id{:}P'{:}R} \qquad \frac{P \xrightarrow{\mathbf{transmit}(m:c,ch)} P' \quad (ch \neq \underline{\texttt{idle}})}{id{:}P{:}R \xrightarrow{\mathbf{traffic}(\{(r,\,m:c)\,|\,r\in R\},\{(id,\,ch)\})} id{:}P'{:}R}$$

$$\frac{P \xrightarrow{\mathbf{deliver}(d)} P'}{id{:}P{:}R \xrightarrow{id:\,\mathbf{deliver}(d)} id{:}P'{:}R} \qquad \frac{P \xrightarrow{\mathbf{newpkt}(d,dest)} P'}{id{:}P{:}R \xrightarrow{id:\,\mathbf{newpkt}(d,dest)} id{:}P'{:}R} \qquad \frac{P \xrightarrow{\tau} P'}{id{:}P{:}R \xrightarrow{\tau} id{:}P'{:}R}$$

$$id{:}P{:}R \xrightarrow{\mathbf{connect}(id,id')} id{:}P{:}R \cup \{id'\} \qquad id{:}P{:}R \xrightarrow{\mathbf{disconnect}(id,id')} id{:}P{:}R - \{id'\}$$

$$id{:}P{:}R \xrightarrow{\mathbf{connect}(id',id)} id{:}P{:}R \cup \{id'\} \qquad id{:}P{:}R \xrightarrow{\mathbf{disconnect}(id',id)} id{:}P{:}R - \{id'\}$$

$$\frac{id \notin \{id', id''\}}{id{:}P{:}R \xrightarrow{\mathbf{connect}(id',id'')} id{:}P{:}R} \qquad \frac{id \notin \{id', id''\}}{id{:}P{:}R \xrightarrow{\mathbf{disconnect}(id',id'')} id{:}P{:}R}$$

All time-consuming actions on process level ($\mathbf{transmit}(m{:}c, ch)$ and $\mathbf{wait}(ch)$) are transformed into an action $\mathbf{traffic}(\mathcal{T},\mathcal{R})$ on node level: the first argument

Table 3. Structural operational semantics for network expressions

$$\frac{M \xrightarrow{a} M'}{M\|N \xrightarrow{a} M'\|N} \qquad \frac{N \xrightarrow{a} N'}{M\|N \xrightarrow{a} M\|N'} \qquad \frac{M \xrightarrow{a} M'}{[M] \xrightarrow{a} [M']} \qquad \left(\forall a \in \left\{\begin{array}{l}\tau,\ id\!:\mathbf{deliver}(d),\\ id\!:\mathbf{newpkt}(d, id),\end{array}\right\}\right)$$

$$\frac{M \xrightarrow{a} M' \quad N \xrightarrow{a} N'}{M\|N \xrightarrow{a} M'\|N'} \qquad \frac{M \xrightarrow{a} M'}{[M] \xrightarrow{a} [M']} \qquad \left(\forall a \in \left\{\begin{array}{l}\mathbf{connect}(id, id'),\\ \mathbf{disconnect}(id, id')\end{array}\right\}\right)$$

$$\frac{M \xrightarrow{\mathbf{traffic}(\mathcal{T}_1,\mathcal{R}_1)} M' \quad N \xrightarrow{\mathbf{traffic}(\mathcal{T}_2,\mathcal{R}_2)} N'}{M\|N \xrightarrow{\mathbf{traffic}(\mathcal{T}_1 \uplus \mathcal{T}_2,\mathcal{R}_1 \uplus \mathcal{R}_2)} M'\|N'} \qquad \frac{M \xrightarrow{\mathbf{traffic}(\mathcal{R},\mathcal{R})} M'}{[M] \xrightarrow{\mathbf{tick}} [M']}$$

$\mathcal{T}$ maps *dest* to $m{:}c$ if and only if the chunk $m{:}c$ is transmitted to *dest*. The second argument $\mathcal{R}$ maps *id* to $m{:}c$ if and only if the chunk $m{:}c$ is received on process level at node *id*. For the sos-rules of Table 2 we use the set-theoretic presentation of partial functions. The two rules for **wait** set $\mathcal{T} := \emptyset$, as no chunks are transmitted; the rules for **transmit** allow a transmitted chunk $m{:}c$ to travel to all nodes within transmission range: $\mathcal{T} := \{(r, m{:}c) \mid r \in R\}$. In case that during the transmission or waiting no chunk is received ($ch = \underline{\texttt{idle}}$) we set $\mathcal{R} = \emptyset$; otherwise $\mathcal{R} = \{(id, ch)\}$, indicating that chunk *ch* is received by node *id*.

The actions id: **newpkt**$(d, dest)$ and id: **deliver**(d) as well as the internal actions τ are simply inherited by node expressions from the processes that run on these nodes.

The remaining rules of Table 2 model the mobility aspect of wireless networks; the rules are taken straight from AWN [12, 13]. We allow actions **connect**(id, id') and **disconnect**(id, id') for $id, id' \in \texttt{ID}$ modelling a change in network topology. These actions can be thought of as occurring nondeterministically, or as actions instigated by the environment of the modelled network protocol. In this formalisation node id' is in the range of node *id*, meaning that id' can receive messages sent by *id*, if and only if *id* is in the range of id'. To break this symmetry, one just skips the last four rules of Table 2 and replaces the synchronisation rules for **connect** and **disconnect** in Table 3 by interleaving rules (like the ones for **deliver**, **newpkt** and τ) [12]. For some applications a wired or non-mobile network need to be considered. In such cases the last six rules of Table 2 are dropped.

Whether a node $id{:}P{:}R$ receives its own transmissions depends on whether $id \in R$. Only if $id \in R$ our process algebra will disallow the transmission from and to a single node *id* at the same time, yielding a $\underline{\texttt{conflict}}$.

2.3 A Language for Networks

A *partial network* is modelled by a *parallel composition* $\|$ of node expressions, one for every node in the network. A *complete network* is a partial network within an *encapsulation operator* $[\_]$, which limits the communication between network nodes and the outside world to the receipt and delivery of data packets to and from the network layer.

The syntax of networks is described by the following grammar:

$$N ::= [M^T_T] \qquad M^T_{S_1 \cup S_2} ::= M^T_{S_1} \| M^T_{S_2} \qquad M^T_{\{id\}} ::= id\!:\!(\xi, P)\!:\!R\ ,$$

with $\{id\} \cup R \subseteq T \subseteq \mathtt{ID}$. Here M^T_S models a partial network describing the behaviour of all nodes $id \in S$. The set T contains the identifiers of all nodes that are part of the complete network. This grammar guarantees that node identifiers of node expressions—the first component of $id\!:\!P\!:\!R$—are unique.

The operational semantics of network expressions is given in Table 3. Internal actions τ as well as the actions id: **deliver**(d) and id: **newpkt**(d,id) are interleaved in the parallel composition of nodes that makes up a network, and then lifted to encapsulated networks (Line 1 of Table 3).

Actions **traffic** and **(dis)connect** are synchronised. The rule for synchronising the action **traffic** (Line 3), the only action that consumes time on the network layer, uses the union $\uplus$ of partial functions. It is formally defined as

$$(\mathcal{R}_1 \uplus \mathcal{R}_2)(id) := \begin{cases} \underline{\mathtt{conflict}} & \text{if } id \in \mathtt{dom}(\mathcal{R}_1) \cap \mathtt{dom}(\mathcal{R}_2) \\ \mathcal{R}_1(id) & \text{if } id \in \mathtt{dom}(\mathcal{R}_1) - \mathtt{dom}(\mathcal{R}_2) \\ \mathcal{R}_2(id) & \text{if } id \in \mathtt{dom}(\mathcal{R}_2) - \mathtt{dom}(\mathcal{R}_1)\ . \end{cases}$$

The synchronisation of the sets $\mathcal{R}_i$ and $\mathcal{T}_i$ has the following intuition: if a node identifier $id \in \mathtt{ID}$ is in both $\mathtt{dom}(\mathcal{T}_1)$ and $\mathtt{dom}(\mathcal{T}_2)$ then there exist two nodes that transmit to node id at the same time, and therefore a frame collision occurs. In our algebra this is modelled by the special chunk $\underline{\mathtt{conflict}}$. The sos rules of Tables 2 and 3 guarantee that there cannot be collisions within the set of received chunks $\mathcal{R}$. The reason is that each node merely contributes to $\mathcal{R}$ a chunk for itself; it can be the chunk $\underline{\mathtt{conflict}}$ though. Therefore we could have written $\mathcal{R}_1 \cup \mathcal{R}_2$ instead of $\mathcal{R}_1 \uplus \mathcal{R}_2$ in the sixth rule of Table 3.

The last rule propagates a **traffic**$(\mathcal{T}, \mathcal{R})$-action of a partial network M to a complete network $[M]$. By then $\mathcal{T}$ consists of all chunks (after collision detection) that are being transmitted by any member in the network, and $\mathcal{R}$ consists of all chunks that are received. The condition $\mathcal{R} = \mathcal{T}$ determines the content of the messages in $\mathcal{R}$. The **traffic**$(\mathcal{T}, \mathcal{R})$-actions become internal at this level, as they cannot be steered by the outside world; all that is left is a time-step **tick**.

2.4 Results on the Process Algebra

As for the process algebra T-AWN [2], but with a slightly simplified proof, one can show that our processes have no *time deadlocks*:

Theorem 2.1. *A complete network N in our process algebra always admits a transition, independently of the outside environment, i.e. $\forall N, \exists a$ such that $N \xrightarrow{a}$ and $a \notin \{$**connect**(id, id'), **disconnect**(id, id'), id:newpkt$(d, dest)\}$. More precisely, either $N \xrightarrow{\textbf{tick}}$, or $N \xrightarrow{id:\, \textbf{deliver}(d)}$ or $N \xrightarrow{\tau}$.*

The following results (statements and proofs) are very similar to the results about the process algebra AWN, as presented in [13]. A rich body of foundational meta theory of process algebra allows the transfer of the results to our setting, without too much overhead work.

Identical to AWN and its timed version T-AWN, our process algebra admits a translation into one without data structures (although we cannot describe the target algebra without using data structures). The idea is to replace any variable by all possible values it can take. The target algebra differs from the original only on the level of sequential processes; the subsequent layers are unchanged. The construction closely follows the one given in the appendix of [2]. The inductive definition contains the rules

$\mathscr{T}_\xi(\textbf{deliver}(data).P) = \textbf{deliver}(\xi(data)).\mathscr{T}_\xi(P)$ and

$\mathscr{T}_\xi([\![\texttt{var} := exp]\!]P) = \tau.\mathscr{T}_{\xi[\texttt{var} := \xi(exp)]}\,(P)$.

Most other rules require extra operators that keep track of the passage of time and the evolution of other internal variables. The resulting process algebra has a structural operational semantics in the (infinitary) *de Simone* format, generating the same transition system—up to strong bisimilarity, $\leftrightarrows$—as the original. It follows that $\leftrightarrows$, and many other semantic equivalences, are congruences on our language [23].

Theorem 2.2. *Strong bisimilarity is a congruence for all operators of our language.*

This is a deep result that usually takes many pages to establish (e.g. [25]). Here we get it directly from the existing theory on structural operational semantics, as a result of carefully designing our language within the disciplined framework described by de Simone [23]. □

Theorem 2.3. *The operator $\|$ is associative and commutative, up to $\leftrightarrows$.*

Proof. The operational rules for this operator fits a format presented in [6], guaranteeing associativity up to $\leftrightarrows$. The *ASSOC*-de Simone format of [6] applies to all transition system specifications (TSSs) in de Simone format, and allows 7 different types of rules (named 1–7) for the operators in question. Our TSS is in de Simone format; the four rules for $\|$ of Table 3 are of types 1, 2 and 7, respectively. To be precise, it has rules 1_a and 2_a for $a \in \{\tau, id\!:\textbf{deliver}(d), id\!:\textbf{newpkt}(d, dest)\}$, rules $7_{(a,b)}$ for

$$(a,b) \in \{(\textbf{traffic}(\mathcal{T}_1,\mathcal{R}_1),\textbf{traffic}(\mathcal{T}_2,\mathcal{R}_2)) \mid \mathcal{R}_1,\mathcal{R}_2,\mathcal{T}_1,\mathcal{T}_2 \in \texttt{ID} \rightharpoonup \texttt{CHUNK}\}$$

and rules $7_{(c,c)}$ for $c \in \{\textbf{connect}(id, id'), \textbf{disconnect}(id, id') \mid id, id' \in \texttt{ID}\}$. Moreover, the partial *communication function* $\gamma : \text{Act} \times \text{Act} \rightharpoonup \text{Act}$ is given by $\gamma(\textbf{traffic}(\mathcal{T}_1,\mathcal{R}_1),\textbf{traffic}(\mathcal{T}_2,\mathcal{R}_2)) = \textbf{traffic}(\mathcal{T}_1 \uplus \mathcal{T}_2, \mathcal{R}_1 \uplus \mathcal{R}_2)$ and $\gamma(c,c) = c$. The main result of [6] is that an operator is guaranteed to be associative, provided that γ is associative and six conditions are fulfilled. In the absence of rules of types 3, 4, 5 and 6, five of these conditions are trivially fulfilled, and the remaining one reduces to

$$7_{(a,b)} \Rightarrow (1_a \Leftrightarrow 2_b) \wedge (2_a \Leftrightarrow 2_{\gamma(a,b)}) \wedge (1_b \Leftrightarrow 1_{\gamma(a,b)})\,.$$

Here 1_a says that rule 1_a is present, etc. This condition is trivially met for $\|$ as there neither exists a rule of the form $1_{\mathbf{traffic}(\mathcal{T},\mathcal{R})}$ nor of the form $2_{\mathbf{traffic}(\mathcal{T},\mathcal{R})}$, or 1_c, 2_c with c as above. As on **traffic** actions γ is basically the union of partial functions ($\uplus$), where a collision in domains is indicated by an error <u>`conflict`</u>, it is straightforward to prove associativity of γ.

Commutativity of $\|$ follows by symmetry of the sos rules. □

3 An Algebra for Link Layer Protocols

We now introduce ALL, the *Algebra for Link Layer protocols.* It is obtained from the process algebra presented in the previous section by the addition of a probabilistic choice operator $\bigoplus_0^n$. As a consequence, the semantics of the algebra is no longer a labelled transition system, but a *probabilistic labelled transition system* (pLTS) [8]. This is a triple $(S, \text{Act}, \rightarrow)$, where

(i) S is a set of states
(ii) Act is a set of actions
(iii) $\rightarrow \subseteq S \times \text{Act} \times \mathcal{D}(S)$, where $\mathcal{D}(S)$ is the set of all (discrete) probability distributions over S: functions $\Delta : S \rightarrow [0,1]$ with $\sum_{s \in S} \Delta(s) = 1$.

As with LTSs, we usually write $s \xrightarrow{\alpha} \Delta$ instead of $(s, \alpha, \Delta) \in \rightarrow$. The *point distribution* δ_s, for $s \in S$, is the distribution with $\delta_s(s) = 1$. We simply write $s \xrightarrow{\alpha} t$ for $s \xrightarrow{\alpha} \delta_t$. An LTS may be viewed as a degenerate pLTS, in which only point distributions occur. For a uniform distribution over $s_0, \ldots, s_n \in S$ we write $\mathcal{U}_{i=0}^n s_i$. The pLTS associated to ALL takes S to be the disjoint union of the pairs ξ, P, with P a sequential process expression, and the network expressions. Act is the collection of transition labels, and $\rightarrow$ consists of the transitions derivable from the structural operational semantics of the language.

Rules (1)–(6), (9), (11) and (12) of Table 1 are adopted to ALL unchanged, whereas in Rules (7), (8) and (10) the state ζ, P' (or ζ, Q') is replaced by an arbitrary distribution Δ. Add to those the following rule for the probabilistic choice operator:

$$\xi, \bigoplus_{\mathtt{i}=0}^{n} P \xrightarrow{\tau} \mathcal{U}_{i=0}^{\xi(n)}\ \xi[\mathtt{i} := i]\ , P$$

Here the data variable i may occur in P. The rules of Tables 2 and 3 are adapted to ALL unchanged, except that P', M' and N' are now replaced by arbitrary distributions over sequential processes and network expressions, respectively. Here we adapt the convention that a unary or binary operation on states lifts to distributions in the standard manner. For example, if Δ is a distribution over sequential processes, $id \in \mathtt{ID}$ and $R \subseteq \mathtt{ID}$, then $id{:}\Delta{:}R$ describes the distribution over node expressions that only has probability mass on nodes with address id and range R, and for which the probability of $id{:}P{:}R$ is $\Delta(P)$. Likewise, if Δ and Θ are distributions over network expressions, then $\Delta\|\Theta$ is the distribution over network expressions of the form $M\|N$, where $(\Delta\|\Theta)(M\|N) = \Delta(M) \cdot \Theta(N)$.

4 Formalising Liveness Properties of Link Layer Protocols

Link layer protocols communicate with the network layer through the actions $id\colon \mathbf{newpkt}(d, dest)$ and $id\colon \mathbf{deliver}(d)$. The typical liveness property expected of a link layer protocol is that if the network layer at node *id* injects a data packet *d* for delivery at destination *dest* then this packet is delivered eventually. In terms of our process algebra, this says that every execution of the action $id\colon \mathbf{newpkt}(d, dest)$ ought to be followed by the action $dest\colon \mathbf{deliver}(d)$. This property can be formalised in Linear-time Temporal Logic [22] as

$$\mathbf{G}\big(id\colon \mathbf{newpkt}(d, dest) \Rightarrow \mathbf{F}(dest\colon \mathbf{deliver}(d))\big) \tag{1}$$

for any $id, dest \in \mathtt{ID}$ and $d \in \mathtt{DATA}$. This formula has the shape $\mathbf{G}\big(\phi^{pre} \Rightarrow \mathbf{F}\phi^{post}\big)$, and is called an *eventuality property* in [22]. It says that whenever we reach a state in which the precondition ϕ^{pre} is satisfied, this state will surely be followed by a state were the postcondition ϕ^{post} holds. In [7, 13] it is explained how action occurrences can be seen or encoded as state-based conditions. Here we will not define how to interpret general LTL-formula in pLTSs, but below we do this for eventuality properties with specific choices of ϕ^{pre} and ϕ^{post}.

Formula (1) is too strong and does not hold in general: in case the nodes *id* and *dest* are not within transmission range of each other, the delivery of messages from *id* to *dest* is doomed to fail. We need to postulate two side conditions to make this liveness property plausible. Firstly, when the request to deliver the message comes in, *id* needs to be connected to *dest*. We introduce the predicate $\mathbf{cntd}(id, dest)$ to express this, and hence take ϕ^{pre} to be $\mathbf{cntd}(id, dest) \wedge id\colon \mathbf{newpkt}(d, dest)$. Secondly, we assume that the link between *id* and *dest* does not break until the message is delivered. As remarked in [13], such a side condition can be formalised by taking ϕ^{post} to be $dest\colon \mathbf{deliver}(d) \vee \mathbf{disconnect}(id, dest)$. Thus the liveness property we are after is

$$\begin{gathered}\mathbf{G}\big(\mathbf{cntd}(id, dest) \wedge id\colon \mathbf{newpkt}(d, dest) \Rightarrow \\ \mathbf{F}(dest\colon \mathbf{deliver}(d) \vee \mathbf{disconnect}(id, dest) \vee \mathbf{disconnect}(dest, id))\big)\end{gathered} \tag{2}$$

We now define the validity of eventuality properties $\mathbf{G}\big(\phi^{pre} \Rightarrow \mathbf{F}\phi^{post}\big)$. Here ϕ^{pre} and ϕ^{post} denote sets of transitions and actions, respectively, and hold if one of the transitions or actions in the set occurs. In (2), ϕ^{pre} denotes the transitions with label $id\colon \mathbf{newpkt}(d, dest)$ that occur when the side condition $\mathbf{cntd}(id, dest)$ is met, whereas $\phi^{post} = \{dest\colon \mathbf{deliver}(d), \mathbf{disconnect}(id, dest), \mathbf{disconnect}(dest, id)\}$ is a set of actions.

A *path* in a pLTS $(S, \mathrm{Act}, \rightarrow)$ is an alternating sequence $s_0, \alpha_1, s_1, \alpha_2, \ldots$ of states and actions, starting with a state and either being infinite or ending with a state, such that there is a transition $s_i \xrightarrow{\alpha_{i+1}} \Delta_{i+1}$ with $\Delta_{i+1}(s_{i+1}) > 0$ for each i. The path is *rooted* if it starts with a state marked as 'initial', and *complete* if either it is infinite, or there is no transition starting from its last state. A state or transition is *reachable* if it occurs in a rooted path.

In a pLTS with an initial state, an eventually formula $\mathbf{G}(\phi^{pre} \Rightarrow \mathbf{F}\phi^{post})$, with ϕ^{pre} and ϕ^{post} denoting sets of transitions and actions, *holds outright* if all complete paths starting with a reachable transition from ϕ^{pre} contain a transition with a label from ϕ^{post}.

Definitions 3 and 5 in [9] define the set of probabilities that a pLTS with an initial state will ever execute the action ω. One obtains a set of probabilities rather than a single probability due to the possibility of nondeterministic choice. This definition generalises to *sets* of actions ϕ^{post} (seen as disjunctions) by first renaming all actions in such a set into ω. It also generalises trivially to pLTSs with an *initial transition*. For t a transition in a pLTS, let $Prob(t, \phi^{post})$ be the infimum of the set of probabilities that the pLTS in which t is taken to be the initial transition will ever execute ϕ^{post}. Now in a pLTS with an initial state, an eventually formula $\mathbf{G}(\phi^{pre} \Rightarrow \mathbf{F}\phi^{post})$ *holds with probability at least* p if for all reachable transitions t in ϕ^{pre} we have $Prob(t, \phi^{post}) \geq p$.

Possible correctness criteria for link layer protocols are that the liveness property (2) either holds outright, holds with probability 1, or at least holds with probability p for a sufficiently high value of p.

Sometimes we are content to establish that (2) holds under the additional assumptions that the network is stable until our packet is delivered, meaning that no links between any nodes are broken or established, and/or that the network layer refrains from injecting more packets. This is modelled by taking

$$\phi^{post} = \{dest\colon \mathbf{deliver}(d), \mathbf{disconnect}(*, *), \mathbf{connect}(*, *), \mathbf{newpkt}(*, *)\}. \quad (3)$$

We will refer to this version of (2) as the *weak packet delivery* property. *Packet delivery* is the strengthening without $\mathbf{newpkt}(*, *)$ in (3), i.e. not assuming that the network layer refrains from injecting more packets.

5 Modelling and Analysing the CSMA/CA Protocol

In this section we model two versions of the CSMA/CA protocol, using the process algebra ALL. Moreover, we briefly discuss some results we obtained while analysing these protocols.

The *Carrier-Sense Multiple Access* (CSMA) protocol is a media access control (MAC) protocol in which a node verifies the absence of other traffic before transmitting on a shared transmission medium. If a carrier is sensed, the node waits for the transmission in progress to end before initiating its own transmission. Using CSMA, multiple nodes may, in turn, send and receive on the same medium. Transmissions by one node are generally received by all other nodes connected to the medium.

The CSMA protocol with Collision Avoidance (CSMA/CA) [17,19][4] improves the performance of CSMA. If the transmission medium is sensed busy

[4] The primary medium access control (MAC) technique of IEEE 802.11 [19] is called *distributed coordination function* (DCF), which is a CSMA/CA protocol.

before transmission then the transmission is deferred for a *random* time interval. This interval reduces the likelihood that two or more nodes waiting to transmit will simultaneously begin transmission upon termination of the detected transmission. CSMA/CA is used, for example, in Wi-Fi.

It is well known that CSMA/CA suffers from the *hidden station problem* (see Sect. 5.2). To overcome this problem, CSMA/CA is often supplemented by the request-to-send/clear-to-send (RTS/CTS) handshaking [19]. This mechanism is known as the IEEE 802.11 RTS/CTS exchange, or *virtual carrier sensing.* While this extension reduces the amount of collisions, wireless 802.11 implementations do not typically implement RTS/CTS for all transmissions because the transmission overhead is too great for small data transfers.

We use the process algebra ALL to model both the CSMA/CA without and with virtual carrier sensing.

5.1 A Formal Model for CSMA/CA

Our formal specification of CSMA/CA consists of four short processes written in ALL. It is precise and free of ambiguities—one of the many advantages formal methods provide, in contrast to specifications written in English prose.

The syntax of ALL is intended to look like pseudo code, and it is our belief that the specification can easily be read and understood by software engineers, who may or may not have experience with process algebra.

As the underlying data structure of our model is straightforward, we do not present it explicitly, but introduce it while describing the different processes.

The basic process CSMA, depicted in Process 1, is the protocol's entry point.

Process 1. The Basic Routine

```
CSMA(id) ≝
1. newpkt(data,dest). INIT(id,0,dataframe(data,id,dest))
2. + [NEW(dataframe(data,src,id))] deliver(data) .
3.   (
4.      ⟦timeout := now + sifs⟧ [now ≥ timeout]
5.      transmit(ackframe(src)) . CSMA(id)
6.   )
```

This process maintains a single data variable `id` in which it stores its own identity. It waits until either it receives a request from the network layer to transmit a packet `data` to destination `dest`, or it receives from another node in the network a CSMA message (data frame) destined for itself.

In case of a newly injected data packet (Line 1), the process `INIT` is called; this process (described below) initiates the sending of the message via the medium. When passing the message on to `INIT` we use a function $\texttt{dataframe}: \texttt{DATA} \times \texttt{ID} \times \texttt{ID} \rightarrow \texttt{MSG}$ that generates a message in a format used by the protocol: next to the header fields (from which we abstract) it contains the injected `data` as well as the designated receiver `dest` and the sender `id`—the current node.

In case of an incoming `dataframe` destined for this node (the third argument carrying the destination is `id`) (Line 2)—any other incoming message is ignored by this process—the `data` is handed over to the network layer (**deliver**(`data`)) followed by the transmission of an acknowledgement back to the sender of the message (`src`). CSMA/CA requires a short period of idling medium before sending the acknowledgement: in [19] this interval is called *short interframe space* (`sifs`). The process waits until the time of the interframe spacing has passed, and then transmits the acknowledgement. The acknowledgement sent is not always received by `src`, e.g. due to data collision; therefore `src` could send the same message again (see Process 4) and `id` could deliver the same data to the network layer again.

Process 2. Protocol Initialisation

```
INIT(id,tries,dframe) ≝
1. [tries ≤ max_retransmit]
2.    ⟦cw := cwmin × 2^tries⟧
3.    ⨁_{b=0}^{cw−1} CCA(id,b,tries,dframe)      /* choose a backoff from {0,...,cw−1} */
4. + [tries > max_retransmit]
5.    deliver(channel_access_failure) . CSMA(id)
```

The process `INIT` (Process 2) initiates the sending of a message via the medium. Next to the variable `id`, which is maintained by all processes, it maintains the variable `tries` and `dframe`: `tries` stores the number of attempts already made to send message `dframe`. When the process is called the first time for a message `dframe` (Line 1 of Process 1) the value of `tries` is 0.

The constant `max_retransmit` specifies the maximum number of attempts the protocol is allowed to retransmit the same message. If the limit is not yet reached (Line 1) the message `dframe` is sent. As mentioned above, CSMA/CA defers messages for a *random* time interval to avoid collision. The node must start transmission within the contention window `cw`, a.k.a. backoff time. `cw` is calculated in Line 2; it increases exponentially.[5] After `cw` is determined, the process `CCA` is called, which performs the actual **transmit**-action. In case the maximum number of retransmits is reached (Line 4), the process notifies the network layer and restarts the protocol, awaiting new instructions from the application layer, or a new incoming message.

Process 3 takes care of the actual transmission of `dframe`. However, the protocol has a complicated procedure when to send this message.

First, the process senses the medium and awaits the point in time when it is idle (Line 6). In case, before this happens, it receives from another node in the network a CSMA message destined for itself (Line 1), this message is handled just as in Process 1, except that after acknowledging this message the protocol returns to Process 3.

[5] A typical value for `cwmin` is 16; it must satisfy `cwmin` > 0.

Process 3. Clear Channel Assessment With Physical Carrier Sense

```
CCA(id,b,tries,dframe) ≝
1.  [NEW(dataframe(data,src,id))] deliver(data) .
2.    (
3.      ⟦timeout := now + sifs⟧ [now ≥ timeout]
4.      transmit(ackframe(src)) . CCA(id,b,tries,dframe)
5.    )
6.  + [IDLE]
7.    ⟦timeout:=now+difs⟧      /* start wait for duration difs */
8.    (
9.      [¬IDLE] CCA(id,b,tries,dframe)
10.     + [IDLE ∧ now ≥ timeout]
11.       ⟦timeout := now + b⟧
12.       (
13.         [¬IDLE]      /* busy during backoff time */
14.           ⟦b := timeout − now⟧ CCA(id,b,tries,dframe)
15.         + [IDLE ∧ now ≥ timeout]      /* idle for backoff time */
16.           transmit(dframe) .
17.           ACKRECV(id,tries,now+max_ack_wait,dframe)
18.       )
19.   )
```

To guarantee a gap between messages sent via the medium, CSMA/CA (as well as other protocols) specifies the *distributed (coordination function) inter-frame space* (difs ∈ TIME), which is usually small,[6] but larger than sifs, so that acknowledgements get priority over new data frames. When the medium becomes busy during the interframe space, another node started transmitting and the process goes back to listening to the medium (Line 9). In case nothing happens on the medium and the end of the interframe space is reached (Line 10), the process determines the actual time to start transmitting the message, taking the backoff time b into account (Line 11). If the medium is idle for the entire backoff period (Line 15), the message is transmitted (Line 16), and the process calls the process ACKRECV that will await an acknowledgement from the recipient of dframe (Line 17); the third argument specifies the maximum time the process should wait for such an acknowledgement. (As mentioned before an acknowledgement may never arrive.) If another node transmits on the medium during the backoff period, the protocol restarts the routine (Lines 13 and 14), with an adjusted backoff value b—the process already started waiting and should not be punished when the waiting is restarted; this update guarantees fairness of the protocol.

The process awaiting an acknowledgement (Process 4) is straightforward. It waits until either it receives a CSMA message destined for itself (Line 1), or it receives an acknowledgement (Line 6), or it has waited for this acknowledgement as long as it is going to (Line 8).

[6] Recommended values for the constant difs are given in [19].

In the first case, the message is handled just as in Process 1, except that after acknowledging this message the protocol returns to Process 4. In the second case the network layer is informed that the sending of `dframe` was successful and the process loops back to Process 1 (Line 7). Line 8 describes the situation where no acknowledgement message arrives and the process times out. Here CSMA/CA retries to send the message; the counter `tries` is incremented.

Process 4. Receiving an ACK

```
ACKRECV(id,tries,acktimeout,dframe) ≝
1. [NEW(dataframe(data,src,id))] deliver(data) .
2.   (
3.     ⟦timeout := now + sifs⟧ [now ≥ timeout]
4.     transmit(ackframe(src)) . ACKRECV(id,tries,acktimeout,dframe)
5.   )
6. + [NEW(ackframe(id))]      /* acknowledgement received */
7.   deliver(success) . CSMA(id)
8. + [now ≥ acktimeout] INIT(id,tries+1,dframe)
```

5.2 The Hidden Station Problem

As mentioned in the introduction to this section, CSMA/CA suffers from the hidden station problem. This refers to the situation where two nodes A and C are not within transmission range of each other, while a node B is in range of both. In this situation C may be transmitting to B, but A is not able to sense this, and thus may start a transmission to B at roughly the same time, leading to data collisions at B.

While CSMA/CA is not able to avoid such collisions as a whole—it is always possible that two (or more) nodes hidden from each other happen to (randomly) choose the same backoff time to send messages—it is the exponential growth of the backoff slots that makes the problem less pressing in the long run, as the following theorem shows.

Theorem 5.1. If <u>`max_retransmit`</u>$=\infty$ then weak packet delivery holds with probability 1.

Proof sketch. Since the number of messages that nodes transmit is bounded, and all nodes select random times to start transmitting out of an increasing longer time span, with probability 1 each message will eventually go through. □

In practice, <u>`max_retransmit`</u> is set to a value that is not high enough to approximate the idea behind the above proof. In fact, the transmission time of a single message may be larger than the maximal backoff period allowed. For this reason the hidden station problem does occur when running the CSMA/CA protocol, as studies have shown [5]. Nevertheless, the above analysis still shows that link layer protocols can be formally analysed by process algebra in general, and ALL in particular.

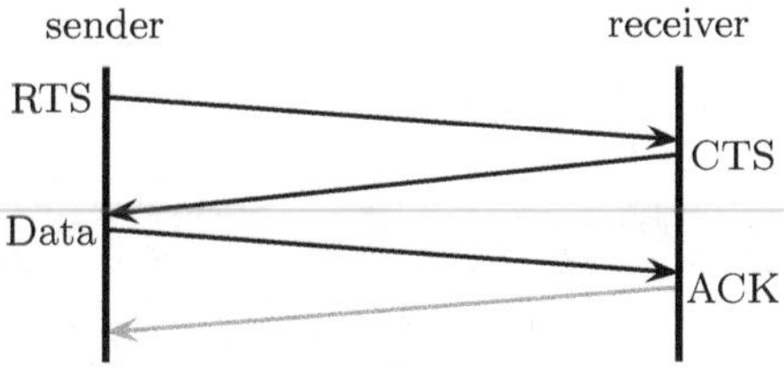

Fig. 1. RTS/CTS exchange

5.3 A Formal Model for CSMA/CA with Virtual Carrier Sensing

To overcome the hidden station problem the usage of a request-to-send/clear-to-send (RTS/CTS) handshaking [19] mechanism is available. This mechanism is also known as *virtual carrier sensing.* The exchange of RTS/CTS messages happens just before the actual data is sent, see Fig. 1. The mechanism serves two purposes: (a) As the RTS and CTS messages are very short—they only contain two node identifiers as well as a natural number indicating the time it will take to send the actual `data` (plus overhead)—the likelihood of a collision is reduced. (b) While the handshaking does not help with solving the hidden station problem for the RTS message itself, it avoids the problem for the sending of `data`. The reason is that a hidden node, which could interfere with the sending of `data` will receive the CTS message from the designated recipient of `data`, and the hidden node will remain silent until the `data` has been sent.

As for the CSMA/CA protocol we have modelled this extension in ALL, based on the model of CSMA/CA we presented earlier.

Our extended model uses two functions to generate `rts` and `cts` messages, respectively. The signature of both is $\texttt{ID} \times \texttt{ID} \times \texttt{TIME} \to \texttt{MSG}$. The first argument carries the sender (source) of the message, the second the indented destination, and the third argument a duration (time period) of silence that is requested/granted. For example, before the message `rts(src,dest,d)` is transmitted, the time period `d` is calculated by
The calculation is straightforward as it follows the protocol logic and determines the amount of time needed until the acknowledgement would be received (see Fig. 2). After the `rts` message has been received the medium should be idle for the interframe space $\underline{\texttt{sifs}}$; then a `cts` message is sent back, which takes time $\underline{\texttt{dur\_cts}}$; then another interframe space is needed, followed by the actual transmission of the message—the sending will take `dur(dataframe(data,id,dest))` time units; after the message is received (hopefully) another interframe space is required before the acknowledgement is sent back.

$$[\![\texttt{d} := \underline{\texttt{sifs}} + \underline{\texttt{dur\_cts}} + \underline{\texttt{sifs}} + \texttt{dur(dataframe(data,id,dest))} + \underline{\texttt{sifs}} + \underline{\texttt{dur\_ack}}]\!] .$$

Process 2 remains essentially unchanged; it is merely equipped with the destination `dest` of the message that needs to be transmitted, and an additional timed variable $\texttt{nav} \in \texttt{TIME}$. These variables are not used in this process, but required later on. Variable `nav` holds the point in time until the process should

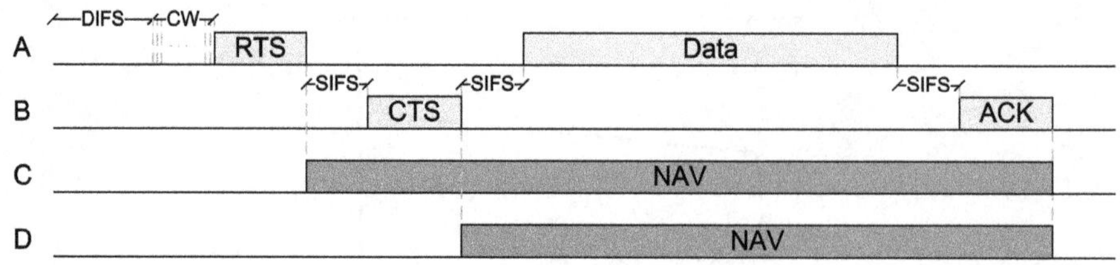

Fig. 2. The use of virtual channel sensing using CSMA/CA [3]

not transmit any `rts` or `cts` message. This period of silence is necessary as the node figures out that until time `nav` another node will transmit message(s).[7]

Process 5 is the modified version of Process 1. Identical to Process 1 it awaits an instruction from the network layer, or an incoming CSMA message destined for itself. Lines 1–3 are identical to Process 1. Lines 4–11 handle the two new message types. In case an `rts` message `rts(src,dest,d)` is received that is intended for another recipient ($\texttt{dest} \neq \texttt{id}$) the node concludes that another node wants to use the medium for the amount of `d` time units; the process updates the variable `nav` if needed, indicating the period the node should remain silent, by taking the maximum of the current value of `nav`, and `now+d`, the point in time until the sender `src` of the `rts` message requires the medium. The same behaviour occurs if a `cts` message is received that is not intended for the node itself (Line 4). If the incoming message is an `rts` message intended for the node itself (Line 6) by default the node answers with a clear-to-send message back to the sender (Line 9). However, when the receiver of the `rts` has knowledge about other nodes requiring the medium ($\texttt{now} \leq \texttt{nav}$), a clear-to-send cannot be granted, and the request is dropped (Line 6). Similar to the sending of an acknowledgement (Line 2), the process waits for the short interframe space (<u>`sifs`</u>) before sending the CTS (Line 6). Line 8 handles the case where the medium becomes busy ($\neg$IDLE) during this period; also here a clear-to-send cannot be granted, and the request is dropped.[8] Only when the medium stays idle during the entire interframe space the node `id` can inform the source of the `rts` message that the medium is clear to send; the `cts` is transmitted in Line 9. The time a receiver of this message has to be silent is adjusted by deducting the time elapsed before this happens. In Line 10 the process resets `nav` to remind itself not to issue any `rts` message until the present exchange has been completed.[9]

---

[7] After a successful RTS/CTS exchange, communicating nodes proceed with transmitting the data and an acknowledgement regardless of the value of `nav`.

[8] The condition $\texttt{now} > \texttt{timeout}-\underline{\texttt{sifs}}$ prevents the process from dropping the request in the very first time slice that `CSMA` is running. Here the medium counts as busy, but only because we have just received an `rts` message.

[9] A case NEW(`cts(src,dest,d)`) $\wedge$ $\texttt{dest} = \texttt{id}$ is not required as a `cts` message is only expected in case an `rts` was sent, and hence handled in process `RTSREACT`.

Process 5. The Basic Routine (RTS/CTS)

```
CSMA(id,nav) ≝
1.  newpkt(data,dest). INIT(id,dest,0,dataframe(data,id,dest),nav)
2.  + [NEW(dataframe(data,src,id))] deliver(data) . ⟦timeout := now + sifs⟧
3.    [now ≥ timeout] transmit(ackframe(src)) . CSMA(id,nav)
4.  + [(NEW(rts(src,dest,d)) ∨ NEW(cts(src,dest,d))) ∧ dest ≠ id ∧ nav < now+d]
5.    ⟦nav := now+d⟧ CSMA(id, nav)
6.  + [NEW(rts(src,id,d)) ∧ now > nav] ⟦timeout := now + sifs⟧
7.    (
8.      [¬IDLE ∧ now > timeout−sifs] CSMA(id, nav)
9.      + [IDLE ∧ now ≥ timeout] transmit(cts(id,src,d−dur_cts−sifs)) .
10.       ⟦nav := now+d−dur_cts−sifs⟧ CSMA(id, nav)
11.   )
```

Process 6. Clear Channel Assessment With Virtual Carrier Sense

```
CCA(id,dest,b,tries,dframe,nav) ≝
1.  [NEW(dataframe(data,src,id))] deliver(data) . ⟦timeout := now + sifs⟧
2.    [now ≥ timeout] transmit(ackframe(src)) . CCA(id,dest,b,tries,dframe,nav)
3.  + [(NEW(rts(src,dest,d)) ∨ NEW(cts(src,dest,d))) ∧ dest ≠ id ∧ nav < now+d]
4.    ⟦nav := now+d⟧ CCA(id,dest,b,tries,dframe,nav)
5.  + [NEW(rts(src,id,d)) ∧ now > nav] ⟦timeout := now + sifs⟧
6.    (
7.      [¬IDLE ∧ now > timeout−sifs] CCA(id,dest,b,tries,dframe,nav)
8.      + [IDLE ∧ now ≥ timeout] transmit(cts(id,src,d−dur_cts−sifs)) .
9.        ⟦nav := now+d−dur_cts−sifs⟧ CCA(id,dest,b,tries,dframe,nav)
10.   )
11. + [IDLE ∧ now > nav]
12.   ⟦timeout:=now+difs⟧
13.   (
14.     [¬IDLE] CCA(id,dest,b,tries,dframe,nav)
15.     + [IDLE ∧ now ≥ timeout]
16.       ⟦timeout := now + b⟧
17.       (
18.         [¬IDLE]        /* busy during backoff time */
19.           ⟦b := timeout − now⟧ CCA(id,dest,b,tries,dframe,nav)
20.         + [IDLE ∧ now ≥ timeout]        /* idle for backoff time */
21.           ⟦d := sifs + dur_cts + sifs + dur(dframe) + sifs + dur_ack⟧
22.           transmit(rts(id,dest,d)) .
23.           CTSRECV(id,dest,tries,now + max_cts_wait,dframe,nav)
24.       )
25.   )
```

Process 6 is the modified version of Process 3. The goal of this process is to send an rts message (Line 22). Before it can start its work, it waits until the medium is idle, and any time it is required to be silent has elapsed (Line 11).

Until this happens incoming data frames, `rts` or `cts` messages are treated just as in Process 5: Lines 1–10 copy Lines 2–11 of Process 5, except that afterwards the process returns to itself. Then Lines 12–20 are copied from Lines 7–15 from Process 3. Line 21 calculates the time other nodes ought to keep silent when receiving the `rts` message, and Line 23 passes control to the process CTSRECV, which awaits a `cts` response to the `rts` message transmitted in Line 22. The fourth argument of CTSRECV specifies the maximum time that process should wait for such a response; a good value for <u>`max_cts_wait`</u> is <u>`sifs`</u> + <u>`dur_cts`</u>.

Process CTSRECV listens for this time to a `cts` message with source `dest` and destination `id`. In case the expected `cts` message arrives in time (Line 1), the node waits for a time <u>`sifs`</u> (Line 2) and then transmits the data frame and proceeds to await an acknowledgement (Line 3). The fourth argument of ACKRECV specifies the maximum time the process should wait for such an acknowledgement; a good value for <u>`max_ack_wait`</u> is <u>`sifs`</u> + <u>`dur_ack`</u>. If the `cts` message does not arrive in time (Line 6), the process returns to INIT to send another `rts` message, while incrementing the counter `tries` (Line 7). While waiting for the `cts` message, any incoming `rts` or `cts` message destined for another node is treated exactly as in Process 5 (Lines 4–5). Incoming data frames cannot arrive when this process is running, and incoming `rts` messages to `id` are ignored.

Process 7. Receiving a CTS

```
CTSRECV(id,dest,tries,ctstimeout,dframe,nav) ≝
 1. [NEW(cts(dest,id,d))]
 2.    ⟦timeout := now + sifs⟧ [now ≥ timeout]
 3.    transmit(dframe) . ACKRECV(id,dest,tries,now + max_ack_wait,dframe,nav)
 4. + [(NEW(rts(src,dest,d)) ∨ NEW(cts(src,dest,d))) ∧ dest ≠ id ∧ nav < now+d]
 5.    ⟦nav := now+d⟧ CTSRECV(id,dest,tries,ctstimeout,dframe,nav)
 6. + [now ≥ ctstimeout]
 7.    INIT(id,dest,tries+1,dframe,nav)
```

Process 8. Receiving an ACK

```
ACKRECV(id,dest,tries,acktimeout,dframe,nav) ≝
 1. [NEW(ackframe(id))]
 2.    deliver(success) . CSMA(id,nav)
 3. + [(NEW(rts(src,dest,d)) ∨ NEW(cts(src,dest,d))) ∧ dest ≠ id ∧ nav < now + d]
 4.    ⟦nav := now+d⟧ ACKRECV(id,dest,tries,acktimeout,dframe,nav)
 5. + [now ≥ timeout]      /* nothing received */
 6.    INIT(id,dest,tries+1,dframe,nav)
```

Process 8 handles the receipt of an acknowledgement in response to a successful data transmission. If an acknowledgement arrives, it must be from the node to which `id` has transmitted a data frame. In that case (Line 1), the network layer is informed that the sending of `dframe` was successful and the process loops back to Process 5 (Line 2). Line 5 describes the situation where no acknowledgement message arrives and the process times out. Also here CSMA/CA retries to send the message; the counter tries is incremented. Lines 3–4 describe the usual handling of incoming rts or cts messages destined for another node.

5.4 The Exposed Station Problem

Another source of collisions in CSMA/CA is the well-known *exposed station problem*. This refers to a linear topology $A - B - C - D$, where an unending stream of messages between C and D interferes with attempts by A to get a message across to B. In the default CSMA/CA protocol as formalised in Sect. 5.1, transmissions from A to B may perpetually collide at B with transmissions from C destined for D. CSMA/CA with virtual carrier sensing mitigates this problem, for a cts sent by B in response to an rts sent by A will tell C to keep silent for the required duration. In fact, we can show that in the above topology, if max_retransmit=∞ then packet delivery holds with probability 1. A non-probabilistic guarantee cannot be given since nodes A and C could behave in the same way, meaning if one node is sending out a message the other does the same at the very same moment, and if one is silent the other remains silent as well. In this scenario all messages to be sent are doomed.

Based on our formalisation, we can prove that once the RTS/CTS handshake has been successfully concluded, meaning that all nodes within range of the intended recipient have received the cts, then packet delivery holds outright. So the only problem left is to achieve a successful RTS/CTS handshake. Since rts and cts messages are rather short, even by modest values of max_retransmit it becomes likely that such messages do not collide.

In spite of this, CSMA/CA with (or without) virtual channel sensing cannot achieve packet delivery with probability 1 for general topologies. Assume the following network topology

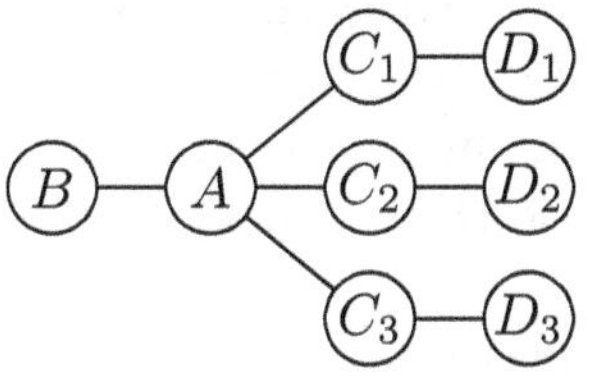

Here it may happen that one of the C_is is always busy transmitting a large message to D_i; any given C_i is occasionally silent (not sending any message), but then one of the others is transmitting. As C_i is disconnected from C_j, for $j \neq i$, coordination between the nodes is impossible. As a consequence, the medium at A will always be busy, so that A cannot send an rts message from B.

6 Related Work

The CSMA protocol in its different variants has been analysed with different formalisms in the past.

Multiple analyses were performed for the CSMA/CD protocol (CSMA with collision detection), a predecessor of CSMA/CA that has a constant backoff, i.e.

the backoff time is not increased exponentially, see [10,11,20,21,26]. In all these approaches frame collisions have to be modelled explicitly, as part of the protocol description. In contrast, our approach handles collisions in the semantics; thereby achieving a clear separation between protocol specifications and link layer behaviour.

Duflot et al. [10,11] use probabilistic timed automata (PTAs) to model the protocol, and use probabilistic model checking (PRISM) and approximate model checking (APMC) for their analysis. The model explained in [26] is based on PTAs as well, but uses the model checker UPPAAL as verification tool. These approaches, although formal, have very little in common with our approach. On the one hand it is not easy to change the model from CSMA/CD to CSMA/CA, as the latter requires unbounded data structures (or alike) to model the exponential backoff. On the other hand, as usual, model checking suffers from state space explosion and only small networks (usually fewer than ten nodes) can be analysed. This is sufficient and convenient when it comes to finding counter examples, but these approaches cannot provide guarantees for arbitrary network topologies, as ours does.

Jensen et al. [20] use models of CSMA/CD to compare the tools SPIN and UPPAAL. Their models are much more abstract than ours. It is proven that no collisions will ever occur, without stating the exact conditions under which this statement holds.

To the best of our knowledge, Parrow [21] is the only one who used process algebra (CCS) to model and analyse CSMA. His untimed model of CSMA/CD is extremely abstract and the analysis performed is limited to two nodes only, avoiding scenarios such as the hidden station problem.

There are far fewer formal analyses techniques available when it comes to CSMA/CA (with and without virtual medium sensing). Traditional approaches to the analysis of network protocols are simulation and test-bed experiments. This is also the case for CSMA/CA (e.g. [4]). While these are important and valid methods for protocol evaluation, in particular for quantitative performance evaluation, they have limitations in regards to the evaluation of basic protocol correctness properties.

Following the spirit of the above-mentioned research of model checking CSMA, Fruth [15] analyses CSMA/CA using PTAs and PRISM. He considers properties such as the minimum probability of two nodes successfully completing their transmissions, and maximum expected number of collisions until two nodes have successfully completed their transmissions. As before, this analysis technique does not scale; in [15] the experiments are limited to two contending nodes only.

Beyond model checking, simulation and test-bed experiments, we are only aware of two other formal approaches. In [1] Markov chains are used to derive an accurate, analytical model to compute the throughput of CSMA/CA. Calculating throughput is an orthogonal task to our vision of proving (functional) correctness.

An approach aiming at proving the correctness of CSMA/CA with virtual carrier sensing (RTS/CTS), and hence related to ours, is presented in [3]. Based on stochastic bigraphs with sharing it uses rewrite rules to analyse quantitative properties. Although it is an approach that is capable to analyse arbitrary topologies, to apply the rewrite rules a particular topology needs to be modelled by a directed acyclic graph structure, which is part of the bigraph.

7 Conclusion

In this paper we have proposed a novel process algebra, called ALL, that can be used to model, verify and analyse link layer protocols. Since we aimed at a process algebra featuring aspects of the link layer such as frame collisions, as well as arbitrary data structures (to model a rich class of protocols), we could not use any of the existing algebras. The design of ALL is layered. The first layer allows modelling protocols in some sort of pseudo code, which hopefully makes our approach accessible for network and software researchers/engineers. The other layers are mainly for giving a formal semantics to the language. The layer of partial network expressions, the third layer, provides a unique and sophisticated mechanism for modelling the collision of frames. As it is hard-wired in the semantics there is no need to model collisions manually when modelling a protocol, as it was done before [21]. Next to primitives needed for modelling link layer protocols (e.g. **transmit**) and standard operators of process algebra (e.g. nondeterministic choice), ALL provides an operator for probabilistic choice.

This operator is needed to model aspects of link layer protocols such as the exponential backoff for the Carrier-Sense Multiple Access with Collision Avoidance protocol, the case study we have chosen to demonstrate the applicability of ALL. We have modelled and analysed two versions of CSMA/CA, without and with virtual carrier sensing. Our analysis has confirmed the hidden station problem for the version without virtual carrier sensing. However, we have also shown that the version with virtual carrier sensing overcomes not only this problem, but also the exposed station problem with probability 1. Yet the protocol cannot guarantee packet delivery, not even with probability 1.

To perform this analysis we had to formalise suitable liveness properties for link layer protocols specified in our framework.

Acknowledgement. We thank Tran Ngoc Ma for her involvement in this project in a very early phase. We also like to thank the German Academic Exchange Service (DAAD) that funded an internship of the third author at Data61, CSIRO.

References

1. Bianchi, G.: Performance analysis of the IEEE 802.11 distributed coordination function. IEEE J. Sel. Areas Commun. **18**(3), 535–547 (2000). https://doi.org/10.1109/49.840210
2. Bres, E., van Glabbeek, R.J., Höfner, P.: A timed process algebra for wireless networks with an application in routing. In: Thiemann, P. (ed.) ESOP 2016. LNCS, vol. 9632, pp. 95–122. Springer, Heidelberg (2016). https://doi.org/10.1007/978-3-662-49498-1_5

3. Calder, M., Sevegnani, M.: Modelling IEEE 802.11 CSMA/CA RTS/CTS with stochastic bigraphs with sharing. Formal Aspects Comput. **26**(3), 537–561 (2014). https://doi.org/10.1007/s00165-012-0270-3
4. Chhaya, H.S., Gupta, S.: Performance modeling of asynchronous data transfer methods of IEEE 802.11 MAC Protocol. Wirel. Netw. **3**, 217–234 (1997). https://doi.org/10.1023/A:1019109301754
5. Comer, D.: Computer Networks and Internets. Pearson Education Inc., UpperSaddle River (2009)
6. Cranen, S., Mousavi, M.R., Reniers, M.A.: A rule format for associativity. In: van Breugel, F., Chechik, M. (eds.) CONCUR 2008. LNCS, vol. 5201, pp. 447–461. Springer, Heidelberg (2008). https://doi.org/10.1007/978-3-540-85361-9_35
7. De Nicola, R., Vaandrager, F.W.: Three logics for branching bisimulation. J. ACM **42**(2), 458–487 (1995). https://doi.org/10.1145/201019.201032
8. Deng, Y., van Glabbeek, R.J., Hennessy, M., Morgan, C.C., Zhang, C.: Remarks on testing probabilistic processes. In: Cardelli, L., Fiore, M., Winskel, G. (eds.) Computation, Meaning, and Logic: Articles Dedicated to Gordon Plotkin, Electronic Notes in Theoretical Computer Science, vol. 172, pp. 359–397. Elsevier (2007). https://doi.org/10.1016/j.entcs.2007.02.013
9. Deng, Y., van Glabbeek, R.J., Morgan, C.C., Zhang, C.: Scalar outcomes suffice for finitary probabilistic testing. In: De Nicola, R. (ed.) ESOP 2007. LNCS, vol. 4421, pp. 363–378. Springer, Heidelberg (2007). https://doi.org/10.1007/978-3-540-71316-6_25
10. Duflot, M., et al.: Probabilistic model checking of the CSMA/CD, protocol using PRISM and APMC. In: Automated Verification of Critical Systems (AVoCS 2004). Electronic Notes in Theoretical Computer Science Series, vol. 128, pp. 195–214 (2004). https://doi.org/10.1016/j.entcs.2005.04.012
11. Duflot, M., et al.: Practical applications of probabilistic model checking to communication protocols. In: Gnesi, S., Margaria, T. (eds.) Formal Methods for Industrial Critical Systems: A Survey of Applications, pp. 133–150. IEEE (2013). https://doi.org/10.1002/9781118459898.ch7
12. Fehnker, A., van Glabbeek, R.J., Höfner, P., McIver, A.K., Portmann, M., Tan, W.L.: A process algebra for wireless mesh networks. In: Seidl, H. (ed.) ESOP 2012. LNCS, vol. 7211, pp. 295–315. Springer, Heidelberg (2012). https://doi.org/10.1007/978-3-642-28869-2_15
13. Fehnker, A., van Glabbeek, R.J., Höfner, P., McIver, A.K., Portmann, M., Tan, W.L.: A process algebra for wireless mesh networks used for modelling, verifying and analysing AODV. Technical report 5513, NICTA (2013). http://arxiv.org/abs/1312.7645
14. Friend, G.E., Fike, J.L., Baker, H.C., Bellamy, J.C.: Understanding Data Communications, 2nd edn. Howard W. Sams & Company, Indianapolis (1988)
15. Fruth, M.: Probabilistic model checking of contention resolution in the IEEE 802.15.4 low-rate wireless personal area network protocol. In: Leveraging Applications of Formal Methods, Second International Symposium (ISoLA 2006), pp. 290–297. IEEE Computer Society (2006). https://doi.org/10.1109/ISoLA.2006.34
16. IEEE: IEEE standard for ethernet (2016). https://doi.org/10.1109/IEEESTD.2016.7428776
17. IEEE: IEEE standard for low-rate wireless networks (2016). https://doi.org/10.1109/IEEESTD.2016.7460875
18. ISO/IEC 7498-1: Information technology—open systems interconnection—basic reference model: The basic model (1994). https://www.iso.org/standard/20269.html

19. ISO/IEC/IEEE 8802-11: Information technology—telecommunications and information exchange between systems—local and metropolitan area networks—specific requirements—part 11: Wireless LAN medium access control (MAC) and physical layer (PHY) specifications (2018). https://www.iso.org/standard/73367.html
20. Jensen, H.E., Larsen, K.G., Skou, A.: Modelling and analysis of a collision avoidance protocol using Spin and Uppaal. In: The Spin Verification System. Discrete Mathematics and Theoretical Computer Science, vol. 32, pp. 33–50. DIMACS/AMS (1996). https://doi.org/10.7146/brics.v3i24.20005
21. Parrow, J.: Verifying a CSMA/CD-protocol with CCS. In: Aggarwal, S. (eds.) IFIP Symposium on Protocol Specification, Testing and Verification (PSTV 1988), North-Holland, pp. 373–384 (1988)
22. Pnueli, A.: The temporal logic of programs. In: Foundations of Computer Science (FOCS 1977), pp. 46–57. IEEE (1977). https://doi.org/10.1109/SFCS.1977.32
23. de Simone, R.: Higher-level synchronising devices in MEIJE-SCCS. TCS **37**, 245–267 (1985). https://doi.org/10.1016/0304-3975(85)90093-3
24. Simpson, W.: The point-to-point protocol (PPP). RFC 1661 Internet Standard (1994). http://www.ietf.org/rfc/rfc1661.txt
25. Singh, A., Ramakrishnan, C.R., Smolka, S.A.: A process calculus for mobile ad hoc networks. Sci. Comput. Program. **75**, 440–469 (2010). https://doi.org/10.1016/j.scico.2009.07.008
26. Zhao, J., Li, X., Zheng, T., Zheng, G.: Removing irrelevant atomic formulas for checking timed automata efficiently. In: Larsen, K.G., Niebert, P. (eds.) FORMATS 2003. LNCS, vol. 2791, pp. 34–45. Springer, Heidelberg (2004). https://doi.org/10.1007/978-3-540-40903-8_4

9

Compiling Sandboxes: Formally Verified Software Fault Isolation

Frédéric Besson[1(✉)], Sandrine Blazy[1], Alexandre Dang[1], Thomas Jensen[1], and Pierre Wilke[2]

[1] Inria, Univ Rennes, CNRS, IRISA, Rennes, France
frederic.besson@inria.fr
[2] CentraleSupélec, Inria, Univ Rennes, CNRS, IRISA, Rennes, France

Abstract. Software Fault Isolation (SFI) is a security-enhancing program transformation for instrumenting an untrusted binary module so that it runs inside a dedicated isolated address space, called a sandbox. To ensure that the untrusted module cannot escape its sandbox, existing approaches such as Google's Native Client rely on a binary verifier to check that all memory accesses are within the sandbox. Instead of relying on *a posteriori* verification, we design, implement and prove correct a program instrumentation phase as part of the formally verified compiler CompCert that enforces a sandboxing security property *a priori*. This eliminates the need for a binary verifier and, instead, leverages the soundness proof of the compiler to prove the security of the sandboxing transformation. The technical contributions are a novel sandboxing transformation that has a well-defined C semantics and which supports arbitrary function pointers, and a formally verified C compiler that implements SFI. Experiments show that our formally verified technique is a competitive way of implementing SFI.

1 Introduction

Isolating programs with various levels of trustworthiness is a fundamental security concern, be it on a cloud computing platform running untrusted code provided by customers, or in a web browser running untrusted code coming from different origins. In these contexts, it is of the utmost importance to provide adequate isolation mechanisms so that a faulty or malicious computation cannot compromise the host or neighbouring computations.

There exists a number of mechanisms for enforcing isolation that intervene at various levels, from the hardware up to the operating system. Hypervisors [10], virtual machines [2] but also system processes [17] can ensure strong isolation properties, at the expense of costly context switches and limited flexibility in the interaction between components. Language-based techniques such as strong typing offer alternative techniques for ensuring memory safety, upon which access control policies and isolation can be implemented. This approach is implemented e.g. by the Java language for which it provides isolation guarantees, as proved by Leroy and Rouaix [21]. The isolation is fined-grained and very flexible but the security mechanisms, e.g. stack inspection, may be hard to reason about [7]. In the web browser realm, JavaScript is dynamically typed and also ensures memory safety upon which access control can be implemented [29].

1.1 Software Fault Isolation

Software Fault Isolation (SFI) is an alternative for unsafe languages, e.g. C, where memory safety is not granted but needs to be enforced at runtime by program instrumentation. Pioneered by Wahbe *et al.* [35] and popularised by Google's Native Client [30,37,38], SFI is a program transformation which confines a software component to a memory sandbox. This is done by pre-fixing every memory access with a carefully designed code sequence which efficiently ensures that the memory access occurs within the sandbox. In practice, the sandbox is aligned and the sandbox addresses are thus of the form $0xYZ$ where Y is a fixed bit-pattern and Z is an arbitrary bit-pattern *i.e.*, $Z \in [0x0 \ldots 0, 0xF \ldots F]$. Hence, enforcing that memory accesses are within the sandbox range of addresses can be efficiently implemented by a *masking* operation which exploits the binary representation of pointers: it retains the lowest bits Z and sets the highest bits to the bit-pattern Y.

Traditionally, the SFI transformation is performed at the binary level and is followed by an *a posteriori* verification by a trusted SFI verifier [23,31,35]. Because the verifier can assume that the code has undergone the SFI transformation, it can be kept simple (almost syntactic), thereby reducing both verification time and the Trusted Computing Base (TCB). This approach to SFI can be viewed as a simple instance of Proof Carrying Code [25] where the compiler is untrusted and the binary verifier is either trusted or verified.

Traditional SFI is well suited for executing binary code from an untrusted origin that must, for an adequate user experience, start running as soon as possible. Google's Native Client [30,37] is a state-of-the-art SFI implementation which has been deployed in the Chrome web browser for isolating binary code in untrusted pages. ARMor [39] features the first fully verified SFI implementation where the TCB is reduced to the formal ARM semantics in the HOL proof-assistant [9]. RockSalt [24] is a formally verified implementation of an SFI verifier for the x86 architecture, demonstrating that an efficient binary verifier can be obtained from a machine-checked specification.

1.2 Software Fault Isolation Through Compilation

A downside of the traditional SFI approach is that it hinders most compiler optimisations because the optimised code no longer respects the simple properties that the SFI verifier is capable of checking. For example, the SFI verifier expects that every memory access is immediately preceded by a specific syntactic code pattern that implements the sandboxing operation. A semantically equivalent but syntactically different code sequence would be rejected. An alternative to the *a posteriori* binary verifier approach is Portable Software Fault Isolation (PSFI), proposed by Kroll *et al.* [16]. In this methodology, there is no verifier to trust. Instead isolation is obtained by compilation with a machine-checked compiler, such as CompCert [18]. Portability comes from the fact that PSFI can reuse existing compiler back-ends and therefore target all the architectures supported by the compiler without additional effort.

PSFI is applicable in scenarios where the source code is available or the binary code is provided by a trusted third-party that controls the build process. For example, the original motivation for Proof Carrying Code [25] was to provide safe kernel extensions [26] as binary code to replace scripts written in an interpreted language. This falls within the scope of PSFI. Another PSFI scenario is when the binary code is produced in a controlled environment and/or by a trusted party. In this case, the primary goal is not to protect against an attacker trying to insert malicious code but to prevent honest parties from exposing a host platform to exploitable bugs. This is the case *e.g.* in the avionics industry, where software from different third-parties is integrated on the same host that needs to ensure strong isolation properties between tasks whose levels of criticality differ. In those cases, PSFI can deliver both security and a performance advantage. In Sect. 8, we provide experimental evidence that PSFI is competitive and sometimes outperforms SFI in terms of efficiency of the binary code.

1.3 Challenges in Formally Verified SFI

PSFI inserts the masking operations during compilation and does away with the *a posteriori* SFI verifier. The challenge is then to ensure that the security, enforced at an intermediate representation of the code, still holds for the running code. Indeed, compiler optimisation often breaks such security [33]. The insight of Kroll *et al.* is that a safety theorem of the compiled code (i.e., that its behaviour is well-defined) can be exploited to obtain a security theorem for that same compiled code, guaranteeing that it makes no memory accesses outside its sandbox. We explain this in more detail in Sect. 2.2.

One challenge we face with this approach is that it is far from evident that the sandboxing operations and hence the transformed program have well-defined behaviour. An unsafe language such as C admits undefined behaviours (e.g. bitwise operations on pointers), which means that it is possible for the observational behaviour of a program to differ depending on the level of optimisation. This is not a compiler bug: compilers only guarantee semantics preservation *if* the code to compile has a well-defined semantics [36]. Therefore, our SFI transformation must turn any program into a program with a well-defined semantics.

The seminal paper of Kroll *et al.* emphasises that the absence of undefined behaviour is a prerequisite but they do not provide a transformation that enforces this property. More precisely, their transformation may produce a program with undefined behaviours (*e.g.* because the input program had undefined behaviours). This fact was one of the motivation for the present work, and explains the need for a new PSFI technique. One difficulty is to remove undefined behaviours due to restrictions on pointer arithmetic. For example, bitwise operators on pointers have undefined C semantics, but traditional masking operations of SFI rely heavily on these operators. Another difficulty is to deal with indirect function calls and ensure that, as prescribed by the C standard, they are resolved to valid function pointers. To tackle these problems, we propose an original sandboxing transformation which unlike previous proposals is compliant with the C standard [13] and therefore has well-defined behaviour.

1.4 Contributions

We have developed and proved correct CompCertSfi, the first full-fledged, fully verified implementation of SFI inside a C compiler. The SFI transformation is performed early in the compilation chain, thereby permitting the generated code to benefit from existing optimisations that are performed by the back-end. The technical contributions behind CompCertSfi can be summarised as follows.

- An original design and implementation of the SFI transformation based on well-defined pointer arithmetic and which supports function pointers. This novel design of the SFI transformation is necessary for the safety proof.
- A machine-checked proof of the **security** and **safety** of the SFI transformation. Our formal development is available online [1].
- A small, lightweight runtime system for managing the sandbox, built using a standard program loader and configured by compiler-generated information.
- Experimental evidence demonstrating that the portable SFI approach is competitive and sometimes even outperforms traditional SFI, in particular state-of-the-art implementations of (P)Native Client.

The rest of the paper is organised as follows. In Sect. 2, we present background information about the CompCert compiler (Sect. 2.1) and the PSFI approach (Sect. 2.2). Section 3 provides an overview of the layout of the sandbox and the masking operations implementing our SFI. In Sect. 4 we explain how to overcome the problem with undefined pointer arithmetic and define masking operations with a well-defined C semantics. Section 5 describes how control-flow integrity in the presence of function pointers can be achieved by a sligthly more flexible SFI policy which allows reads in well-defined areas outside the sandbox. Section 6 specifies the SFI policy in more detail, and describes the formal Coq proofs of safety and security. Section 7 presents the design of our runtime library and how it exploits compiler support. Experimental results are detailed in Sect. 8. Section 9 presents related work and Sect. 10 concludes.

2 Background

This section presents background information about the CompCert compiler [18] and the Portable Software Fault Isolation proposed by Kroll *et al.* [16].

2.1 CompCert

The CompCert compiler [18] is a machine-checked compiler programmed and proved correct using the Coq proof-assistant [22]. It compiles C programs down

$$\begin{aligned}
constant \ni c &::= i32 \mid i64 \mid f32 \mid f64 \mid \&gl \mid \&stk \\
chunk \ni \kappa &::= is_8 \mid iu_8 \mid is_{16} \mid iu_{16} \mid i_{32} \mid i_{64} \mid f_{32} \mid f_{64} \\
expr \ni e &::= x \mid c \mid \triangleright e \mid e_1 \Box e_2 \mid [e]_\kappa \\
stmt \ni s &::= \mathbf{skip} \mid x := e \mid [e_1]_\kappa := e_2 \mid \mathbf{return}\ e \mid x := e(e_1 \ldots, e_n)_\sigma \\
&\mid \mathbf{if}\ e\ \mathbf{then}\ s_1\ \mathbf{else}\ s_2 \mid s_1; s_2 \mid \mathbf{loop}\ s \mid \{s\} \mid \mathbf{exit}\ n \mid \mathbf{goto}\ lb
\end{aligned}$$

Fig. 1. CMINOR syntax

to assembly code through a succession of compiler passes which are shown to be semantics preserving. COMPCERT features an architecture independent front-end. The back-end supports four main architectures: x86, ARM, PowerPC and RiscV. To target all the back-ends without additional effort, our secure transformation is performed in the compiler front-end, at the level of the CMINOR language that is the last architecture-independent language of the COMPCERT compiler chain. Our transformation can obviously be applied on C programs by first compiling them into CMINOR, and then applying the transformation itself.

The CMINOR language is a minimal imperative language with explicit stack allocation of certain local variables [19]. Its syntax is given in Fig. 1. Constants range over 32-bit and 64-bit integers but also IEEE floating-point numbers. It is possible to get the address of a global variable *gl* or the address of the stack allocated local variables (i.e., *stk* denotes the address of the current stack frame). In COMPCERT parlance, a memory chunk κ specifies how many bytes need to be read (resp. written) from (resp. to) memory and whether the result should be interpreted as a signed or unsigned quantity. For instance, the memory chunk is_{16} denotes a 16-bit signed integer and f_{64} denotes a 64-bit floating-point number. In CMINOR, memory accesses, written $[e]_\kappa$, are annotated with the relevant memory chunk κ. Expressions are built from pseudo-registers, constants, unary ($\triangleright$) and binary ($\Box$) operators. COMPCERT features the relevant unary and binary operators needed to encode the semantics of C. Expressions are side-effect free but may contain memory reads.

Instructions are fairly standard. Similarly to a memory read, a memory store $[e_1]_\kappa = e_2$ is annotated by a memory chunk κ. In CMINOR, a function call such as $e(e_1 \ldots, e_n)_\sigma$ represents an indirect function call through a function pointer denoted by the expression e, σ is the signature of the function and $e_1 \ldots, e_n$ are the arguments. A direct call is a special case where the expression e is a constant (function) pointer. CMINOR is a structured language and features a conditional, a block construct $\{s\}$ and an infinite loop **loop** s. Exiting the nth enclosing loop or block can be done using an **exit** n instruction. CMINOR is structured but **goto**s towards a symbolic label *lb* are also possible. Returning from a function is done by a return instruction. CMINOR is equipped with a small-step operational semantics. The intra-procedural and inter-procedural control flows are modelled using an explicit continuation which therefore contains a call stack.

CompCert Soundness Theorem. Each compiler pass is proved to be semantics preserving using a simulation argument. Theorem 1 states semantics preservation.

Theorem 1 (Semantics Preservation). *If the compilation of program p succeeds and generates a target program tp, then for any behaviour beh of program tp there exists a behaviour of p, beh′, such that beh* improves *beh′.*

In this statement, a behaviour is a trace of observable events that are typically generated when performing external function calls. CompCert classifies behaviours depending on whether the program terminates normally, diverges or goes wrong. A *goes wrong* behaviour corresponds to a situation where the program semantics gets stuck (i.e., has an undefined behaviour). In this situation, the compiler has the liberty to generate a program with an *improved* behaviour i.e., the semantics of the transformed program may be more defined (i.e., it may not get stuck at all or may get stuck later on).

The consequence is that Theorem 1 is not sufficient to preserve a safety property because the target program *tp* may have behaviours that are not accounted for in the program *p* and could therefore violate the property. Corollary 1 states that in the absence of going-wrong behaviour, the behaviours of the target program are a subset of the behaviours of the source program.

Corollary 1 (Safety preservation). *Let p be a program and tp be a target program. Consider that none of the behaviours of p is a going-wrong behaviour. If the compilation of p succeeds and generates a target program tp, then any behaviour of program tp is a behaviour of p.*

As a consequence, any (safety) property of the behaviours of *p* is preserved by the target program *tp*. In Sect. 2.2, we show how the PSFI approach leverages Corollary 1 to transfer an isolation property obtained at the Cminor level to the assembly code.

Going-wrong behaviours in CompCert. As safety is an essential property of our PSFI transformation, we give below a detailed account of the going-wrong behaviours of the CompCert languages with a focus on Cminor.

Undefined evaluation of expressions. CompCert's runtime values are dynamically typed and defined below:

$$values \ni v ::= \mathbf{undef} \mid \mathbf{int}(i_{32}) \mid \mathbf{long}(i_{64}) \mid \mathbf{single}(f_{32}) \mid \mathbf{float}(f_{64}) \mid \mathbf{ptr}(b, o)$$

Values are built from numeric values (32-bit and 64-bit integers and floating point numbers), the **undef** value representing an indeterminate value, and pointer values made of a pair (b, o) where b is a memory block identifier and o is an offset which, depending on the architecture, is either a 32-bit or a 64-bit integer.

For Cminor, like all languages of CompCert, the unary ($\triangleright$) and binary ($\square$) operators are not total. They may directly produce going-wrong behaviours *e.g.* in case of division by $\mathbf{int}(0)$. They may also return **undef** if (i) the arguments are not in the right range *e.g.* the left-shift $\mathbf{int}(i) << \mathbf{int}(32)$; or (ii) the arguments are not well-typed *e.g.* $\mathbf{int}(i) +_{int} \mathbf{float}(f)$. Pointer arithmetic is strictly conforming to the C standard [13] and any pointer operation that is implementation-defined according to the standard returns **undef**.

$$
\begin{array}{lll}
\mathbf{ptr}(b,o) \pm \mathbf{long}(l) & = \mathbf{ptr}(b, o \pm l) & \\
\mathbf{ptr}(b,o) - \mathbf{ptr}(b,o') & = \mathbf{long}(o - o') & \\
\mathbf{ptr}(b,o) \,!\!= \mathbf{long}(0) & = \mathbf{tt} & \text{if } W(b,o) \\
\mathbf{ptr}(b,o) == \mathbf{long}(0) & = \mathbf{ff} & \text{if } W(b,o) \\
\mathbf{ptr}(b,o) \star \mathbf{ptr}(b,o') & = o \star o' & \text{if } W(b,o) \wedge W(b,o') \\
\mathbf{ptr}(b,o) == \mathbf{ptr}(b',o') & = \mathbf{ff} & \text{if } b \neq b' \wedge V(b,o) \wedge V(b',o') \\
\mathbf{ptr}(b,o) \,!\!= \mathbf{ptr}(b',o') & = \mathbf{tt} & \text{if } b \neq b' \wedge V(b,o) \wedge V(b',o') \\
\multicolumn{3}{c}{\text{where } \star \in \{<, \leq, ==, \geq, >, !=\}}
\end{array}
$$

Fig. 2. Pointer arithmetic in CompCert

The precise semantics of pointer operations is given in Fig. 2. For simplicity, we provide the semantics for a 64-bit architecture. Pointer operations are often only defined provided that the pointers are valid, written V, or weakly valid, written W. This validity condition requires that the offset o of a pointer $\mathbf{ptr}(b, o)$ is strictly within the bounds of the block b. The weakly valid condition refers to a pointer whose offset is either valid or one-past-the-end of the block b. Any pointer arithmetic operation that is not listed in Fig. 2 returns **undef**. This is in particular the case for bitwise operations which are typically used for the masking operation needed to implement SFI.

The indeterminate value **undef** is not *per se* a going-wrong behaviour. Yet, branching over a test evaluating to **undef**, performing a memory access over an **undef** address and returning **undef** from the `main` function are going-wrong behaviours.

Memory accesses are ruled by a unified memory model [20] that is used throughout the whole compiler. The memory is made of a collection of separated blocks. For a given block, each offset o below the block size is given a permission $p \in \{\mathbf{r}, \mathbf{w}, \dots\}$ and contains a memory value

$$
mval \ni mv ::= \mathbf{undef} \mid \mathbf{byte}(b) \mid [\mathbf{ptr}(b,o)]_n
$$

where b is a concrete byte value and $[\mathbf{ptr}(b,o)]_n$ represents the nth byte of the pointer $\mathbf{ptr}(b,o)$ for $n \in \{1 \dots 8\}$. A memory write $storev(\kappa, m, a, v)$ is only defined if the address a is a pointer $\mathbf{ptr}(b,o)$ to an existing block b such that the memory locations $(b,o), \dots, (b, o+ \mid \kappa \mid -1)$ have the permission $\mathbf{w}$ and the offset o satisfies the alignment constraint of κ. A memory read $loadv(\kappa, m, a)$ is only defined under similar conditions with the additional restriction that not reading all the consecutive fragments of a pointer returns **undef**.

Control-flow transfers may go-wrong if the target of the control-flow transfer is not well-defined. Hence, a **goto** lb instruction goes wrong if, in the current function, there is no statement labelled by lb; and an **exit** n instruction goes wrong if there are less than n enclosing blocks around the statement containing the exit instruction. A conditional **if** e **then** s_1 **else** s_2 goes wrong if the expression e does not evaluate to $\mathbf{int}(i)$ for some i. Also, the execution goes wrong if the last statement of a function is not a **return** instruction. Last but not least, a function call $x := e(e_1 \ldots, e_n)_\sigma$ goes wrong if the expression e does not evaluate to a pointer $\mathbf{ptr}(b, 0)$ where b is a function pointer with signature σ.

We show in Sect. 4 how our transformation ensures that pointer arithmetic and memory accesses are always well-defined. Section 5 shows how we make sure indirect calls are always correctly resolved. Section 6 shows that, together with other statically checkable verifications, our PSFI transformation rules out all possible going-wrong behaviours.

2.2 Portable Software Fault Isolation

Kroll, Stewart and Appel have pioneered the concept of Portable Software Fault Isolation (PSFI) [16] whereby SFI is enforced by a pass of the compiler front-end that is architecture independent. The main expected advantage is that isolation is implemented, once and for all, for any target architecture. Moreover, the generated code is optimised by the back-end passes of the compiler. Compared to traditional SFI, there is no architecture-specific binary verifier but instead the compiler enters the TCB. The key insight of Kroll *et al.* is to leverage a formally verified compiler, namely CompCert, to transfer a security proof of isolation obtained at the Cminor level through the compiler back-end, with minimal proof effort. In the following, we recall the only basic properties that a Cminor SFI transformation needs to satisfy so that isolation holds at assembly level.

In CompCert's terms, the sandbox is identified by a dedicated memory block sb. A Cminor program is secure (Property 1) under the condition that all its memory accesses are performed within the sandbox.

Property 1 (Program security). A Cminor program p is secure if all its memory accesses are within the sandbox block sb.

After compilation, the assembly code is secure if its observable behaviours are the same as the observable behaviours of the Cminor program. In order to apply CompCert's semantics preservation theorem (more precisely Corollary 1), it remains to ensure that the Cminor program has a well-defined semantics (Property 2).

Property 2 (Program safety). A Cminor program p is safe if all its behaviours are well-defined, i.e., not wrong.

Kroll *et al.* state Property 1 by means of an instrumented Cminor semantics which gets stuck in case of memory accesses outside the sandbox. They prove formally that the additional semantic safeguards are never triggered for a transformed program.

Kroll *et al.* also sketch some necessary steps to prove the Property 2 of safety but do not propose a formal proof. This leaves open a number of challenging issues such as whether it is feasible to define a masking operation that has a defined Cminor semantics and how to deal with indirect function calls through function pointers, More generally, the work leaves open whether a formal proof of Property 2 on safety is possible given the restrictions of CompCert's semantics (notably pointer arithmetic) and without relying on axioms asserting properties of an external masking primitive. One of the central contributions of this work is to provide a positive answer to this question and propose solutions to these issues where neither the sandboxing of memory accesses nor the sandboxing of function pointers is part of a TCB. The transformation that circumvents the limitations imposed by pointer arithmetic is original and, we surmise, is a necessary component to transfer security down to assembly. For a precise comparison with Kroll *et al.* see Sect. 9).

3 A Thread-Aware Sandbox

The memory address space of a C program is partitioned into a runtime stack of frames, a heap and a dedicated space for global variables. The address space of a sandboxed program is re-organised to fit into a single global variable, *sb*, where the global variables, the heap and the stack frames are relocated. Figure 3a depicts the memory layout of the program after our SFI transformation. Each global variable is relocated and allocated in the sandbox at a given offset, and each global memory access of the program is translated into a memory access in the sandbox. For managing the heap it suffices to use a sandbox-aware `malloc` implementation that allocates memory inside the sandbox.

To prevent buffer overflows, a standard approach consists in introducing a so-called *shadow stack* that is used to store the function stack frames. Our implementation supports multi-threaded applications and therefore there are as many shadow stacks as there are threads. Upon thread creation, we allocate a novel shadow stack in the sandbox. The shadow-stack pointer is passed as an additional argument to each function call. This is efficient when arguments are passed by register, with the only drawback of reserving an additional register. Frames are allocated by incrementing the shadow-stack pointer at function entry. All accesses to the original stack are then translated into accesses to the sandbox shadow stack. The following Example 1 and the code snippet in Fig. 3 illustrate the essence of the transformation.

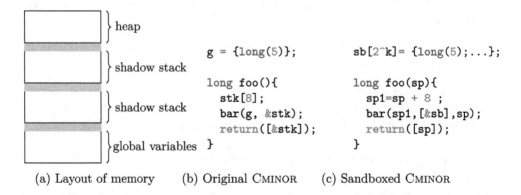

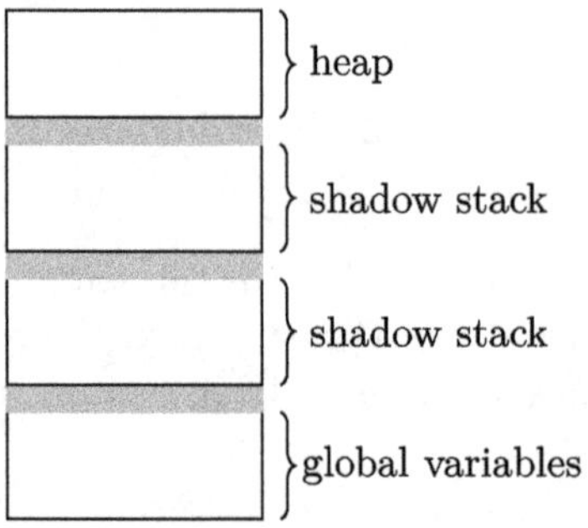

(a) Layout of memory

```
g = {long(5)};

long foo(){
  stk[8];
  bar(g, &stk);
  return([&stk]);
}
```

(b) Original CMINOR

```
sb[2^k]= {long(5);...};

long foo(sp){
  sp1=sp + 8 ;
  bar(sp1,[&sb],sp);
  return([sp]);
}
```

(c) Sandboxed CMINOR

Fig. 3. Sandbox transformation

Example 1. The CMINOR program of Fig. 3b declares a global variable `g` initialised to the 64-bit integer 5. The function `foo` allocates a stack frame of 8 bytes that will be used to store a 64-bit local variable. By convention, the current stack frame is called `stk`. The function `foo` calls the function `bar` with as arguments the value of `g` and the address of the local variable `stk`; and returns the value, presumably updated by `bar`, of the local variable.

Syntactically, the program of Fig. 3c only performs memory accesses on the global sandbox `sb` variable. The size of `sb` variable is 2^k for some predefined k. At thread creation, a shadow stack is allocated by our sandbox-aware `malloc` in the sandbox after the statically allocated global variables. For our program, the unique global variable `g` is stored at offset 0 and spans over 8 bytes. Therefore, the initial value of the shadow-stack pointer `sp` is 8. After the transformation, the function `foo` reserves the space for the local variable `stk` by incrementing the pseudo-register `sp`. The function `bar` is called with the incremented shadow-stack pointer `sp1`, the value stored at offset 0 in the sandbox (i.e., the value of the global variable `g`) and the address of the local variable `stk` which is given by the value of the stack pointer `sp`. At function exit, the value of the local variable `stk` is returned by dereferencing the shadow-stack pointer `sp`.

Our SFI transformation enforces the isolation security policy stipulating that all memory accesses are performed within the sandbox *sb*—at the CMINOR level. However, this holds because the semantics gets stuck (i.e., the semantics *goes wrong*) whenever the program performs an access outside the bounds of the sandbox. As explained earlier, the compiler is free to translate this into an insecure program that would escape the sandbox at runtime. To get a formal security guarantee, it is necessary to transform further the CMINOR program to rule out any behaviour that *goes wrong* i.e., ensure Property 2. Given the numerous undefined behaviours of the C language, ruling out any *going-wrong* behaviour may seem a daunting task. In general, this requires to ensure both memory safety and control-flow integrity. The following two sections describe how we can exploit the SFI transformation and the knowledge that all memory accesses are inside the sandbox to ensure both memory safety and control-flow integrity.

4 Memory-Safe Masking

For SFI, memory safety is obtained by making sure that every memory access is performed inside the sandbox. Starting from an analysis of the standard SFI solution, we present our own design which satisfies the additional requirements of being compliant with the semantic restrictions of COMPCERT and with a strict interpretation of the C standard.

4.1 Standard SFI Masking of Addresses

Standard SFI transformations ensure memory safety by masking memory accesses. The gist of it is to allocate a sandbox *sb* of size 2^k at a 2^k aligned memory address, say $\&sb = tag \times 2^k$. Under those constraints, enforcing that an address A is within the bounds of the sandbox can essentially be done by replacing the high-address bits by those of *tag*. Using bitwise operations, this can be done by the expression $(A\&(2^k-1))|tag \times 2^k$, where & is the bitwise *and* and | is the bitwise *or*. More visually, this can be written $(A\&\underbrace{1\cdots1}_{k})|tag\underbrace{0\cdots0}_{k}$.

At binary level, this masking transformation is defined and the cost is modest: two bitwise operations. However, this masking operation has no well-defined C semantics. This is also the case for the semantics of CompCert and in particular for the Cminor language. The reason is twofold: bitwise operations over pointer values return **undef** and concrete addresses (e.g. $tag \times 2^k$) are not pointers for CompCert where they are represented by a block and an offset (see Fig. 2).

4.2 Specialised Masking for 32-Bit Sandboxes

For 32-bit sandboxes, there exists a variant of the sandboxing primitive which has the advantages (1) that the sandbox address does not need to be aligned; (2) that the cost of masking may be reduced to a single instruction. In its simplest form, the masking primitive is defined by

$$\&sb + (A - \&sb)_{64 \to 32 \to 64}$$

where $\&sb$ is the symbolic address of the sandbox. The subtraction of $\&sb$ extracts the offset of the pointer and the double (unsigned) cast $64 \to 32 \to 64$ has the effect of truncating the offset to a 32-bit quantity that is therefore within the bounds of a 32-bit sandbox. At first sight, this masking is less efficient than the standard masking but it is efficient for typical address computations which require both displacement and scaling (e.g. $A = t + k + k' * i_{32 \to 64}$ where t is a 64-bit address, k and k' are constants and i is a 32-bit integer). Assuming that each cast or arithmetic operation is mapped to a single instruction[1], the masked address A can be computed using 8 instructions: 4 instructions for computing the address A and 4 more for the sandboxing primitive. Using simple properties of modular arithmetic, it is possible to distribute the $64 \to 32$ cast over addition and multiplication to obtain the following equivalent formulation of the sandboxed address:

$$\&sb + A'_{32 \to 64} \quad with \quad A' = t_{64 \to 32} + c_1 + c_2 * i$$

where c_1 and c_2 are compile-time constants: $c_1 = (k - \&sb)_{64 \to 32}$ and $c_2 = k'_{64 \to 32}$. Using this formulation, the address A' still requires 4 instructions but the cost of the sandboxing is reduced to 2 instructions making it on par with the standard sandboxing. On x86, 32-bit registers are just zero-extended 64-bit registers. Therefore, the cast $A'_{32 \to 64}$ is actually redundant and the overhead induced by the sandboxing is reduced to a single instruction. Our experiments (see Sect. 8.2) validate the practical advantage of this encoding.

Still, as for the standard sandboxing, this sanboxing primitive has no semantics in CompCert due to the limitations of pointer arithmetic. As a consequence, the solution of Kroll *et al.* [16] does not give actual code for the masking primitive, but rather axiomatise its behaviour as an external function. This prevents optimisations such as common subexpression elimination or function inlining from happening and induces the cost of a function call for each memory access.

4.3 Towards Well-Defined Pointer Arithmetic

To illustrate the limitations of pointer arithmetic, we examine the semantic behaviour of the standard sandboxing primitive (the specialised sandboxing primitive has similar

[1] Some architecture have rich addressing modes allowing for more compact encodings.

issues). The standard sandboxing primitive can be written $(A\&(2^k-1)) \mid \&sb$ where $\&sb$ is the address of the sandbox variable. If sb is allocated at runtime at address $tag \times 2^k$ for some tag, this formulation is equivalent at binary level. Again, this heavily relies on pointer arithmetic that is undefined and on information about where the sandbox is linked at runtime.

Consider the alternative formulation $(A\&(2^k-1)) + \&sb$ where the bitwise $\mid$ is replaced by a $+$. This formulation has the advantage that incrementing a pointer, here sb, is well-defined (see Fig. 2). As on modern hardware, both addition and bitwise operations take a single cycle, the difference in efficiency should be negligible. Moreover, at least for x86, the addition can be compiled into the addressing mode.

Still, this does not solve our issue. To understand this, suppose that A is a pointer. In this case, the bitwise &, whose purpose is to extract the pointer offset, is still undefined. Therefore, the whole expression $(A\&(2^k-1)) + \&sb$ is undefined. Because dereferencing an undefined expression is a *going-wrong* behaviour, the compiled program may have an arbitrary runtime behaviour and escape the sandbox. A prerequisite for our masking primitive is therefore to ensure that the evaluation is defined i.e., different from **undef**. As all the semantic operators of CompCert are strict in **undef** (if any argument is **undef**, so is the result), a necessary condition is that A is not **undef**. As A can be obtained from any expression, a challenge is to ensure that every expression evaluates to a defined value. A particular difficulty is that the many undefined pointer operations (see Fig. 2) cannot be detected by runtime checks.

4.4 Arithmetisation of the Heap

To tackle this challenge and ensure that every computation is defined, we propose an original and radical approach which ensures syntactically that pointers are neither stored in memory nor in local variables. As a result, the program is only manipulating integer values and memory addresses are only constructed by the sandboxing primitives. This approach implies, as a side-effect, that our previously undefined masking primitives are defined. Let asb be the runtime address of the symbolic address $\&sb$ of the sandbox. The masking of an address A can be written

$$A' + \&sb$$

where A' is either defined by $A' = A\&(2^k-1)$ or $A' = (A - asb)_{64\to 32\to 64}$. As A is necessarily an integer, A' is necessarily a defined integer and therefore $A' + \&sb$ returns a defined pointer $\mathbf{ptr}(sb, o)$ that is necessarily inside the sandbox.

An additional subtlety is that memory accesses are indexed by a memory chunk κ which mandates an alignment constraint (e.g. the chunk i_{64} mandates an 8-byte aligned address). As a result, the masking primitive is parameterised by the chunk κ and the masking primitive for i_{64} is $A'\&msk_{i_{64}} + \&sb$ where $msk_{i_{64}} = (2^{k-3}-1) \times 2^3$.

Only computing over numeric values is facilitated by the fact that the sandboxed program is only manipulating pointers relative to a single object, the sandbox. Therefore, a solution could be to only compute with pointer offsets. This is not totally satisfactory because the null pointer (i.e., 0) would be undistinguishable from the base pointer $\mathbf{ptr}(sb, 0)$. Instead, we use the integer asb that is the integer runtime address of the sandbox (i.e., we have $asb = \&sb$) and perform the following transformation t over program expressions.

$$
\begin{aligned}
t(\&sb) &= asb \\
t(c) &= c \text{ for } c \in \{i32, i64, f32, f64\} \\
t(\triangleright e) &= \blacktriangleright t(e) \\
t(e_1 \Box e_2) &= t(e_1) \blacksquare t(e_2) \\
t([e]_\kappa) &= [msk_\kappa(t(e))]
\end{aligned}
$$

The operators ▶ and ■ ensure that, if the expressions are well-typed, they never return the **undef** value. Typical examples include division, modulus, and bitwise shifts. We transform expressions so that they evaluate to an arbitrary value when their original semantics is undefined. For example, we transform the left-shift operations on 32-bit integers so that the resulting expression always has a shift amount less than 32:

```
a«b   ⇝   a « (b & 31).
```

Similarly, we transform divisions and modulus in the following way, to rule out the undefined cases of division by zero and signed division of `MIN_SIGNED` by `-1`:

```
a/b ⇝ (a+(a==MIN_SIGNED & b==-1))/(b+(b==0)).
```

We can prove that the resulting division expression is always defined. Most of the other expressions are always defined and do not need further transformations.

5 Enforcement of Control-Flow Integrity

Correct sandboxing of code requires some degree of control-flow integrity. Existing SFI implementations enforce a weak form of control-flow integrity which only ensures that jumps are aligned and within a sandbox of code. This is achieved by inserting a masking operation before indirect jumps, that will mask the target address to ensure that the jump is within the sandbox. Additional padding with no-ops is inserted to ensure that all the instructions are indeed aligned [30,37,38]. We enforce a stronger, more traditional, form of control-flow integrity where any control-flow transfer has a well-defined CMINOR semantics.

5.1 Relaxation of the CMINOR SFI Property

Intraprocedural control-flow integrity is ensured by simple syntactic checks. For instance, they ensure that a **goto** *lb* has a corresponding label *lb* and that an **exit** n has at least n enclosing blocks. The semantics of CMINOR prescribes that function calls and returns necessarily match. For this to still hold at the assembly level where the return address is explicitly stored in the stack frame, it is sufficient to prove that the CMINOR program has no *going-wrong* behaviour. To ensure control-flow integrity, the only remaining issue is due to indirect calls through function pointers. Our control-flow integrity counter-measure implements software trampolines and ensures that an indirect call with signature σ can only be resolved by a function pointer towards a function with signature σ.

For this purpose, the existing CMINOR SFI security policy i.e., Property 1, which rules out any memory access outside the sandbox is too restrictive. As we shall see, the implementation of trampolines necessitates controlled memory reads, outside the sandbox, within compiler-generated variables. To accommodate for this extension, we propose a slightly relaxed SFI security property which, in addition to memory accesses inside the sandbox, authorises other memory reads in read-only regions.

Property 3. A CMINOR program is secure if all its memory accesses are within either the sandbox block *sb* or some read-only memory.

This relaxed property still ensures the integrity of the runtime because all memory writes are confined to the sandbox. Note that Property 3 and Property 1 are equivalent if the trusted runtime library has no read-only memory. This can be achieved at modest cost by modifying slightly the source code and remove the C type qualifier `const` which instructs the compiler that the memory is read-only.

5.2 Control-Flow Integrity of Indirect Calls

In Sect. 4, we have eluded the presence of function pointers. They actually perfectly fit our strategy of encoding pointers by integers. In this case, each function pointer is encoded as an index and the trampoline code translates the index into a valid function pointer.

Consider a function f of signature σ and suppose that the function pointer $\&f$ is compiled into the index i. The reverse mapping from indexes to function pointers is obtained from a compiler-generated array variable A_σ such that $A_\sigma[i] = \&f$. The array variable A_σ is made of all the function pointers with signature σ. The array variable is also padded with a default function pointer such that its length is a power of two. At the call site, the instruction $e(e_1 \ldots, e_n)_\sigma$ is transformed into $[te\&msk_\sigma + \&A_\sigma](te_1, \ldots, te_n)_\sigma$ where $te, te_1 \ldots, te_n$ are transformed expressions such that all memory accesses are masked and msk_σ is the binary mask ensuring that the index te is within the bounds of the variable A_σ. In our actual implementation, we optimise direct calls and in this case bypass the trampoline. Therefore, when the expression e is a constant pointer $\&f$ to an existing function with signature σ, we generate directly $(\&f)(te_1 \ldots, te_n)$. As a result, only C code using indirect calls goes through the trampoline code.

Though our implementation only exploits the relaxation of Property 3 for the sake of trampolines, a more aggressive implementation could sometimes avoid to relocate read-only memory inside the sandbox. This could have a positive impact on optimisations which exploit the immutability of read-only memory.

6 Safety and Security Proofs

We next give an overview of our fully verified Coq proof of security and safety.

6.1 Security Proof

Property 3 is an informal formulation of our security property that is formally stated as a CMINOR instrumented semantics. This semantics mimics the CMINOR semantics with the exception that memory accesses are restricted: a memory read is either performed within the sandbox or in a read-only memory region; a memory write is necessarily performed within the sandbox.

The goal of the security proof is to show that all the memory accesses abide by the restrictions of the instrumented semantics. This is stated by Theorem 2 which establishes that for a transformed program *tp*, no behaviour of the standard CMINOR semantics gets stuck for the instrumented CMINOR semantics.

Theorem 2 (Security). *For any transformed program tp, every behaviour of tp in the standard semantics of* CMINOR *is also a behaviour of tp in the instrumented semantics.*

The proof is based on the standard technique of forward simulation that is used in COMPCERT to ensure the preservation of semantics by compiler passes. Here, the forward simulation has the distinctive feature of relating the same (transformed) program equipped with a standard and an instrumented semantics. Since the only difference between the two semantics is that memory accesses must be secure, the crux of the proof lies in the correctness of the masking primitive, as stated in the following lemma.

Lemma 1. *For any masked expression e, if e evaluates to some pointer* $\mathbf{ptr}(b, o)$*, then b is the block of the sandbox i.e., sb.*

The proof relies on the definition of the masking primitive: a masked expression e is of the form $e' + \&sb$. Since $\&sb$ evaluates to the pointer $\mathbf{ptr}(sb, 0)$, then if the whole expression evaluates to a pointer $\mathbf{ptr}(b, o)$, necessarily $b = sb$.

6.2 Safety Proof

In order to benefit from COMPCERT's semantic preservation theorem and transport our security proof to the compiled assembly program, we must also prove that the sandboxed program is safe, i.e., it never gets *stuck*. We address all the going-wrong behaviours that we enumerated in Sect. 2.1. The well-formedness properties of a program (calling only defined functions, accessing only defined variables, jumping only to defined labels, exiting from no more blocks than currently enclosed in) are checked statically and make the transformation fail if they are violated. Next, the memory accesses require the addresses to be valid and adequately aligned: our masking operation ensures that this is always the case. Then, the evaluation of expressions must always be defined: this has mostly been dealt with the arithmetisation of the memory (Sect. 4.4). Finally, function calls should always be performed with the appropriate number of well-typed arguments. This is easy to check statically for direct function calls, but requires trampolines (as described in Sect. 5.2) for indirect function calls. The following sandbox invariant encapsulates all these conditions.

Definition 1 (Sandbox Invariant). *A state S of program P satisfies the sandbox invariant if the following conditions are satisfied:*

1. *indirect control-flow transfers are well-defined in P (e.g.* `goto` *instructions in the functions of P only jump to defined labels);*
2. *every function of P ends with an explicit return;*
3. *every function of P is well-typed;*
4. *every function of P starts by explicitly initialising its local variables;*
5. *the global array* A_σ *for signature* σ *contains function pointers to functions of signature* σ*;*
6. *the environment for local variables and the memory in S only contain properly initialised, numerical values.*

Properties 1, 2, 3 are ensured by a set of syntactic checks over the bodies of all the functions of the program. Property 4 is enforced by our function transformation which inserts assignments that explicitly initialise all declared local variables. Property 5 is ensured by construction of the arrays for function pointers. All these properties can be established solely on the program body and do not change during the execution of the program. By contrast, Property 6 cannot be checked statically and depends on the state of the program at each point.

Safe Evaluation of Expressions. A necessary condition for the safe evaluation of expressions is that the program is well typed. CompCert does not generate these type guarantees so we have integrated a verified (simple) type-inference algorithm for Cminor programs. Type-checking alone is not sufficient to rule out undefined behaviours of C operators, but together with the transformations explained in Sect. 4.4, we prove the following lemma about the evaluation of transformed expressions.

Lemma 2 (Safe evaluation of expressions). *In a memory state and a well-typed environment for local variables containing only defined numerical values, the transformation of any well-typed expression e evaluates to a defined numerical value.*

Lemma 2 follows directly from the properties of our expression transformation.

Safety of Calls through Trampolines. As mentioned in Sect. 5, we implement software trampolines to secure function calls through function pointers. To ensure the safety of indirect function calls, we maintain a map *smap* from function signatures to the corresponding array identifier and the length of this array. The proof of safety relies on the fact that for every function f of signature σ present in a program, we have $smap(\sigma) = (A_\sigma, l_\sigma)$ such that all offsets lower than l_σ in A_σ contain a pointer to a function of signature σ. The safety proof of indirect calls itself is not hard, but we need to set up this signature map and establish invariants relating it to the global environment of the program.

Safety Theorem. Considering the invariants defined in Definition 1, we prove Lemma 3 which is our main technical result.

Lemma 3 (Safety). *For any* Cminor *program state S that satisfies the invariants, either S is a final state or there exists a sequence of steps from S to some S' such that S' also satisfies the invariants.*

A subtlety of the proof is that at function entry, the local variables carry the value **undef** and therefore the sandbox invariant only holds after they have been initialised by a sequence of assignments (see Property 4 of Definition 1).

Using Lemma 3, we can show Property 2, in the form of Theorem 3.

Theorem 3 (Safety of the transformation). *All behaviours of the transformed program are well-defined, i.e., not wrong.*

Proof. A going-wrong behaviour occurs precisely when a state is reached, from which no further step can be taken, though it is not a final state. Lemma 3, together with a proof that the initial state of the transformed prorgam satisfies the invariants, tells us that no such reachable state exists, concluding the proof. □

As a result, we benefit from CompCert's semantic preservation theorem and can transport the security proof down to the assembly program.

Theorem 4 (Security of the compiled program). *Let p be a transformed* Cminor *program. If p compiles into the assembly program tp, then tp is secure.*

The proof uses Corollary 1 and Theorem 2 to conclude that the behaviours of *tp* are the same as those of *p*, and hence secure.

7 SFI Runtime and Library

Our modified CompCert compiler, CompCertSfi, takes as input a C program unit in the form of a list of C files. Each C file is first compiled down to the Cminor language using the existing passes of the CompCert compiler. Then, all the Cminor programs are syntactically linked [14] together to form the program unit to be isolated inside the sandbox. CompCertSfi comes with a lightweight runtime and a generic support for interfacing with a trusted library (e.g. a libC). An originality of our approach is that the runtime is using a standard program loader. Moreover, the runtime gets some of its configuration through compiler-generated variables.

7.1 Loading the SFI Application

The sandboxed code is linked with our runtime library by a linker script which specifies where to load at runtime the *sb* variable, viewed as the data segment. The compiler also emits a sandbox configuration map which contains the symbolic address of the sandbox, its numeric value at runtime, the total size of the sandbox and the range of addresses reserved for global variables.

Our runtime code is executed before starting the sandboxed `main` function. It first checks that the sandbox is properly linked according to the sandbox configuration map, sets the shadow-stack pointer and initialises the sandbox heap using our sandbox-aware implementation of `malloc` based on `ptmalloc3`[2].

By construction, our runtime stack is free of buffer overruns. Yet, if the recursion is too deep, the stack may overflow. Therefore, the runtime inserts an unmapped page guard at the bottom of the stack and intercepts the segmentation fault. This protection suffices provided that the size of each function stack frame does not exceed a page; which can be checked at compile-time. Eventually, after copying its arguments inside the sandbox, the runtime calls the `main` function of the sandboxed application.

7.2 Monitoring Calls to the Runtime Library

The runtime library is trusted and therefore part of the TCB. To ensure isolation, each call towards the runtime library is monitored to check the validity of the arguments. For this purpose, a call to a library function, say `foo`, is renamed in the object file into a call to a function `sb_foo` which sanitises its arguments before really calling the function `foo`. The verifications are library specific but usually straightforward to implement. For `stdio`, the `FILE` structures are allocated by the runtime outside of the sandbox. Hence, the returned `FILE*` cannot be dereferenced to corrupt the `FILE` structure. To prevent the sandboxed program to forge `FILE*` pointers, the runtime maintains at all time the set of valid `FILE*`. For variadic functions *e.g.*, `printf`, we statically compile the format into a sequence of safe primitive calls. (We reject programs using formats computed at runtime). For functions in `string`, we check beforehand that the range of memory accesses is within the range of the sandbox. We also allow callbacks and therefore a runtime function may take a function pointer as argument. To ensure that the function is valid, the runtime is using the trampoline programming pattern presented in Sect. 5.2.

[2] http://www.malloc.de/malloc/ptmalloc3-current.tar.gz.

7.3 Communication via Global Variables

Programs may not only communicate *via* function calls but also directly *via* global variables. For the libC, this includes e.g. `stdout` or `errno`. To ensure isolation, CompCertSfi relocates those variables inside the sandbox but also generates a global variable map which is an array variable of the form

$$\{\&n_1, o_1, \ldots, \&n_i, o_i, \ldots, \&n_m, o_m\}$$

where $\&n_i$ is the symbolic address of a global variable and o_i is its offset in the sandbox. Using this information, the runtime has the ability to synchronise the values of the variables inside and outside the sandbox. For example, at program startup, the value of `stdout` (a `stream` pointer) is copied inside the sandbox at the relevant offset. This allows the sandboxed program to call `stdio` functions but protects the integrity of the stream. For `errno`, it is the responsibility of each runtime library call to synchronise the value of `errno` in the sandbox.

8 Experiments

We have evaluated our PSFI approach over the CompCert benchmark suite and a port of Quake. All the experiments have been carried over a quad-core Intel 6600U laptop at 2.6 GHz with 16 GB of RAM running Linux Fedora 27. For Quake, we explain how to adapt the code to our runtime library and verify the absence of noticeable slowdown. For the other benchmarks, we make a more detailed performance evaluation and compare CompCertSfi with CompCert, gcc, clang but also the state-of-the-art (P)NaCl implementation of SFI. In our experiments, all the benchmarks are ordered by increasing running time. Moreover, for computing a runtime overhead, the running time is obtained by taking the harmonic mean of 3 consecutive runs.

8.1 Porting Quake

Quake engines come in various flavours and we use the tyr-quake[3] implementation linking with Xlib. The port requires the addition of several functions to our runtime library from Xlib and the libC. Most of them are not problematic and require no or little modification. For instance, the `getopt` function which is used to parse command-line options is using the global variables `optarg`, `optind`, `opterr`, and `optopt`. As explained in Sect. 7.3, the runtime library copies the values of these variables at reserved places inside the sandbox.

Other functions, *e.g.* `gethostbyname`, allocate memory on their own and return a pointer to this piece of data which is therefore not accessible to the sandboxed code. For the specific case of `gethostbyname`, the library provides the function `gethostbyname_r` which, instead of allocating memory, takes as argument a data-structure that is filled by the function. In our case, we pass as argument a sandbox allocated piece of memory. This does not solve our problem entirely as inner pointers may still point outside the sandbox. To cope with this issue, we perform a deep copy of the relevant piece of data inside the sandbox.

A last issue is that the video memory is shared between the application and the X server using the system call `shmat`. Fortunately, the libC provides the relevant flags to

[3] https://disenchant.net/git/tyrquake.git.

bind shared memory at a specific address. Hence, we were able to allocate it inside the sandbox thus allowing a seamless communication with the X server. After these modifications, the sandboxed QUAKE runs without noticeable slowdown which is encouraging and an indication of the good overall performance of our sandboxing technique. In the following, we complement this with a more precise runtime evaluation for the COMPCERT benchmarks.

8.2 PSFI Overhead: Impact of Sandboxing Primitives

Next, we compare the efficiency of a standard masking primitive (Sect. 4.1) with a specialised version for 32-bit sandboxes (Sect. 4.2).

Figure 4 shows the overhead of the standard sandboxing primitive with respect to the specialised sandboxing primitive. There are 6 benchmarks for which the overhead incurred by the standard sandboxing is above 10% reaching 40% for 2 benchmarks. These cases illustrate the significant performance advantage that is sometime obtained by the specialised sandboxing. For some benchmarks, the standard sandboxing outperforms our optimised sandboxing. Yet when it does it is by a very small margin (below 3%). Overall, for the vast majority of our benchmarks, the specialised sandboxing primitive is very competitive.

In Sect. 4.1, we gave theoretical arguments for the advantage of the specialised sandboxing. Another argument comes from the fact that the specialised sandboxing is easier to optimise. First, note that the standard and the specialised sandboxing primitives are both using a bitwise mask but for different purposes. For the standard primitive, it is used to enforce that the pointer is within the sandbox bounds but also to enforce alignment constraints. For the specialised primitive, it is only used to enforce alignment constraints. Using the existing COMPCERT dataflow framework, we have implemented an alignment analysis that is quite effective at removing redundant alignment masks. To enable more optimisations, we explicit alignment constraints in the CMINOR code program (e.g. by specifying that function arguments of a pointer type are necessarily aligned). Thus, our experimental results are explained by both the theoretical advantages given in Sect. 4.2 and the effectiveness of our alignment analysis.

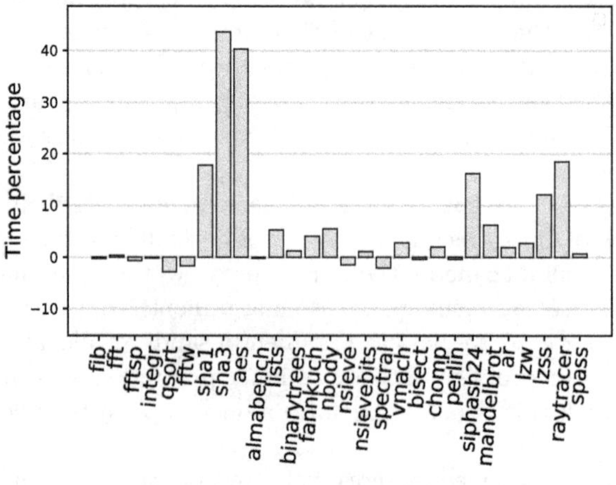

Fig. 4. Overhead of standard w.r.t specialised sandboxing

8.3 PSFI Overhead: Impact of Compiler Back-End

As a second experiment, we evaluate the overhead of our PSFI transformation for various compilers: CompCert, gcc and clang. CompCert is a *moderately optimising compiler* and the benchmarks run significantly faster using gcc and clang. In Fig. 5, the baseline is given by the minimum of the execution times of the three compilers without PSFI instrumentation. The black bar is the overhead of a compiler (e.g. CompCert), with respect to the baseline and the grey bar is the overhead of the same compiler but with the PSFI transformation (e.g. CompCertSfi). In order to use gcc and clang, we implement a trusted decompiler from our secured Cminor programs to Clight, a subset of C in CompCert. These Clight programs are then compiled with gcc or clang.

For a fair comparison, we should compare programs for which we actually have a reasonable security guarantee. We have a formal proof of security and safety (see Sect. 6) for the sandboxed Cminor program, and we are confident that our syntax-directed decompiler preserves this property. For CompCert, this would suffice to preserve the security of the compiled Clight code, but this is not the case for gcc and clang because of semantic discrepancies between the compilers. To limit this risk, we have set the compiler flags to instruct gcc and clang to adhere to the specificity of CompCert semantics: signed integer arithmetic is defined and so are wraps around (flag `-fwrapv`), strict aliasing is irrelevant (flag `-fno-strict-aliasing`), and floating-point arithmetic is strictly IEEE 754 compliant (flags `-frounding-math` and `-fsignaling-nans`). We also instruct the compilers to ignore any knowledge about the C library (`-fno-builtin`).

Our experimental results are shown in Fig. 5. In Fig. 5a, we have the overhead of CompCert and CompCertSfi. The overhead of CompCert over gcc and clang is expected and corroborates existing results[4]. For 10% of the benchmarks, the overhead CompCertSfi over CompCert is negligible and sometimes the PSFI transformation even improves performance. Those are programs for which the PSFI transformation introduces few masking operations, if any. For 41% of the benchmarks, the overhead is below 10% and can be considered, for most applications, a reasonable efficiency/security trade-off. For all the other benchmarks except `binarytrees` and `vmach`, the overhead is below 25%. The two remaining benchmarks have a significant overhead reaching 82% for `binarytrees`. This corresponds to programs which are memory intensive and where sandboxing cannot be optimised.

In Fig. 5b and c, we perform the same experiments but with gcc and clang. The results have some similarities but also have visible differences. For about 60% of the benchmarks the overhead is below 20%. Moreover, for both compilers, the average overhead is similar: 22% for gccSfi and 24% for clangSfi. Yet, on average gccSfi makes a better job at optimising our benchmarks and best clangSfi for about 75% of the benchmarks. For the rest of the benchmarks, we observe a significant overhead, up to 20%, indicating that the PSFI transformation hinders certain aggressive optimisations. The results also seem to indicate that optimisations are fragile as the overhead is not always consistent across compilers. The case of the `integr` benchmark is particularly striking because it runs with negligible overhead for clangSfi but exhibits the worst case overhead for gccSfi. The `integr` program is using a function pointer inside a loop and we suspect that gccSfi, unlike clangSfi, fails to optimise the program due to the inserted trampoline code. Though less striking, the benchmarks `fftw` and `raytracer` follow the opposite trend; these are programs where the overhead of clangSfi is much higher than gccSfi.

[4] http://compcert.inria.fr/compcert-C.html#perfs.

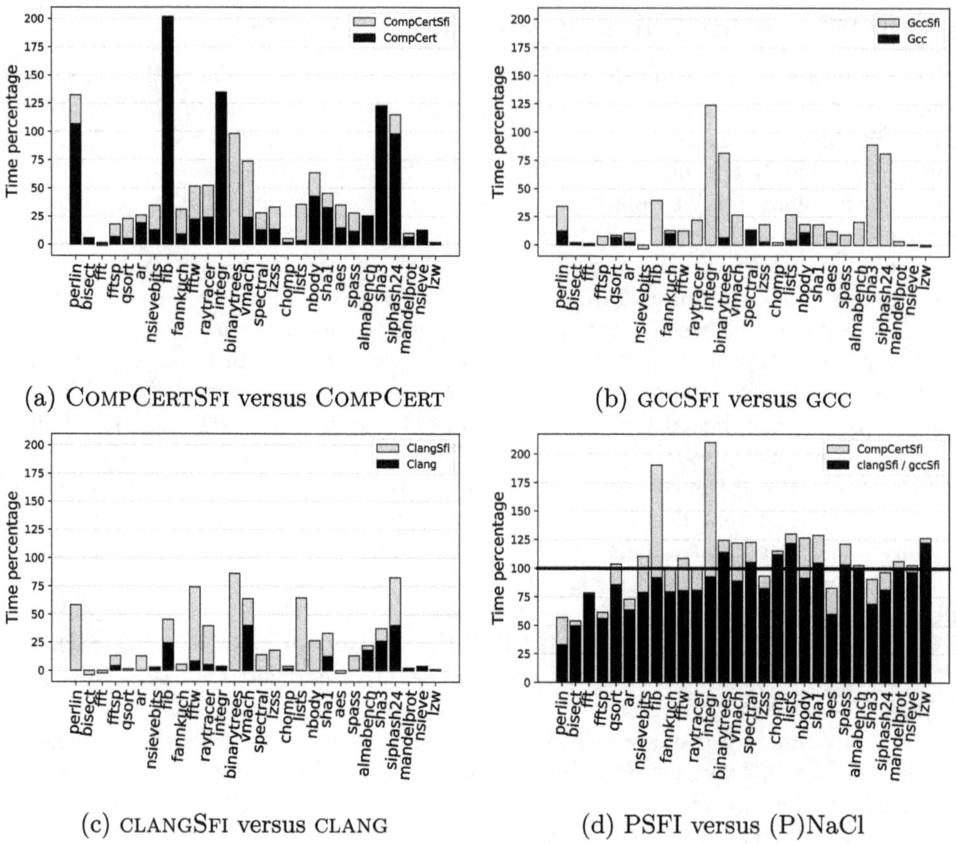

(a) CompCertSfi versus CompCert (b) gccSfi versus gcc

(c) clangSfi versus clang (d) PSFI versus (P)NaCl

Fig. 5. Overhead of PSFI:CompCert, clang, gcc, (P)NaCl

8.4 PSFI Versus (P)NaCl

We also compare our compiler-based SFI approach with (P)NaCl [30], which to our knowledge is one of the most mature implementations of SFI. Figure 5d shows the overhead of CompCertSfi, gccSfi, clangSfi with respect to (P)NaCl. The baseline is given by the best among NaCl and PNaCl. The best of clangSfi and gccSfi is given in dark gray and CompCertSfi is given in light grey.

We first analyse the results of CompCertSfi. Our benchmarks are ordered by increasing runtime. The first 5 benchmarks have a runtime below one second. They are not representative of the performance of both approaches but only illustrate the fact that (P)NaCl has a startup penalty due to the verification of the binary and the setup of the sandbox. The overhead peaks above 75% for two programs (i.e., `fib` and `integr`). As the PSFI transformation keeps `fib` unmodified and only inserts a trampoline call in `integr`, these programs only highlight the limited optimisations performed by CompCert. Of the remaining benchmarks, 40% of them run faster or have similar speed with CompCertSfi. For those benchmarks, the average overhead of CompCertSfi w.r.t (P)NaCl is around 9%. Except for a few programs whose overhead skyrockets due to CompCert not being specialised for speed, we can say that CompCertSfi performance is comparable to (P)NaCl, having programs with better speed in both sides and a large number having similar results.

We also matched GCCSFI/CLANGSFI against (P)NaCl to compare the impact on performance of more aggressive optimisations. Here 60% of the programs are faster with GCCSFI/CLANGSFI. Among the remaining programs, `lzw` and `chomp` are programs for which the (P)NaCl code runs faster than the optimised GCC CLANG code without the PSFI transformation. As (P)NaCl is based on CLANG, more investigation is needed to understand this paradox that may be explained by code running outside the sandbox *i.e.* the trusted runtime library. Among the remaining benchmarks, `binarytrees` and `lists` still show a noticeable overhead. Those are recursive micro-benchmarks for which our PSFI is costly (see Fig. 5). For `lists`, 99% of the time is spent in a tight loop where only a single address is masked. For `binarytrees`, 70% of the time is spent in the runtime code of `malloc` and `free` and therefore this highlights the fact that our implementation is less efficient than the (P)NaCl counterpart. Overall these results indicate that our implementation of SFI is competitive with (P)NaCl, given similar compilers. Furthermore speed can be improved with more sandbox-dedicated optimisations; these would be harder for (P)NaCl to check.

9 Related Work

Since Wahbe *et al.* [35] proposed their initial technique for SFI, there has been a number of proposals for efficiently confining untrusted software to a memory sandbox (see [23, 24, 31, 32, 34, 37, 39]). One of the most prominent is Google's Native Client (NaCl) [37], which provides an infrastructure for executing untrusted native code in a web browser. NaCl was specifically targeted at executing computation-intensive applications without incurring a performance penalty. Certain features (in particular self-modifying code) were ruled out. These restrictions were addressed in a subsequent work [3].

RockSalt [24] is an SFI verifier for x86 code which has been developed and formally verified with the proof assistant Coq. The major contribution of RockSalt is to provide a formal model of the x86 architecture, from which it is possible to extract a decoder for a subset of the very rich set of x86 instructions, and build a verifier for the NaCl sandbox policy. Their experiments show that the formally verified checker performs marginally better than the NaCl verifier. In comparison, our approach avoids the complexities of the x86 instruction set by relying on the COMPCERT compiler back-end to produce binaries whose adherence to the sandbox policy is guaranteed by a combination of a sandbox verification at a higher level (CMINOR) and the COMPCERT's correctness theorem.

ARMor [39] is using the binary rewriter Diablo [28] to implement SFI for ARM processors. Using an untrusted program analysis, a proof of SFI safety is automatically constructed using the HOL theorem prover. ARMor was tested with some programs of the MiBench benchmark [11], namely BitCount and StringSearch. These programs required 2.5 and 8 h respectively to prove the memory safety and control-flow integrity of the executables, which means that the approach is not practically viable as it is.

Kroll *et al.* [16] proposed PSFI as an alternative methodology to the standard, verification-based SFI. In PSFI, the sandbox is built by inserting the necessary masking instructions during compilation. This means that the correctness of the transformation can be argued at an intermediate stage in the compilation where the program representation retains a high-level structure. Our work extends the seminal proposal in a number of ways that we detail below. Unlike Kroll *et al.*, we exclude from the TCB the masking primitive and the trampoline mechanism for calling external functions. In our implementation, these crucial components are written entirely in CMINOR and proved correct without introducing trusted, unproved, code. Kroll *et al.* sketch a proof of safety but do not identify the issue of pointer arithmetic. To sidestep the semantics limitation of pointer arithmetic, we introduce a compile-time encoding of pointer as integers. This transformation is instrumental for our Coq verified proof of safety, which itself is mandatory to transfer security down to assembly.

Since the seminal work of Norrish [27], several works propose formal semantics of the C language [8,12,15]. All these share the limitations of CompCert with respect to pointer arithmetic. Recent works specifically aim at providing a more defined semantics for pointers. The proposal of Besson *et al.* [4] is able to cope with most existing low-level pointer manipulations and has been ported to CompCert [5,6]. Yet, it has nonetheless limitations and the design of our PSFI transformation would not benefit from the increased expressiveness. The semantics of Kang *et al.* [14] is more permissive because, after a cast, a pointer is indistinguishable from an integer value. To our knowledge, their semantics has not been ported to the CompCert compiler. Our SFI transformation has the advantage of being compatible with the existing semantics of CompCert with the caveat that pointers needs to be explicitly compiled into integers.

10 Conclusion

We have presented CompCertSfi, a formally verified implementation of Software Fault Isolation based on the CompCert compiler. Our approach provides security guarantees at runtime when the source code may be malicious or has security vulnerabilities but the build process is trusted. This is typically the case when a final product is built using code originating from multiple third parties. Our work shows that it is possible to perform security-enhancing compilation that is both formally verified and competitive with existing approaches in terms of efficiency. CompCertSfi does not rely on *a posteriori* binary verification for guaranteeing security, and hence has a reduced TCB compared to traditional SFI solutions. The reduction in TCB is obtained through a formal, machine-checked proof of the fact that the security guaranteed by our SFI transformation in the compiler front-end, still holds at the assembly level. Key to achieving this property has been to fine-tune the transformation (and in particular its pointer manipulations) to ensure that the secured program has a well-defined semantics.

The impact of SFI has been evaluated on a series of benchmarks, showing that the transformed code can in a few cases be more efficient, and that the average runtime overhead incurred is about 9%. We have evaluated the impact of back-end optimisation on the transformed code on three different compilers. The gains vary, with clang being more efficient than CompCert and gcc, and CompCert being slightly more efficient than gcc. The experiments show that CompCertSfi combined with an aggressive back-end optimiser can sometimes achieve performances superior to Native Client implementations. In addition, there is still room for further optimisation of the generated code. We have observed that existing optimisations are sometimes hindered by our SFI transformation, so we gain by having more optimisation before the SFI transformation. We also intend to investigate optimisations for removing redundant sandboxing operations and in particular hoisting sandboxing outside loops.

References

1. Supplementary material. https://www.irisa.fr/celtique/ext/compcertsfi
2. Andronick, J., Chetali, B., Ly, O.: Using Coq to verify Java Card™ applet isolation properties. In: Basin, D., Wolff, B. (eds.) TPHOLs 2003. LNCS, vol. 2758, pp. 335–351. Springer, Heidelberg (2003). https://doi.org/10.1007/10930755_22
3. Ansel, J., et al.: Language-independent sandboxing of just-in-time compilation and self-modifying code. In: PLDI, pp. 355–366 (2011)
4. Besson, F., Blazy, S., Wilke, P.: A precise and abstract memory model for C using symbolic values. In: Garrigue, J. (ed.) APLAS 2014. LNCS, vol. 8858, pp. 449–468. Springer, Cham (2014). https://doi.org/10.1007/978-3-319-12736-1_24
5. Besson, F., Blazy, S., Wilke, P.: CompCertS: a memory-aware verified C compiler using pointer as integer semantics. In: Ayala-Rincón, M., Muñoz, C.A. (eds.) ITP 2017. LNCS, vol. 10499, pp. 81–97. Springer, Cham (2017). https://doi.org/10.1007/978-3-319-66107-0_6
6. Besson, F., Blazy, S., Wilke, P.: A verified CompCert front-end for a memory model supporting pointer arithmetic and uninitialised data. J. Autom. Reasoning (2018, accepted for publication)
7. Besson, F., de Grenier de Latour, T., Jensen, T.P.: Interfaces for stack inspection. J. Funct. Program. **15**(2), 179–217 (2005)
8. Ellison, C., Roşu, G.: An executable formal semantics of C with applications. In: POPL. ACM (2012)
9. Fox, A., Myreen, M.O.: A trustworthy monadic formalization of the ARMv7 instruction set architecture. In: Kaufmann, M., Paulson, L.C. (eds.) ITP 2010. LNCS, vol. 6172, pp. 243–258. Springer, Heidelberg (2010). https://doi.org/10.1007/978-3-642-14052-5_18
10. Guanciale, R., Nemati, H., Dam, M., Baumann, C.: Provably secure memory isolation for Linux on ARM. J. Comput. Secur. **24**(6), 793–837 (2016)
11. Guthaus, M., Ringenberg, J., Ernst, D., Austin, T., Mudge, T., Brown, R.: MiBench: a free, commercially representative embedded benchmark suite, pp. 3–14. Institute of Electrical and Electronics Engineers Inc., United States (2001)
12. Hathhorn, C., Ellison, C., Roşu, G.: Defining the undefinedness of C. In: PLDI, pp. 336–345. ACM, June 2015
13. ISO: ISO C Standard 1999. Technical report (1999)
14. Kang, J., Kim, Y., Hur, C., Dreyer, D., Vafeiadis, V.: Lightweight verification of separate compilation. In: POPL, pp. 178–190. ACM (2016)
15. Krebbers, R.: An operational and axiomatic semantics for non-determinism and sequence points in C. In: POPL. ACM (2014)
16. Kroll, J.A., Stewart, G., Appel, A.W.: Portable software fault isolation. In: CSF, pp. 18–32. IEEE (2014)
17. Larus, J.R., Hunt, G.C.: The singularity system. Commun. ACM **53**(8), 72–79 (2010)
18. Leroy, X.: Formal verification of a realistic compiler. Commun. ACM **52**(7), 107–115 (2009)
19. Leroy, X.: A formally verified compiler back-end. J. Autom. Reason. **43**(4), 363–446 (2009)
20. Leroy, X., Appel, A.W., Blazy, S., Stewart, G.: The CompCert memory model. In: Program Logics for Certified Compilers. Cambridge University Press (2014)

21. Leroy, X., Rouaix, F.: Security properties of typed applets. In: Vitek, J., Jensen, C.D. (eds.) Secure Internet Programming, Security Issues for Mobile and Distributed Objects. LNCS, vol. 1603, pp. 147–182. Springer, Heidelberg (1999). https://doi.org/10.1007/3-540-48749-2_7
22. The Coq development team: The Coq proof assistant reference manual (2017). http://coq.inria.fr, version 8.7
23. McCamant, S., Morrisett, G.: Evaluating SFI for a CISC architecture. In: Proceedings of the 15th Conference on USENIX Security Symposium, USENIX-SS 2006, vol. 15. USENIX Association (2006)
24. Morrisett, G., Tan, G., Tassarotti, J., Tristan, J.B., Gan, E.: RockSalt: better, faster, stronger SFI for the x86. In: PLDI, pp. 395–404. ACM (2012)
25. Necula, G.C.: Proof-carrying code. In: POPL, pp. 106–119. ACM Press (1997)
26. Necula, G.C., Lee, P.: Safe kernel extensions without run-time checking. In: OSDI, pp. 229–243. ACM (1996)
27. Norrish, M.: C formalised in HOL. Ph.D. thesis, University of Cambridge (1998)
28. Put, L.V., Chanet, D., Bus, B.D., Sutter, B.D., Bosschere, K.D.: DIABLO: a reliable, retargetable and extensible link-time rewriting framework. In: In IEEE International Symposium On Signal Processing And Information Technology (2005)
29. Richards, G., Hammer, C., Nardelli, F.Z., Jagannathan, S., Vitek, J.: Flexible access control for JavaScript. In: OOPSLA, pp. 305–322. ACM (2013)
30. Sehr, D., et al.: Adapting software fault isolation to contemporary CPU architectures. In: 19th USENIX Security Symposium, pp. 1–12. USENIX Association (2010)
31. Sehr, D., et al.: Adapting software fault isolation to contemporary CPU architectures. In: Proceedings of the 19th USENIX Conference on Security, USENIX Security 2010, p. 1. USENIX Association (2010)
32. Shu, R., et al.: A study of security isolation techniques. ACM Comput. Surv. **49**(3), 50:1–50:37 (2016)
33. Simon, L., Chisnall, D., Anderson, R.J.: What you get is what you C: controlling side effects in mainstream C compilers. In: EuroS&P, pp. 1–15. IEEE (2018)
34. Sinha, R., et al.: A design and verification methodology for secure isolated regions. In: PLDI, pp. 665–681. ACM (2016)
35. Wahbe, R., Lucco, S., Anderson, T.E., Graham, S.L.: Efficient software-based fault isolation. In: SOSP, pp. 203–216. ACM (1993)
36. Wang, X., Chen, H., Cheung, A., Jia, Z., Zeldovich, N., Kaashoek, M.: Undefined behavior: what happened to my code? In: APSYS (2012)
37. Yee, B., et al.: Native client: a sandbox for portable, untrusted x86 native code. In: S&P, pp. 79–93. IEEE (2009)
38. Yee, B., et al.: Native client: a sandbox for portable, untrusted x86 native code. Commun. ACM **53**(1), 91–99 (2010)
39. Zhao, L., Li, G., Sutter, B.D., Regehr, J.: ARMor: fully verified software fault isolation. In: EMSOFT, pp. 289–298. ACM (2011)

Permissions

All chapters in this book were first published by Springer; hereby published with permission under the Creative Commons Attribution License or equivalent. Every chapter published in this book has been scrutinized by our experts. Their significance has been extensively debated. The topics covered herein carry significant findings which will fuel the growth of the discipline. They may even be implemented as practical applications or may be referred to as a beginning point for another development.

The contributors of this book come from diverse backgrounds, making this book a truly international effort. This book will bring forth new frontiers with its revolutionizing research information and detailed analysis of the nascent developments around the world.

We would like to thank all the contributing authors for lending their expertise to make the book truly unique. They have played a crucial role in the development of this book. Without their invaluable contributions this book wouldn't have been possible. They have made vital efforts to compile up to date information on the varied aspects of this subject to make this book a valuable addition to the collection of many professionals and students.

This book was conceptualized with the vision of imparting up-to-date information and advanced data in this field. To ensure the same, a matchless editorial board was set up. Every individual on the board went through rigorous rounds of assessment to prove their worth. After which they invested a large part of their time researching and compiling the most relevant data for our readers.

The editorial board has been involved in producing this book since its inception. They have spent rigorous hours researching and exploring the diverse topics which have resulted in the successful publishing of this book. They have passed on their knowledge of decades through this book. To expedite this challenging task, the publisher supported the team at every step. A small team of assistant editors was also appointed to further simplify the editing procedure and attain best results for the readers.

Apart from the editorial board, the designing team has also invested a significant amount of their time in understanding the subject and creating the most relevant covers. They scrutinized every image to scout for the most suitable representation of the subject and create an appropriate cover for the book.

The publishing team has been an ardent support to the editorial, designing and production team. Their endless efforts to recruit the best for this project, has resulted in the accomplishment of this book. They are a veteran in the field of academics and their pool of knowledge is as vast as their experience in printing. Their expertise and guidance has proved useful at every step. Their uncompromising quality standards have made this book an exceptional effort. Their encouragement from time to time has been an inspiration for everyone.

The publisher and the editorial board hope that this book will prove to be a valuable piece of knowledge for researchers, students, practitioners and scholars across the globe.

List of Contributors

Taro Sekiyama
National Institute of Informatics, Tokyo, Japan

Atsushi Igarashi
Kyoto University, Kyoto, Japan

Xuan Bi, Ningning Xie and Bruno C. d. S. Oliveira
The University of Hong Kong, Hong Kong, China

Tom Schrijvers
KU Leuven, Leuven, Belgium

Stephanie Balzer and Frank Pfenning
Carnegie Mellon University, Pittsburgh, USA

Bernardo Toninho
NOVA LINCS, Universidade Nova de Lisboa, Lisbon, Portugal

Ken Sakayori and Takeshi Tsukada
The University of Tokyo, Tokyo, Japan

Rob van Glabbeek and Peter Höfner
Data61, CSIRO, Sydney, Australia
Computer Science and Engineering, University of New South Wales, Sydney, Australia

Michael Markl
Data61, CSIRO, Sydney, Australia
Institut für Informatik, Universität Augsburg, Augsburg, Germany

Laura Bocchi
University of Kent, Canterbury, UK

Maurizio Murgia
University of Kent, Canterbury, UK
University of Cagliari, Cagliari, Italy

Vasco Thudichum Vasconcelos
LASIGE, Faculty of Sciences, University of Lisbon, Lisbon, Portugal

Nobuko Yoshida
Imperial College London, London, UK

Mario Alvarez-Picallo and C.-H. Luke Ong
University of Oxford, Oxford, UK

Alex Eyers-Taylor and Michael Peyton Jones
Semmle Ltd., Oxford, UK

Paolo G. Giarrusso
LAMP—EPFL, Lausanne, Switzerland

Yann Régis-Gianas
IRIF, University of Paris Diderot, Inria, Paris, France

Philipp Schuster
University of Tübingen, Tübingen, Germany

Frédéric Besson, Sandrine Blazy, Alexandre Dang and Thomas Jensen
Inria, Univ Rennes, CNRS, IRISA, Rennes, France

Pierre Wilke
CentraleSupélec, Inria, Univ Rennes, CNRS, IRISA, Rennes, France

Index